ANCIENT GREECE

The Triumph of a Culture

ROBERT PAYNE

New York · W · W · NORTON & COMPANY · INC ·

» ANCIENT GREECE «

FOR ALEXANDER ARTEMAKIS

AND ALL THE GREEKS

⠀⠀CONTENTS⠀⠀

CONTENTS

⇒ ILLUSTRATIONS ⇐

PLATES

Between pages 32 and 33

Mount Olympus. (National Tourist Organization, Athens)
Interior of the Erechtheum facing east. (Robert McCabe)
The Lions of Delos. (Robert McCabe)
Hadrian's Temple of Zeus at Athens.
The Erechtheum. (National Tourist Organization, Athens)
The Parthenon.
Aegina, Temple of Aphaia. (Royal Greek Embassy, London)
Temple of Athena at Lindos. (Nick Stournaras)

Between pages 64 and 65

Head of a Griffin. Found in the Kladeos at Olympia. (Collection of Walter C.
    Baker, Metropolitan Museum of Art, New York)
The Lion Gate at Mycenae. (Robert McCabe)
Grave Circle at Mycenae. (Robert McCabe)
Ladies of the Court fresco, Palace of Knossos. (Greek Embassy, Information
    Office, London)
Ivory Group—the Great Mother, Daughter, Divine Child. (Hirmer Fotoarchiv,
    Munich)
Statuette of Snake Goddess in Ivory and Gold. (Museum of Fine Arts, Boston)
Bronze statuette of Apollo from Thebes. (Museum of Fine Arts, Boston)
Gold Mask from Mycenae. (Royal Greek Embassy, London)

Between pages 128 and 129

Demeter of Cnidus. (The Trustees of the British Museum)
Victory of Paeonios, at Olympia.
Victory of Samothrace. (The Louvre)
Aphrodite Rising from the Sea. (Alinari)
Aphrodite of Cyrene. (Richter)

9

ILLUSTRATIONS

Athena from the Temple of Aphaia on Aegina. (Staatliche Antikensammlungen, Munich)
Athena of Piraeus.
Athena Parthenos. (Alexander Artemakis)

Between pages 160–161

"Chatworth" Apollo, from Tamassos in Cyprus. (Trustees of the British Museum)
Poseidon, found at sea off Artemision. (Alexander Artemakis)
Apollo from west pediment of Temple of Zeus, Olympia.
Zeus and Ganymede, from Olympia. (Royal Greek Embassy, New York)
Heracles from east pediment of Temple of Aphaia, Aegina. (Staatliche Antikensammlungen, Munich)
Apollo of Piombino. (The Louvre)
Ares by Alcamenes. Roman copy. (The Louvre)
Apollo of Piraeus. (Hirmer Fotoarchiv, Munich)

Between pages 224 and 225

Young Citharoedus singing. Detail from amphora. (Metropolitan Museum, New York)
Heracles at war with Birds. Detail from amphora. (Trustees of the British Museum)
Women at the Well, between Dionysus and Satyr. Detail from amphora. (Trustees of the British Museum)
Young nobleman on horseback. Detail from vase. (Trustees of the British Museum)
Young peasant on horseback. Detail from vase. (Trustees of the British Museum)
Women putting away clothes. Attic kylix, by Douris. (Metropolitan Museum, New York)
Dancers—boy with double flute, girl with castanets. (Trustees of the British Museum)
Horse's head in collar of acanthus. (Roger-Viollet)

Between pages 256 and 257

Head of Zeus by Phidias, from coin of Elis. (Burton Y. Berry Collection)
Head of Apollo from Leontini tetradrachm. (Museum of Fine Arts, Boston)
Head of Apollo from Catana tetradrachm. (Trustees of the British Museum)
Head of Arethusa from Syracuse tetradrachm. (Museum of Fine Arts, Boston)
Silver decadrachm of Syracuse, with head of Persephone. (Museum of Fine Arts, Boston)
Spartan soldier wearing Corinthian helmet. Height 4½ inches (Wadsworth Atheneum)
Veiled dancer from Alexandria. (Walter C. Baker collection, Metropolitan Museum, New York)
Jockey. (Royal Greek Embassy, New York)

ILLUSTRATIONS

FIGURES

⇒ PREFACE ⇐

My purpose is to describe the emergence and the early growth of the Greek spirit, of the ideas first formulated in Greece and in the lands held in intellectual fee by men trained in the schools of Athens. That spirit and those ideas were so powerful that even today we are their willing prisoners, still pursuing the debate which the Greeks held with themselves. So I have attempted to clothe that debate in living colors and to show them at the work of building up the civilization which became the foundation of our own, so dangerous and imperfect, and yet so much more responsible than any other devised by man. I wanted to see the living men behind the words, the faces behind the ideas. Their humanness and their sense of responsibility is as much a part of the story as the cascade of ideas which poured out of them; and in telling their history it would be unfair to forget the very human qualities they brought to bear on their intellectual adventures.

They were of the earth earthy, and so I have depicted them; but they were also the first explorers through vast and uncharted areas of the human soul. Those wide-eyed, daring people sometimes seem to resemble seamen hurling themselves recklessly over unknown oceans, but if we look closer we see that they are continually taking sounding, measuring the force of the winds, and calculating their distance from land. They were skillful navigators who took their responsibilities seriously for all their air of improvidence and impulsive courage. They did not always know where they were going, but they knew that the journey was worth pursuing.

The Greeks discovered themselves. It was their most signal discovery and their greatest gift to mankind, for ever since they embarked on the journey into themselves men have been compelled to ask the same questions and follow them through the same perilous landscapes. They discovered that the world inside them was as bright and intricate as the world outside. They invented the word "idea." Out of this invention, this way of looking at the world, came the detached intelligence which could weigh events and thoughts without tampering with the scales. The sovereign intelligence did not rule their lives, but it ruled their understanding of their lives. "O Solon, Solon," said the priest of Egypt, "you Greeks are always children." It was perhaps more true than the priest realized, for they retained the eagerness of children long after they had acquired the wisdom and intellectual energy which comes with age.

Our civilization is still so closely welded to its Greek origins that it is sometimes difficult to know where the Greeks end and we begin. They haunt us in our poetry and drama; they are present in our sciences; and their philosophers still stand at our shoulders. We like to think that in the past fifty years we have advanced at unprecedented speed, but within a comparable space of time the Greeks made discoveries in the arts and sciences on a scale which has never since been equaled. They brought the infant to birth, and we have merely nurtured it. We are the inheritors of the traditions they established.

I cannot see any simple patterns of challenge and response, or rise and fall, manifesting themselves in the history of Greece. A nation is not like a man who comes to maturity, grows old, and dies, for a nation may have many births and many deaths. Athens, which was the heart and core of Greek civilization, perished in the winter of 405. For more than a quarter of a century she had fought a losing war, at the mercy of the traitors in her midst. She had no spirit left, no will to fight, nor any great desire to survive. She had no army, no ships, no purpose. By order of her enemies everything that could serve to protect Athens was destroyed. The long defensive wall was pulled down, while the flute-players played and the people wept. She was ruined, powerless, crushed. So she died, and within ten years she was alive again, dominating the intellectual and spiritual life of Greece.

We need to know why civilizations suffer so many mortal blows, and still survive. We need a history of the resurrection of civilizations.

The Greeks, of course, had advantages over the nations that came after them. They had a dazzling youthfulness. We remember them chiefly for their love of life, their astonishing energy, their intellectual stamina, their quick perceptions. It is the custom to say of them that they saw life whole, but nothing could be further from the truth. They saw life in brilliant fragmentation, as the young see it, blazing with color, as clear as their own cliffs and seas, yet broken into a multiplicity of small fragments which they were able to see and understand. We speak of their classic calm, but they were the most nervous and excitable of peoples, always in dread of death, while furiously embracing life. They were more Oriental than we suspect, and the moments of calm when they came were often dreadful. They spoke too often about pursuing "the middle way" to be quite convincing, for they were always running after extremes. Today we see the white bones of the Parthenon crowning the Acropolis, and we tend to forget that the original Parthenon was painted in gaudy colors. The crowded streets of ancient Athens were not filled with men walking in impeccable white gowns, but in colorful rags. They were a rowdy, undisciplined, argumentative people, who loved nothing better than to embark on litigation, quarrelsome and very mercenary. Yet out of their quarrels in the market-place came freedom under the reign of law.

They adored all gleaming things, seed, frost, dew, seafoam, fountains, the leaves in spring, all fruits and flowers, the light of oil-lamps and the starry night, the eternal seashore bathed in the sun. They were so intoxicated with the shapes of the naked bodies of men and women that they became for the first time, and for all time, the artists of the ideal human form. They seem to enter the stage at the morning of the world, and there was always something curiously virgin about them: it was not only Sappho who cried across the centuries: *Aiparthenos essomai.* "Forever shall I be virgin." There was something virgin in all of them, even in Socrates, who talked all day and all night about a universe which seemed to have come into existence only a few days before. There was dew still on their eyes, and through this dew they saw everything slightly magnified, so that it appeared strange and entrancing and infinitely delightful—so delightful indeed that we with the dust of atomic powder in our eyes look back across the centuries with expressions of envy, wishing to be among them.

There was a dawn in Greece, but there was no high noon or sunset: there was no period of maturity followed by an inevitable decline: the light never faded from the sky, and there was no death.

We are still living in the long morning of the Greek world.

As life on this planet grows more dangerous, we can derive some comfort from the knowledge that our civilization springs from ancient Greece, which gave us the concepts of freedom under law and the right of men to rule themselves according to their desires. For it was their particular triumph that they gave dignity to our lives.

⫸ ANCIENT GREECE ⫷

1 » THE BARREN LAND

GREECE is a barren land, the earth so stubborn and austere that it breaks the hearts of the men who farm the narrow valleys and the small patches of arable land at the foot of the steep-sided limestone mountains. There are few rivers, few plains, few beaches. There is a host of small craggy islands which are the fragmented eminences of mountains drowned long ago, and the islands are as austere as the mainland. In this hard land, where men must live close to the earth, life goes on very much as it did in the heroic age. Within a few miles of Athens you will come upon horses and mules stamping around a threshing floor in a corner of a field as they did in ancient times, and the winnowing is still done with the help of wind and flails. The thin black goats still give milk and cheese and meat, and the same olives sleep on the slopes of the hills. Birds are still trapped in nets, and the country women still gather the wild honey. So it was, and so it has always been: a land which has been cut to the bone, fit for a race of ascetics, a desert of broken rocks.

The traveler coming to Greece from the west for the first time is shocked by the pervading barrenness, the prickling-sharp outlines of mountains and shores, the absence of trees, the rare springs. The winds have rubbed the mountains smooth, giving them a polished look: the light glances cleanly off them. Once perhaps the mountains were covered with trees, and the roots held the soil. Plato speaks of the land as the skeleton of a person who was wasting away, all the fat burned off him, but remembers that there was a time, fifty years before his day, when some great forests remained and the timbers were used in the building of temples he had seen with his own eyes. The goats and charcoal burners had deforested the land, and the rains had washed the topsoil away; the few remaining forests were probably fired by the invading Persians. It is not a late barrenness, but one of long standing.

This barren land is bathed in a light unlike any other light on the surface of the earth—a light that is almost palpable, full of ripeness and strength, giving clear outlines to things and possessing a life of its own. Almost the Greek light is sentient. It crowds the heavens, it shouts, it exults. It swings across the sky like a presence conscious of its divinity, and therefore the Greeks gave it the appearance of a youthful god with streaming golden hair, whom they called Phoebus Apollo, the god of the divine radiance, and they chose for his birth-place the small white glittering island of Delos in the purple seas of the Aegean.

The Greeks spoke of "the rosy-fingered dawn," but beyond those fingers were hands, arms, shoulders, a face. The whole body of Apollo poured across the sky, intensely virile, flashing with a million points of light, healing everything it touched, germinating the seeds and defying the powers of darkness. He was not the sun only, but all the brightness of the world: he was the moon, the planets, the Milky Way, and the faintest stars; he was the sparkle in the waves, the gleam in eyes, the glistening of bleached cloth, the light in a girl's face, the shining of wine in the mouth. He was the strange glimmer of fields on the darkest nights; and whenever a spring issued from a mountain, he was present at the moment when it emerged into the light.

He was not the most powerful of the gods, but the one who gave the greatest blessing of all—the divine light flooding down from the divine sky. So gradually he became the god of accurate perception, of the clean and sharp outlines of things, and the enemy of obscurant-ism and the legendary dragons once believed to haunt the earth. From him came order and the definitions of things. At the beginning of the *Homeric Hymn to the Delian Apollo* we see Apollo entering the hall of Zeus with bow drawn taut while all the gods spring trembling from their seats.

The Greeks gloried in the light, especially the light gleaming from moist things—the light of the sea, of rivers, of freshets and springs, and the light flowing from the healthy flesh of young bathers, the water rippling over the skin. For them darkness was a nightmare, something that had to be borne as old men bear pain and suffering, but they seem to have felt that darkness was an enemy to be placated with offerings of lamps, and like the modern Greeks they kept their lamps burning late.

For Homer almost everything that was shining was holy. When he wanted to describe the goddess Athena, he called her "the bright-eyed one," and when he wanted to depict Helen walking along the ramparts of Troy, he did not describe her face or how she walked; it was enough to say she wore a shining veil. Light was the sap of life; and if one must die, it is best to die in the sun:

> *Make the sky clear, and grant us to see with our eyes.*
> *In the light be it, though thou slayest me!*

So Ajax prays to Zeus in the *Iliad*, a prayer which wells up from the very depths of the Greek consciousness. The Greeks made Homer blind, because this was the most tragic fate that could overtake a man, and for the same reason they made King Oedipus tear out his eyes with golden pins: the spectacle of a blind hero leaning on the arm of his daughter was calculated to make them reel with horror however many times they had seen it before. The Greeks were perfectly aware of the perfection of their light and spoke about it a little self-consciously, as though they could not quite believe that so much beauty had been given to them alone. The prodigality of the light almost made up for the barrenness of the land.

Throughout their history the Greeks remained poor, having few resources of their own. No fertilizing Nile poured through their narrow valleys; there were no great river systems like those which threaded through Syria. With no large grazing grounds, with no great shoals of fish in their seas, with no abundant resources of precious stones or metals, the Greeks were forced to look toward Asia and Egypt. More than anything else it was the barrenness of the land that turned them into conquerors.

For conquerors they were. Long before Alexander the Great led his pathetically small armies to the conquest of Persia and northern India, the Greeks had a tradition of fighting overseas. All the coastal cities of Asia Minor were theirs by right of conquest. They sent armies against Egypt and raiding parties to France, Spain, and North Africa: they possessed colonies and settlements all around the Mediterranean, which became a Greek lake, guarded by armed merchantmen and privateers. The colonies they established in Egypt and Italy rivaled their own cities in the splendor of their temples and the luxurious appointments of their public buildings. Cyrene, Sybaris, and Marseilles were all richer than Athens. Unhappily, the colonies were always quarreling with one another, and sometimes a single colony would defy the armed might of the mainland. Troy would appear to have been a colony which rebelled, and suffered a ten-year war for its audacity. The history of Greek colonization in the Mediterranean is the history of an interminable civil war.

There was a tragic fatality in the Greeks which led them to quarrel continually among themselves, even when they were on the edge of disaster, even when they were confronted with the overwhelming power of a common enemy. At the battle of Plataea three separate Greek armies wandered forlornly among the foothills of Mount Cithaeron, the commanders quarreling bitterly, incapable of a common plan of action. The Persians possessed a vast superiority in numbers and firepower. They had well-trained cavalry, while the Greeks had no cavalry at all. The advantages were all in favor of the Persians, who were fighting on a battleground of their own choosing. Yet the Greeks won the battle, which decided the fate of Europe. They did not win it because their strategy and tactics were superior to the Persians'. They won the battle because an obscure Spartan wielding a weapon no more lethal than a stone cracked the head of Mardonius, the Persian commander in chief, and the Persians panicked when they heard of the loss of their leader. From that lucky stone came democracy and the Periclean age in Athens, and the Greeks very properly ascribed the victory not to themselves but to Zeus, whose intervention came only just in time.

One might have thought the ferocious quarrels on the battlefield of Plataea would have taught the Greeks a lesson, but the quarrels continued. They were a bold and argumentative race, stubbornly independent, every man regarding himself as the equal of every other man. They were, and still are, virtuosos in the art of defamation and in the stratagems of intrigue. They were virulent haters and conspiratorial by nature, lovers of argument for argument's sake. Geography, which shaped their poverty, gave them a hard-bitten independence and self-reliance, for men accustomed to live in narrow and well-guarded valleys are intolerant of government and likely to defend themselves all the more passionately when their land is poor.

It is customary to speak of the Greek city-states as the ultimate units forming the national polity, but in fact there was no national polity and the ultimate units were the valleys with their hill-forts and strings of villages extending along the plain beneath the mountains. They were valley dwellers who found their best protectors in the mountains. Living in the sheltering valleys, they were able to maintain their individuality and their enduring traditions, with the result that a wide variety of dialects survived. Hence, too, the multiplicity of their gods and goddesses, and the continuing role played by the local heroes, whose power to command their lives was only a little less than that of the gods. They had the defects and virtues of valley dwellers. They lived in closed communities and regarded the inhabitants of the neighboring valleys as their dedicated enemies. Fierce bonds of kinship held them together.

Greece, then, was a network of small valley states in an undeclared war against one another, never at peace except during the great national festivals called into existence to remind them of their common origin; for, while the people were argumentative, the gods admitted no argument and the rule of Zeus was sovereign. He was the all-wise, all-powerful divinity, ruler of the skies and mountains, living in the inaccessible sharp-sided peaks of Mount Olympus, himself shaped like a mountain bearded with mist. He was the Thunderer, and his messengers were eagles. For him, and for him alone, the valley dwellers were prepared to make peace in order to assemble before his altars and offer sacrifices in honor of their common heritage.

The Greeks rarely asked themselves what their common heritage was. What had a Spartan in common with an Athenian, or a Boeotian with an Arcadian? There were astonishing differences from one valley to another, and a man journeying across Greece in classical times might have the feeling at the end of the day's march that he had entered another country, and so with each succeeding day he would find new customs, new rituals, new habits of thought. Whatever unity the Greeks possessed flourished on variety, and it was difficult to express what they had in common.

Herodotus assumed there were four criteria for being a Greek: common descent, religion, language, and culture. There was no common descent, for they were the children of many tribes and many migrations. When Thucydides looked back across the centuries he saw only the dark waves of immigrants pouring across the land, making war with the original settlers, pushing them back into the hills: wave after wave of immigrants. There was a common religion, but only in the sense that all over Greece gods with the same names were worshiped, yet the naked Aphrodite of Athens had almost nothing in common with the armed Aphrodite who was worshiped in Sparta. The religion of the Greeks was in a continual flux, the new gods rising, the old gods dying. As for the Greek language, this too varied in different places, so that an Athenian had difficulty in understanding an Arcadian, and he had even greater difficulty in understanding the islanders. All over Greece there were little pockets where only Pelasgian, the ancient language of the original inhabitants, was spoken.

Greek unity, to the extent that it existed, had little to do with common descent, religion, or the spoken language. It was essentially a cultural unity, being the gift of Homer to the Greek people. Without Homer, without the legendary poems describing the feats of the Greek tribes before the walls of Troy, there would have been no sense of a united people. Homer gave them the names of their gods and of their ancestral leaders. He gave them pride in a common achievement and the sense of a mission to be fulfilled. He may never have visited the mainland of Greece, but it was he, more than anyone else, who created the Greek nation, and if Homer had no existence, if in fact as some people still believe the epics are merely folk songs from many different sources joined together by committees of poets to form consecutive stories, then it remains true that the sense of unity sprang from poetry. The epics gave birth to Greece.

To the Greeks, therefore, all roads led back to Homer. They knew obscurely that there must have been other roads going back into the distant past, but they could not map these roads and had very little desire to do so. Homer was the angel with the flaming sword who stood at the gates of paradise, wearing his singing robes of gold; and they were so dazzled by his presence, and so proud of his accomplishment, that they were content to be his children.

There were some who believed that Homer was the inventor of the Greek language: they were not wholly wrong. There is nothing in the least primitive in those clear and copious verses, intended to be chanted and never to be spoken. Before Homer there must have been a slow and cautious development, centuries of trial and error, a deliberate effort to build a complex grammar out of whatever tools lay close at hand. Many dialects and many obsolete tongues went to form that language, and the vast vocabulary was derived from a vast number of different sources, so that, like English, Greek is a language in which the same statement can be made in many ways with many different overtones of meaning. It is a language of clear outlines, very swift on the tongue, possessing an extraordinary sweetness, and with a grammar so intricate that it takes schoolboys seven or eight years to master the fundamentals. If necessary, it can be abrupt and strident, but there is none of the heavy metallic quality of Latin, where each word seems to be cast in bronze. Spoken Greek gives the effect of a mountain stream foaming between steep banks, throwing up fountains of spray, now sliding over smooth rocks so that it acquires the colors of the stone and now racing darkly in the shadows. Even on the written page it gives the effect of a language in the sunlight.

Homer, then, made two bequests to the Greeks. He gave them a nation and he gave them a poetic language, which all could learn, though it was not a language that anyone spoke in their homes. By upholding the heroic ideal, he gave them faith in themselves. It is not only that he stands at the beginning of Greek civilization, but his thought and his particular way of looking at life permeated the Greek ethos up to the coming of Christianity, and even beyond. To say that he was the first and greatest of the Greek poets is to grant him only a small portion of his proper fame. Sometimes it seems that the whole course of Greek civilization sprang from his fiery imagination, and that nothing was ever done or spoken which did not have its origins in his mind. He was the seed that fell and flourished on the barren land.

For just as there is no Greece without Homer, so, too, there is no Greece without that wild and enchanted landscape. Those skies, that peculiar clarity in the air, the earth which demanded so much toil to produce a few bean sprouts, the seashore riddled with coves, the bleak promontories and the knifelike mountains where the winds howled—these were also essential elements in the coming to birth of Greek civilization. Even today more than three quarters of Greece is barren, but the barren land produced a fertile people. A few men living on porridge and wine and a little cheese produced a civilization which was the greatest of its time; and some believe it was the greatest there has ever been.

2 « THE FERTILE ISLAND

THE TRAVELER coming to Crete by sea sees range upon range of stark and jagged hills against the skyline. These hills have an austere and unapproachable beauty, as though they were the private preserve of the gods. The bare rocks, blue and white and silver, gleam in the sun under skies glowing with an Oriental ripeness. We are far from Greece, on our way to Syria and Egypt.

Once we have stepped ashore, the scene changes and we are no longer so acutely aware of the sharp-sided mountains and the rocky cliffs. A country which seemed to be all rock becomes a nest of wide and fertile plains and valleys. Ash and cypress grow along the banks of the streams, the vines grow shoulder-high, and thickset olive trees stretch for miles. There are sixteen feet of topsoil and inexhaustible layers of fresh water lie below. Compared with the gaunt valleys of Greece, Crete is paradise.

No wonder the ancient Greeks looked with longing toward Crete and invested the island with an air of mystery and enchantment. According to Greek folk memory, behind those frowning cliffs there once lurked King Minos, lord of a hundred cities and many islands, grand admiral of the eastern seas, who ruled from his great palace at Knossos amid unexampled splendor. To his court came the Athenian engineer Daedalus, whose name means "the cunning craftsman," to fashion a wooden cow for Queen Pasiphaë and a labyrinth in which to hide the monstrous man-headed bull she gave birth to, and he built a dancing place for her daughter, Princess Ariadne. For some reason King Minos threw Daedalus into prison, but he escaped when

Princess Ariadne showed him the secret doors, and when the king heard of it he ordered all his ships to remain at anchor and refuse to take on passengers, so that Daedalus was forced to invent wings and in this way escaped to Sicily. About the same time Theseus, Prince of Athens, came to Crete with seven maidens and six other youths on the occasion of the annual offering to the man-headed bull. He slew the monster with a sword given to him by the princess and escaped from the labyrinth with the help of a thread she had provided for him. Minos reigned three generations before the Trojan War: so Herodotus tells us, and there is no particular reason why we should disbelieve him.

Who was Minos? Who was Daedalus? Who was the Minotaur, the man-headed bull?

The truth is that we do not know, and until recently it would have been quite impossible to make even an informed guess. Our knowledge of ancient Crete begins with the present century, with the excavations of Sir Arthur Evans at Knossos, and even now, after sixty years of intensive digging, we are only a little closer to the heart of the mystery. The excavations at Knossos raise as many problems as they solve; and Minos, Daedalus, and the Minotaur are scarcely more than vague presences looming through the mists of prehistory. Sir Arthur Evans thought the Minotaur could be explained by the bull-like bellowing of the earth during the periodic earthquakes that are visited upon the island, but this is scarcely an explanation which will satisfy historians. Some mysterious and powerful human force was once exerted from the island. Vast navies sailed from its coasts. Great fortresses dominated the approaches to the cities of this small kingdom which extended its power far beyond its frontiers or its apparent resources. But the navies have vanished, and there is no trace of a fortress anywhere on the island. We are still far from the day when we shall be able to write a connected history of Minoan Crete at the height of its glory.

For glory there was, but it was not in the least the glory we associate with great naval powers. When Sir Arthur Evans uncovered Knossos, he found to his surprise a kind of fairy palace, delicately ornamented, a storehouse of jewels and frescoes and painted reliefs. The arts of Knossos were rounded and complete. There was nothing hesitant. There was the sense of a people living in quiet enjoyment of life, loving the earth, enjoying bright colors and possessing exquisite

taste, with an impressive serenity. There were no vast portraits of the
gods; indeed, there were scarcely any gods, and the few that were
discovered usually took the form of pottery figurines only a few
inches high. The overwhelming impression produced by these discoveries was of a gay, sensual people innocent of any delight in war.
They enjoyed bullfights where no blood was shed: the fighting consisted in mastering the bull and leaping delicately over its head. They
worshiped and were quietly devoted to the Great Mother, whose
sanctuary was the shade of a small tree in an enclosed garden. From
the evidence of their art, they seem never to have suffered from a
sense of guilt and appalled horror before the mysteries of life evident
in most of the ancient civilizations which have left sufficient remains
to enable us to penetrate into their minds.

A strange modernity colored the civilization at Knossos. The
houses were well-built, sometimes five stories high, with oiled parch-
ment windows. The drainage system—at least in the palaces—was far
superior to anything known in the Western world until the time of
Queen Victoria. Light for the inner apartments came from light
wells. Sometimes they built their houses with setbacks, and they
planted trees on the roofs. Across the walls of the houses they painted
bands of color. They seem to have painted all their household utensils,
and the gay curling S line is everywhere, becoming flower or wave
or the wheeling stars according to the whim of the painter. The line
sings joyfully in the Neolithic pottery found outside the palace, and
it is continually appearing on the palace walls.

Wherever Evans dug he came upon evidence of their quiet charm,
their forthrightness, their open-eyed wonder at the beauty of life.
They painted no goblins, no demons, no dark gods. There was nothing
heavy in their jewelry; it was always light and graceful and intricately
feminine. Their women wore brilliantly colored flounced skirts reaching to the ground; breasts and arms were left bare; they fashioned
their hair in sumptuous curls and ringlets. Sometimes they wore puff
sleeves, which were simply slipped over the arms. The skirts rustled
pleasantly when they walked, swinging in the familiar S curve. They
wore ribbons and necklaces, and embroidered bodices sometimes appear on the frescoes. The famous fresco with the portrait of a young
girl with enormous eyes, bright crimson lips, and arrogantly tilted
nose, called *La Parisienne* by the workmen who discovered it in 1903,
suggests a pure, leaping joy in the world outside her. She was a

priestess, as we know from the sacral knot she wears on her shoulders, and once she formed part of a long gallery of priests and priestesses sitting in pairs as they ritually passed a sacred goblet around in a rite which cannot have been very dissimilar to Holy Communion. On another fresco we see court maidens gossiping, and all of them wear exotically curled ringlets and have jeweled combs in their hair: while one of them, the most beautiful, idly fingers the necklace at her throat.

The men, it seems wore nothing but brightly colored loincloths rather in the manner of Elizabethan codpieces, but pulled up over the belly and fastened to an ornamental belt: similar narrow codpieces are known from primitive statuettes to have been used in Libya. They wore their hair long, with side locks flowing over their shoulders. On one of the wall paintings we find a youthful elegant wearing a pair of red gloves. The men have astonishingly narrow hips and waists. Alarmed by their slenderness, Sir Arthur Evans developed the theory that they must have worn tight, metal belts from the time of their youth. It is more probable that they cultivated slenderness through their athletic exercises. Their stark-nakedness must have acted as a foil to the sumptuous panoply of the women. On all these frescoes they are depicted in profile, and seem to be looking past us into some remote and visionary world of their own.

No doubt these frescoes represent the court beauties and the young princes and princesses. They are the superb aristocrats of a leisurely age, moving with a happy elegance, dedicated to their own pleasures, and not therefore typical of the islanders as a whole. Such refinement is rare in all ages, and to find their equals we must go to the Gandhara age in India or to Japan under the Fujiwara emperors. Even in Athens at the time of Peisistratus, when a discreet elegance was cultivated, we shall not find anything to compare with the pure refinements of Minoan Crete.

The palace at Knossos tells us very little about the lives of the common people: for this we must go to the graves scattered about the island with their clay toys and broken pottery painted with designs which imitate at a great remove the delicate designs of the court. The Harvesters' Vase, found at Hagia Triada, gives an astonishingly vivid picture of peasants joining in procession as they celebrate the harvest festival, led by the long-haired landowner who wears for the occasion a heavy fringed cloak ornamented with wavelike patterns. Probably they are celebrating the olive harvest, for they carry over their shoulders long staves provided with sickle blades. The peasants are naked except for their round flat caps and long slender codpieces. So they march along, on that crowded steatite vase, singing at the top of their lungs while a priest shakes a sistrum; and one of them, with a drunken, happy expression, falls to his knees and in falling clings to the thighs of the man in front, who turns and laughs cheerfully at his companions as though he wanted them to be sure to observe his own discomfiture. It is all done with humor and grace. The faces are recognizably the faces of peasants, but with their straight foreheads and noses and pointed chins they clearly belong to the same general type as the princes of Knossos.

The priest with his sistrum points to Egyptian influence, but in fact little Egyptian influence can be detected in Minoan Crete. Trade with Egypt was extensive, and there may have been times when the Egyptians possessed or believed they possessed suzerainty over the island. Cretan tribute bearers carrying on their shoulders great cups and vases decorated in typically Minoan styles appear on a wall painting in the tomb of Senmut, the architect of Queen Hatshepsut. These offerings may have been no more than presents given by a Cretan embassy, for nowhere can there be found any trace of Egyptian domination. There are no pyramids in Crete, no massive stone images of gods and kings, no vast and labyrinthine temples. Only occasionally do we come across designs which are a faint echo of Egypt.

Among the treasures found at Hagia Triadha was a stone sarcophagus painted on all four sides in fresh madders, rose pinks, orange, yellow and blue. Within a pattern of blue and white suns wheeling across the heavens we see the sacrifices and offerings being prepared for a dead prince, who is shown wearing a shroud as he emerges from his palacelike tomb to stand in the shade of a sacred tree beside an altar. He watches impassively while three priests with sheepskins round their waists come forward bearing gifts—two brindled calves and a boat which has evidently been carved out of an elephant's tusk. These priests have an Egyptian air about them: such tribute bearers to the dead are seen frequently in Egyptian tombs. But these are no ordinary priests, for they come out of the darkness, out of a square of blue-painted background which separates them from the brightness falling on the dead prince and on the great ceremonial vase standing between high pillars behind them. To this ceremonial vase comes a priestess with a pitcher of wine, and another woman wearing a crown, and a lyre player plucking the strings with a plectrum. Their backs are turned to the Egyptian priests, and they pour their libations according to another ritual altogether. On top of the high pillars guarding the ceremonial vase are double axes made of gold, being the emblems of divine power.

Figure 1. The Hagia Triadha Sarcophagus.

On the other side, too, we find rituals which are separate and even opposed to one another, for in the center a great bull lies shackled with scarlet cords on an altar and blood pours from the neck into a vase, while only a little way off a priestess standing in the shade of a sacred tree offers a bloodless sacrifice of fruit and wine. Here, too, are the double axes made of gold and a small shrine bearing the horns of consecration. A dark-winged bird has just alighted on the double axes.

Mount Olympus.

Interior of the Erechtheum facing east.

The Lions of Delos.

Hadrian's Temple of Zeus at Athens.

The Erechtheum.

The Parthenon.

Aegina, Temple of Aphaia.

Temple of Athena at Lindos.

The bird is not a messenger of death, but signifies the presence of the Great Mother, who ruled benignly over the living and the dead.

These beautiful panels painted on a limestone sarcophagus tell us nearly all we know about the rites attending upon the dead in Minoan Crete. The paintings are gay and delicate, and at the same time very solemn. The actors in the drama move with an enviable dignity and grace; and though there is grief, there is also joy in the expectation of deliverance from death. If there is a suggestion of Egyptian influence in the priests with their gift of calves and a boat to take the dead man across the dark rivers he will meet on his journey, the women taking part in the rites and the sturdy lyre player belong wholly to Minoan Crete. The women are robust, high-breasted, quivering with life. The sun of Europe shines on the scene, and we are far from the East.

For what is most extraordinary about Minoan art is that it expresses so little of the Orient. There is always the sense of immediacy, the quick line flowing free. There is no constraint, no heaviness. A painter will paint an octopus on the surface of a vase, relishing every curve of its long waving arms, so that the octopus still seems to be alive. So it is with their paintings of birds and dolphins and flying fish and butterflies and flowers. Authorities on Minoan art like to speak of these "free-field designs." This is an ambiguous way of saying that they painted with an angelic freedom and a divine grace. Not until our own times have men painted with such joyous abandon.

There are mysteries in Minoan Crete which we may never solve, but there is no mystery about the artists. They spoke so clearly in the language of painting that we can hear every word they said; and they seem to have rejoiced in the thought that they would be heard over the centuries. There are Minoan vases painted in 1500 B.C. which are closer to us in feeling than vases made fifty years ago. There are Minoan paintings which look as though they had been painted yesterday.

The painters provide the clue to the strange institution of bull-leaping which seems to have formed the chief amusement of the princes and princesses at the Minoan court. To paint an octopus on a vase, to suggest its living essence in a few deft strokes, the artist must make an imaginative leap into the very soul of the octopus. He must have studied it for many years, taking careful note of all its changing forms and transmutations, attentive to all its moods, until at last, in a moment of illumination, having learned all that it is possible to learn, he abandons himself to his inspiration and in a few seconds he pours onto the curving surface of the vase the pure form which represents all the octopuses he has ever seen and known. In much the same way the Chinese painters sometimes studied bamboos for twenty years before putting brush to paper in joyful surprise that they had at last mastered the essence of the bamboo. The joy is in the sudden leap which reproduced the essence of a soul.

Something of the same kind seems to have happened with the bull-leapers. They leaped for the pure joy of it, for the sense of mastery that it gave them. They leaped like dancers, and on their faces there was an expression of blissful unconcern. There was no blood, no feeling that blood was necessary or desirable. As we see them on gems and frescoes, they come to the bull naked, wearing only their loincloths, their hair carefully dressed, and the girls wear necklaces and bracelets, and sometimes red and blue frontlets. They carry no weapons, and it is far from their intention to injure the bull in any way. They come as friends and they are oblivious of danger as they run up to the bull, grasp the horns, and make the great leap, the *salto mortale*, over its back, landing safely on their feet after their headlong flight. In that single leap many things have been accomplished, many worlds have been conquered, and all are peaceful. In the mysterious way of artists they have made the leap that brings them into possession of the bull. Only the most daring could accomplish the feat, and only those who had accomplished it could say that they possessed the strength of bulls for having mastered them. Clean-limbed and sinewy, these leapers pitted themselves against bulls for the sheer joy of it.

Everything we know about Minoan civilization suggests a reverence for life so great that the public display of sacrificial victims would have been unthinkable. Occasionally, as we saw on the Hagia Triadha sarcophagus, a bull might be sacrificed on the death of a great prince, but such occasions were probably rare. The bulls were sacred, for had not Zeus come to Pasiphaë in the shape of a bull? Throughout the mythology of Minoan Crete we are presented with bulls possessing divine or regal power, and there is no end to the legends associating Minos with bulls. Minos becomes Minotaur. The royal cups and vases have the bull's head painted on them. The bull was the emblem of kingly power, as the lion and the unicorn are the emblems of the

British crown.

The double-headed ax, or *labrys*, was just as certainly the emblem of the spiritual power of the Great Mother whose rule embraced the heavens, the earth, and everything beneath the earth. She was *Diva triformis*, ruling over the three worlds, attended by doves when she was riding through the air, by lions and bulls when she walked the earth, and by serpents when she journeyed into the underworld. She was the Lady of the Wild Woods and of the Wild Beasts in one of her manifestations, and in this disguise she was known by the Greeks as Artemis. Some of her symbols, the pillar, the snake, and the owl, were taken over by Athena. She fed into all the streams of Greek mythology.

No one traveling through Crete need be surprised by the presence of the goddess. Strange things happen under those incredibly blue skies. Sometimes the sea seems to be floating in the air, and sometimes olive groves can be seen suspended over the high mountains. Even now in the remote valleys the ancient prehistoric words are spoken, and the ancient goddesses are worshiped.

But while the sense of divinity is abundantly present, it is more difficult to understand the sources of Minoan power. The jewellike palace at Knossos tells us only about the fastidious taste of a small cultivated élite, and we must go to Phaistos near the south coast to see the naked power exerted by the Minoan kings in all their glory. Here the Italians have excavated a vast palace overlooking the plain of Messara. Sir Arthur Evans found a small stairway in Knossos, about five feet wide, and called it the Great Stairway. At Phaistos there is a stairway forty feet wide, and the ruins around it are built on a corresponding scale. There are few references to Phaistos in Greek literature. Homer speaks of the ships leaving the harbor— "their blue prows borne to Egypt by the strength of wind and wave." He may have entered the harbor, for he describes it accurately: "At the time of the southwesterly gales the great rollers drive towards a headland hard by Phaistos, where only a small reef holds them back." Idomeneus, King of Crete, returned to Phaistos after the Trojan War, but he remains as shadowy as Minos.

There are no histories of Phaistos, no collections of the songs sung by her poets, no records except the tablets written in the language known as Linear B. There is the famous Phaistos disk with delicate stamped ideograms, the earliest example of printing, which has not yet been deciphered, though by substituting some of the syllabic values from the Ventris grid it would seem to be an elaborate hymn to Hera sung by the priestesses of her temple on Mount Ida.

Phaistos, standing on a rock above a brightly carpeted valley, suggests royal power with a vengeance. This power evidently derived from command of the seas, for Crete is not, and was not then, an island rich in minerals. There were no great lodes of silver in her mountains like the great silver lodes of Laurium in Attica, which provided the foundation for the wealth of Athens. There were small copper mines, and there was a large export of olive oil and purple dye from the murex shellfish. Gold was imported from Egypt and silver from the Cyclades. The wealth of Crete came from her strategic trading position and the power of her sailors to keep the sea lanes open.

Also, there were pirates. How formidable they were and continued to be we know from the accounts of the Romans, who were putting down Cretan pirates fifteen hundred years after the decline of the Minoan empire. Odysseus, coming to Ithaca in disguise at the end of his long voyage, is asked where he came from, and gives a long and happy account of his life as a Cretan, the owner of a fleet of pirate ships. "I had no liking for work," he says. "Nine times before we fought against Troy, I led my well-found fleet against foreign shores and acquired a great deal of booty. So my house grew great, and I was respected and feared by my fellow Cretans." Then he went on to tell how, with Idomeneus, he led the Cretans against Troy, and there was more booty. Another raid against Egypt was less successful, for a detachment of the Egyptian army surprised them while they were plundering farms on the banks of the Nile, and Odysseus himself escaped only by running up to the king's chariot and embracing the king's knees and invoking the royal mercy. Odysseus, of course, is lying in his teeth, but his account of the life of a Cretan pirate is clearly authentic.

The power of Crete reposed on her ships, and of these no vestiges remain. No dockyards, no naval forts have survived: we do not know how the Minoan navy was administered, or where its chief ports were to be found, or even what kind of ships were used. Some rare gems, discovered by archaeologists, show lean, high-prowed three-masters, but the designs give us few clues about the ships' armament and maneuverability. Trading stations where the Cretans sold their own produce for foreign wares are known to have existed in Egypt, Sicily, Rhodes, Cyprus, and along all the coasts of the Levant, but there is still a considerable mystery about the nature of Minoan sea power. Thucydides, who was very careful when it came to weighing up the evidence, firmly believed that Minos brought peace to the eastern Mediterranean. "When Minos built up his navy, communication by sea became safer," he wrote. "He was able to expel the raiders who were colonizing most of the islands, and thereafter the dwellers on the seacoast grew rich and began to live a more settled life." But this is the merest outline, and we would like to know far more about how it was done.

The mystery of Minoan sea power remains. There are hints, allusions, vague suggestions, moments when we seem to see clearly, and then the mist closes in again. Herodotus and, later, Diodorus tell a circumstantial story of a great armada organized by Minos against Sicily. Just as the Trojan War was supposed to have been brought about by the abduction of Helen, so this war was supposed to have been brought about by the abduction of Daedalus, the engineer. Minos was killed fighting against the Sicilian king Kokalos; thereupon, in obedience to some kind of warning from Heaven, the entire population of Crete except for the towns of Polichne and Praisos sailed for Sicily to continue the siege. At last they were compelled to abandon the siege and sailed back to Crete, but their ships were wrecked off the coast of Calabria and the survivors settled in Italy. Herodotus says that the Greeks, learning that Crete was depopulated, came to settle there, and that all these adventures took place three generations before the Trojan War.

It is an odd story, and we have no more reason to doubt it than we have to doubt the fact that there was a Trojan War. Some confirmation of the story comes from Theron, the tyrant of Acragas, who in the fifth century B.C. discovered what he claimed to be the bones of Minos and solemnly returned them to Crete. Diodorus tells us that the tomb took the form of a temple to Aphrodite with a crypt containing the bones. Just such a tomb-temple was discovered by Sir Arthur Evans in the neighborhood of the palace at Knossos.

Herodotus relates that when the Cretans returned from the Trojan War they were welcomed with famine and plague, "and then for the second time the land was depopulated." The fertile island became a graveyard.

Unless we discover an ancient history of Crete we shall never know how many times it was destroyed. Time after time the islanders reeled under the impact of natural disasters. Floods, plagues, earthquakes, tidal waves, famines struck the island; and if the worst disaster was the earthquake and tidal wave resulting from a volcanic eruption which took place near the island of Santorin about 1450 B.C., there were others nearly as dreadful. The Lady of the Wild Beasts ruled the island, but it was Poseidon the Earthshaker, with the sound like the roaring of a bull, who held it in fee.

Crete stands at the beginning of Western civilization. Long before the emergence of the Mycenaeans, the Minoans hammered out a way of life which in its freedom from prejudice and convention demonstrated that they were no longer bound helplessly to the fearful gods. They walked with their eyes wide open, and they were unafraid. Those frescoes and jewels dug out of the earth speak to us directly across the centuries, and we recognize our kinship to these people who stand at the dawn of the Western world. Sometimes they seem closer to us than the Athenians of the time of Pericles, closer by far than the Romans. They had an innocence which we have lost, and a delighted awareness of the springs of life which is almost beyond our comprehension.

Lying at the crossroads between Egypt, Palestine, Asia Minor and Greece, Crete seems to have been one of those rare places where ideas and customs and traditions from many different civilizations are focused and fused together into something entirely new. From this fusion of ancient cultures, on that island, Europe had its beginnings.

3 «« THE MYCENAEANS

ABOUT 2000 B.C. there came down the Balkan Peninsula the first of many waves of conquerors who forced their way into the heart of Greece. They were armed shepherds, speaking a form of Greek, and they were an offshoot of the great migratory wave which had come out of Southern Asia centuries before. They were armed with bronze weapons, short swords and spears, and they lived in simple horseshoe-shaped houses, no doubt because such houses permitted them to herd their sheep in the courtyard at times of danger. They lived in tightly knit clans ruled by their war chiefs, and we hear very little about their gods, far more about their goddesses. The language they spoke was akin to Sanskrit, belonging to the Indo-European group of languages, but they had no writing. They conquered the original inhabitants of Greece, the Pelasgians, and probably enslaved them. They seem to have been red-haired and blue-eyed, tall and vigorous, with a gift for building impregnable fortresses out of great blocks of hewn stone. For nearly a thousand years they were the acknowledged rulers of the mainland of Greece; then they were conquered by the Dorians and nothing more was ever heard of them.

Of the Pelasgians we know only what Greek tradition has recorded. According to Herodotus, these obscure people worshiped the god of the erect phallus according to a ritual which survived up to classical times on the island of Samothrace, and they consulted the oracle at Dodona, where the rustling of the leaves of the sacred oak was interpreted by the priests and recited as verses, very much as the Pythian priestess at Delphi would at a later time make wild utterances which the priests put into conventional hexameters. They spoke a language which was not Greek, but many of its words were incorporated into the language of the conquerors: words ending in *inthos, assos,* and *essos* are believed to be Pelasgian. "I cannot say for certain what language the Pelasgians spoke," wrote Herodotus, "but if I may conjecture from those Pelasgians who still remain among us, it must have been a barbarian tongue." There were small pockets of people speaking this tongue all over Greece, but chiefly in Arcadia.

No one knows what elements of the Pelasgian religion survived to be incorporated in the religion of the conquerors, except that Zeus inherited from them his crown of oak leaves. Pausanias, coming to Dodona in the second century A.D., records a verse chanted by the dove-priestesses who attended the sacred tree, which sounds as though it was originally composed thousands of years before:

> *Zeus was, Zeus is, Zeus shall be! O great Zeus!*
> *The Earth brings fruit: therefore pray to the Earth Mother!*

The conquerors had brought with them the Indo-European god of the thunder, Diaus or Zeus, and the cry of the priestesses is perhaps a lament over the passing of the Earth Mother from her high estate.

By the sixteenth century B.C. the conquerors had already established themselves in their fortress palaces at Mycenae, Tiryns, Thebes, and Pylos, and they were building ships and trading among the islands. They may have served as mercenaries in Egypt, and certainly they traded with the Egyptian ports, for scarabs and pots bearing inscriptions in Egyptian hieroglyphics have been found in their tombs, and their jeweled swords were sometimes engraved with scenes of ducks and herons wading in a river which can only be the Nile. The arts of Minoan Crete also influenced them, and it may have been from Crete that they derived the syllabary in which they wrote out their accounts, those endless lists of possessions found by Carl Blegen and Alan Wace at Pylos and Mycenae.

We shall call these conquerors the Mycenaeans, in the absence of a better word. At Mycenae they built a palace of unexampled splendor with a lion gate which has survived through the centuries, and the stonework of the huge protective walls flanking the gate testifies to their skill in engineering. They built vaulted stone tombs shaped like beehives, and these too are spectacular engineering feats, the lintel across the entrance to one of these tombs weighing more than 130 tons. No one knows how these things were accomplished. But while they built massively, with stupendous blocks of stone, they also built delicately. The great *tholos* which has come to be known as "the Treasury of Atreus" was decorated with delicate green columns beside the entrance, and these columns were inlaid with mosaics of white stone in chevron patterns, with here and there slender ribbings of gold.

In the *Iliad* Mycenae is a city "rich in gold," but the city flourished and perished long before Homer sang of its glory. Pausanias wandered among the ruins and wrote that he had seen the grave of Agamemnon and of the two children of Cassandra, and little more was heard of Mycenae until Heinrich Schliemann in 1876 sent his dramatic telegram to King George of Greece, announcing that he had discovered the tombs of Agamemnon, Cassandra, and her children, "together with an immense treasure of the most ancient objects of pure gold." With these alone, he wrote, it would be possible "to fill a great museum, the most wonderful in the world." This immense hoard of treasure was found within the royal grave circle inside the Lion Gate, but even in Schliemann's day there was considerable doubt whether the gold masks and jeweled swords belonged to the period of Agamemnon. Now we know that they belonged to Mycenaean kings who lived three and a half centuries before the siege of Troy. The treasure proved that a hitherto unknown civilization had existed, leaving so little trace on Greek history that neither Herodotus nor Thucydides was aware of it. To the day of his death Schliemann believed that he had gazed upon the face of Agamemnon, which crumbled as he looked at it.

Schliemann's name is now indissolubly connected with Mycenae, but it is to the more cautious archaeologists who followed that we owe our detailed knowledge of the site. Chrestos Tsountas went on patiently digging in the royal palace, the cemeteries, and the nearby ruins. Alan Wace showed conclusively that the palace must have belonged to a king who ruled long before the Trojan War. The discoveries proved that by 1600 B.C. Mycenae was the chief city of the Argolid with its trade extending throughout the Mediterranean world, and with the collapse of Minoan Crete around 1450 B.C. it inherited the power of the Minoan kings and became the leader of the Greek world.

The Mycenaeans built like men who took no thought of the

passing of time, like conquerors who intended to remain. According to Greek tradition, those vast walls could only have been built by the Cyclops, the one-eyed giants of legend. It is more likely that they were built by slaves recruited from the original Pelasgian population. Everything we know about these people suggests that they built their power on slave labor; and the inscribed tablets found at Mycenae and Pylos suggest that they were careful bureaucrats, continually recording the numbers of slaves, horses, ceremonial tripods, and chariots that fell into their hands.

They were a people in love with grandeur, but also with delicacy. The gold masks that covered the faces of their dead kings were delicately modeled to convey a sense of godlike power strangely combined with a sense of human frailty. They painted the walls of their palaces with dazzling frescoes, and not even the Minoans excelled them in the art of gem carving.

Religion at Mycenae seems to have revolved around the Great Mother who appears on many seals and signet rings. These minute carvings present her in vivid detail, in attitudes of blessing or of quiet repose. She is always bare-breasted; she wears the long flounced skirt, and is usually accompanied by her handmaidens.

The most magnificent of the seals so far discovered shows her sitting beneath the sacred tree with flowers in her hair and holding three poppies in her hand, while two priestesses and a handmaiden come to pay tribute to her. One of the priestesses, wearing a long pigtail, comes empty-handed, with one arm stretched out to touch the sacred poppies in a gesture that suggests that merely by touching them she will receive the powerful influence of the goddess. There is a small cairn of sacred stones beside the goddess, and on one of these a slender handmaiden is standing as she reaches up to pluck the fruit of the tree.

Above the outstretched arm of the priestess there are two double axes, the smaller one superimposed upon the other; they are the symbols of the goddess, the emblems of her spiritual power. Beyond the double axes there floats high in the air a presiding genius who is helmeted, holding a spear in one hand, the other hand free and perhaps waving a blessing. She hides behind a shield shaped like a figure 8. Such shields are often represented, and like the double ax the double shield suggests divine powers. The destructive ax is balanced by the protecting shield.

High above the sacred grove the sun shines in full splendor beside the crescent moon: it is at once noonday and the depth of night.

But what is most remarkable about the signet is the quiet composure and serenity of these people partaking in the worship of the goddess. The signet is extremely small, scarcely more than an inch across, but the artist has poured into it all his affection for the goddess and has clearly indicated the relationship between the participants in the drama. The goddess has recognizable features—a long straight

Figure 2. Gold signet ring from Mycenae with Great Mother and her Attendants.

nose, a broad forehead, a delicate chin, the head balanced on a long and slender neck. As she holds the three poppy heads on their long stalks she gives an impression of imperious power. Power wells up from the goddess, while the power of the heavens flows down in rings of light. In the attitudes of the priestesses there is no humility; they come to her as though by right, gravely, making their offerings out of affection for her, towering over her, with none of the servility that can be seen in Egyptian paintings showing offerings to the gods.

A very human dignity informs them. Bathed in the light of the sun and the moon, they stand and move according to their own volition.

We cannot hope to understand the full meaning of the signet. For example, we do not know the significance to be attached to the poppies, which appear on the crowns of Cretan goddesses and were associated in classical times with Demeter. We know that opium was extracted from poppies, and was given to the ill and wounded, but the three poppies on the signet seem to have a sacramental purpose. The poppies are as mysterious as the strange objects on the side facing the tree. They may be flowers, helmets, ox skulls, but more likely they are the skulls of lions. No one knows what kind of tree is represented. Schliemann pronounced the fruit to be pineapples or perhaps breadfruit, such as he had seen in Central America. He thought the women wore visors, and he was puzzled by their masculine appearance; he also noted that the curved bands of their skirts mirrored the crescent shapes which are to be seen everywhere on the signet. For some reason he thought the waving lines beneath the sun and moon represented the sea, though it is more likely that they represent rings of heavenly light or the Milky Way.

The signet of the Great Mother hints at an unexpected tenderness in the religion of the Mycenaean Greeks. It does not stand alone. Many other signets have been discovered, showing her before her altars or on the summits of her mountains. So far only one representation of the Great Mother in ivory has been discovered. Found in 1939, this small carving, only three inches high, shows her sitting with her daughter while a divine child plays at her knees. Once again we see the heavy flounced skirt, the short sleeves, and the tight jacket that leave the breasts bare; in addition there is a long, curiously woven scarf curling around the back of the Great Mother and her daughter, joining them together. The Great Mother throws her arm over her daughter's shoulder, and the daughter in her turn places a protective hand on the shoulder of the divine child, who wears a long robe with a ropelike girdle. Tenderness encloses them. They belong to one another, forming an enclosed circle, but the power of their affection radiates outward like the ripples on a pond when a stone is flung into it.

The Great Mother is of course the same goddess who ruled over Minoan Crete, and no doubt she was borrowed by the Mycenaeans, who made her more gentle, charming, and affectionate. We know the names of some of the Mycenaean gods, for they are recorded on the Linear B tablets, usually in connection with offerings. Zeus (*Diwo*), Hera (*Era*), Athena (*Atana*), and Poseidon (*Posedao*) are clearly indicated, while *Diwia* and *Posedaeia* may be the female counterparts of the gods or the names of priestesses. Iphimedia, who appears briefly and mysteriously as a semidivine figure in Homer, appears also on the tablets. There is no Aphrodite, no Apollo, no Dionysus, the name *Diwonusoyo* on a Pylos tablet apparently having nothing to do with the god. The gods received large offerings. On one tablet we find Poseidon accepting offerings of a bull, four rams, many measures of wheat, wine and honey, as well as twenty cheeses and two sheepskins. We also find gifts of oil intended for "a spreading of couches," no doubt the ceremonial coupling of the images of the gods well known in later Greek and Roman rites.

With the help of Homer and the archaeologists, it is possible to piece together an account of the daily lives of the Mycenaeans. We know what they wore and how they decorated themselves and what they ate. We know some, but not all, of the gods they worshiped, and what language they spoke, and how they built their houses, and how they buried their dead. We are beginning to know them so well that if we saw them walking across a field we would recognize them instantly.

The men wore their hair long and bound with fillets; the rich bound their hair with gold and silver ribbons. In summer they wore long-sleeved cloaks reaching to their knees, which they exchanged in winter for long woolen capes. They delighted in ornamental belts, earrings, necklaces; they wore gloves and furs. They had chairs and tables, but no plates; food was eaten off the table, which was afterward washed with sponges. They ate meat: mutton, goat's flesh, pork, and more rarely beef. All these animals were domesticated. Fowl were kept in their farmyards, and geese wandered in and out of their houses. Game included wolves, deer, wild boar, wild goats, and rabbits. They ate fish, and especially delighted in oysters. They grew wheat, barley, millet, beans, peas, and lentils, and cultivated vines and olive trees. They sweetened their wine with honey, and enjoyed the fruit of their orchards. In the garden of Alcinoüs there were pears, apples, figs, and pomegranates. Children ate meat, marrow, relishes, and wine, but there seems to have been no milk. Cheese was the commonest dish: they almost lived on it. There were no cats—the cat appeared in

Greece about the sixth century B.C.—but they had hunting dogs and watchdogs.

Soldiers were armed with round shields, swords, and spears, while the commanders bore enormous tower-shields which covered them from their feet to the neck: on the inside of the shields they hung their battle-axes and whatever other weapons they found necessary. Schliemann discovered the famous Warrior Vase, showing Mycenaean soldiers marching off to battle while their women sadly bid them farewell. They wear fringed kilts, stockings up to their knees, leather jerkins, and crested helmets with cheekpieces. From the front of each helmet protrudes a bull's horn. Such horns are men-

Figure 3. The Warrior Vase discovered by Schliemann.

tioned in Homer, who also describes a curious helmet made of felt plated with rings of boars' tusks. Wace was able to show that a collection of boar tusks found at Mycenae would make just such a helmet as Homer describes.

The organization of society in Mycenaean times seems to have resembled the organization of society in the early Middle Ages, with the kings exercising arbitrary power over the nobles who in turn exercise arbitrary power over the rest of the population. The nerve center of Mycenaean society was the fortress, usually built on rocky outcrops dominating a wide valley: sometimes the fortress retained the familiar horseshoe shape, though it was built of enormous blocks of stone. Within the fortress walls were the apartments of the king, his wife, and his servants. Here was the treasury, the armory, the storehouse for surplus grain, and the stables for the royal horses. Near the fortress gate were the graves of the royal ancestors, whose beneficent influence was believed to protect the ruling family. Schliemann found in some of the graves a strange funnellike opening, through which he thought offerings of wine were made to the illustrious dead; they may have been the funnels through which the living conversed with their ancestors.

Burial and cremation were both practiced, as they were later in classical Greece. The bodies of the kings seem to have been embalmed, for Schliemann found considerable evidence of embalming and was even able to recognize the features of kings who had died thirty-five centuries before he opened their tombs. The gold masks, with the holes in the ears so that they could be tied to the dead face, seem to have been the Mycenaean equivalent of the far more sumptuous masks of the Pharaohs.

In this simple and primitive society organized around the sacred person of the king, the nobility enjoyed lives of quiet luxury. We see them reclining languidly at the windows of their houses, or amusing themselves in chariot races. The women possessed mirrors of polished bronze backed with ivory. They wore richly embroidered garments, and on ceremonial occasions they wore coronets and tiaras of hammered gold leaf. Minoan fashions were followed slavishly, and the Minoan way of life seems to have been scrupulously observed. There was, however, one important difference. Crete was protected by its ships, and there is almost no trace of military equipment, while the Mycenaean economy was geared for war, harsh, militant, and piratical.

In the past few years we have come to know the language spoken by the Mycenaeans. Largely through the efforts of Alice Kober and Michael Ventris, an English architect and cryptographer, the inscriptions written in the language known as Linear B have been deciphered. Unfortunately, most of the tablets refer to tax assessments, landholdings, military stores, and temple offerings, and though they throw considerable light on Mycenaean bureaucracy, they tell us little about the organization of the state or the ordinary lives of the people. The enormous sustained effort which went into deciphering the inelegant characters scratched on mud was rewarded with such tidbits as:

> One pair wheels bound with silver,
> One pair wheels bound with bronze, unfit for service.

The language proved to be Greek in a very ancient and primitive form, but recognizably related to the Greek spoken in the classical age. The sound of the language would approximate the sound of a modern Greek peasant speaking jerkily with a mouthful of stones, in a high wind. There appear to have been no diphthongs, and all words ended in vowels. The script was syllabic, the inscribed characters representing a vowel or a vowel with a consonant, so that the familiar Greek name Eteocles was represented as *E-te-wo-ke-re-we-i-jo*, found in the genitive case and presupposing the name Etewoklewēs. Ventris was able to decipher a surprisingly large number of personal names, including Antenor, Eumenes, Idomeneus, Hector, Pirithoüs, and Theseus. The proof that Ventris had broken the code lay in the astronomical odds against coincidence—far too many of his readings make excellent sense. It was already a language with a fair degree of sophistication, ready for use, and the songs sung at court and the chronicles compiled for the Mycenaean kings may yet be discovered.

The Linear B script seems to have come into existence about 1500 B.C. and to have survived for about three hundred years. The Mycenaeans employed it when they settled in the ruins of Minoan Crete, where they compiled the same careful records that they compiled on the mainland. Here they remained until about 1200 B.C., when Mycenaean civilization vanished from the face of the earth. The great palaces were destroyed, the kings were killed or driven out, the art of writing was lost, and the arts and crafts of the Mycenaean age left no trace on the imaginations of the Greeks. It was as though they had never been.

To this day no one knows who destroyed the Mycenaeans, but where historical records fail, poetry may provide the necessary clues. The *Iliad* describes an attack by the confederated Greek tribes on a city in Asia Minor. Homer tells us that plague broke out among the invading armies and that there were palace revolts during the absence of the kings. Plagues, revolts, the vast bloodletting on the coast of Asia Minor, all these may have accounted for the destruction of Mycenaean power. The *Iliad* and the traditional legends concerning the murder of Agamemnon and the doom on the house of Atreus may be dramatic representations of the last years of Mycenaean civilization before it was silenced forever. Thucydides believed that eighty years after the Trojan War the Mycenaeans were themselves conquered, but he does not say and evidently did not know who conquered them.

Perhaps the conquerors were the Dorians, who appeared about 1100 B.C. in northern Greece and pushed their way steadily southward. They came along the valley of the Vardar and divided into two streams, one going down the east coast and the other down the west coast, until they ultimately converged in the Peloponnese in the region which came to be known as Sparta. On their southward march they left small settlements and colonies behind. The small state of Doris in central Greece and the island of Leucas off the west coast remained Doric up to classical times, but the Peloponnese was their main stronghold. Not all of the Peloponnese fell into their hands, for Elis, Arcadia and Achaea remained unconquered. Dorian influence swept up to the gates of Athens, and it was one of the proudest boasts of the Athenians that the Dorians never entered their city.

One by one the great Mycenaean strongholds fell before the invaders. Tiryns, Pylos, and Mycenae fell. Wherever they could, the Dorians destroyed the evidence of Mycenaean civilization. There was a puritanical streak in them; they were stern, disciplined, impassive, as though they felt it a duty to present a mask to the world. Their kings claimed descent from Heracles, and they claimed to be returning to their lost possessions. Savagely authoritarian, they built up a civilization on a slave economy, which permitted a large number of nobles to live strenuously in the small ugly villages under the frowning slopes of Mount Taygetus, which constituted their capital. Some, discontented with their gloomy valleys, built ships and sailed off to more luxurious pastures. They stormed Knossos and destroyed the last remnants of a civilization which had endured for two thousand years. They captured Rhodes, a still more fertile island, and neighboring Cos, which was to become a holy island sacred to Asclepius, the god of medicine. Halicarnassus, too, fell to them, so that they commanded the narrows between Rhodes and the mainland and might have become a great Mediterranean naval power if they had possessed the quick intelligence and mobility of the mainland Greeks who were even then colonizing the islands of the Aegean and building new cities along the western coast of Asia Minor.

The Dorian invasion did not take place suddenly. For hundreds of years waves of these new invaders fought their way through Greece. It was a time of uproar, of terrible dislocations and strains, for though the Mycenaean power had been destroyed there was as yet nothing to take its place. The Dorians used weapons of iron, and were merciless in employing these new weapons against weaker bronze, but they were heavily outnumbered on the mainland, and except in the Peloponnese they were never able to achieve physical mastery over the native population. Yet no one dared live any longer in the open villages; everyone hurried to the comparative safety of the few walled cities, hoping to live out the storm. The Dorian invasions shook Greece to her foundations. For centuries the hurts were to be remembered and the wounds remained unhealed.

Gradually a kind of peace settled over the mainland—a peace of exhaustion. Trade began to flourish; coinage was introduced; and the riches of Asia flowed from the colonies back into the parent cities which had sent out their young men to settle in the new lands. At the foot of the Acropolis in Athens, in the marshlands south of the crag dominating the plains, a small city was rising. In time this city would become the school of Greece, but in those days it was still a small huddle of makeshift houses in the shadow of a gaunt hill.

Athens was to grow and gather to herself nearly all the intellectual fire of Greece, but her beginnings were slow and undistinguished. She was to claim later that the intellectual resurgence of Greece came from her own colonists settled on the shores of Asia Minor, and so it did, but the people of Asia Minor also played their part by intermarrying with the Athenians. Out of that confrontation came the real beginnings of Western civilization.

4 ≪ THE COMING OF THE GODS

WHEN Homer was writing the
Iliad and the *Odyssey*, some two or three hundred years after the
Dorian invasions, the gods were still new. They came flocking to
Greece and Ionia from all the points of the compass. Some, like Zeus,
came with the great migrations, while Dionysus came from Thrace
and Aphrodite from ancient Sumer by way of Ashkelon. Some came
from Egypt, while still others have recognizable Hittite ancestors.
All were refashioned according to the shaping imagination of the
Greeks, assuming the forms demanded by the times. By about 800 B.C.
the Greek Pantheon was complete: the government of the universe
belonged to twelve gods who reigned on Mount Olympus. To them
was entrusted full power over heaven and earth and the regions below
the earth.

In a revealing passage Herodotus tells us that the oldest divinities
of Greece were Hera, Hestia, Themis, the Graces and the Nereids—
all feminine. Only one survived to join the ranks of the Olympians,
and her position was always tentative and uncertain. The twelve
canonical Olympians were Zeus, Hera, Demeter, Athena, Apollo,
Poseidon, Aphrodite, Dionysus, Artemis, Ares, Hephaestus, and
Hermes. Of these the first five wielded by far the greater powers,
while the last four wielded almost no power at all. Seven gods and
five goddesses were included in the Olympian canon, but in fact four
gods and four goddesses divided the effective power among themselves.

According to the mathematics of divinity, there was in Homeric
times a rough balance of power between the male and female princi-

ples. The ancient female goddesses of the Pelasgians were supplanted by gods and goddesses of a divine family derived from many origins.

We know these gods and goddesses so well that we are sometimes in danger of taking them for granted. We tell ourselves that Zeus is the father of the gods, Demeter the Earth Mother, Athena the guardian of cities, Apollo the lord of the clear intelligence, but when we examine them more closely, all that appears to be simple, clear-cut, and intelligible about them begins to grow obscure. They shade into one another, continually assuming new shapes and acquiring new powers. They pursue their own independent lives according to a divine logic, and they are continually encroaching upon each other. They borrow the robes, emblems, and machinery of other gods. They form small intimate groups, but the groups tend to break up, to become new splinter groups. Dionysus, the last to enter Olympus, was originally the god of the erect phallus, of orgiastic and barbarian rituals, but he too is tamed at last, and Apollo's temple at Delphi becomes his natural home.

Not only Proteus was continually changing his shape. Even Zeus, originally a sky-god, whose voice was heard in the thunder and whose face could be seen in the clouds when the lightning struck, acquired qualities which almost removed him entirely from the raging elements. He acquired wisdom, benevolence, the sense of justice, and from being a violent youth he entered into serene old age. So Phidias depicted him at Olympia in gold and ivory: not stern but gentle in the consciousness of power. So powerful and so gentle that the image of Olympian Zeus became in time the image of the Byzantine Christ.

In Homer, Zeus is still youthful and impulsive, even, it would seem, unsure of himself, for he boasts prodigiously:

Hearken unto me, all you gods and goddesses,
I shall say unto you what my heart biddeth me.
Let no gods or goddesses come between me and my desire,
Or attempt the thing I shall do.
Come, make trial, O you gods, that you may know—
Bind to the heavens a chain of gold,
Lay hold of it, see whether you can throw me down,
Though you labor, from my highest heavens.
But should I desire to draw you up by my chain,

Then would I draw up with you the whole earth and the sea,
And tie the chain like a ribbon around Olympus,
Leaving you hanging in space.
So am I greater far than any gods or men.

So he boasts like any Herod in the miracle plays, and like Herod he seems to be running for a fall. This is not the voice of the thunder, but that of a god who has acquired a large and unruly family and is not yet sure how he can cope with them.

In time the god of thunder becomes the god of the peaceful skies. The savagery is burned away; the heart of darkness is transformed into a calm and all-pervading light. Homer records the progress from stormy boasting to serenity when he describes the abode of the gods on Mount Olympus:

Here is the abode of the gods, the everlasting
Place of their sojourn.
This place is never shaken by winds,
Nor is it ever moistened by the rain,
Nor does any snow ever fall there,
But the wide air is made eternally clean and cloudless,
Shining in the light of a hovering whiteness.

In such a world there is no place for thunder, nor for the sharp claws of eagles. Already we have reached the ideal world which was to be celebrated by Plato: the world in which all the images are hushed in the silence of contemplation.

So it happens all through the early history of the gods. Apollo, the terrible avenger, becomes the god of healing. Athena, the goddess of the wilds, becomes the protector of industry and cities. Aphrodite from being a goddess of lust becomes the symbol of immortal beauty. The thunder-god comes at last to a place where no thunder is ever heard.

Sometimes we can watch these changes taking place, but more often we must be content to watch them at so great a distance that we can only guess what is happening. Then, toward the end of the eighth century B.C., the process of change comes to a stop. Quite suddenly the gods appear fully formed, clothed in divine flesh, and conscious of their mission to bring civilization down to earth.

Athena

THE goddess with a name like the whisper of the wind among olive
leaves may have been the most ancient of all the Greek goddesses.
She was older than Athens, and perhaps older than any settlement in
Greece by the fair-haired Achaeans, belonging to the original Pelasgic
inhabitants of the place, who may have worshiped her in the form of
an owl. Like the owl she was always wise and stealthy, a creature of
the dusk and the night, with shining eyes of unfathomable quickness
in seeking her prey, and with sharp talons which could kill in a
moment. To the very end, even when she was transformed into a
majestic warrior-goddess, with gleaming shield and spear, there was
something of the woodland about her.

At a very early period Athena was worshiped as a virgin goddess,
remote and unapproachable, cut off from the ordinary life of mankind
and of the gods, reigning in lonely splendor. The Mycenaeans knew
her as *Potnia Atana*, the Lady Athena, as we know from the inscribed tablets found at Pylos, and in gems found at Mycenae we
see her already helmeted and almost invisible behind her protective
shield shaped like a figure 8. She is not of the earth, for we see her
hovering in the air above the priestesses who are making offerings
to the Great Mother. She brandishes a sword, and in so doing offers
the benediction of the heavenly powers on the fertile earth. She is the
virgin and inviolate spirit of the heavens mysteriously presiding over a
festival celebrating fecundity. Perhaps she was Queen of Heaven,
while the Great Mother was Queen of Earth.

How vast and terrible were her powers we know from Hesiod's
Theogony, where he speaks of her as "the Lady with the eyes of an
owl, the strange and awful one, the strife-stirring, the unwearying
leader of the army, who delights in tumults and wars and battles."
Hesiod is speaking of a time before men were made, and therefore
the wars are heavenly wars. He goes on to describe how she emerged
in full armor from the head of Zeus, but so strange a birth suggests
that she was never born. Zeus conquered the heavens only to discover
that there were whole regions where she still reigned supreme; and
even when she was admitted into the circle of the Olympian gods she
remained always secret and apart from them. The *Homeric Hymn to*

Athena describes her rising from the head of Zeus with "warlike arms of flashing gold," striking fear into the hearts of the gods:

There she stood, shaking her sharp spear,
While Olympus reeled at the sight of the owl-eyed goddess,
And the earth wept pitifully, and the sea rose in dark waves,
Which suddenly burst into foam, while the Son of Hyperion
Caused his swift-footed horses to halt on their journey
For a long age, until at last the goddess Pallas Athene
Stripped from her immortal shoulders her heavenly armor,
Making Zeus glad.

But one cannot imagine Athena stripping herself of her armor and standing naked before the gods, though it might have amused the gods to think that such things were possible.

The Greeks saw no difficulty imagining her both as an owl and as a virgin. Sometimes at night or at dusk, coming upon an olive grove in Attica, you can see the transformation taking place. The olive tree, even on the darkest night, wears a ghostly shimmer of silver, and the eyes of an owl perched on the high branches seems to transform the whole tree into the appearance of a woman moving toward you. Then the eyes vanish, there is a mysterious whirring of wings, followed by a thin scream in the darkness as a field mouse is caught in the owl's talons.

Long before she emerged from the head of Zeus, Athena was the owl with the terrible eyes, the lady of the darkness, associated with sudden screams and a mysterious whirring noise, and very wise in her ways. So she became the divine sister, the wise counselor, the relentless avenger in war, the herald of victories, and the virgin whose body no one had ever looked upon. She had the wisdom of an owl sitting contemplatively on the branches of an olive tree and the aroused fury of an owl swooping on its prey; and her wisdom and her fury were not contradictory.

For the Athenians she was always the owl, and she was always associated with olive trees. They stamped the owl on their coins, and when an owl fluttered over the shipwrecked Persian fleet at Salamis, they knew she had come as a herald of victory. On their vases they depicted her wearing the wings of an owl, but they gave her the slender body of a young woman, with a look of defiance on her stern features, and they put a helmet on her head.

Figure 4. Athena, wearing the wings of an owl.

Athena did not belong to Athens alone; all over the Greek world she had her sanctuaries and shrines. In time she became the most powerful of the goddesses, as Apollo was to become the most powerful of the gods, while Zeus sank further and further back into the mists of Mount Olympus, thundering occasionally but no longer wielding effective lordship over men. Zeus was far away, but Athena was always near. Like Zeus, she carried the aegis with the Gorgon's head on her breast, and she also wielded the thunderbolt, hurling down sudden death and all manner of disasters when anything happened to displease her, and while she borrowed her more terrible powers from Zeus, she retained her ancient role as the beneficent Queen of Heaven, sending down light and warmth and fruitful dew to give prosperity to fields and plants.

By the time Phidias carved her in gold and ivory in the Parthenon she had absorbed so many powers from so many different sources that the contraries were all mixed up in her. She was the goddess of war, of peace, of lovers, of childbearing, of industry, of the fertile fields; she was the goddess who protected children, but she also protected the city councilors. Almost she was whatever anyone wanted her to be so long as she could be represented as a virgin of severe beauty and deliberate purpose.

She was perhaps the greatest of the inventions of the Greeks, for without being bloodless, possessing no prophetical powers, strangely independent of the world of the gods, gravely and serenely serving the human intelligence, she represented all that was pure. At the heart of her mystery, under whatever form she was seen, there was purity incarnate.

Demeter

LONG after Athena was firmly established among the Greeks, Demeter appeared as a wanderer along the cost of Attica, coming perhaps from Sicily, though no one knew for certain where she came from. She was the Earth Mother, but when we hear about her first in a poem composed during the eighth century or the beginning of the seventh, she appears as one who has discarded the panoply of mythology and wears a very human face. She is no longer, if she ever was, the ancient primitive goddess of fertility, bringer of abundance. She is a woman overwhelmed by grief as she wanders helplessly in search of her lost daughter.

In the beginning there were only the footfalls of the weeping woman along the echoing shores. At last, coming to Eleusis, she rested below the citadel of King Keleos, and forever afterward the stone where she rested was known as the Laughless Stone.

No one knew she was the sister of Zeus, queen of the underworld and of all growing things, "the lady of the golden sword," her swords being the stalks of wheat and the shoots of flowers. The king's daughters pitied her and brought her into the palace, but she refused to be comforted: only once, and that was when the old nurse Iambe uttered an obscene oath, did she melt a little. Once, seeing the old crone by the fireside with nothing to do, King Keleos entrusted her with his sickly son. She gave the boy a bath and then raked a deep hole in the embers of a fire, and put him in. The boy's mother was hiding in the nursery and snatched her son from the flames. Demeter sprang forward to snatch the son back, but the screaming of the queen of Eleusis unnerved her. "Unhappy woman, for having broken the spell," the goddess said, and suddenly she removed her hood, and her corn-colored hair fell to the ground, and she had the burning eyes of a goddess, and the look of power.

It is all the wildest of fairy tales: the old crone, the broken spell, the child in the fire. But Demeter in her grief is a completely convincing figure, being the most human of the goddesses. She is all women weeping for their lost children. As the *Homeric Hymn to Demeter* describes her, she does not know and cannot guess what has happened to her daughter Persephone, but the poet knows:

She was gathering flowers with the deep bosomed daughters of Ocean:
Roses, crocuses, lovely violets, irises and hyacinths
In the soft grassy meadows, and the narcissus also,
A marvelous shining flower fashioned by Earth
At the bidding of Zeus to please the god of the underworld,
A snare for the blossoming maiden, and all who set eyes on it,
Whether gods or mortals, were awed at the sight.
Out of its roots a hundred flowers sprang.
It scented the air with sweetness:
All heaven and earth and the sea-swell laughed with joy.
Marveling, the girl stretched out her hand to the lovely bauble,
But the earth with its many roads gaped open,
And there on the plain of Nysa the King of Terrors
With deathless horses sprang out upon her,
Aïdoneus, son of Cronus, lord of the many names.
He caught her up in his golden chariot; weeping,
She cried out to her father, the perfect, the most high,
And none heard her voice, the enduring gods were silent:
Silent were mortal men and the olive trees laden with fruit.

Persephone vanished, only to emerge from her imprisonment under the earth four months later. She had become Korê, the corn maiden, and thereafter the mystery of the Mother and the Maiden were to be celebrated at Eleusis for centuries in a rite so secret that even today we can only guess what happened in the great temple that looked out at Salamis and the sea.

There were gay processions from Athens, with pauses at the wayside shrines for libations, sacrifices, and ceremonial dances, and much banter, and some obscenity. Aristophanes heard a fragment of conversation along the Sacred Way and duly reported it in his play *The Frogs:* "Just now I saw through the corner of my eye a ravishing girl with her nipples bursting through a rent in her garment. O Dionysus, king of the dance, guide my footsteps!"

So they went gaily to Eleusis, which they reached at night, when torches were lit and the worshipers ran wildly along the shore with their torches held aloft, imitating Demeter searching for her lost daughter. In the morning more solemn rites were announced by the herald with the summons: "You who are about to die, come near!" For the mystery of Demeter took the form of a death—a death into life.

"The things done, the things said, the things shown": these were the basis of the ceremonies, which took the form of recitations and the display of the ear of wheat, the golden sword, and a sacred marriage consummated by the priest and priestess of Demeter to shouts of "Rain! Conceive!" During part of the ceremony the initiate was led through blind alleys and corridors in total darkness, while thunder echoed against the walls, and he was in a state of abject terror when he came out suddenly into the blinding lights in the presence of the revealed mystery, which may have been the sacred marriage, or perhaps it was only the priestess lifting up in silence an ear of wheat. In the end Persephone was reconciled with her mother.

No one knows exactly what happened during the mystery; only that there was a triumph over death. "Blessed is he," wrote Pindar, "who, having seen all this, goes beneath the earth; he knows the end of life, and he knows its god-sent beginning."

From an old woman who had once wept helplessly along the seashore in search of her lost daughter came the promise of eternal life. Demeter was the goddess who touched men's hearts most deeply. In her person all sorrows and griefs were represented, and at the same time she represented the changing seasons and she blessed the ripening of the wheat. Zeus, Apollo, and Athena were cold to human sorrow. They assumed vast emblematic shapes of power, immortal, death-defying, but those who knew death and were not immortal could find little consolation from their lips. They were admired and adored, but not loved as Demeter was loved. Demeter was Mother Earth, the gentle nurse of creation, sorrowing for the lost seeds when they vanished beneath the earth, radiant with joy when they rose from the earth again. Zeus and Athena wielded their thunderbolts, and Apollo his silver bow: Demeter wielded an ear of wheat.

Apollo

THE story was told that when Apollo left the holy island of Delos to conquer Greece, a dolphin guided his ship to the little town of Crisa in Phocis, lying beneath the Shining Cliffs. The young god leaped from his ship disguised as a star at high noon; flames poured out of him, and the flash of his splendor lit the sky; and then the star vanished, and there was only a young god armed with a bow and arrow marching up the steep road that led to the dragon's lair. When he had slain the dragon he announced in a clear ringing voice to the gods that he claimed possession of all the territory he could see from where he was standing. For his own lodging he had chosen the loveliest place in Greece, and thereafter the hills beneath the Shining Cliffs were always associated with him.

But when Apollo killed the Python at Delphi and built his palace there, he was already old, though represented in the guise of a youth. He had traveled through many places and accumulated many legends; he had fathered children in many widely scattered countries, and he had assumed so many strange and sometimes conflicting powers that there was always an element of mystery about him. He was the god of healing, and the god of sudden death. He was the god who protected the flocks and the cattle, and was therefore beloved by the country-men, but he was also the god who presided over the foundation of cities and the establishment of civil constitutions. He was the god of prophecy and mysterious forewarnings, but he was also the god of song and music. He was the god of mysteries and miracles, and he was the god of the clear intelligence. No other god had so many op-posites mixed up in him, and none rode over so many contradictions so triumphantly.

At the opening of the *Iliad*, Apollo, the Shining One, descends from Olympus "with a face as dark as night." In hot rage he destroys the invaders of Troy. He has reason to hate them because of the harm they have done to his priest, and so he shoots them down mercilessly with his invisible arrows which bring the plague to their camp. The *Iliad* opens with the Trojan plain lit by the funeral pyres of the Achaeans who died of the plague. At the beginning we hear very little of the wrath of Achilles: that will come later. For the moment there is only the far greater wrath of Apollo, the nine-day twanging of his bowstring as he destroys dogs, mules, and men indifferently. This is not the god who was to say "Know thyself" and "Follow the mean" at Delphi. This is the god of pure unbridled terror.

At the end of the *Iliad*, Apollo has changed almost beyond recog-nition. He has become the wise counselor, the god of pity and re-morse, hating all displays of arrogance. Achilles has dragged Hector's body around the tomb of Patroclus; he has committed evil upon the defenseless dead. "Great he may be," Apollo says, "but he should beware of our just wrath. In his fury he is dishonoring the dumb earth." The gods approve his words, and the mangled body of Hector is healed by their divine power, so that no wounds show, and there is no dust on him. From being the god of terror and the plague he has become a god of blessings.

Homer seems to have been writing when the character of Apollo was still not completely formed, when the contrary forces had not yet settled down into an uneasy alliance. As protector of the Trojans, he was a god of Ionia, and perhaps the greatest of their gods. Vitruvius tells us that the Ionian cities built a Doric temple to Panionian Apollo, and in this temple the proportions of the Doric order were first worked out: and he adds that these proportions were designed to reflect the character of the male body at its most beautiful. The Doric temple was therefore an abstract portrait of Apollo himself, superbly masculine, rising triumphantly from the earth, the stately Doric columns representing the power surging in him, his limbs, his torso, the beautiful head. That portrait may have subtly modified the character of the god: through architecture he became the god of order and the clear intelligence and the protector and champion of the arts.

Something of this kind must have happened, for his deepest roots are with the dark gods of the earth. All that was death-dealing, prophetic, and mysterious about him seems to have come from that earlier existence before architecture seized him by the throat and transformed him.

We think of Apollo as the god of the sun, but it was not as a sun-god that he came to wield his empire over men. For Homer Helios was the sun-god, and Apollo was close to the earth. He was the guardian of the earth's purity, the hater of pollutions, and therefore the enemy of the Achaeans, who polluted the sacred earth of Troy by their mere presence. The Ionians, building their new and gleaming cities on the coasts of Asia Minor, self-consciously striving for artistic form, would seem to have impressed the god into their service; and from being the god who safeguarded the purity of the earth he became the god who touched their cities and their arts with his holiness and bathed them in the light of his purity, his enchanting beauty, and his formidable power.

Apollo, then, was an Ionian god who made the journey to Greece

by way of the sacred island of Delos. In the beginning, according to
the *Homeric Hymn to Delian Apollo*, the island doubted whether
it could support the presence of the god:

How shall I receive the god, the proud one,
The arrogant one who stands in the highest place
Above all the gods and people of the teeming earth?
My heart is fearful at the thought of his coming,
For when he sees me at the first leap of the sunrise
Surely he will despise me, a heap of barren stones!
He will press his foot on me, he will thrust me
Into the depths of the sea, and the waves will wash over me,
And then he will turn away into another place
And build his temple in a land of fruitful trees,
And I shall be lost in the dark sea. Only the black seals
And the many-footed creatures of the sea shall dwell on me . . .

Apollo, according to the legend, not only came to the island, but
chose to be born there, and the Greeks never tired of celebrating his
miraculous birth. Theognis in the sixth century B.C. spoke of how his
mother, the goddess Leto, "grasped the palm tree in her tender hands
and gave birth to the fairest of immortals beside the wheel-shaped lake,
and the whole earth laughed for joy," and three centuries later Callimachus described how the island blazed in a golden glory at the
moment of birth:

Gold were the foundations of the island,
Gold were the ripples in the wheel-shaped lake,
Gold was the sheltering palm tree,
Gold were the rolling floods of the river Inopus,
And gold was the ground from which the Mother lifted up her Son.

They said that to celebrate his birth the islands of the Cyclades
wheeled round in holy joy, and strange perfumes were wafted over
the island and white swans suddenly appeared on the lake. Leto did
not give her son milk from her breast: she gave him ambrosia and
nectar, and he grew up tall and straight in the twinkling of an eye.
For centuries a palm tree marked the place where he was born, and
Odysseus remembered the fresh beauty of the palm tree beside the
lake when he emerged naked from the reeds and saw Nausicaä playing
ball with her maidens. "I never saw anyone so beautiful, neither man

nor woman," he declared. "I am blinded by admiration, and I can only compare you with the young palm tree which I saw when I was at Delos near the altar of Apollo."

Apollo ruled the world from Delphi, young and victorious. Aeschylus called him "the young god who has ridden down powers gray with age." His temple at Delphi testified to his triumph, for though Zeus claimed him as a son, yet he had no very visible father and was in fact the rival of Zeus in men's affections. And just as Athena became associated with a kind of intellectual maturity which derived from the purity of her mind, so Apollo became associated with a conception of strenuous masculine purity. He was the defender of the winged intelligence as it soared through the untraveled spaces.

Yet to the end there was something strangely foreign about him, and he was never completely at home in Greece. In the fighting at Troy he resolutely defended the Trojans. He destroyed the Greek host, championed Hector, and was responsible for the death of Achilles. He had many homes, and one of them was in the far north, in the country of the Hyperboreans, and every year he rode into the unknown and uncharted regions beyond the frontiers of Greece. He was "the god who vanishes," *deus absconditus*, returning with the first swallows.

At the table of the gods he led the Muses in dance and song, accompanying them on his lyre. He was the protector of poets, and spoke in careful verses from his oracle at Delphi. His last recorded words were spoken to Julian the Apostate, who visited his shrine in A.D. 362 on the eve of his disastrous campaign in Persia. The Roman emperor asked what he could do to preserve the glory of the god, who replied:

> *Tell the King the fair-wrought house has fallen.*
> *No shelter has Apollo, nor sacred laurel leaves.*
> *The fountains now are silent; the voice is stilled.*

The voice was stilled, but Apollo remained to haunt the Western imagination with his shining glory. As the god who presided over youthful daring, swift and intrepid as his own thoughts, he retained his empire over men and was never completely forgotten.

When the Greeks portrayed him they poured into him all their worship of the intellect. They represented him always with a bow in one hand and an offering bowl in the other, with a body that was

Head of a Griffin. Found in the Kladeos at Olympia.

The Lion Gate at Mycenae.

Grave Circle at Mycenae.

Ladies of the Court fresco, Palace of Knossos.

Ivory Group—the Great Mother, Daughter, Divine Child.

Statuette of Snake Goddess in Ivory and Gold.

Bronze statuette of Apollo from Thebes.

Gold Mask from Mycenae.

strenuously masculine and features of an almost feminine sensitivity, with the light of thought dawning in him. Imperious and pensive, he betrays his divine power by intellectual beauty and by a certain grave serenity. The Greek artists depicted him in many aspects, but even when they represented his tenderness, as in the boyish ringleted Apollo of Piombino, we are aware of his divinity, and the beauty of the Apollo of Leontini with the delicate ivy tendril, as we see him on a coin struck by Phrygillos, is clearly related to the earlier portrait, though now he is older, more mature, and infinitely more subtle. Grown older still, in early manhood, he appears in the "Chatworth" Apollo in the British Museum, in a mask of terrible power and transcendent divinity, and so he appears again in the beautiful coin struck by Heracleidas in Catana with his sunburst of bay leaves and fountain of golden hair. And still older, still graver, the face now gaunt with thought, he appears in his superb nakedness in the bronze statue recently discovered at Piraeus. If he grew any older, he would become Zeus.

Aphrodite

ATHENA belongs wholly to the Greek imagination, her roots so deep in the past that it is unlikely that we shall ever find them. Aphrodite came late on the scene, and never wholly made her peace with the Greek gods. This beautiful and rebellious goddess only came to birth, according to Hesiod, when Uranus, the god of Heaven, spread himself lovingly at dusk over Earth, and at the moment of the embrace Cronus cut off his private members with a sickle of gray flint and sent them plunging into the sea; and out of the spilled seed swirling on the waters or the white foam following in the wake of the floating members Aphrodite was born. Then she floated across the sea, passing close to the island of Cythera and coming to land at Cyprus, where the earth flowered under her feet. Hesiod tells the story unconvincingly, as though he only half believed it, and he evidently regarded her as a creature born in the night, half cousin to the Titans and the Giants. He says, too, that from the very beginning she had the honor of entering among the assembly of the gods, bringing with her "the whisperings of maidens and smiles and deceits and sweet raptures and embraces and caresses." It is a lengthy catalogue, which seems to have been added as an afterthought.

Hesiod is no more convincing than Homer, who tells us that
Aphrodite was born of Zeus and Dione, who is only the feminine
aspect of Zeus. In the *Homeric Hymn to Aphrodite* she is half the
Lady of the Wild Beasts and half vision of immortal beauty. The
author of the hymn seems to be describing two goddesses combined
in a single divine body:

First the Graces bathed her with the heavenly oils,
Those oils that bloom upon the eternal gods.
Divinely sweet they were, filling the air with perfumes.
Then the laughter-loving one was vested in rich raiment,
Gold jewels were hung around her: then she flew
Swiftly from scented Cyprus, hurrying on to Troy,
Flying above the clouds until she came
To Ida of the many fountains, mother of wild creatures,
Searching for her home among the mountains.
Then came the gray wolves fawning all around her,
Lions with fierce eyes, bears, and leaping leopards
Ravenous for deer; and all these pleased her.
Therefore she placed desire within their breasts,
So that they might lie together in shadowy caves.
Only for herself she chose a well-built shelter,
Where Anchises was waiting for her, beautiful as the gods,
Alone while all his fellows were out at pasture,
Playing upon his lyre, roaming hither and thither.
Then Aphrodite stood before him in her perfect beauty,
Very tall, but not so tall that men should fear her.
He gazed upon her height and shining robes
Splendid and gold-embroidered,
Like moonlight shimmering on her tender breasts,
So marvelous . . .

Marvelous she was, but this Aphrodite among the lions is as
incredible as the Aphrodite who rises from the sea foam. She tells
Anchises she was born in Phrygia, and perhaps she was—we know too
little of the Phrygian goddesses to be able to dismiss her claim. She
lies down beside Anchises, who fathers on her Aeneas, the Trojan
hero who was later to become the ancestral hero of the Romans.
Then, as he sleeps, she appears to him no longer as a beautiful woman
but as a goddess indeed, so immensely tall that he can only gaze up

at her in disbelief.

Homer, Hesiod, and the *Homeric Hymn* all give the impression of making up their accounts of Aphrodite out of the whole cloth: either they do not know where she came from or else they are content to conceal her origin. In fact, she was the Philistine goddess Ashtoreth, as Herodotus makes clear when he says that the temple to Celestial Aphrodite in Ashkelon "was the oldest of all the temples to the goddess." Ashtoreth derived from the Syrian Astarte and the Babylonian Ishtar. She was always a fertility goddess, though she had the power also to make men sterile. Herodotus says that when the Scythians plundered her great temple at Ashkelon, the goddess sensibly afflicted them with impotence: but other historians have offered more reasonable explanations for the notorious impotence of the Scythians. Herodotus says too that in Cyprus it was freely admitted that Aphrodite came from Ashkelon, while her temple on the island of Cythera was originally built by the Phoenicians.

Aphrodite, then, goes back to the most ancient Babylonian times and the beginning of mythology. Until she reached the coast of Palestine she remained the goddess of the fertile earth and all fecundity, represented as a beautiful woman with the tail of a fish. She seems to have come first to Cyprus, where the Arcadians had established a colony: Homer knows her as Cypris, and Hesiod thought she was born there, for he calls her Cyprogeneia. Here, in the town of Paphos, she had her sanctuary and her temple harlots, and was therefore especially beloved by sailors. In Dorian Corinth, too, she had her temple on the Acropolis, and here too she was attended by temple harlots. In Athens she was worshiped as Pandemos, in whose power lay the loving care for the sexual vigor of "all the people"; and there was a temple to Aphrodite of the Gardens outside Athens on the banks of the Ilissus. In Athens she was tamed. She displayed her nakedness, her inviting smile, her precarious modesty, but she wielded no thunderbolts. "I am Cypris, famous and powerful on earth and heaven," she says in the prologue to Euripides' *Hippolytus*. "Those who come to me in humility receive my blessings, those who are proud I bring low." For the Athenians she represented the humility of perfect beauty, surprisingly gentle for one so well endowed. Sophocles called her "the unconquerable," and so she was, but she was more a creature of caresses than of violent passions. She was the goddess of the frail flowers, myrtles and roses, and she helped maids who wanted to get married when they offered her their prayers.

Like Dionysus, she seems to be restless among the great gods, conscious of her strange origins, and she wears her immortality as though she were mortal.

Dionysus

WE would know considerably less than we do about the origins of Dionysus if Herodotus had not studied the march of Xerxes' army into Greece and reported on the wild tribesmen of Thrace. Among these tribes were the Satrae, "who as far as we know were never conquered, being the only Thracians who have retained their independence down to our own day. The explanation lies in the nature of their country which consists of high mountains thickly wooded with all kinds of trees and covered with snow. They are first-rate fighters. They possess a shrine of Dionysus situated in the loftiest mountain ranges. The service of the temple is in the hands of the Bessi, a branch of the Satrae; and there is a priestess as at Delphi who delivers the oracles, the oracles being no more complicated than the Delphic ones."

In time Dionysus was to become one of the twelve canonical gods of the Olympian hierarchy, presiding equally over tragedy and the cultivation of vineyards, represented always as a youth with a faintly Oriental grace, accumulating legends about mysterious journeys to India. In Homer he does not appear as one of the great divinities: he is simply a god who knows something about the preparation of wine. Hesiod says he was the son of Semele, daughter of Cadmus, by Zeus, and the fragmentary *Homeric Hymn to Dionysus* says he was born in some remote region of the earth on "a high mountain richly timbered, somewhere in Phoenicia near the streams of Aegyptus." Yet there seems to be no doubt that he entered Greece from the north during the period of confusion and exhaustion following the turmoil of the Dorian invasion, and that originally he was a god of great power exerting his influence in prophecies and strange orgiastic ceremonies by which the growth of vegetation and animals was assured. He was a hard-limbed and savage Thracian god with a wild light in his eyes before he became drowsy with wine.

There was nothing gentle or decorous about him; he had to be tamed before he could be fitted comfortably among the calm splendors of the Olympian gods. Originally it would seem that he was a bull—a wild and rampaging bull, making a sound like thunder as he roared across the pasture lands in a rage of sexual excitement, until at last he was caught and the people killed him and tore him apart while the flesh was still hot, hoping to acquire his strength and virility. His worship was attended by ferocious excitement and ecstasies in which men and women performed feats of strength far beyond their normal powers. Having eaten the raw flesh of the bull, his votaries believed they had entered into communion with the god and had become gods themselves.

> *O Dionysus, come to us!*
> *Come as a bull,*
> *Come as a many-headed serpent,*
> *Come as a lion in a blaze of fire!*

says the chorus in Euripides' *Bacchae*, and we are far indeed from the languorous youth with the vine wreath who is so often depicted on the vases.

Euripides, living during the last years of his life in his Macedonian exile, carefully studied the Dionysiac mystery. The Bessi and Satrae tribes were still living in their mountains not far from where he was staying, and he was temperamentally incapable of putting aside an opportunity to watch them at close quarters. What he saw and learned about the orgiastic worship of Dionysus is put into the mouth of a herdsman who saw some women resting in the hills. The herdsman and his companions thought they were fair game, and pounced upon them, but learned quickly enough that these women were not for their pleasure. The women threw themselves on the cattle grazing on the slopes of the hill:

> *They hurled themselves with naked, swordless hands*
> *Upon the heifers grazing on the grass. One stretched wide*
> *The legs of a well-fed calf which bellowed to high heaven.*
> *Heifers were torn limb from limb. Ribs and cloven hooves*
> *Were scattered piecemeal, while blebs of bloody flesh*
> *Hung dripping from the pinewoods. The wanton bulls—*
> *Forgotten now the menace of their horns—fell beneath*
> *These women's hands; were tripped and dragged to the earth,*
> *And quicker were the entrails torn away*

Than drop the lids over your royal eyeballs.
Then like an invading army they went wild
Through Hysiae and Erithrae beneath Cithaeron's crags,
With terror in their wake. They pillaged homes,
Snatched up babes, slung them on their shoulders,
And there the babes remained, not falling.
Nothing to the dark earth fell: nor brass nor iron:
Upon their hair unscorching flames rose.
And some who saw this pillage drew their swords,
And then was seen a still more marvelous thing.
From them the pointed javelins drew no blood.
They carried staves with vine leaves wound around them,
And these they hurled, till the men turned and ran.
Women defeating men! A god came with them!
Then slowly these strange women turned away
To the fountains which the god created,
And washed the blood away, while the snakes
Licked with their tongues the blood from women's cheeks.
And therefore, King, thou seest that a god
Has come, desiring entry to thy city.
They say he is powerful. Also they say of him
He brings the wine which puts an end to grief.
If he does not exist, then Love is forfeit,
And all our joys have vanished from the earth.

(Bacchae, 735–775)

As Euripides tells the story, the women with the *thyrsoi* are caught up in a savage trancelike state; some god has possessed them and filled them with a strange power of immunity against swords and an even stranger power to tear bulls apart with their bare hands. They toss children onto their shoulders, and the children stay there, caught up in the same trance. A fountain springs up when they need to bathe the blood of bulls from their faces, and snakes curl round their cheeks and lick the last drops of blood away. The scene is observed through a distorting lens: something very much like this had happened, but the order of events has been subtly altered, and some details are omitted or left unexplored. The god who brings the wine is not the god who inspired the raging women.

Dionysus, lord of the wine, the upright phallus, and of tragedy, leader of the Bacchants, mysterious wanderer from the east riding in sumptuous elegance upon a panther, combines within himself so many gods that they are past counting. His ultimate origin was probably in Thrace, where as a god of fertility he was worshiped with orgiastic rites. Thracians who later settled in Phrygia allied him to the local god Diounsis, lord of the vineyards and of tombs, believed to have entered Phrygia on a panther from the east. From Phrygia, then, the new god came to Greece, only to meet himself upon the way. According to tradition, he paused on the road to Attica at the village of Eleutherae lying on the slopes of Mount Cithaeron. Hence the god was always Eleutherus, in Athens, and the title is inscribed on the throne of his priest in the theater to this day. "Eleutherus" can mean either "from Eleutherae" or "the free," and Dionysus took both meanings of the word in his stride. Every year his *xoanon*, the ancient wooden cult image, made an effort to escape back to Eleutherae and was always caught before it got very far beyond the Dipylon Gate. The Athenians celebrated his capture with songs of thanksgiving: out of those songs poetic tragedy may have begun.

The beginnings of poetic tragedy are still obscure, and all we know for certain is that Dionysus was deeply involved, the first performances of drama taking place within the precincts of his temple in the marshy lands south of the Acropolis. Tradition has it that the subject of the first plays was the god's own adventures as he wandered over Asia and the Thracian forests. Peisistratus instituted the annual festival of the Great Dionysia, celebrating the resurrection of the god of the vine after his long winter sleep, and it may have been during his reign over Athens that the *Homeric Hymn to Dionysus*, with its enchanting picture of Dionysus assuming the form of two lions and a bear was composed:

I sing of Dionysus, son of glorious Semele,
He who stood between the cliffs and the barren sea,
A youth in his first manhood, with dark hair streaming,
A purple robe flowing from his wide shoulders,
When over the wine-dark sea the pirates came—
Tyrrhenian pirates on a high-decked ship, not knowing
How they were doomed as they made signs to one another,
And slipping off the ship, they quickly made him their own.
So they exulted, "He must be the son of a King,

One of those who are fed with the dews of heaven."
Then they roughly bound him, but in vain,
For the shackles fell away, the ropes and the withies,
And his dark eyes sparkled with laughter.
Only the helmsman knew who he was, and shouted in alarm:
"Madmen, who is this god you have seized?
See how strong he is! Even this well-built ship
Is not strong enough to hold him, for surely he is Zeus,
Or Apollo of the Silver Bow, or else Poseidon.
This is no mortal man, but one who lives on Olympus!
Set him free on the dark shore, and lay no hands upon him.
Touch him, and the tempests will come!"
     Then the tempest arose—a tempest of sweet running wine
Streamed through the black ship, heavenly odor of godhead,
And the sailors were startled to see the vine-shoots appearing
High on the mast, thick clusters of grapes dangling,
The dark ivy with gleaming berries twining,
The thole-pins covered with garlands,
Flowers everywhere, and the seamen frightened out of their wits,
For in the bows, where once there stood a god, a fearful lion roared.
And in the well deck a shaggy bear stood ravening,
Another lion glared fiercely in the forepeak.
The lion sprang, the sailors threw themselves overboard,
And all escaped their doom, being changed into dolphins.
The prince of the gods spoke to the helmsman:
"Courage, my dear, I shall take you to my heart,
I am Dionysus . . ."

Accompanied by these legends, Dionysus entered into his inheritance. He was the flesh made holy and more desirable, and from the beginning there was more than a hint of mortality in him. Apollo presided over the lyric song, the voice singing alone, while Dionysus presided over the poetic tragedies, where voices spoke to one another. One was spirit, the other flesh, and in Delphi they lived together in the same temple, where, according to Plutarch, "the share of Dionysus equals that of Apollo."

That the Greeks could honor the body and the spirit in the same temple was one of their most signal achievements. They adored the phallus and carried it garlanded through the streets, and at the same time they adored the sunlit intelligence; they saw no reason why one should be more praised than another, for both were mysteries. When they went on pilgrimage to Delphi, they might carry in one hand an arrow tipped with silver for Apollo and in the other a phallus-shaped cake for Dionysus; and they would not have thought it strange.

The Greek gods never died. They survive into our own day, and they are likely to survive for many generations to come. Zeus, Athena, Demeter, Apollo, Aphrodite, and Dionysus still exert their influence on our lives. Homer depicted them as divine presences possessing remorseless powers. For us they represent archetypal aspects of the embattled human spirit: immortal and compassionate.

Figure 5. The birth of Tragedy, with sacrificial altar, goat attended by satyrs, and performers in mule-cart.

5 «« HOMER

WHEN the face of Homer was forgotten, men set about to invent an ideal image of the poet who stands at the very beginning of Greek civilization. They gave him a broad and furrowed brow, a heavy nose, a thick and coiling beard, hair falling in wild curls about his ears, lips pursed and trembling on the edge of speech. It was a face of great power, of almost kingly majesty. They showed him with eyes half closed to emphasize his blindness, though on the coins of the island of Ios he appears with eyes wide open to emphasize that he lived among them and was not always blind. All the portraits agree in representing him as an old man who is still vigorous, determined, capable of dominating an audience, though troubled by dreams. If his brow were smoothed, he would bear a close resemblance to the gold and ivory Zeus at Olympia. The resemblance was not fortuitous. Homer, like Zeus, was the creator of worlds.

Of the circumstances of Homer's life nothing is known with certainty. Herodotus says he lived four hundred years before his own time, but Herodotus is often generous with time, and we can only guess that Homer was born toward the end of the ninth century, perhaps in Smyrna, which is not far from Troy, and it is possible that he died on Ios. Unlike the nineteenth-century scholars who were inclined to regard Homer as a tribe of poets, the Greeks themselves never doubted his real existence. For them he was a living presence, a source of energy and power, a man of almost godlike understanding and godlike pity; they would have recognized him if he entered the room. The Greeks knew him at least as well as we know Shakespeare,

74

for he was a man who revealed himself in his poetry. What they respected in him was something which is rarely associated with him—his formidable *charm*. He had the magician's trick of making you believe everything he said, and the magician's slow bemused wonder at his own creation. He could—and did—say the most extraordinary things without batting an eyelid. One moment he will be speaking about completely mundane things, the next moment he will be describing some completely incredible event on a mysterious island where the gods are in possession, and he will go from one world to another as easily as a man passes through an open door. No wonder there were Greeks who imagined he was an Egyptian and the son of Hermes!

Homer was no bookish, house-bred man, but one who lived in the open, a companion of soldiers and sailors, an occasional farmer, a great trencherman, with a lust for wandering. He suffered from sleeplessness, believed in auguries and the miraculous intervention of the gods, and knew beggary and perhaps slavery. He had seen war but seems never to have fought in battle, for his descriptions of fighting are less convincing than his descriptions of battlefields when the fighting is over—he had seen the dead and dying, and knew the aftermath of defeat, and he had spent many nights sitting around campfires waiting for the morning's slaughter. He had known grief and longing, and he may have seen his own city put to the flames by raiding pirates in the days when, according to Thucydides, the seas were infested by freebooters and cutthroats of all kinds; and though he spoke of Troy, which had perished hundreds of years before his time, he seems never to have walked on the Trojan plain. He had seen cities burning, people sold into slavery, old men praying for the bodies of their dead sons. He knew shipwrecks, for he had himself been shipwrecked, and like all men who lived along the coasts or on the Greek islands, he knew a good deal about the building of ships. The *Iliad* and *Odyssey* are too personal, too close to the bone, to permit us to believe that he was merely relating an ancient story; and like Shakespeare, he tells as much about himself as about his heroes. The defeat of the Trojans and the wanderings of Odysseus are colored by defeats and wanderings nearer home.

Again and again in the course of those immense epics, we see Homer plain. Odysseus is not always Odysseus: sometimes he is Homer remembering some half-forgotten journey to the Greek islands, a cliff, a broken coast, a strange mountain, violent seas. He, too, has clambered through the wild weeds on a deserted shore and caught a glimpse of Nausicaä playing ball, and no one can read of the Wanderer returning home after his long and desperate journey without the knowledge that Homer too had made many desperate journeys and yearned for the comfort and safety of his own hearth-fire. Then there is the old dog Argus lying on a dungheap, full of fleas, forgotten and neglected by the household, but rising on his haunches when he hears the footsteps of his master, wagging his tail and drooping his ears as he crawls wearily toward Odysseus, only to die before his master has seen him. Such brilliant episodes are too personal to be poetic inventions. They are things that a man has seen and known at his heart's core, and are transformed into poetry because the heart demands it.

We see Homer plain whenever he speaks about food, and he is always speaking about it. He knew poverty and suffering, sickness and despair, starvation, and ignominy; he knew the dregs of life. Because he had starved so long, he possessed the hungry man's enjoyment in describing banquets. There is that terrible night scene in which Priam and Achilles confront one another, the bereft king and the murderer of his son giving voice to their griefs. The doomed and the damned stand together, and one of them clasps the hand still dark with his son's blood. It is a scene of shuddering terror, of violence hurtling through the air. From that terror there can be no relief until the crimes are expiated. The young prince and the sorrowing king talk gravely to one another, and when they have finished talking, both men are hungry and sit down to a banquet. So on another occasion Achilles will say of Niobe: "She remembered to eat when she was worn out with weeping."

Homer's dreams of food, the succulence of food, are among his happiest obsessions. He could conjure up the tang and the taste of it, and the smell of the juices. Near the end of the story of Odysseus, when our feelings are at fever pitch and the crisis with the wooers is not far away, Odysseus spends a sleepless night debating with himself what needs to be done. Homer must describe him turning uncomfortably on his bed. How shall it be done? He uses the first image which comes to his mind, and it is inevitably of food. "His body kept tossing from side to side. He might have been a good fat black pudding going round in front of a blazing fire, while the cook basted it on the spit to roast it quickly." Food, raiment, shelter, all these are very close to his thoughts. Only a man who had been poor and worn patched clothes could take such pleasure in describing the embroidered raiment of heroic men and the sumptuous apartments of kings. He saw everything against the background of his own sufferings and sorrows. He does not hide himself: the man comes through the poetry almost too vividly for comfort.

There can be no doubt about it: Homer was a man who lived and breathed, as Herodotus says, "some four hundred years before my time." The Greeks believed he was born in one of the coastal towns of Asia Minor, and that he composed his epics on the island of Chios, where for centuries afterward there lived a family of rhapsodists calling themselves the Homeridae and claiming descent from him. Chios was an artistic center, famous for its figs and wines, its sheer mountains and dangerous harbors, and being ten miles off the coast of Asia Minor, at the crossroads of the Aegean, it was admirably suited as a poet's residence. Somewhere on the island of Chios there may one day be found the tablets on which he wrote his poems.

That Homer had a real and substantial existence is not of course the opinion of the scholars who for more than a hundred and fifty years have been writing elaborate commentaries on his work, on the assumption that the *Iliad* and the *Odyssey* are the products of entire schools of poets. Homer, it is said, is merely the trade name of a factory engaged in the mass production of epics. All this might be true enough if it were not so abundantly clear that each epic is informed with a single breath from a singer of monumental power. There can be no doubt that he borrowed and stole as he pleased, and that he even incorporated fragments from traditional songs, as Shakespeare borrowed from Plutarch and Holinshed, scarcely troubling to change a word. He was no niggardly thief, but stole generously, with both hands. Yet what remains is so distinctly the product of one mind that we can safely dismiss the idea of the Homer-factory. What he stole he touched with his genius, and it became his own.

So we are led to imagine Homer living in that shadowy period following the upheaval of the Dorian invasion, when a comparative calm settled on the eastern Mediterranean. The great wars were over, and the Greeks on the coastal fringe of Asia Minor were settling down into the pattern which persisted until Alexander the Great hurled his armies against Asia, and even much later. Trade was flourishing in those principalities ruled by tyrants—in those days the word "tyrant" had no evil connotation, meaning scarcely more than "prince." With trade came wealth and ease, comfort and leisure to explore the wonders of the physical world. In the tyrants' courts the poets gathered to celebrate a heroic tradition already vanishing in the face of a mercantile civilization.

It was a time of intellectual ferment, of vast and continual explosions of intellectual energy, with cultures from many shores streaming into the Ionian melting pot. The center of Greek mercantile power was not on the mainland of Greece, but in Ionia, where a dozen great cities were coming to birth, while Mycenae and Athens remained little more than struggling villages. And with mercantile power came trade in ideas, as the merchantmen sailed across uncharted seas and returned with spoils and treasure and the products of interminable barter— glass from Phoenicia, jewelry and cloth from Egypt, strange stones from Libya, and marble from the Cyclades. New techniques, new metals, new ways of building ships and houses and palaces and chariots and armor came with the high-masted ships, to rejoice the hearts of the artisans. With the new ideas came the new gods, and it must have been about this time that Philistine Ashtoreth, half woman and half fish, was transformed into Aphrodite. Apollo, too, emerged into the full light of the Ionian day. Most useful of all the new instruments imported into Ionia was the Semitic alphabet, brought by Phoenician traders. The cumbrous hieroglyphs derived from ancient Crete and Mycenae gave place to the simple and elegant letters devised by herdsmen and shepherds. The alphabet appeared in Ionia between 1000 and 800 B.C. Homer, who must have lived between those dates, came on the scene when the alphabet was still fresh in men's minds. His writings smell of the lamp, and we would be wrong to imagine him as a man who simply declaimed his verses on the spur of the moment. He composed on tablets or on papyrus, and the rhapsodists who recited the epics were able to consult the original manuscripts.

It is the characteristic of tyrants once they are in power to celebrate the glory of their real or imagined ancestors. The half-Oriental tyrants of Ionia were sustained in their belief in their heroic ancestors by the poets who flocked to their courts. We shall understand the *Iliad* and *Odyssey* better if we see them as compositions produced to honor reigning princes who claimed descent from Achilles and Odysseus.

We speak of the world of Homer, but in fact there were many worlds. There was the mythological world in which the long-dead heroes moved and had their being: a world full of ghosts to be revived by a poet's lips. There was the world of the tyrants and their courts, with their chroniclers and traditions going back to the distant past, to Troy and beyond. The traditions may have been spurious, and the legends may have been invented, but there is no doubt that both traditions and legends were handed down from antiquity, and could be used to serve a tyrant's purpose. There was the world of the merchants, whose wealth provided the tyrant with his revenue: this was the immediate world, visible in the crowded ports and chambers of commerce, in the shipyards and workshops. There was the world of the priests and religious festivities, a world traditionally allied to the court, so that a poet, after singing before the tyrant's throne, might go on and sing the same song during the religious processions. Then there was the world of the poor, the outcasts and wanderers, and the peasants who scraped a bare living from the soil. Finally, there was the private world of the poet, whose own memories and sufferings are indelibly burned into his poems.

The range of Homer's poetry is vast, for it embraces the world of the gods and the world of his heart, and all that lies between. The commentators who wondered how he could so easily mix up the Bronze and Iron Ages, and why he described chariots and armor which could not have existed at the time of the Trojan War, are clouding the issue. The surprising thing is that there are so few incongruities, for the poet was writing at a time when Greek civilization was developing at many different levels. Ideas were taking wings; words were being melted down and hammered into new shapes; traditions, long dead, were being revived. The coins were new, gleaming, fresh from the mint, and they could not be put into circulation fast enough. The Ionians were discovering themselves at breakneck speed.

Homer, then, came at the right time, in the right place. All the circumstances that go to the making of great poetry were present. There was peace or the semblance of peace; there was the sense of the world's newness; and the free exchange of cultures. Great undertakings were afoot, and the horizons were widening. People were clamoring for poetry, and there were patrons wealthy enough to pay for it. In this strange, exciting world the singer fulfilled a function acknowledged and approved by society. So Plato describes the bards standing in glorious raiment in the hushed market place.

In such a society, essentially mercantile and unheroic, the heroic ideal was formed, feeding on memories of ancient battles and voyages. It was a society not unlike Elizabethan England, but with the difference that there were a dozen princes vying for the services of poets. Sometimes the heroic ideal was attached to the service of the tyrant, at other times to the service of the city. In the true heroic age Achilles fought for his own glory, for his own anarchic ends, caring little for the fate of the Achaeans who accompanied him, careless even of his commander, towering Agamemnon. His destructive temper expended itself in feats of arms which dazzled even himself, and there were no laws of war or affection which he felt bound to uphold. His task was to accumulate so much honor that he would become almost indistinguishable from the gods. He was the tyrannical prince raised to the highest degree of power and honor. With Hector, the heroic ideal is seen under another aspect altogether, for this young prince has no quarrel with the enemy and his whole concern is to defend and protect his native city. He asks for nothing, only that the city should survive with all its people. Achilles and Hector confront each other from different levels of ambition and experience, almost from different realms, so that we sometimes find ourselves wondering how the sword of one can touch the other. Achilles is all vaulting speed and defiant action, treating his women like slaves and all his friends except Patroclus as though they were impediments to glory. Hector, on the contrary, is all caution, deeply and even helplessly in love with his wife and his son, and he speaks to all men reverently. Yet they have much in common: what they have most in common is simply their heroism. They are both fated to live short lives, and they know it. They are both dedicated to honor, though their conceptions of honor are at variance with one another. Heroism was to be aware of doom and to run toward it, but not joyfully. Doom was the common enemy, and they openly railed against it and writhed under its blows. They had taken the measure of their deaths long before they had begun to die.

On the portraits of these two antithetical heroes Homer expended some of his greatest art. The lean, hard, sinewy Achilles is described in three dimensions: we come to know that swashbuckling stride, the defiant toss of his head, the yellow hair streaming from under the crested helmet. There is nothing complex in him; he has the soul of an axhead. He has never known sorrow or tenderness, and would not recognize them if they came his way: there is neither sorrow nor tenderness in his grief for Patroclus, only a sudden and unavailing despair. Hector knows sorrow and tenderness only too well. Almost he is Hamlet, suffering from a superfluity of sorrows. He is the man caught in the web, dissembling, hoping for a way of escape, falling into dreams and out of them, remembering his childhood when he should be polishing his weapons, more aware than anyone else of the evanescence of life and the terrible burdens he bears. Here he bids farewell to his wife Andromache on the eve of battle:

The day will come, my soul knows it is coming,
When our holy Troy will go down into ruins,
Troy and the brave King and the King's people with him,
And I am not moved so much by the grief of the Trojans—
Grief will come—Hecuba's grief, and the grief of my father,
The grief of so many good men dying
In the bloody earth under the feet of our enemies.
I think of my death, and then your grief hurts me:
And I am grieved when I think of you being carried away weeping
By the enemy armored in bronze into certain slavery.
They will set you to work over somebody's loom in Argos
Or carrying a pitcher in some remote village somewhere,
And always against your will, because you're a captive.
When they look on you weeping, they will say:
"See, there's the wife of Hector who was a great captain
Of the horsemen of Troy, in the days when they fought for their
*   city."*
And hearing them, your grief will grow greater,
Knowing there will be no man like me to free you from slavery.
O let me be dead and let the earth be heaped over me
Before I hear you weeping or how you were enslaved."
* So the shining one spoke, and stretched his arms to his son,*
And the boy cried out to his nurse with the beautiful girdle—
Afraid of the glint of steel and the horsehair crest of the helmet,
And suddenly both the father and mother were laughing.
Then the shining Hector put his helmet away,
Set it shimmering on the ground, and threw out his arms to his son,
Kissing the boy and rocking him in his arms.

No one could have written such a scene of intolerable poignancy without being overwhelmed with affection for the character he has created. Everything is stripped from Hector except the essential thing, his humanity. The forces that will destroy him are already crowding upon him; death is only a nightmare away, while he rocks his son in his arms and laughs with Andromache because the child is frightened by the crested helmet. Pain and suffering have marked him for their own, and already he belongs more to death than to life, but he continues to live his earthly existence to the full. Even in his death he belongs to humanity, to the living.

We come to know Hector well, for he wears a peculiarly modern face. He is the disenchanted one, for whom no magic wand is ever waved. He defies augury. He will do everything humanly possible to escape his fate, but he knows that it is inescapable. He will behave at all times with exquisite nobility, but he knows that honor will never win any wars. As Homer says, he has the look of nightfall on his face. Despair is written all over him, but with despair goes high courage, the determination to play his allotted role faithfully to the very end. So in the end he is stabbed in the throat, stripped of his armor, and dragged through the dust, because the gods have aided his enemy and forsaken him, and all this was known to him from the very beginning.

Living, Achilles belongs already to his death. The portrait of that implacable and imperious warrior is sketched in violent colors. He kills for the pure joy of killing, contemptuous of danger, certain only of the blessedness of destruction. To say that he is ruthless and vengeful is to underrate his terrible sobriety. He kills aimlessly, as huntsmen kill. When Odysseus says to Eumaeus in the *Odyssey:* "My delight was in ships, fighting, javelins and arrows—things that make men shudder to think about," we hear again the authentic voice of Achilles. He is a nihilist, who feels no guilt and asks for no pardon, despising the world and content to surrender all his priviliges for the pleasure of destroying the world. He did not take part in the Trojan War to rescue Helen: he took part because he wanted to kill and because he wanted to see all Troy reduced to flame and ashes.

There is nothing petty in his violence—he kills the young and defenseless with the same exuberant joy with which he kills mature and well-armed soldiers. Lycaon, one of King Priam's sons, scarcely more than a boy, falls into the river Scamander during a heavy fog while being hard pressed by the enemy. Exhausted, he climbs up the bank and rests for a while, abandoning helmet, shield, and spear. When the fog clears, Achilles comes upon him. It is a moment of exquisite triumph, the proud warrior confronting the shivering youth. Achilles has his spear and sword, the young prince has nothing. So for a moment they watch one another, and suddenly Achilles hurls his spear, but the youth ducks and it passes over his head. There remains the sword, and when Lycaon comes pleading for his life, Achilles has fun with him, remembering that some months before the prince had been his captive and was sold into slavery at Lemnos, returning to Troy only when a huge ransom was offered for him.

"Well, you escaped that time," Achilles says, "but I would like to know how you will escape from the place where I am going to send you. Earth has many strong men in her lap, and usually she keeps them there!"

Lycaon offers to pay a large ransom.

"No," replies Achilles, "I shall take no payment for you! All must die—even you! Patroclus died, and he was a better man than you will ever be. I, too, shall die! I have a goddess for a mother, and a great father, and I am strongly built and beautiful to look upon. Nevertheless I shall die! There will come a morning or an evening or a noon when someone will kill me with a throw of his spear or with an arrow shot from a bow."

Then Achilles draws his sword and kills the young prince, striking between the shoulder blades into the heart.

He has not yet finished with the murder. There are still the rites of vengeance to be performed. There are degrees of destruction, and the dead youth must still receive the ultimate disgrace, the ultimate annihilation. Suddenly Achilles leans down, takes the youth by the foot, and hurls him into the river.

"Go," he says. "The fish will lick the blood from your wounds at their leisure!"

In this way Achilles brings about the youth's *continuing* death, the death which does not come to an end until every vestige of humanity is stripped from the corpse. Achilles is not satisfied with killing; he is also the agent of the body's corruption. First he kills the soul, then the body, then he corrupts the body. For the same reason he will destroy Hector and defile his body by dragging him in the dust behind his chariot, and he will do this not once but every day until even the gods cry out for mercy, and Apollo the Healer is called upon to restore the perfect beauty of the young hero. Apollo and Achilles therefore stand at opposite poles. Achilles is darkness and chaotic power, while Apollo is the messenger of light and reasonableness and human sympathy. In the end Apollo guides the arrow that kills Achilles.

Apollo, however, is not the only god who despairs over Achilles. The river, into which he has thrown so many corpses, rebels against desecration and pollution, and the senseless ignominy it is made to bear. In all of Homer there is nothing quite so nightmarish as the sudden fury of the river as it strikes back at Achilles, hoping to drag him down into its depths. The river demands its sacrifice, and since the river is a god, being the son of Zeus, father of all "heaven-fed" streams, the combat is very nearly equal:

Then the great spearman Achilles leaped into midstream,
And the River, roaring with rage, rushed upon him,
Bellowing like a bull, the waters foaming,
As it swept the dead onto dry land,
The many dead, all slain by Achilles,
But the living were saved in the sweet waters
Or hidden in the depths of whirlpools.
So the wild River rose, Achilles plunging
His shield upon it, but there was no foothold:
He clutched at a full-grown elm, but scarcely had his hands
Grasped it when the bank fell away and the tangled branches and
roots
Were flung across the River, forming a dam, choking its lovely flow.
Then out of a whirlpool rose Achilles in panic fear, his feet hurrying,
But the great god had not yet done with him, though he was running
across the plain—
It sent after him the darkening crest of a wave, to prevent him
From laboring too well on the ruin of the Trojans,
While Achilles ran the space of a spearthrow with the speed of an
eagle,
Black-feathered and valiant, strongest and swiftest of winged things.
Like an eagle he hurried away to the ringing and clanging of bronze
Armor on his chest, and swerved to avoid the River,
Roaring and raging still as it followed after him in wild uproar.

So it is when a man runs a channel from a dark spring,
Guiding its waters among fruit trees and gardens,
Clearing a fresh path with his spade, and the pebbles are swept along,
And smooth as a whispered song is the flow downhill,
Outstripping the man who would follow—so did the River
Outstrip swift Achilles. Gods are stronger than men.
But Achilles leaned with all his might on the River, wondering
Whether all the gods were up in arms against him,
While the enormous wave of the heaven-fed River
Hung poised above his shoulders ready to spring at him.
With the strength of despair he leaped upward, while the River
Seized him by the knees, the earth shifting underfoot,
And he groaned aloud, and gazed into the far heavens, praying:
"O Father Zeus, shall none of the gods have pity on me
And save me from the River? . . ."

So it happens that Zeus has pity on him, sending Poseidon and Athena to the rescue, and for a little while longer Achilles is permitted to live out a life dedicated to destruction. But only a man who is himself like a force of nature could dare to oppose a river in spate, singlehandedly striking back at the elemental powers, being himself an elemental power. Achilles is man raised to the power of storms, floods, lightning and volcanoes. Some terrible heaven-sent force has taken possession of him. "Murder comes from the divine," wrote the German poet Friedrich Hölderlin, and he added that "one may fall into the heights as well as into the depths." Both statements may be regarded as commentaries on Achilles.

The theme of the *Iliad*, announced in the opening lines, is the wrath of Achilles, but what is implied is far more than human anger. The wrath is a sacred wrath. At one point Homer compares Achilles setting forth to a snowy mountain. It is a superb image, deliberately contrived to suggest the fierce, glittering, elemental power of the young hero, but it is worth observing that it represents Achilles as seen by his enemies or as he appears in their fearful imaginations: a relentless impersonal presence which will crush them and leave no trace behind.

Of such large and powerful images Homer is the absolute master. He will describe two armies standing immobile as they face one another as tombstones—"As the pillar on a tomb of a dead man or woman, so they stood immovably in their beautiful chariots, bowing their heads to the earth." The astonishing image echoes through the corridors of the mind. Grief is forearmed and forewarned, as the waiting armies are strangely transformed into a single stone and the bowed heads of the mourners. He will speak of cicadas "singing like lilies," of ships with "vermilion cheeks," and of Odysseus' coat "like the skin of an onion, smooth and shining in the sun." War is "the sleep of bronze." It is in these sudden things that he achieves his poetical aim of bringing the reader into the immediate presence of the gods and heroes. There are no veils between the poetry and the reader. We see what the poet intended us to see with startling clarity.

Not that there is clarity throughout the story: there are intervals of darkness, sometimes set pieces are introduced for no apparent reason, and there is a deliberate jaggedness in the outline which corresponds to the jaggedness of war. The poet sees stray moments of the battle with the sharpest imaginable vision, as though a searchlight had been thrown onto the scene so that everything appears in high relief, but a moment later the plain, the river, the trenches, and the ships may be covered in mist; desperately he attempts to see what is happening; rumors and the din of confused skirmishes come to his ears; darkness descends, and there is only the gleam of campfires; then suddenly, as though dawn had risen in the middle of the night, we see the heroic warriors falling upon one another, brilliantly illuminated. In the end we are deafened by the clang of bronze and blinded by the shining of the armor, and there are times when we hardly care who conquers or who is conquered, for the gods have weighted the scales and the terror is unending.

A century of wars is contained in the *Iliad*, and in the *Odyssey* there is a century of wandering. The action of the *Iliad* very largely takes place on a narrow strip of land between Troy and the sea. The action of the *Odyssey* takes place in most of the known regions of the world, and in the mythological countries of the imagination.

Homer's Odysseus is wise beyond all knowing, but he is still a man, with a man's cunning and a man's desires. He can be as murderous as Achilles, but never murders from pride, never assumes the posture of a divine being. Achilles taunts the wretched boy he finds lying helpless and naked beside the river, and then kills him. Odysseus discovers the youthful Dolon making his way at night through the Achaean lines with a ferret-skin cap on his head and a wolf's pelt draped over his body, and when the spy is caught Odysseus cross-examines him. He wants to know where Hector is, and where the sentries are posted, and where the horses are, and what plans are being made. He must find out everything before he decides on the fate of the youth, and it is not Odysseus but Diomedes who in the end cuts off Dolon's head, "which was still speaking when it hit the dust."

Odysseus, when we meet him again in the *Odyssey*, is no longer the great commander of armies, but a man tormented and buffeted by the elements as he tries to make his way back to Ithaca. In the *Iliad* he moves in straight lines, but in the *Odyssey* he wanders in circles, caught in the world's maze. There is no peace for him, no certainty, no sense of being the master of his fate: Zeus plays with him, shattering his ship, hurling him against rocky shores inhabited by strange gods, sending down visions of paradise and then snatching them away. The *Odyssey* is the story of interminable defeats, made even less palatable by the vain promises of the gods and the knowledge that disaster lies at the end of every road. Odysseus is "one of those who survive," and in this sense he is very close to modern man.

The story is told on many levels, from many different angles, but always with a kind of half-savage gusto. Homer is determined to extract what amusement he can from it, but he knows there is more sorrow than joy in the enterprise. Because the wanderings are dark and circuitous, so the manner of telling it is dark and circuitous. Odysseus tells his own story four times: once at great length to Alcinoüs, once to Eumaeus, and twice to Penelope. In no case does he tell the whole truth. With the *Odyssey* the modern psychological novel is born. There are endless doubts and hesitations, curious interweavings, and the hero is continually looking into a mirror and debating with himself whether he can afford to pursue all or any of the courses of conduct he has embarked upon. He wanders alone, and wears his loneliness like a garment.

Homer presents him to us as the eternal wanderer, almost too weary of wandering to care where he will find the next night's repose, but he wears his ragged coat and carries his mysterious wallet full of holes with a proper disdain. "There is nothing more evil to mortals than this wandering," he says, "but for our wretched bellies' sake men must endure the evil blows." So Homer composes his psychological novel, but inevitably it becomes a morality play: we are all wanderers.

Occasionally, of course, there are compensations. There are brief intervals when the curtain rises to disclose a world of settled comforts, where the wanderer can warm his hands by the fires of the rich and slake his thirst on their wine and eat their food, which is too rich for beggars. When Homer describes the palace of Alcinoüs, he is dreaming of luxuries which even the richest Ionian princes cannot have possessed, for in their gardens it is spring all the year round:

Like the flashing of the sun or the moon shone the high-roofed house
Of the noble Alcinoüs. Bronze walls enclosed its courts,
The cornices enameled with blue tiles, and the golden gates
Guarded the inner rooms: silver door posts rose from the bronze
*   threshold;*
The lintels were silver, the door handles of gold.
Flanking the entrance are sculptured hounds, also of silver and gold,
Fashioned wonderfully by Hephaestus to keep watch over the palace,
Undying hounds for the house of noble Alcinoüs.
Along the walls stand the high thrones,
Smooth draperies cunningly woven by women thrown over them:
Here the Phaeacian dukes sit feasting and drinking,
Largess all round them, while the boys of hammered gold
Throw light on the feasters from their blazing torches.
Fifty slave-girls grind the yellow corn on millstones,
Others are at their looms or twirling yarn, fingers flying
Like the leaves of wind-driven poplars, linen woven so close
That the finest oil could not pass through it.
These Phaeacians are skilled at seafaring,
And their women are cunning workers at the loom:
Athena gave them this art, and their hearts
Are tempered with grace and sweetness.
While beyond the palace doors within hedgerows
Are the vast orchards, pears and pomegranates,
Apple trees with fruit smooth and shining,
Sweet figs, fat olives.
The fruit never failed on these trees winter or summer.
Yearlong they remain, the west wind breathing on them,
So that each comes to its prime—
Heaps of pears, mountains of apples, armfuls of figs,
In unceasing ripeness!

(*Odyssey*, VII, 84)

So might a man write after wandering for many days in winter, sleeping on the cold ground at night, living off berries and roots. The *hunger* of Homer is a thing to wonder at. He hungers after everything —food, rich appointments, palaces, gods, certainties. There is a terrible restlessness in those verses which have been chiseled smooth as though to hide the hungers of his body and his soul.

Odysseus, too, looks out on the world from the heights of his hunger. His name means "the angry one," and like Achilles, he is full of wrath: but his wrath is directed at himself and the world around him. He could weep for the misery the gods have brought on his head; and he does weep. When Hermes, the messenger of the gods, is sent to find him on Calypso's island, he is nowhere to be found. At last Hermes discovers him sitting among the rocks on a deserted strip of coast. "Grief was shaking him, and the tears were rolling down his cheeks as he gazed out to sea."

In time the Greeks were to inscribe on the walls of Apollo's temple at Delphi two inscriptions: "Know thyself" and "Nothing in excess." Odysseus is the man who knows himself only too well, and loves all manner of excess. He is "the man of many devices," never at a loss for words or for some crafty trick. He is multitudinous, for he is all men in their common humanity. Achilles is one man: the triumphant strident nihilist, who cares nothing at all for the havoc he causes. Odysseus can flare up like any outraged murderer; he will hang the suitors on the house-beam, and all their maidservants with them, but his essential humanity remains to testify to the strength and generosity of his character. He tells lies exceedingly well. One cannot imagine Achilles even troubling to tell a lie.

Odysseus is seen in the round; he is all complexity. He knows— who could know better?—that the world is at odds with itself. He is no knight at arms, whose simple purpose is to rescue the maiden from her tower, nor is Penelope a maiden sighing for her lover. They are both middle-aged, and wise in their ways. For them merely to survive is to triumph, and their greatest pleasure is to sit quiet at home with their children around them.

In Odysseus, Homer achieved his greatest triumph. He depicted a hero who was recognizably a man.

6 ⋘ THE BITTER HARVEST

ABOUT a century after Homer, an obscure farmer in Boeotia wrote his own account of the heroes and the gods. He was the son of an Ionian merchant who had hoped to live as luxuriously as the Ionian nobility, but unwise speculation brought disaster, and he sailed off to Greece to live on a farm at Ascra on the slopes of Mount Helicon. "A dreary hole of a place, rotten in winter, tiresome in summer, and there were no good seasons."

There were no good seasons for his son Hesiod, who spent his life in a continual battle with the weather, his litigious brother Perses, and the local gentry. When the father died, Perses bribed the local officials to give him the lion's share of the estate, but he was an incompetent farmer and was soon reduced to penury. He was a liar and a braggart, who hated work and preferred stealing. When he could not steal, he would borrow until Hesiod was weary of seeing his brother coming to the door for the loan of an oxcart or a pair of oxen. There was no love between them.

Hesiod was of the earth earthy, and when he talks you can smell the mud and feel the wind on your face. He has all the instincts of a peasant, hoarding his small possessions, only content when he has accumulated a surplus of grain. He has heard the epics celebrating the heroes, and he knows what is wrong with them. They are not the true heroes. The true heroes are the patient peasants and farmers who eke out a living from the soil so that all men can eat.

For the princes of the earth, and for all those in positions of power, he had only a brooding contempt. They were little more than thieves and murderers disguised in their panoply. For their benefit, if they will listen, he tells the famous parable of the Hawk and the Nightingale:

I will tell a fable for princes: they will understand it.
The nightingale with speckled neck was caught fast in the talons
Of the hawk, which went soaring among the clouds.
The nightingale, spitted on the claws, wept pitifully,
But the hawk proud of his mastery answered her:
"Wretched one, what are you crying for? Why all this screaming?
I have you in my power, for all your singing.
If I like, I can make a meal of you, or let you go.
Only a fool tries his strength with a stronger.
He will fall by the wayside, and be covered with shame."
So spoke the hawk, the swift-flier with the long wings.

(*Works and Days,* 202)

The hawk might be Achilles, "the swift runner," or the local princes, or Perses himself. Hesiod goes on to warn his brother against the promptings of *Hubris*, of that pride which destroys men when they leap too high and disobey *Dike*, Justice. Justice rules. She brings the proud low. Men in their folly must all confront Justice in the end. If you ask who Justice is, he will answer that she is the virgin daughter of Zeus and she sits by his right hand, whispering into his ear all the injustices committed by men as she has heard them from her thirty thousand angels who roam invisibly across the earth. "So take heed, you princes, and put crooked judgments altogether from your thoughts." At such times we see Hesiod hammering out his own morality and inventing a mythology as he goes along out of the scraps remembered from a very dark, irrational past.

For Hesiod, work and justice go hand in hand. "Through their labors men grow rich in flocks and possessions, and are more beloved by the gods." A man has a right to own his own ox and his slaves and to have recompense for his labor; the princes have no right to dispossess men. Perses with his thieving and his conniving was Achilles writ small: all of *Works and Days* can be read as an implicit attack on the heroic ideal. Hesiod is saying: "Not by treachery or cunning, and least of all by war can a man make his peace with heaven. All the treasures of the world are not worth the man who works himself to the bone." And he paints a wonderful picture of the peace and contentment of the honest tillers of the soil:

They and their cities flourish, and sweet Peace,
Nurse of their children, takes up her home in their land.
And Zeus, who sees far and wide, commands no wars among them,
Nor does famine or terror haunt those who follow Justice,
But tenderly they tend their fields through the fruitful days.
Earth bears God's plenty; the oaks are on their hills,
From the crowns of the trees spill acorns, and the bees
Build their houses in the bark. The sheep wear their heavy fleeces.
The children look like their parents, Prosperity rules.
No need for traveling in ships: the grain from the earth
Suffices for all their needs.

(Works and Days, 227)

It is, of course, the eternal dream of the husbandman, and we shall hear it again among the Roman poets and even more despairingly in the Middle Ages. But even as he dreams Hesiod has his eye on the predatory nobles and princes, who are continually despoiling the peasants and reducing them to beggary. Still, there is an all-seeing Zeus in the heavens, and surely he will protect the peasants, if not now, then in some distant future. "Truly I believe it will come to pass," he says hopefully. "It is not God's purpose that the unrighteous should prevail."

Homer's heroes never spoke in this way. When Thersites spoke up for his rights, he received a whipping and was accounted an insolent upstart. Now the boot is on the other foot, for the princes have become the insolent upstarts and those who agitate against them are under the protection of Zeus. Hesiod is saying that the nightingale must go free and the hawk must have his talons taken from him, his wings must be clipped, and he must learn to follow in the paths of righteousness.

Hesiod dreams his powerful dreams, and suddenly we are aware that he is announcing the end of an age and the beginning of another. In this new age Zeus is no longer the great Prince sitting on his throne on Mount Olympus casually loading the scales on behalf of his favorites. What was wanted now—what the human imagination demanded —was a more august, a more benevolent Zeus who never loaded the scales but acted with perfect justice toward all men. Far from being the friend of princes and heroes, the new Zeus was their enemy. In the end it was Hesiod's, not Homer's, Zeus who prevailed in the imaginations of the Greeks.

Meanwhile the work of the farm must go on, and Hesiod sets out to describe the farmer's life: how he goes about his work, and what he plants, and when. He tells the whole cycle of the farmer's year: the felling of wood in autumn for wagons and fresh plows, the barn building and planting, sowing and harvest. The plowman, he tells us, should be a brisk farmhand of about forty summers, who keeps his mind on his work and "is past the age of gaping at his fellows." There are prayers to be said to the Earth Mother to ensure a good crop, and almost in the same breath he adds that it is good to have a slave following a little behind the mattock, making trouble for the birds by hiding the seed. February comes, wretched days all of them, while the wind howls and the forests creak and the beasts shudder and put their tails between their legs:

The wind goes through the hide of an ox: nothing stops it.
It goes through a fine-haired goatskin. The north wind goes through
all skins
Except sheepskins, for the thick fleece keeps the wind at bay,
Though it bends an old man into a hoop.
The wind cannot blow through the young maiden
Who remains indoors with her loving mother,
Knowing nothing as yet of the mysteries of golden
Aphrodite, while she washes her smooth skin tenderly,
Anointing it with oil, and then lying down in an inner room
On a winter's day.

(Works and Days, 515)

He seems to be speaking of his young daughter, but we never learn her name or hear anything more about her. February with its winds and biting rains is the worst month of all, but with this tender invocation of his daughter he plucks some felicity out of it.

He has the farmer's eye for the stars, for the animals that wander on the edge of the farmland, and for the colors of the sky, and like farmers everywhere he is full of taboos. "Never cross a river until you have looked at the lovely ripples, and prayed to them, and washed your hands in their enchantment." He likes to employ euphemisms to avoid evil demons, and so he tells us: "Never, at a happy festival of the gods, cut the dry from the green on the five-branched flower with shining iron"—he means that it is improper to pare the fingernails during divine service. He has the peasant's queer nonsense about virility. "Never let a twelve-year-old boy sit on anything that cannot be moved; no, don't do it, it will make you lose your virility." Don't show too much interest in women: they are all after your barns. Wake early, work long hours, honor the gods, take proper care of your dogs, and keep a tight rein on your tongue. The fifth day is the worst of the month, and the ninth is never wholly bad. So he goes on in his friendly, cantankerous fashion, dispensing advice and old saws, jogging our elbows, and periodically cursing Perses, the brother who nearly succeeded in taking his patrimony away. We are unimaginably far from the Ionian banqueting halls, and sometimes it is as though all the shining of the gods and the heroes was a dream and we had awakened in the gray dawn.

Sometimes; but not always. Sometimes he brings the heroic ideal down to earth, and we see ordinary men living in a state of contentment which the gods might envy. After the arduous work of spring, summer comes as a blessed relief:

When the Snail, the little house-carrier, climbs among leaves
Away from the earth to escape from the Pleiades,
Then it is no longer the season for trenching vineyards:
Whet your bright sickles, rouse up the slaves, for the harvest has come,
And there is no time for sleeping until dawn or for resting in the shade.
The sun is a scorcher, but still you must work
At gathering the fruits of the harvest, and the early riser
Is sure of earth's bounty if he works from the earliest dawn—
A third of a day is dawn, dawn summons
Men on their journeys and advances them in their work.
Dawn sets the yokes on oxen and sends men out into the road.
Then at the time of the flowering artichoke,
When the cicada hops on the tree, singing daylong,
In the weary heat clapping music from under its wings,
Then the goats are plumpest, wine sweetest, women most wanton,
But men lose their vigor—Sirius parches them.
Head, knees and skin are sucked dry by the heat.
O in those days let me lie in the shade of a rock
With wine from Biblis, whey and the milk of goats,
And the flesh of kid or a heifer fed on the woodlands,
Sitting in the shade with the shining wine in my mouth,
My soul refreshed with food, and my face turning

To the summer winds, and then pouring
From virgin springs everflowing a threefold offering
Of purest water, and another of wine.

(*Works and Days*, 571)

So he wrote, and sometimes as we read his verses we find it easy to believe that the Muses taught him song one day when he was pasturing sheep on Mount Helicon. If his light is not so bright as Homer's, it is shed over a more familiar earth. He tells us what he knows, and lifts up a corner of the curtain to show us what life in the Dark Ages was like; and what is strange and consoling is that it is very like the life in Greece today. Heroes may come and go, but the old peasants still stumble through the muddy fields and shelter in summer in the shade of rocks, a jug of wine within reach. The earth is what it was, though the gods died long ago.

They were dying in Hesiod's time, and he wrote just over a thousand lines of a strange work called the *Theogony*, or "The Generation of the Gods," to describe them in their death throes. No doubt he was describing the gods who were still remembered in Boeotia: Coeus and Crius and Iapetus, who ruled in the ancient heavens, their ugly names looking all the uglier when set beside the beautiful names of their wives and daughters: Tethys and Themis and Mnemosyne and Phoebe of the Golden Crown. There are so many gods and goddesses crowding the ancient pantheon that he almost gives up hope of being able to enumerate them all, and sometimes he contents himself with aimless catalogues; and when he says he will name the fifty daughters of Nereus, he does so, and adds two more for good measure. Half the time he is painting a primitive nightmare: we see the ghosts moving about in the darkness, and sometimes they assume bodily shape only to vanish again. We see the Giants in their gleaming armor, holding long spears in their hands, but they vanish soon enough to give place to the nymphs of the ash trees "who are known all over the wide earth." We meet Echidna, who was the face of a nymph and the speckled body of a huge serpent: she lives at the bottom of a deep cave and spends her time eating raw flesh. She became the mother of monsters: the fearful Chimera with its three heads, lion, goat, and snake, was one of them, and the hound of Hades, the fifty-headed Cerberus, was another. Most terrible of all were the fifty-headed gods Cottus, Briareus, and Gyes, who had three hundred arms among them. He seems to be telling stories he has heard from the lips of some village crone muttering over a witch's brew.

Hesiod's *Theogony* is an account of a long war in Heaven, where no quarter is given. The gods tear at each others' throats, children are swallowed by their parents, monsters die and are reborn, and flames shoot out of the gods as they hurtle to earth and set the woods on fire. There are brief interludes of quietness as when Leto of the Blue Robe inexplicably appears to receive honor from the hand of Zeus, the victor of the heavenly wars. She is the nurse of the young, the guardian of flocks, and the giver of victories in the athletic contests. She presides over the deliberations of princes, and she is present when the people discuss affairs of state in the market place. She will become the mother of Apollo and Artemis, and Hesiod is clearly granting her a role of very special importance in the divine government of the universe, but no sooner has he described her calm and majestic presence than he must gorge himself again with bloodlettings and mysteries. Cronus has fathered six children on Rhea. They are Hestia, Hera, Demeter, Hades, Poseidon, and Zeus. In time these gods will wield vast powers, but the moment they drop from the womb Cronus swallows them. Thus Hesiod weaves the old and the new myths together in alternations of darkness and brightness. It is a strange way to describe the generation of the gods, but oddly satisfying.

Hesiod knew what he was doing. Nowhere is there any touch of the peasant littérateur in his work. He is a farmer, but he has his library of books for reading on long summer evenings, and he has listened to the old wives' tales and thought deeply about the gods. He knows they are a desperately serious matter, and he is determined to come to terms with them. In his lost village on the slopes of Mount Helicon the old gods are still being worshiped, but the new gods are coming in. His disjointed way of writing about them reflects with a kind of dispassionate accuracy the claims of the rival gods.

A small bronze statue found in Boeotia, now in Boston's Museum of Fine Arts, depicts the process at work. The statue represents Apollo and was produced in the first half of the seventh century B.C. Enormous eyes peer out of a pinched face of remarkable power and nobility; the thick braided hair emphasizes the thrust of the towering neck; the limbs have no muscles; the torso is merely sketched in; and the genitals are so small that they have almost vanished. Roughly made, it could be the handle of a dagger. But what is remarkable about the

small statue is the combination of heavy sausagelike limbs with a face
of superb intelligence, and this intellectual face is removed as far as
possible from the body by the simple means of extending the neck,
so that he comes to resemble a bird. He is as alert as a hawk. Soon
he will put on the flesh of a handsome athlete, but he will have the
hawklike gaze to the end.

The *Theogony* is our only comprehensive source book for the
gods who reigned before Zeus. Unhappily Hesiod himself seems to be
wondering whether he has got his facts straight; occasionally there is
an air of improvisation; we are never quite sure how much he is inventing. So, in his halting fashion, he will sometimes pause and deliver himself of a little sermon or a diatribe against women in the intervals of mapping out the heavens. He tells us that when Prometheus
stole the fire from heaven, the earth was inhabited only by men.
Thereupon Zeus commanded that a plague should be sent down to
earth, and this plague took the form of a woman clothed by Athena
in a silver gown, wearing a garland of flowers on her head, and above
the flowers a golden crown. She is made out of common clay, and
she is let loose among men:

> *From her comes the damnable race of women,*
> *Who are no help to men in poverty; only to the rich*
> *Are they helpful; and they cause great trouble.*
> *As in the thatched hives the honeybees*
> *Feed the drones who are always up to their tricks—*
> *The bees work all day, laying their white combs,*
> *While the drones laze in their covered skeps,*
> *Reaping the toil of others in their bellies—*
> *So in the same way did Zeus the Thunderer*
> *Make women to be an evil curse on men,*
> *Being by nature evil . . .*

(Theogony, 591–602)

Quite clearly Hesiod is no longer mapping out the heavens; he
is more concerned to map out his private discontents. His griefs interfere with his mapmaking; the damnable race of women interfere with
his dreaming. But the Muses comfort him. On the subject of the
Muses he speaks with authority and conviction. He has seen them
dancing on the hills, those ethereal waifs who never make demands on
men, but on the contrary give of their blessings:

Let my song begin with the choir of the Muses
Who own the great and holy mountain of Helicon.
They dance around a spring as dark as violets,
Around the altar of Almighty Zeus.
To Hesiod one day they taught the art of song
While he shepherded his lambs under holy Helicon.
They were Muses from Olympus, daughters of Zeus,
The bearer of the Terrible Flame,
Saying, "Shepherds of the wilderness, poor creatures,
We can say many false things as though they were true,
And when we want to, then we have also the power
To speak the truth truthfully."
So sang the neat voices of the daughters of Zeus,
As they plucked from a gnarled olive tree a spray,
A most marvelous spray, and breathed upon me
The power of a divine voice, celebrating
All things past and future.

Possessed of such a voice he could forget the evil years and the
evil in the hearts of women, and he could even forget the brutal battles of the gods. In the end there were always the Muses dancing
around the spring as dark as violets, teaching him how "to speak the
truth truthfully."

7 ⋘ THE FAR-FLUNG SETTLEMENTS

Even before the Dorian invasion the Greeks were establishing colonies in the islands and trading with the Levant. The Mycenaeans, as we have seen, had conquered the dying Minoan empire and settled in Crete, to add still another strain to the many strains already existing on the island. So it was throughout the eastern Mediterranean. Men fled the barren valleys of Greece and settled wherever they could find a more fruitful earth. Most of them fled to the coasts of Asia Minor where, as Herodotus says, "the climate is the most beautiful in the whole world and there is no other region so blessed."

When Alexander the Great was riding through Asia Minor on his way to destroy the Persian Empire, he was accompanied by geographers and historians who carefully collected the traditions of the towns they passed through and consulted the local historians and mapmakers. At the town of Side, on the south coast of Asia Minor, they learned that there was a tradition that the first settlers came from Aeolia in northern Greece, "and they promptly forgot their native language and began to talk in a foreign tongue—not the language spoken by the local people, but an entirely new dialect of their own." So Arrian reports in his *Life of Alexander the Great*, throwing a curious light on the intense provinciality of the first settlers as they deliberately contrived to develop a local patois which would distinguish them from all other people. Each settlement was a world in itself. Greece was expanding beyond its frontiers, but there was as yet no consciousness of Greek unity.

The northern Greeks settled along the upper coast of Asia Minor, which came to be known as Aeolis. From southern Greece came the great wave of Ionic migration which led to the settlement of twelve towns and cities along the lower coast of Asia Minor. These Ionians were proud of their bloodlines, regarding themselves as the fine flower of Greece. Herodotus, born in the Dorian city of Halicarnassus, thought too much had been said about the purity of their descent. "They have no right to pride themselves on their purity," he declared, "for some of them are Abantes from Euboea, who are not Ionians at all, even in name, to say nothing of the admixture of Minyans from Orchomenos and of Cadmeans, Dryopians, and Phocians, who seceded from their native state, and Molossians, and Pelasgians from Arcadia and Dorians from Epidaurus, and many other races are mingled with them, and those of them who set forth from the prytaneum (town hall) of Athens and who believe themselves to be of the purest Ionian blood, these, I say, brought no women with them, but took Carian women, whose parents they had killed."

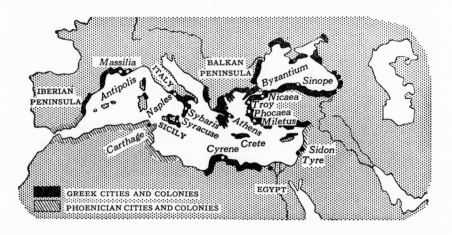

The Greek conquest of the West began from the shores of Asia.

Herodotus rarely raises his voice in anger, but there is no hiding his anger here. As he well knew, the Ionians, the most brilliant and versatile of the Greeks, were not a homogeneous race, but the result of a marriage between Greece and the Orient. Many tribes had gone into their making, and many languages fed their dialects. Out of that richness there would come Homer and the scientific spirit of inquiry and the beginnings of Greek philosophy. Out of the mingling of many bloodstreams there would come the first fruits of Western civilization. Ionia was the springboard. Then from Ionia the sacred fire would be passed to Athens, and then to Rome, and then to France and England, until in the end it lit most of the known world.

From Ionia went the expeditions which conquered the littoral of the Black Sea, and sailed up the Adriatic, and reached out to France and Spain to found colonies in remote and unknown places. The Greek conquest of the West began from the shores of Asia.

Phocaea

THE most northerly city of the Ionian confederation was built on an isolated headland running off the bay of Smyrna, the cliffs encircling it and islands protecting it. Herodotus says the Phocaeans were the first of the Greeks to make long voyages, the first to show their countrymen the way to the Adriatic, Tyrrhenia, and Spain as far as Tartessus. They were in fact the first Greeks who dared to sail from one end of the Mediterranean to the other, and Herodotus points out, as a mark of their courage, that they did not sail in deep, broad-beamed merchant ships but in narrow galleys manned by fifty oarsmen.

After the Carthaginians, the Phocaeans possessed the most powerful naval force in the Mediterranean. Their far-flung settlements were scattered all over the southern coast of Europe. All the islands of the western Mediterranean fell into their hands. Ischia, Sardinia, Corsica, Elba, Majorca, Minorca and Ibiza became Phocaean outposts. They sailed through the Gates of Hercules and entered the Atlantic. Nothing daunted them. Of their city on the headland Diogenes Laertius said "it had no great size, and was skilled in nothing but to rear brave men."

The Phocaeans founded Marseilles (Massilia). Strabo tells a pleasant story about their coming to France. Aristarche, a priestess of the temple of Artemis of the Ephesians, dreamed that Artemis had come to her, ordering her to join an expedition to the west, taking with her the cult statue of the goddess. So she joined two merchants, Simos and his son Protis, who were planning to take their merchandise through the Strait of Messina. Finally they came to France and dropped anchor in a wide bay where a hundred ships could ride out a storm in comfort. There were islands in the bay, which reminded them of their own safe anchorage in Phocaea. There were no other ships in sight, no towns, no fortresses. They landed and went up into the bare hills, where they learned that all this coast was owned by King Nannos, who was about to hold a feast in honor of his daughter Gyptis. According to the custom, all the young princes for miles around were invited to the feast, and at a certain moment Gyptis would be brought in, carrying a cup of pure water which she would offer to the youth who found most favor in her eyes. The Phocaeans were invited to the feast, and the cup was given to young Protis, who drank the pure water and was given the harbor of Massilia as a wedding present. Protis, the happy bridegroom, changed his name to Euxinos, "the honored guest," and Gyptis changed her name to Aristoxena, "the best of guests." Because Gyptis came of royal blood, she became coruler with her Greek husband of the harbor and the wild shores, and because Artemis had directed the Greeks along their dangerous journey and was responsible for the marriage, she became the guardian goddess of the land, and on the headland a temple was erected for her. All this happened about 600 B.C., but her cult statue survives to this day in the museum at Avignon.

The Phocaeans went on to found Antipolis (Antibes) and Nicaea (Nice), but Massilia remained their chief city in the western Mediterranean. They traded in timber, cattle, honey, skins, and fish, until the Carthaginians attacked them and then they fled for a few years, only to return when the danger was over. They left their stamp on southern France, and changed the face of the land, for they brought with them the vine, the fig tree, the cherry tree, the chestnut, and the olive. For nearly six hundred years Massilia remained the most powerful Greek outpost in the western Mediterranean, and even when the Romans conquered her the people continued to speak Greek and to worship Artemis, the sister of Apollo.

When the Persians invaded Asia Minor, they offered easy terms to the Phocaeans. Harpagus, the Persian commander, offered to lift the siege if the Phocaeans would pull down one of the towers in the battlements and dedicate one dwelling house for the king. The Phocaeans promised to answer on the following day, on condition that Harpagus withdraw his forces, and Harpagus seems to have been perfectly aware of their intentions. When at last he entered the city it was empty. The Phocaeans had fled, putting all their women and children, their temple statues and treasure and household goods, on their fifty-oared galleys. They sailed for the island of Chios, offered to buy the neighboring islands of Oenussae which lie off the Sea of Erythrae, and the Chians prudently refused, fearing that their own trade would be strangled. By this time a Persian garrison had been installed in Phocaea, and the Phocaeans sent some armed galleys back, killed the Persians in a hit-and-run raid and, having thrown an iron anchor into the sea, swore they would never return until the anchor rose to the surface. But they had not counted on the Phocaeans waiting on the islands of Oenussae. About half were so much in love with their city that they decided to return, while the rest sailed off to Corsica.

From their base in Corsica they became pirates and sea raiders, to such effect that the Carthaginians and Tyrrhenians led a fleet of sixty ships against them. The naval battle, which was fought off Sardinia, gave a technical victory to the Phocaeans, forty of their ships being destroyed, and the rest being so battered that they were very nearly useless for further service. The Carthaginians and Tyrrhenians took some prisoners, and promptly stoned them to death. Herodotus reports that where the dead Phocaeans lay, any living thing that passed by, whether man, sheep, or ox, suffered a paralytic stroke. Finally the Phocaeans abandoned Corsica and settled in southern Italy. "Phocaea and Teos were the only two cities to prefer their liberty to their homes," wrote Herodotus; he could pay them no greater honor.

Miletus

OF all the cities founded by the Greeks on the coast of Asia Minor Miletus was the richest, the most cultivated, the most self-consciously aware of the power of the intelligence. It was wonderfully situated near the mouth of the Meander River with four sheltered harbors, with rolling meadow land beyond flanked by low hills covered with vineyards. Wheat grew in the valleys, sheep pastured in the plateau beyond the hills, and there were small forests nearby. Everything had been arranged to give Miletus the perfect setting for a trading port which could control much of the traffic between the Greek world and the kingdoms of the Asiatic hinterland.

The Milesians reveled in trade. They were skilled craftsmen famous for their furniture—especially for their beds—and for their fine purple cloth and vivid carpets. The wool of Phrygia and the iron of Colchis passed through their hands. Their chief exports were hemp, timber, ironware, cloths of all kinds, and wines from the interior provinces, and it was said of them that "they would sell anything." They were traders by instinct, with the result that Miletus became the largest, most populous, and richest of all the Greek cities, with sixty colonies of its own scattered over the eastern Mediterranean and the Black Sea.

Trade gave them leisure, as it gave them power. Trade, too, was responsible for the large influx of foreigners who came to settle in the city—Egyptians, Scythians, Phoenicians, Babylonians, even Indians could be seen walking through its streets. Out of the marriage of so many minds there emerged an aristocracy of culture such as the world has rarely seen. Science had its beginnings in that sunlit Asiatic city.

Traditionally the first scientist was Thales, who appears to have come from a Phoenician family long resident in Miletus. He was born about 640 B.C., and when quite young traveled in Egypt, where he measured the height of the pyramids by comparing their shadows with a shadow thrown by a man. Diogenes Laertius says he was the first to study astronomy, meaning perhaps that he was the first to work out a theory about the revolution of the stars without benefit of mythology. Herodotus says he predicted the eclipse of the sun, and he was credited with being the first to construct a sextant. He taught seamen to navigate by the Little Bear. Once he diverted the course of a river in order to help the advance of a Lydian king against Persia. He believed Water to be the first principle, out of which all things were made. Aristotle suggested that he chose Water because "the nutriment of everything is moist, and all seeds have a moist nature," but that is to accuse him of a simplicity he did not possess. He believed that the universe was living, "being alive with the gods," and this conception of a living, breathing universe was to haunt Greek philosophers to the end.

Mathematician, astronomer, engineer, philosopher—he was all these, but in his own time he may have been chiefly regarded as a statesman. Thrasybulus, the tyrant of Miletus, frequently consulted him, and he seems to have been the first to suggest a federation of Ionia. All his works except a few scattered fragments are lost. Once, when he was asked why he had fathered no children, he answered: "Because I love them too much." He was asked when he was young why he had not married, and said: "It is not yet time," and when he reached middle age and was asked the same question, he replied: "It is too late." He was the first to proclaim that it was the duty of the philosopher "to know himself." He wrote: "God is the most ancient of all things, for he had no birth; the earth is the most beautiful of all things, for it is the work of God; space is the greatest of all things, for everything is contained within it; intellect is the swiftest of all things, for it runs through everything; necessity is the strongest of things, for it rules everything; time is the wisest of things, for it finds out everything." In this pleasant way he summed up his knowledge of the universe, and it is a measure of our loss that this is the only complete sentence of his that has come down to us.

He was followed by his pupils, Anaximander and Anaximenes, both of Miletus, and both continuing the tradition of scientific inquiry. Anaximander constructed a sundial and a globe of the heavens, and he made a map of the known world for his friend Hecataeus, the historian. Anaximander believed a sphere of flame surrounded the earth, as bark surrounds a tree. He suggested that men were descended from fish, and he was puzzled because babies are so helpless, while young animals gather food for themselves soon after they are born. He said the first principle was "the Boundless" (*to apeiron*), which is perhaps only an interpretation of Thales' Water. There was not one world, but instead innumerable worlds were eternally coming into existence and eternally passing away.

Anaximenes studied lunar rainbows and marine phosphorescence. For him the first principle was "infinite air," by which perhaps he meant what we mean by "ether." The rarefaction of air gives fire, its condensation results in the creation of winds, clouds, water, earth, even rock. "Our souls are air," he wrote. "Air holds us together, as wind and air encompass the whole world." Such gnomic utterances are all that remain, and we can only surmise how far he traveled along the road opened out by Thales and Anaximander.

When Cyrus conquered Ionia and placed his satraps in command, most of the cities of Asiatic Greece contrived to live peacefully with the invaders. The Milesians were regarded as the most loyal vassals of the Persian king. Their trade was protected by the Persians, and their taxes went to fill the Persian exchequer. Pride, love of freedom, resentment against paying taxes—all these went into the Ionian revolt, which broke out in 499. The revolt was led by Aristagoras, tyrant of Miletus, who sailed to Sparta and Athens in search of allies. The

Spartans, traditionally friendly with the Persian kings, refused their help. The Athenians to the number of thirty thousand gathered in the Agora and listened to the pleading of Aristagoras and passed a decree for the dispatch of twenty warships to Ionia. "The sailing of this fleet," said Herodotus, "was the beginning of evil for the Greeks and the barbarians."

In the spring of 498 the expedition reached Ionia. The twenty Athenian warships, with five more from Eretria, sailed to Ephesus, and then the sailors marched inland to Sardis, which they set on fire, destroying the famous temple of Cybele on the Pactolus. Thereafter the Persians had a pretext for destroying every Greek temple that came into their hands. The Greeks retreated, having, as they thought, accomplished their purpose, while Ionia waited in trepidation for the Persian giant to rouse himself and in his own time destroy the rebels. When the Persian king sat down to dinner he ordered a servant to repeat three times: "Lord, remember the Athenians."

At last in 494 the Persians gathered a huge fleet composed of Phoenicians, Cilicians, Egyptians, and loyal Cypriots, and decisively defeated a smaller Ionian fleet off the island of Lade. Then it was the turn of Miletus. The Persians dug tunnels under the walls, brought up catapults, blockaded the sea lanes, and battered the city into subjection. They killed most of the men, enslaved the women and children, and razed the city. For many years the greatest of Greek cities in Asia was a huddle of ruins inhabited only by a small Persian garrison.

Syracuse

THE Corinthians boasted that they founded the colony at Syracuse in 734 B.C., thus making it the most ancient of Greek colonies in Sicily. At first they settled only on the island of Ortygia, but gradually their power spread until it included most of the eastern part of Sicily. They spoke the Dorian dialect of Corinth, regarded themselves as of pure Corinthian descent, and maintained the closest relations with the mother city. "We're as Corinthian as Bellerophon himself," says Praxinoa in the fifteenth idyl of Theocritus. "There is no harm in speaking Doric, is there?"

None, perhaps, except to the Athenians, who found themselves uncomfortably close to a Corinth grown wealthy and powerful by reason of its Sicilian connections. In classical times Syracuse was larger and more prosperous than Corinth, and even more self-assertive. Nearly seven hundred years after its foundation Cicero visited the city and described it even then as "the largest of Greek cities, and the most splendid of all capitals," thus putting it above Rome and Athens. "It has a strong natural position," he went on, "and is quite wonderful to look at, whether you approach it by land or sea. So vast is Syracuse that it may be said to consist of four very large cities." Then, for four or five pages, he describes the wealth and splendor of a city that had no rivals even after a Roman governor had despoiled it of its greatest artistic treasures.

According to the Syracusan legend, the island of Ortygia was sacred to Artemis, who was born in Delos. Once Delos bore the name of Ortygia, and this island off the coast of Sicily was regarded as second only to Delos in its sanctity. A fresh-water spring bubbled up on the southeast side of the island, very close to the sea, and its existence was explained by the presence of the nymph Arethusa, one of Artemis' attendants, who was hunting on the plains of Elis in the Peloponnese when she was spied by the river-god Alpheus, and to elude him she swam out to sea. When she reached Ortygia, she rose again into the upper world, metamorphosed into a fountain. Of the nymph's beauty we have ample witness in the coins struck by Euainetos, the greatest of all die engravers, who depicted her with magnificently robust curls and with dolphins tumbling in the waves about her head. He was so proud of the silver decadrachms of Arethusa that he sometimes signed them in bold letters, his own name appearing where we might expect to find the name of the city.

The beautiful coinage of Syracuse testified to the power and magnificence of a city which had known uninterrupted prosperity since its foundation. The navy of Syracuse kept the Carthaginians at bay. Above the wide, sheltered harbor stood the low cliffs, and the fertile plains stretching for ten miles to the foothills of the Iblean Mountains. White villas crowded the cliffs, and spilled out over the surrounding plains. On Ortygia, beside the fountain of Arethusa, stood the temple of Artemis, and there was another temple to Athena with doors of ivory and gold, and the golden shield on the roof of the temple was a beacon to sailors.

Democracy collapsed in Syracuse about 485 B.C., and there followed a long period of rule by princely tyrants. Ortygia became a fortress given over to an army of Sikels and Campanians who formed the praetorian guard of the ruling tyrant, and sometimes they would dethrone the tyrant and elect another in his place. The wealth of Syracuse survived its unruly guardsmen.

In time Syracuse became the largest city in the Greek world, and the wealthiest, so that it seemed in danger of collapsing of its own magnificence. Yet it survived the Romans as it survived its tyrannical guardsmen, and the Greek city did not die until A.D. 878, when the Saracens conquered it, killed all its inhabitants, and leveled it to the ground. A few temple columns remained, and today we can still see the archaic columns of a temple to Apollo and the ruins of the fortress of Euryalos, the seat of the ancient tyrants. But far more important toward an understanding of Syracuse are those lovely coins, so clear and full of precisely observed detail, conveying with illimitable grace, in the space of two inches, the charm and beauty of a people.

Sybaris

BY all accounts the wealthiest and most luxurious of the colonies was Sybaris, which lay in a wide and fertile plain within a semicircle of wooded mountains overlooking the Gulf of Tarentum. Founded by Achaeans about 720, it soon became the most prosperous of all the settlements overseas, its wealth coming from portage rights over the hills enabling goods to be taken overland from the Ionian to the Tyrrhenian Sea, so avoiding the dangerous passage through the Strait of Messina. Sybaris traded extensively with Asia Minor, especially with Miletus, and from Miletus it seems to have derived its passionate indulgence in luxury.

The grammarian Athenaeus is our chief authority for its habits and customs. He tells of the people's fondness for food and hot baths, their addiction to fine raiment, their pride in their splendid trappings. They were the first to cover their streets with awnings as a protection against the hot Mediterranean sun, and the first to invent chamberpots. They were the inventors of pipelines, constructed to enable wine to flow from the vineyards to the port, where it was poured into jars and sealed for export. They invented the menu, and sat down to complicated six-course meals, using spoons for drinking soup—an unheard-of luxury among the Greeks. They liked to sleep late, and they hated noise so much that metalworkers and carpenters were ordered out of the residential part of the city; roosters also were forbidden to crow. When a citizen of Sybaris left the city, he always went by chariot rather than on foot, and he would take his time on the journey, spending three or four days on the road if it pleased him, though any ordinary Greek would have traveled the same distance in a day. They wore robes dyed in Tyrian purple and braided their hair with gold ribbons. They were passionately fond of fish mayonnaise, fruit syrups and cabbage, which they used to eat before drinking. They adored eels, and eel sellers were exempt from taxes, a distinction they shared with the importers of purple dyes.

Once the Sybarites passed a law to the effect that women taking part in celebrations should be given a whole year to prepare their dresses and ornaments. This was taken as a proof of their self-indulgence and their peculiar generosity to women.

Athenaeus tells the story of a Sybarite invited to attend a public eating place in Sparta. There were wooden benches instead of couches, and the food was meager. "Well," said the Sybarite, "there was a time when I was greatly impressed with Spartan bravery in battle. Now I have come to know you, I fail to see anything remarkable about it. The most pitiable coward would sooner die than live the way you do." Athenaeus tells the story twice, and evidently considered it fair comment.

In Sybaris the very rich were attended by dwarfs, and they enjoyed the companionship of lap dogs imported from Malta. If the meal was successful, the host was likely to say: "Please dine with me a year from today!" They were too lazy to pour water on their hands during meals; this service was performed by slaves who stood at their elbows.

Sybaris became the most powerful and influential city in Magna Graecia, with twenty-five daughter-colonies of her own scattered around the Mediterranean. Poseidonia (Paestum), at the western end of the portage, was the favorite colony, having been founded about 524. The Sybarites had only a few years in which to cultivate this colony, for their own city was captured and razed fourteen years later by the army of the neighboring city of Croton. It was a long and murderous war fought for the possession of the portage rights. At one time the Sybarites murdered thirty ambassadors from Croton and left their bodies to rot outside the walls. There is a story, told by Athenaeus, of how the commanders of the Croton army tricked the

Sybarites to defeat by bringing up flute players who played the same dance tunes which the Sybarite horses danced to when on parade. So, dancing, the horses went over to join the flute players. There is only one thing wrong with the story. Exactly the same story was told of other armies. Sybaris did not fall because her horses defected to the enemy. The hard-fought battle lasted seventy days, and came to an end only when Croton received reinforcements from Sparta.

Croton took a terrible revenge on Sybaris. The walls were razed and a river was diverted to flow over the ruins. Nothing was allowed to remain. The survivors were sold into slavery, and the capital of Magna Graecia vanished from the earth. Many years later Pericles established a colony nearby in a place called Thurii in an attempt to revive the ancient city, and Herodotus became one of the founders. But the new city never achieved the celebrity or power of Sybaris, which entered into legend, becoming for all time the symbol of supreme luxury.

Cyrene

IF we can believe Herodotus, the largest of the Greek colonies in Africa came into being because a man from the island of Thera suffered from a speech defect and consulted the oracle at Delphi in the hope of receiving advice on curing it. In reply Apollo commanded him to set sail for Libya and found a colony there. Mortified, he returned to Thera, still suffering from the speech defect. He could make nothing of the words of the oracle. On his own island everything went wrong, and so he sent again to Delphi, only to receive the same reply from the priestess. At last he set off for Libya in two fifty-oared galleys with his chosen companions, but when he reached the coast he felt sure the oracle had made a mistake and set sail again for Thera, abandoning the enterprise. The islanders refused to let him land. Once more he set out for Libya, and on a small island off the coast he founded a colony, which did not prosper. Two years passed. The settlers suffered from hunger and misery, and at last they came to the conclusion that there was nothing to be gained by staying there any longer. They abandoned the island, and when they reached Delphi they were commanded to return. They were told that they had not been to Libya, only to an island off the coast. So they returned for the third time, landed on the mainland, found guides, and were taken to a place where a spring gushed out of the earth. The guides said: "This is a place for you to settle, for here there is a hole in the sky."

According to tradition, Aristotle of Thera with his two hundred companions settled in Libya in 631 B.C. By "a hole in the sky" the guides meant an abundant rainfall, and the wealth of the land soon attracted more settlers. There was good arable soil and ample pasture for sheep. In time Aristotle became the *battus* or king of Libya, and his descendants proved strong enough to defeat the armies of Egypt. Libya became Greek, with a string of Greek cities along the coast. "You are a king over great cities, and this great privilege is a shining heritage of your house," wrote the poet Pindar in an ode addressed to King Arcesilaus IV of Cyrene in 462 B.C. Another king, called Magas, was sufficiently famous to be mentioned in a monument set up by King Asoka in India. He ruled for fifty years, led his armies against Egypt, and died at last, "suffocated by his own bulk." Till the time of the Roman conquest Cyrene remained a power to be reckoned with, deriving its wealth largely from the export of wool and a strange plant called silphium which grew in the arid steppes and was believed to have medicinal qualities. Perhaps silphium is asafetida, but no one is quite sure.

The kings and princes of Cyrene shared with the tyrants of Sicily a lust for grandeur. They built vast temples to Apollo, cultivated the arts, protected poets, and staged plays in the theater. Here Greek civilization flourished under the African sun. More than six hundred sculptures have been discovered under the ruins of the abandoned city, where the great columns of the temple of Apollo, and twenty other temples, rise toward the skies.

Cyrenaic art came to possess a quality of its own, warmer and more sensual than the art of the Greek mainland. The Cyrenaic philosophers believed profoundly in the pursuit of happiness, and many stories were told of their affection for reasonable luxury. When Aristippus, the pupil of Socrates, was rebuked for his habits of luxury, he answered: "If extravagance were a fault, it would have no place in the festivals of the gods." When he was rebuked for taking the famous courtesan Lais as his mistress, he replied: "I possess her, but I am not possessed by her. The best of all things is to enjoy pleasures without being their slave, not to deprive oneself of pleasure." Cyrene was Sybaris without its effeminacy: gay, pleasure loving, sensitive, in love with life under the sun.

Today you can wander for miles through the deserted city, which still bears the impress of the Greek imagination. There, if anywhere, you see a city built to house a people who believed that the human spirit should be clothed in a calm luxury.

8 ⋘ THE EARLY SONGS

Homer and Hesiod spoke with the calm wisdom of age: they were old or at least middle-aged men who composed their verses out of a deep experience of life. Their themes were the high and serious themes of war and destiny, of the generation of the gods and man's dependence on them. They wrote with a settled gravity, perfectly aware of their moral purposes, and it is scarcely possible to imagine they were ever young. Gaunt, bearded figures, they stand at the beginning of Greek poetry like the angels with flaming swords who guarded the gates of Paradise.

Though Homer is incomparably the greater poet, they have much in common. They were both poets of the market place, chanting their verses to the multitudes in a style deliberately designed for public recital, keenly aware that the gods and the heroes were listening to them, their audience extending to the outermost spaces of the heavens. They saw themselves as the chosen vehicles of mythology, creators of legend, guardians of the mysteries; theirs was a priestly rather than a poetic function. Their task was to relate the gods to heroic men, and the very nature of their verse precluded them from composing the simple songs of love and marriage and harvesting and drinking which were part of the ordinary round of life. They were remote from the preoccupations of private innocence.

We know that dance songs were sung in Homeric times, and there must have been love songs and drinking songs, but none has survived. When Homer is describing the shield of Achilles, decorated with scenes from the lives of gods and heroes, he points to the small corner where youths and maidens wreathed with flowers dance on a dancing floor made by the lame god Hephaestus. It is evidently not a village dance, for it takes place in a palace. The youths wear "finely woven doublets glistening with oil, with gold daggers hanging from their silver belts." They hold hands and dance in circles, while musicians play and acrobats perform among them. They were evidently singing lustily to the tune of the music. The earliest song that has come down to us is an invocation to Dionysus sung by the women of Elis:

> *Come, hero Dionysus,*
> *To thy temple at Elis,*
> *To the holy temple with the Graces,*
> *Raging with thy bull hooves.*
> *O noble bull! O noble bull!*

Plutarch, who preserved the fragment, was considerably exercised by the question of why the women were summoning Dionysus in the shape of a bull. We know more now about the bull cults in ancient Greece, and are not so perturbed. The rhythm of the song suggests that it was a chorus punctuated by the stamping of feet on the floor.

Another "leaping" song of venerable antiquity was found engraved on both sides of some broken tablets at Palaikastro in Crete at the beginning of the century. The hymn proclaims the worship of the youthful Zeus, "the lord of the splendid gleaming." Armed youths surround the altar of the young god, leaping and singing to the music of flutes and harps:

> *Io!*
> *O most great Youth we greet thee,*
> *Kronian lord of the splendid gleaming,*
> *Who comest at the head of thy Daimons.*
> *Year by year thou comest to Dikte,*
> *Rejoicing in songs.*
> *For thee we strike harp-strings*
> *Mingled with the music of flutes,*
> *We stand singing before thy well-guarded altar.*
>
> *Io!*
> *O most great Youth we greet thee,*

Kronian lord of the splendid gleaming.
To this place away from Rhea
The shield-bearing heralds have brought thee
To the sound of stamping feet.

Io!
O most great Youth we greet thee,
Kronian lord of the splendid gleaming.
We leap for the jars brimming over,
And for the fleecy flocks we leap,
We leap for the orchards and for rich hives.

Io!
O most great Youth we greet thee,
Kronian lord of the splendid gleaming.
We leap for our cities,
And for our seafaring ships,
We leap for our good people and for lovely Themis.

Though these songs take the form of ritual hymns, we are already aware that a personal energy is being poured into them. Where the Homeric poet is often curiously impersonal, the worshiper as he leaps for the brimming jars and the fleecy flocks is already beginning to employ poetry for his own personal ends, and soon enough there would be poems of desire and affection and mourning. Greek tradition preserves the names of many poets living before the time of Homer—we hear of Linus, Orpheus, Musaeus, Eumolpus, Thamyris, Amphion. Most of these were lyric poets, and a long lyric tradition must have been in existence when there emerged in the seventh and sixth centuries a body of poets exulting in their freedom to compose songs on any theme that occurred to them.

These early songs have a freshness and innocence which suggest that a curtain has been raised on a new kind of song. Gone are the great rolling hexameters with their fixity and finality; instead there are light-footed verses, gay and rippling like a summer stream. There are no legendary heroes, and almost there are no gods, though Aphrodite will be invoked nightly. The thunderclouds have gone, and the last heavy rains have fallen. Now the earth gleams in the sunlight, brighter than ever because it is wet and gleaming.

Archilochus

THE first major lyric poet who has come down to us was a scoundrel who, according to Pindar, "fattened on the abuse of his enemies." His real name was Telesiclides, but he chose to call himself Archilochus, which can be translated "the great commander." That was only one of the jokes he played on posterity, which took its revenge by calling him simply "the Scorpion." He was the bastard son of an aristocratic father and a slave woman, and to the end there was something in him of the aristocrat and the slave.

According to the legend, he fell violently in love with a girl called Neobule, daughter of Lycambes. They were engaged to be married, and then for some unknown reason the girl broke off the engagement. Archilochus took his revenge by attacking both the daughter and her father in verses filled with furious venom, attacking the good name of one and the good faith of the other; and there is a legend that they both hanged themselves.

Only a miserable handful of his works have survived, but there is enough to suggest his savage power mingled with a strain of tenderness. Many of his poems describe his adventures in and about the island of Thasos in the north Aegean Sea. He told how he left his native island of Paros in poverty and despair—

> *Let me say*
> *A fond farewell to Paros with its wretched figs and fish*

—and went to Thasos for a change of enemies. He found the second island no better than the first. There was the further disadvantage that on Thasos he was forced to fight in a war from which he could derive little profit. He hated war, old women, the deaths of his friends, and he especially hated the island of Thasos, "a wretched place, bare and rough as a hog's back in the sea." He seems to have been a good soldier, but he thought nothing of throwing his shield away on the battlefield and running for his life.

> *Some savage, finding my shield, will give himself airs.*
> *I left it under a hedge, and there's no crime in it.*
> *I was sorry to see it go, but the devil take it!*
> *I can get another shield if I ever have to.*

The old order was surely dead or doomed when a man could speak of his shield in the same tones that he speaks of a harlot. He enjoyed harlots—they were the only women available to hired mercenaries—but he thought their fees too high and their legs too fat. He liked the company of his fellow scoundrels, and went fighting and whoring through Thrace and Euboea, always unhappy in his loves, quarreling with his friends, taking his greatest joy in being venomous. He was the first poet of hate, but he was also, which was much more important, the first poet of lyric tenderness.

> She wore a spray of myrtle in her hair,
> And in her hands the glory of the rose,
> While on her back and shoulders fell
> Her hair like darkness.

He would say of a girl that "her breasts and her dark hair were perfume—even an old man would love her," and somehow, by some miracle, we are transported back across the centuries into his presence. Once he wrote that no man ever receives honor from his own countrymen when he is dead. It was not true. The Greeks remembered him, hating the man and loving the poet all the more because he was believed to be the first who ever wrote in iambics. He wrote his own perfect epitaph:

> I am the servant of the God of War
> And gifted in the art of poetry.

Alcman

THE Spartan poet Alcman flourished in the middle of the seventh century B.C. Unlike Archilochus, he was a professional poet whose most important function was to compose choral songs for whatever temple or group would pay for them. Clement of Alexandria said he was the first writer of choral odes, Suidas that he was the first to compose love poetry. The critic Antipater of Thessalonica said he was "the commander of the Nine Muses," and sometimes we feel that this is exactly what he was.

Where Archilochus is all fire and venom, Alcman is all lyric sweetness. He never raises his voice, never reaches out beyond the compass of his own experience; he conceals his art, which is all the more evident because it is carefully concealed. He came, it appears, from Sardis, the capital of Lydia, and settled in Laconia. All that we know about him, on the dubious authority of Athenaeus, is that he fell in love with a young woman with the very odd name of Mega-lostrata, and it may have been to her that he wrote his beautiful fragment on the milk of lionesses:

> *How many times amid the mountaintops,*
> *While the gods feasted at the feasting places*
> *And torches gleamed,*
> *You brought me one of those jars that peasants carry,*
> *Filled by your lovely hand with milk of lionesses,*
> *And thereof made a great cheese*
> *Shining and whole.*

The man who could write such things inevitably attracted legends to himself. Some said he was the slave of Agesilaus the Spartan, others that the Cimmerians captured him from Sardis and eventually sold him to Sparta, where his songs procured him his freedom. But the legends fail to throw any light on him. Archilochus said he was the servant of the God of War, Alcman replied that he was the servant of the goddess Artemis, the sister of Apollo.

He seems to have been the first to make use of the pathetic fallacy—the deliberate projection of human feelings and emotions into nature. The most exquisite of his surviving fragments depicts the coming of sleep:

> *Now sleep the mountain peaks and cliffs,*
> *The headlands and the valleys lie asleep,*
> *And all the creeping things the black earth feeds,*
> *The beasts whose lying is upon the hillside,*
> *The hived bees, the monsters in the blue seas' depths,*
> *They sleep now while the birds*
> *Lie drowsy in their wings.*

Except for these fragments and a few more, we should know very little about Alcman if it had not been for the happy discovery of one of his long choral odes in the Egyptian desert. In 1855 Auguste Mariette, the French archaeologist who discovered the Serapeum at Memphis, found near the second pyramid at Saqqara a papyrus

containing a fragment of a *partheneion*, a hymn to be sung by a
chorus of girls in honor of the Spartan goddess Orthia. It is a mysterious fragment, for we do not know on what occasion it was sung
or why the girls, who were perhaps priestesses, speak of the beauty
of one rivaling that of another. The names, too, are mysterious, for
while some are common names, others seem to be priestly titles. Altogether eleven girls take part in the song, led by Hagesichora, which
means "the choir leader." There is no clear indication where one
singer leaves off and another begins:

> *A vengeance comes from the God:*
> *Happy are those who spin*
> *Their web of days*
> *Shedding no tears.*

> *I sing the light of Agido.*
> *I see her like the sun—*
> *And now Agido conjures up*
> *The flooding rays.*

> *She who is the lovely choir leader*
> *Will not let me praise her,*
> *Or say she is fair.*
> *Well she knows she is beautiful,*
> *As if among a herd of cattle*
> *We chanced upon a race horse,*
> *Swift, sinewy, with thundering hooves,*
> *Creature of a winged dream!*

> *Look upon her! She is like*
> *A fleet race horse coming from Venice.*
> *The hair of our cousin Hagesichora*
> *Is a blossom of the purest gold,*
> *Her face shining silver below.*
> *How can I speak more plainly?*
> *You have only to look upon Hagesichora.*
> *In beauty she may be second to Agido,*
> *But she has the pace of a Scythian horse*
> *Compared with a Lydian racer.*

As we carry the plow of Orthia,
So the Pleiades rise against us,
Blazing like the flame of Sirius
Through the divine night.

We have no wealth of purple stuffs,
Nor serpent-bracelets of gold
On neck and wrists to make us beautiful,
Nor Lydian coifs on the brows
Of silk-eyed girls.
The hair of Nanno is not as beautiful,
Arete's beauty fails us, though her beauty
Is like the beauty of the gods:
Thulakis and Kleasisera fail us also.

And we who cling to Agido
Honor the day with our songs.
O gods, accept their prayers,
For the end of the enterprise
Belongs to God. As for me
My virgin singing is the hoot of an owl
From the rooftops. I sing in vain.
I yearn to please the Goddess of the Dawn,
She who gives balm to our wounds.
Maidens, Hagesichora has led us
To the place of peace.

Sappho

WHEN the Greeks spoke of Sappho they called her simply "the Poetess," as they called Homer "the Poet." It was not only that there was no one to compare with her, but she represented in herself everything they demanded from a woman poet—the clear ringing note of fierce passion enclosed in verses of impeccable purity. There were many other women poets, but by common consent none ever approached Sappho in perfect command of language. She was one of the lords of language, and in the whole course of Greek literature there were only perhaps three others who achieved that stature.

She was born in Eressos on the island of Lesbos sometime in the middle of the seventh century, her family moving to Mytilene when she was a child. Tradition says of her that she was small and frail, not particularly beautiful, her hair, eyes, and skin being darker than usual among the Greeks. One early commentator described her as a nightingale with ill-shaped wings enclosed within a tiny body. One of her brothers was a cupbearer, another a wine merchant sailing between Mytilene and Naucratis, and legend has it that he accumulated enough money to buy the notorious courtesan Doricha "at a high price." All we know with reasonable certainty is that she was banished by the tyrant Pittacus when the nobles attempted to rise in rebellion, visited Syracuse, and later returned to her birthplace. There is a story that she threw herself off the Leucadian cliff in unrequited love for the ferryman Phaon, but there is no basis for the story. Many of her poems are addressed to young girls, and it has been assumed that she presided over a school of young poetesses whom she encouraged in the writing of love songs, but there is nothing in her poems to warrant the assumption. Nor is it certain that she was a Lesbian, a word conveniently invented on her imagined love affairs. She married a man from the island of Andros, had children, and lived a long life.

Of her surviving works there remain about a hundred scattered fragments and a handful of complete poems. The entire body of her work seems to have survived well into the sixteenth century, for Peter of Alcona remembered being told by Demetrius Chalcondyles that the bishops of the Greek church had only recently burned her poems, together with those of Anacreon, Bion, Alcman, and Alcaeus. The loss is all the harder to bear in the knowledge that they survived intact for more than two thousand years.

Sappho's greatest claim to memory is that she introduced a note of piercing tenderness absent before. "My heart is like that of a child," she said once, and she has a child's directness, a child's waywardness and generosity. She holds nothing back. In simple, precise words she pours out "not one passion, but a congress of passions." Such was the verdict of Longinus, who saved one of her poems from oblivion:

> *Like a god in my sight is the man who*
> *Sits beside you, looking into your eyes,*
> *Listening to the sweet murmur of your voice,*
>   *The enticing laughter.*

It breaks my spirit to think of it:
My heart beats fast in my breast,
My speech comes short and fails me,
 And my tongue is broken.

A delicate sweet flame leaps within me
Like liquid fire, my eyes grow dim.
I see nothing before me: only I hear
 A silent thunder.

Sweat dews my brows; I am trembling
In every limb, and it seems to me
I have grown paler than dry grass,
 And death is near.

So she wrote with a kind of quiet inevitability, each word falling in place as though it had been invented only that moment. She never pauses for breath. Behind all the lament for lost loves, for absent lovers, and for the impermanence of the affections, there is always a core of serenity. The broken tongue will mend, the autumn grasses will grow green again. She is the poet of hopeless loves, but out of her poems springs the undying hope of lovers.

We are told that she wrote nine books of poems, which may have amounted to perhaps four hundred pages, but we know her best through the vivid fragments quoted by ancient scholiasts or uncovered from the Egyptian sands. These fragments have the resonance of whole poems, and sometimes we find ourselves wondering how anything else could be added:

I have a daughter, my darling Cleis,
Who seems to me as pretty as a gold flower:
For her I would not take all the treasures of Lydia,
Or even of Lesbos.

There was a time when Leda found
Among the hyacinths a white egg,
Whiter than any seen before.

In ancient days the Cretan maidens danced
Once to the music round the holy altar,
Pressing the soft smooth flowers of the grass.

I loved you, Atthis, long ago,
When I was virgin like the flowers,
And then you seemed a small ungainly child.

You are a sweet-apple hanging, O maiden,
From the uttermost twig of the highest bough,
Forgotten by the harvesters who could not reach so high,
Or like the hyacinths trodden by shepherds in the mountains
Until only a purple stain remains on the earth.

With such simple things, with apples, flowers, eggs, did she build up a world with effortless ease, a world as radiant and joyous as the one depicted by Minoan artists. Indeed, she seems less Greek than Minoan, and the frescoes uncovered by Sir Arthur Evans are still the best illustrations for her poems. She wrote of the weariness of love before the weariness had time to set in, and of all the early poets she is the freshest. The morning dew shines on the lips and eyes of her young lovers.

Her longer poems are sometimes set pieces, evidently written for special occasions. An ode to "Glittering-throned, undying Aphrodite" recounts the terrors of love with quiet candor and ends with a formal invocation to the goddess, seeking her protection. Such poems were probably composed for recital at one of the festivals in honor of the goddess. They have a formal elegance and a sustained excitement, but we no longer feel close to her. The fragments tell us most, as when she said:

I love delicacy, and I believe
All bright and beautiful things
Spring from desire of the sun.

Alcaeus

WHILE Sappho proclaims her intense joy in womanhood, Alcaeus, who was her friend, proclaims his intense joy in masculinity. He, too, came from Lesbos, and like Sappho was forced to flee from the island during the reign of the tyrants. He was something of a swashbuckler, enjoying his life too much to throw it away in a war. We hear of him fighting against the Athenians for possession of Sigeum, and throwing his shield away as he ran from the battlefield: his enemies found the shield and hung it on a tree as a memorial to his cowardice. He is said to have traveled in Thrace and in Egypt before returning to Lesbos in 580.

Quintilian said of him that he might have been the equal of Homer if he had not stooped to buffoonery and bawdry. Not that Homer was lacking in these accomplishments, but Alcaeus was too much the swashbuckler to maintain the high and serious line. The surviving fragments show him to be a man who loved nodding plumes and glittering headpieces, but he preferred to see them hanging quietly on the walls:

> *The great house gleams with bronze; the ample rafters*
> *Are patterned with gleaming helmets, and the plumes*
> *Of horsehair wave in the wind, those martial ornaments.*
> *Plates of armor hang on their pegs, greaves also*
> *Of glistening bronze, defense against javelins,*
> *And there are corslets of new linen and curving shields*
> *With many flowing kilts and cinctures:*
> *Nor are these to be forgotten when the dread work begins.*

Not to be forgotten, but also not to be remembered too fondly, for there are other and more important matters like drinking and wenching to be attended to. "Wash your gullet with wine," he sings, and makes a reasoned plea for winebibbing on hot summer days.

> *Wash your gullet with wine, for the dog star returns*
> *Now when the searing heat scorches the parched earth.*
> *Now the cicada's cry is heard from under the leaves,*
> *And the artichoke flowers, and women are warm and wanton,*
> *While men grow lank, as the dog star withers their brains*
>   *and their knees.*

Alcaeus finds excellent excuses for drinking in the summer, and equally good excuses for drinking in winter.

> *Zeus rains down on us: from the sky there falls*
> *Enormous winter. The rivers are frozen over.*
> *Then damn the winter! Throw a log on the fire,*
> *Mix honey with the wine, and round your brows*
> *Bind fleecy wreaths. No more brooding!*
> *O Bacchus, you have a way of improving matters—*
> *Wine is the best medicine there is!*
> *Therefore drink deep.*

Alcaeus is Archilochus without the venom, which explains why Horace liked him. Urbane, friendly, tolerant of everything except tyranny, he seems to have lived his life quietly in the backwaters. His verses are saved from vulgarity by their masculine vigor and by his undisguised delight in the joys of the flesh; there is a toughness underneath the effortless facility. When he describes girls bathing in a river, he changes them into the inevitable goddesses, but he introduces us into their company:

> *O Ebro, fairest of rivers, beside Aeno,*
> *Descendest thou to the purple sea from Thrace*
> *In glittering floods of foam.*
> *Many maidens stand around thee,*
> *Pouring fountains of water over themselves,*
> *With soft hands smoothing their liquid thighs*
> *With soothing unguents.*

Anacreon

THERE is a pleasant conceit that, after a life spent in lechery and drunkenness, Anacreon died at the age of eighty-five of a grape pip which stuck in his throat. Yet it is probable that he was neither very lecherous nor very fond of wine, and he may have died quietly of old age. His erotic verses smell too often of the lamp to be wholly convincing. He presents himself to us as a fellow of infinite venery, and he would like us to believe that he was a resourceful lover, but in this he is rarely convincing. His imitators were legion—poets went on writing *Anacreontea* well into the Renaissance—but no one rivaled him in his chosen field, the compliments of love.

He was born in Teos about 570 and was driven from the city by the Persian conquest of Ionia twenty-five years later. He settled in Abdera in Thrace and was one of the founding members of that Teian colony; he saw some fighting, and carefully explains that like Archilochus and Alcaeus he threw away his shield. He lived for a while at the court of Polycrates, tyrant of Samos, until he was summoned to Athens, where he so commended himself to the Athenians that many years later they put up a statue of him on the Acropolis; Plutarch tells us that the statue represented him "singing in his cups." There were no other statues of poets on the Acropolis, and it is unlikely that the Athenians would have offered him so much veneration if he was not a poet of astonishing power.

Only the tattered remnants of his work have survived: his real power can only be guessed at in the handful of poems that have come down to us. He could write as venomously as Archilochus when he chose, as his poem on the fortunes of young Artemon, who climbed from poverty to grandeur, demonstrates:

> *He went about in filthy clothes, his hair like a mop,*
> *Buttons of wood in his ears, and around his ribs*
> *The hide of a threadbare ox scraped off some shield or other.*
> *He made his living pimping: cake-girls and whores*
> *Gave him some of their money: for his pains*
> *His neck was framed in a pillory: they whipped him raw,*
> *And tore out the hairs of his beard.*

> *See him now: he rides like a generous lord*
> *In a coach and four, magnificent in golden earrings,*
> *While over his head there hovers an ivory parasol*
> *Like some great lady.*

The portrait of Anacreon as the happy servant of his lusts was fostered by his imitators. He wrote about garlands of roses and sprays of myrtle, but these were the decoration of his occasional poems. When he wrote about the coming of old age, he spoke with greater authority:

> *The love god with the golden curls*
> *Threw into my hands a purple ball,*
> *Whispering to me to make love*
> *To the girl in the bright sandals.*

> *So I went to her, this beauty from Lesbos,*
> *Who turned up her nose disdainfully*
> *At my white hair, and then went running*
> *To hide behind another girl.*

Once when he was asked why he wrote no hymns to the gods, he answered, "Because our loves are our gods." Not abstract love, but fierce desire is the theme of his greatest poem; and the gentle *Anacreontea* pale before the passion of *The Grape Harvest*:

Come the black-skinned grapes
On shoulders of men and maidens,
Heaped high in baskets,
Thrown in the winepress
And then trodden down
Till the must flows out,
And the Great God rejoices
In the clamor of vintage songs,
And there in the wine vat seethes
Bacchus in his lovely youth.
See how the old men drink,
Reeling as they dance,
Gray hair swinging free;
And when the young man comes
Upon the delicate girl
Lying amid frail leaves,
He takes her in his arms
Fierce before the bridals,
And not with words he comes
But takes her against her will:
Since Bacchus in the young
Rejoices fiercely.

The Greek genius for lyric poetry flowered first in Asia and the islands. Archilochus of Paros, Alcman of Sardis, Sappho and Alcaeus of Lesbos, and Anacreon of Teos laid the foundation for the poetry of the classical age, but it is important to observe that they came from the east, bringing with them an amplitude and an opulence foreign to the character of the Greeks of the mainland. After them, none ever sang quite so freshly. Pindar will soar, Aeschylus will compose with a full orchestra, and Sophocles will write verses of such chiseled clarity that they seem to demand to be inscribed on marble, but the Greeks themselves always looked back to the age of their earliest poets with a feeling of longing.

Today we can barely glimpse the magnitude of our loss. Of the great beginning of Western song there are only ruins.

Demeter of Cnidus.

Victory of Paeonios, at Olympia.

Victory of Samothrace.

Aphrodite Rising from the Sea.

Aphrodite of Cyrene.

Athena from the Temple of Aphaia on Aegina.

Athena of Piraeus.

Athena Parthenos.

9 « THE SPLENDID CONTESTS

O my heart, if you would sing of the glory of the games,
Then as beyond the Sun there are no stars shining
With a brighter light in the empty spaces of Heaven,
So there are no more splendid contests than those at Olympia.

(Pindar, First Olympian)

In the heroic age life was essentially parochial, deeply rooted in the local soil. Farmers became soldiers, and then farmers again at the order of their princes, but now a new generation of Greeks was arising out of the shadows, footloose, eager for experience, no longer afraid of the power of the tyrants. In a peaceful age men did not need tyrants or princes for their protection.

Rivalry was in the air. Hesiod had spoken of two kinds of strife: one led to war, the other to healthy competition and prosperity. "The neighbor," he wrote, "envies the neighbor who presses on toward wealth." There was rivalry among the colonies and among individuals, and gradually it was becoming accepted that there could be peaceful rivalry between the cities and the city-states. The stage was being set for the great games held on the mainland of Greece at which peaceful competition would be put to the test.

The people of Elis, near the western coast of the Peloponnese, claimed that the Olympian games were originally founded by Heracles and later refashioned and reorganized by King Iphitus in 776 B.C., or else—for no one was quite sure on these matters—they were originally founded by King Oenomaus who ruled over Elis in the days following Deucalion's flood. According to the legend, King Oenomaus was commanded by an oracle to give his daughter Hippodamia to anyone who could beat him in a chariot race, and death was the penalty for anyone he vanquished. It was a long course for a chariot race, for it began near Elis and ended at Corinth, a good fifty miles. The candidate was allowed a head start, but King Oenomaus had received magic horses from Poseidon and always caught up with them until Pelops, the ancestor of the house of Atreus, succeeded in bribing Myrtilus, the royal charioteer, who conveniently replaced the metal linchpins of his master's chariot with wax, with the result that the king fell and broke his neck. Pelops married Hippodamia, and when he died funeral games were held in his honor. For centuries afterward, right up to the time of Pausanias, the coffer containing the bones of Pelops and his golden-hilted sword were exhibited at Olympia together with the grave of King Oenomaus and the graves of the suitors of Hippodamia.

All we know with reasonable certainty is that about the year 776 B.C. a small local festival in honor of Heracles, or of Pelops, or of both, was founded at Elis. Its fame grew steadily, and soon more and more legends accumulated around the site. The goddess Hera came to preside over the ceremonies. Zeus seems to have followed his wife, and Cronus may have followed Zeus. Over a period of perhaps a hundred years the pot of legends was kept boiling, and at last Zeus rose to the top. From being a small local festival, it became the great national festival of all the Greeks, and all events were dated from the inauguration, which may or may not have occurred in 776 B.C.

In honor of Zeus the rubble over the city of Pisa, destroyed in the wars, was named Olympia. Here the temples were built and the race courses laid out. At first there was only a simple foot race, but later a complete repertoire of races was included. There were competitions for throwing the javelin, for boxing, for wrestling, for chariot racing, even for mule racing, though this last was later abandoned. The games grew so important that a Hellenic truce was arranged, and heralds assuming the garb and dignity of high priests went out from Olympia under safe-conduct to proclaim the games throughout the Greek-speaking world. To harm one of these heralds was to incur the anger of Zeus, and heavy punishments were invoked. Every four years, during the eighth month following the winter solstice, there was peace. It was summer, and the farmers were resting from their labors.

The games provided an outlet for Greek energies, which might otherwise have been expended in predatory wars. No longer was it necessary to invade neighboring territories for loot and treasure: far greater treasure could be acquired at the games. Outwardly the treasure consisted of little more than a wreath of the leaves of the sacred wild olive, said to have been originally planted by Heracles, cut with a golden knife by a noble youth with both parents living. The olive wreath would soon crumble into dust, but it was no more than the symbol of an enduring honor. They would be remembered as conquerors.

In the fifth century B.C. an Elean scholar called Hippias compiled a list of all the winners of the foot race since its founding in 776. Plutarch scoffed at the list, saying it "reposed on no credible authority," and it is likely enough that Hippias was moved by piety to his own city. Yet it is almost certainly accurate from about 600 B.C., and since the list was continued until A.D. 394, under the reign of the Emperor Theodosius, we have a thousand-year record of the Olympian games, accurate in all its particulars and throwing an extraordinary light on the people who took part in the games.

The splendor of the festivals at Olympia outdid all other festivals. The *Hellenodikai*—the judges of the Hellenes—superintended the arrangements for the games, wearing robes of royal purple. Trumpeters announced the beginning of each race. There were solemn offerings to Zeus, with the thighs of white oxen burning on his altar. The foot race was always the first, but it was the chariot race that caused the greatest excitement, because it was the most dangerous. The race began when "the Eagle rose and the Dolphin dived": probably a pivoted beam with a very heavy dolphin at one end and a considerably lighter eagle at the other. It was a nine-mile course. Sometimes forty four-horsed chariots took part in the contest. Chariot racing was for the rich, and the gilded princes of Sicily were great contenders for the prize, not always successfully, for once when Dionysius of Syracuse entered the race his chariot was deliberately upset by those who hated his tyranny.

The chariot races were held in the morning. In the afternoon came the Pentathlon, a combined contest of running, jumping, wrestling, and throwing the javelin and the discus. In the evening, under the golden moon, the victors marched in procession and sang hymns.

The third day saw more sacrificial victims offered upon the altar of Zeus, and in the afternoon there was the boys' contest. They ran races, wrestled, and boxed with the cestus, and it was said that after these matches even the boxers' dogs could hardly recognize them. But if boxing was bad, the Pancration, which took place on the fourth day, was worse. It was unarmed combat of the most ferocious kind, with arm twisting, eye gouging, and kicking permitted. It sometimes ended in death, and when a certain Arrhacion of Phygalia died at the moment of victory he was awarded the crown.

The festival ended on the fifth day with the victors wearing their crowns and offering sacrifices at the altar of Cronus on a nearby hill. There followed a great banquet, and all that night there was the singing of triumphal songs. On the sixth day the athletes returned to their homes.

The victorious athletes were regarded with a reverence such as was given only to great military leaders. They were thought of as being in some special way more than human, almost godlike, for by acquiring honor in the games they had raised themselves above the common people. Their names were recorded in the sacred books kept by the priests, and they were themselves the priestly servants of their country's honor. When they returned to their native cities, robes of royal purple were thrown over their shoulders and they were drawn by white horses in procession before an admiring populace, and sometimes a section of the city walls would be torn down for their entry, as though they were conquerors. In the market places bronze statues were erected, showing them as they were when they triumphed in the glory of their young manhood. Privileges such as were granted to no others were granted to them, for had they not endowed their cities with honor and renown? What they had brought to the city was sanctity, a share of the divine splendor, a portion of the power and also the benevolence of the gods. In their lives they were worshiped, and after their deaths special ceremonies were held to pay tribute to their heroism, not because they were successful athletes but because they had once been the equals of the incarnate gods.

Around these victorious athletes the Greek imagination worked with astonishing fecundity, seeing in these young heroes the very reason for the continuing existence of the Greek people. They were the fountain of honor, the source of all blessings, the mediators between heaven and earth. In them reposed the strength of the nation, and from them came the certainty of victory in whatever wars were fought by their native cities. So it happened that a city would sometimes offer bribes to one of these athletes, inviting him away from his own city and then sending him to the games as their representative; and soon enough we hear of the commercialization of heroes. Sometimes, too, enormous rewards were announced, and athletes who were successful in the games might expect to receive so much prize money that they could be independently wealthy for the rest of their lives. According to Plutarch, Solon, the great Athenian lawgiver, offered Athenian victors at the Olympic games prize money amounting to 500 drachmas. With that money a man could buy 500 sheep or 100 oxen, and he could live like a lord.

But it was not only in their religious and athletic aspects that the great games so powerfully influenced the imaginations of the Greeks. They saw in the games the concrete embodiment of an idea—the sentiment of Panhellenic unity, the conception of a national ethos overshadowing and encompassing all local and tribal loyalties. While the games added honor and renown to the native cities of the victors, so, too, by the peculiar mathematics of victory, they added honor and renown to the whole of the Greek community. The games were a perpetual reminder that the Greeks were all members of a single commonwealth, and that this commonwealth existed to preserve the freedom of the individual members. None but Greeks could attend the games; all who took part had to produce certificates authenticating that they were truly citizens of the commonwealth. When the Macedonian princes claimed the right to take part in the games, their claim was allowed only when satisfactory proof of their Hellenic ancestry was furnished. Foreigners might attend the games as observers, but not as participants.

These contests formed an exercise in national consciousness, their chief purpose being to bring honor to the entire commonwealth through the accumulation of honors acquired by the victors, and by spreading peace and civilization among the many nations forming the Greek community. There was the sense of partaking in a solemn mystery at which the gods descended from the skies and walked among men, but in the minds of the Greeks the presence of the gods was scarcely more important than the presence of a common purpose and common traditions. In the imaginations of the Greeks the mere coming together of youthful athletes from all the regions of the commonwealth was a sacred act.

How these ideas came to birth, and exactly what prompted them, is still unknown; nor is it likely that we shall ever be able to learn the names of the men who first explored the possibilities of developing a national consciousness by substituting peaceful contests for wars. We can observe a deliberate design leading with unfaltering purpose to a deliberate conclusion, but the names of the architects are lost in the mists of time.

The Olympic games set the pattern for all other games. In 581 the Pythian games were inaugurated in honor of Apollo at Delphi; the first Isthmian games were held near the isthmus of Corinth in honor of Poseidon during the same year; six years later the Nemean games were founded at Nemea in Argolis in honor of Zeus. But this was only the beginning. Nearly all the Ionian and Sicilian tyrants vied with one another to produce games in honor of the local gods, and in far-off Cyrene games were held in honor of Apollo. But though there came a time when nearly every city enjoyed its own games, there was never any question of the supremacy of the Olympic games. Olympian Zeus reigned supreme.

When Pausanias came to Olympia, he described all the statues and buildings with the careful patience of a cataloguer determined to record everything in exact detail. There was little poetry in him, but at Olympia he remembered a famous chorus of Sophocles and burst out in a sudden chorus of his own. "Many wondrous sights there are," he exclaimed, "and many are the marvelous tales that may be heard in Greece, but one thing I know—the blessing of God falls in the greatest measure on the mysteries of Eleusis and the Olympic games." Eleusis was the supreme private mystery, concerning the life and soul of the individual, as Olympia was the supreme public mystery, concerning the life of the Greek communities. One could not choose between them, for together they embraced the whole world.

About the year 468 the architect Libon of Elis designed a new and more sumptuous temple for Olympian Zeus a stone's throw from the track where the races were held. It was not in itself a very imposing temple, being slightly smaller than the Parthenon and having no great commanding position. The great temples to Athena at Athens, Lindos, and Aegina were superbly situated on cliffs, while the temple of Zeus at Olympia nestled quietly in a valley, surrounded by a host of other temples and buildings used for training athletes and for the government of the games. But what distinguished the temple of Olympian Zeus above all others were the astonishing sculptures by Phidias,

Alcamenes, and Paeonius which decorated it.

Among the ancients there was universal agreement that the statue of Zeus inside the temple was a work of extraordinary beauty and majesty. Quintilian wrote that the majesty of the statue equaled the majesty of God, and Dion Chrysostom called it "the most beautiful statue on earth and the most beloved by the gods," and he went on to declare, in a famous oration which reads like a prayer: "Let no one who has drained the cup of sorrows and suffered sleepless nights fail to stand before the statue, for standing there he will forget all his griefs and troubles."

From these descriptions one might imagine a statue of vast simplicity, but in fact it was of the utmost intricacy. It took Pausanias three pages to describe the exquisite details, the splendors of the jewel-like design. The god was seated on a throne, with robes of gold and flesh of ivory: his right hand held a Victory, his left a scepter surmounted by an eagle. His golden robes were embroidered with animals and lilies, his throne with ebony, gold, ivory, and precious stones. But this was only the beginning, for the throne itself, its legs and supporting pillars, and the golden footstool, were all intricately carved with figures. Prometheus in his fetters, Penthesilea dying in the arms of Achilles, Theseus making war on the Amazons, the Hours, the Seasons, and the Graces, all were represented, so that throne and pedestal became a repository of Greek mythology in miniature swirling below the forty-foot high figure of Zeus, whose golden hair almost touched the roof-beams.

Countless ornamental details lapped around the legs and waist of the god, but the chest was bare except for the folds of the gown flowing over the left shoulder. The ivory chest was painted to give an effect of warm and ruddy life, and so too was the majestic face. Pausanias says nothing about the features, but coins minted in Elis in classical times give us a fair approximation of his face. He had deep-set eyes, a low forehead, a long straight nose which followed the forehead's line, a heavy mustache which curled over the edges of the mouth, and a thick, tangled beard which was carved with great vigor and beauty. There was something of the lion in that face, magnificently virile, and yet benevolent. The lips were parted, as though he were about to speak, and he wore the wreath of sacred olive leaves, the victor's prize.

If the coins can be trusted, the upper part of the face was curiously young. Remove the beard, and there is a man about thirty, very grave, meditative, heavy with responsibility. There is even a hint of feminity in the long curling strands of hair, seven or eight rivers of hair, which fall over his shoulder. He has small ears and a powerful neck, and the eyes, made of inlaid semiprecious stones, glowed beneath overhanging brows. There are also coins which show him sitting on his throne, and from these it seems that he gazed straight ahead as though lost in dreams, paying no attention to his worshipers. Asked how he intended to represent Zeus, Phidias is said to have replied with three lines of Homer:

> *Zeus spoke and with thundering brows nodded assent,*
> *While his ambrosial hair on his immortal head*
> *Waved forward; and Olympus quaked with terror.*

But all the coins and the surviving accounts of the statue agree on his unearthly calm, the sense of brooding power and effortless majesty emanating from him. Describing the Thunder-bearer, the lord of the lightning-lit skies, Dion Chrysostom said: "He is the god of peace, supremely gentle, dispenser of being and life and all good things, the father and savior and guardian of men."

The German archaeologists who have been working uninterruptedly at Olympia since 1875 were among the luckiest there have ever been. They did not discover the figure of Zeus, which was removed to Constantinople and destroyed in a fire, but very early in their excavations they brought to light the figures of the pediments. Though some were brutally damaged when they were shaken off the temple by an earthquake, many of them were in a quite extraordinary state of preservation with traces of paint still visible, and without too much difficulty the original grouping of the figures could be reconstructed.

The discovery of the figures of the western pediment was especially valuable because they showed to what heights Greek sculpture could attain. Nothing greater than the young God who stands in the center of the pediment has yet been found. He stands there naked, a red scarf falling over his right shoulder and his right arm outstretched in a gesture of command, and on his face there is an expression of complete repose and unyielding assurance. The Centaurs have brazenly interrupted the wedding feast of Pirithoüs and Hippodamia, and a wild struggle is taking place all round them. Amid this violence the young god stands resolute to put an end to it; he has thrown out his arm in a gesture of command; and immediately the contestants are frozen into immobility. For the first time in sculpture we see a god exerting his divine power.

The young god wears a human form, and there is even a very human elegance in the way he stands; and there is about the full lips and rounded cheeks some hint of his Asiatic upbringing. His intelligence is married to sensuality; he has seen and tasted all that can be seen and tasted; and he knows where he is going. The face expresses at once the plenitude of power and of experience.

Who is he? Pausanias, who saw the sculpture when it was painted and shining on the pediment fifty feet above the ground, was quite sure it was Pirithoüs, one of the innumerable sons of Zeus. Modern scholars are inclined to think it is Apollo, and they point to the fact that Zeus occupies the corresponding position on the eastern pediment. It scarcely matters. This majestic figure, who rises so superbly above the conflict, stilling the tempest with a gesture of imperious authority, so calm, so pitiless, so supremely confident of his powers, is carved with incomparable grace and refinement, and no one seeing him can doubt his divinity. One leg has been broken at the knee, a hand is missing, his golden crown has long ago been melted down, but these injuries have no effect on him. There are moments in Greek literature and sculpture when we are conscious that a pinnacle of glory has been reached, when neither art nor artistry could go further. In this young god the pinnacle of glory has been reached.

The artist was Alcamenes, the pupil and rival of Phidias, chiefly famous for his Aphrodite of the Gardens which was long regarded as the perfect representation of the goddess. The statue is lost, but Lucian, imagining a perfect statue, said it should have eyes and forehead by Praxiteles, the nostrils and the contours of the face by Phidias, "and the round cheeks and front of the face, and the beautiful flow of the wrists and the hands and the delicately shaped tapering fingers of the Aphrodite of the Gardens by Alcamenes." Lucian had studied sculpture, and he clearly regarded Alcamenes as the master of the fluent line, the clean-cut curve. In his lifetime Alcamenes was praised for his delicacy rather than his robust strength. But it is the marriage of delicacy and strength which appears on the western pediment.

The triumph of Alcamenes is that he was the first to depict the European intelligence, and he accomplished this in a figure of grave majesty. That commanding figure is recognizably human while remaining a god. He is no Prometheus storming heaven, for he belongs to heaven. That gesture of authority comes easily to him; and his hidden brows are wild with imagination. He stands on that pinnacle where, for a brief while, the Greeks were able to see the world around them with pitiless lucidity, everything arranged in order under the calm sun. From those loins sprang science, and from that gesture came authority over all the things of the earth.

There are many other sculptures in the small museum at Olympia. There is the Hermes of Praxiteles, so disturbingly graceful and feminine that it is almost impossible to imagine that he was ever the swift messenger of the gods. There are the brilliant metopes showing the labors of Hercules. There is the Victory by Paeonius, which stood on a pedestal close to the temple of Zeus, an offering by the Messenians and Naupactians for their victory over the Spartans, a figure of divine grace as she wings her way to earth, her transparent robes swirling around her. She has only just this moment touched the earth, and the impact sends a trembling through the robes. She descends from heaven as authoritatively as Apollo-Pirithoüs stills the tempest, and though her head is broken and she has no hands, she is charged with divine energy and therefore possesses a wholeness which no accidents can efface. There are no more than a dozen Greek sculptures of consummate perfection, and this Victory is one of them.

These are the statues the young athletes saw when they attended the contests in the days when Olympia was the center of pilgrimage, the place of splendor. Here they acquired honor and renown, and were closer to the gods than elsewhere. Returning to their homes, they carried with them the light of their glory; and all Greece bathed in their light.

Pindar believed that their fame resounded through the halls of heaven and echoed through the dark underworld. Those leaping athletes in their beauty testified to the divinity in man, as the statues of the gods testified to their humanity. So in the last and quietest of the Olympian odes Pindar calls on the Muses to tell Apollo of the victory of a young runner from Orchomenos, and then he asks that Persephone, goddess of the underworld, should also be informed:

Go, Echo, to the dark-walled house
Of Persephone the goddess, and take this message
To Cleodamus, the boy's father. Say his son
Once at the noble contests of Olympia
Wore on his young hair the winged crown of glory.

10 «« THE RESOUNDING SONGS

AMONG the treasures of the National Museum at Athens there is a standing youth found in 1936 at Anavysos in Attica. He is six feet tall, but seems larger than life. One leg is a few inches in front of the other, but he gives an impression of a man striding boldly and powerfully across a landscape in which he is sovereign. He wears his hair in closely knit braids, his hands are clenched at his sides, and an archaic smile plays on his lips. We know his name and how he died, for there is an inscription carved on the pedestal:

Stand and mourn beside the tomb of dead Kroisus,
Whom the wrath of Ares snatched from the leaders of battle.

From the style of the carving we know he died about 510 B.C., when tyranny in Athens was giving place to democracy.

What is chiefly remarkable about the statue is the extraordinary power it seems to generate. This youth who has been dead for twenty-five centuries seems far more alive than the people who cluster round him. His flesh is solid on him, and he has the look of a young conqueror. Such power could come into existence only at a time when the Greek spirit was vigorous and demanding, ready for conquest.

The splendid times called forth a splendid poet. Splendor was Pindar's natural home and habitation, the world he lived in. It never seems to have occurred to him that there was any other world. Magnificence was his theme, and he permitted himself no other.

All of Pindar's surviving poems are concerned with the young and strenuously disciplined athletes who took part in the games at the four great festivals of Greece—the Pythian games at Delphi, the Isthmian games at Corinth, the Nemean games in the Argolid, and the Olympic games at Olympia. Pindar celebrated the victors, and at the same time he celebrated the gods, so marrying and matching their accomplishments that they almost shade into one another. The task he gave himself was nothing less than to find the equation between the victories of these youths and the victories of the deathless gods. And since he possessed an aristocratic disdain for anything less than perfection, he spoke of the youths at the moment when their highest endeavors were crowned with success and he spoke of the gods when they were accomplishing their highest purposes. No one ever wrote with such high seriousness about the divine splendor that sheds its light on men.

Pindar was born a citizen of Thebes about 522, being the descendant of the noble family of the Aegeidai. He learned poetry in the schools of Thebes and Athens, and at one time was a pupil of the poetess Corinna, who advised him "to sow with the hand and not with the full sack," evidently in an effort to put a halt to his phenomenal fluency. His surviving poems show him still "sowing with the full sack," but for long passages he writes with conscious mastery, carefully, polishing the jewels until they shine with an almost intolerable brilliance. There are times when he writes like a man who has seen the gods with his own eyes and who soars after them in full flight. Yet always he is the conscious artist, aware of the responsibility he carries.

Legends accumulated around his last days. He spent his last years in the court of the tyrant Hiero of Syracuse with Aeschylus, Bacchylides, and Simonides as his companions in exile. Pausanias tells the story that the goddess Persephone came to him ten days before his death and demanded a hymn, and he died when the hymn was completed. There is another story that he died in Argos in the arms of the boy Theoxonos, whom he had celebrated in his poetry. He died at the age of eighty, having written altogether seventeen books, of which only four and a few fragments have come down to us. Six hundred years after his death there was still to be seen at Delphi the iron chair on which he had declaimed his verses.

Pindar's poetry is difficult. His bold changes and sudden transitions from one theme to another can be oddly disconcerting until we realize that they were demanded by the very nature of his god-intoxicated vision: that flashing, winding, abrupt progress exactly mirrors his pursuit of the gods across the heavens. He sees them in blinding glimpses; they vanish, and when he catches sight of them again they are in another quarter of the heavens pursuing altogether different adventures, but the same holy light plays on them. His greatest and most characteristic verses are simply descriptions of visions seen in quiet ecstasy. Here he describes a holy baptism in the waters of the Alpheus at Olympia:

> *The five-day child*
> *Lay in the long grasses and thickets, his tender body*
> *Heaped with the blue and yellow of the field flowers,*
> *And therefore his mother gave him an immortal name,*
> *Iamus. In time the boy came*
> *Into his golden-helmeted youth, acquiring*
> *A ripe bloom. In his youth he waded*
> *Into the waters of the Alpheus, into midstream,*
> *Crying in a loud voice for his great forefather,*
> *Poseidon, and to his father Apollo,*
> *The Archer who dwelt in heavenly built Delos,*
> *In the darkness of the night, praying*
> *For the crown of honor and the love of the people.*
> *Then from close at hand there came his father's voice,*
> *Saying, "Arise, my son, follow my voice,*
> *Come to the place of welcoming!" So they climbed*
> *Together the sheer rock of towering Kronios,*
> *And the god placed in his hands the gift of prophecy,*
> *The power to command . . .*

The whole story of Iamus, the founder of the princely family of hereditary soothsayers at Olympia, is told in twenty visionary lines in a poem ostensibly celebrating the victory of a young Syracusan in the mule chariot races. Since the victor claimed descent from Iamus, Pindar was perfectly within his rights in describing the birth and growth of the mysterious young god. The ode in celebration of the victor became the excuse for a sudden leap into the world of the gods.

What is startling in Pindar is his very closeness to the gods, even to the highest gods. Zeus, "the lord of the red lightning," becomes his familiar, and he talks with Zeus as sternly as he talks with men. Not surprisingly Pindar believed that men and gods derived from the same mother. "There is one race of men, and one of gods, and both these races take breath from a single Mother," he wrote in a poem on a young wrestler from Aegina, and then he added somberly that even through they spring from the same parent, the gods live in their eternal citadels, while the life of man is fleeting. "Still we bear a likeness to the eternal gods in our intelligence and strength." It is this likeness which amazes, delights, and obsesses him. So he turns continually from men to the gods and back again, restlessly comparing them and bringing them together.

When Homer introduces the gods, we see them in the middle distance, vast and majestic presences, but still out of reach. When Pindar speaks of them, they stand in the foreground, almost tangible and almost human. In a few swift lines the entire presence of a god is depicted. He has an amazing pride, and will describe how a singer once sent the Eagle of Zeus to sleep:

> *On the scepter of Zeus*
> *The Eagle is sleeping, having folded his quick wings,*
> *O King of Birds!*
> *You have shed a dark mist on his drooping head,*
> *His eyelids are closed with a sweet seal,*
> *He dreams, and his lithe back ripples*
> *In the quivering spell of your song.*

There is no doubt that Pindar is portraying himself here as the superb poet who has cast a spell on the Eagle of Zeus, lulling it to sleep with his song. It is an audacious picture, all the more audacious because Pindar clearly intends us to see the Eagle as a metaphor for Zeus himself. It is the proudest boast ever uttered by a Greek poet, and it is astonishing how easily we accept him at his own valuation.

Pindar has been accused of passionless austerity, but nothing could be further from the truth. There is heat in the rush and brilliance of his verse, and if he is austere, it is the athletic austerity of a man who consorts with young princes at the games. He belongs so completely to the aristocratic tradition that he will never permit himself even for a moment to drop into colloquial speech; and he is so immersed in the vision of handsome athletes that we wonder whether he ever spoke to a peasant in his life. Women, children, servants, even soldiers have no place in the world he chose to celebrate. He has none of Homer's humanity.

Although there are times when a veil falls between us and Pindar, there remain the many intellectual beauties of his craft, and no one can mistake the power of his imagination. He must be read with the whole breath. He soars high, with many darts and sudden turnings, displaying the sidelong flash of wings, never at rest. Short passages fail to give the flavor of the man as he leaps from one sunlit cloud to another. He has a superb sense of narrative, but unlike Homer he never pauses long enough to permit you to take in the full details of the scene. He hurries from one brilliantly glimpsed moment to the next, and the reader is expected to fill in the gaps. Here is part of an ode addressed to Telesicrates of Cyrene who won the foot race in full armor at the Pythian games in 474. The ode says very little about Telesicrates: it is chiefly concerned with Apollo's desire to possess the white-armed Cyrene, titular goddess of the young athlete's native country.

Cyrene, the white-armed, had no love for pacing before the loom,
Nor for banqueting with those of her own age;
She loved to stand up against wild beasts,
Slaying them with bronze throwing spears and with swords,
So that the herds of her father might sleep peacefully,
But her eyelids gathered only a small store of sleep, the sweet bed-
    fellow
Nor did sleep rest long over her eyes
With the coming of dawn.

Apollo, Lord of the broad quiver, the far-traveler,
Found her one day spearless, wrestling alone
With a fearful lion. Then at once,
Lifting his voice high,
He called for Chiron to come forth from his cave, saying:
"Come from thy sacred cave, son of Philyra,
Admire the strength of this virgin,
Bend low before her spirit, her cool courage—
A spirit so fierce it suffers no distress,
And no fear has ever clutched at her heart.
Of what race is she? Whence cometh she? From what seed torn,
Who dwells in the secret hollows of the shadowed hills?

See: there is no end to her fierce courage!
Tell me whether I should lay
My famous hands upon her, plucking

Sweet flowers in her bed?"
Then spoke the prophetic Centaur with an easy smile, his brows
    lifting:
"Secret, O Phoebus, are the keys of wise Persuasion
Which unlock the doors of maidens. Both gods and men
Blush to enter the bridal bed in the full daylight.

And you, who are a god forbidden to lie—
Surely you are using dissembling words
In speaking so pleasantly. Whence cometh she? you ask.
Yet who knows better than you the appointed ends of all things,
And their beginnings. You know
The number of the leaves blossoming in the spring, the number
Of the sands in the sea and in the rivers,
Sands driven before the waves and the streaming winds,
Whatever shall come to pass and whence it comes. All this you know,
And if I must measure myself against your wisdom, then—
Then I must say:
You have come to this glade to be her bridegroom, and you will carry
    her
Over the sea into the loveliest garden of Zeus,
Where you shall make her queen of a city, assembling
The islanders upon the plain-encircled cliff, where Libya,
Queen of the lovely meadows, shall proclaim
With golden palaces a welcome to your bride and to her glory,
And she shall be given straitway a portion of earth, her private garden,
Not without destiny of fruit, teeming with
Beasts of the chase.

She will bear a son whom glorious Hermes
Shall take from the womb of his beloved mother, bearing the child
    away
To the Hours and to the Earth Mother on their magnificent thrones.
And they shall place the child on their knees, admiring
His bright luster, feeding him
With ambrosia and nectar, so making
A god out of him—an immortal Zeus, a holy Apollo,
Beloved guardian of flocks, a delightful companion of men,
To be called spirit of the wilds and the pastures, and some will give him

The name of Aristaios." So he prompted
The god to accomplish his bridals . . .

Pindar tells the story with unusual grace and tenderness, a little amused, and staying long enough with Apollo and Chiron to enable them to relate their opinions. He clearly knows the city of Cyrene, and has a quiet affection for it. There is a tradition reported by the commentators that Telesicrates was celebrating his victory by taking home a bride from Delphi, and the whole coloring of the ode suggests the likelihood of the tradition. For once the poet keeps close to the earth. Both Apollo and Cyrene shine in the divine light. Throughout the conversation between the god and the centaur we are aware of the sunlit presence of the girl strangling a lion singlehanded.

This power to throw the light wherever he desired is Pindar's supreme achievement, and he seems to have been perfectly aware of it. He will pour a brilliant light on one of his young heroes, illuminating a face, a shoulder, a torso, sometimes the whole body, like a man from some remote corner of the dark gallery throwing a spotlight upon the stage. The effect is often fragmentary, but there is no doubting the intensity of the illumination. And with his knowledge of brightness there went a corresponding knowledge of the surrounding dark:

> *He who has worn in green youth*
> *Splendor of high-flying pride*
> *Hopefully rides the air*
> *On wings of his human strength,*
> *Rising above pursuit of wealth.*
> *Brief in its time is the joy*
> *Of man's rising, before he falls*
> *Struck by a wayward doom.*

> *We are creatures of a day. What are we?*
> *What are we not? Shadows of dreams are men.*
> *But when a brightness comes, and God gives it,*
> *There is a glory of light upon them, and life is sweet.*
> *Aegina, dear mother, guard this city in the ways of freedom*
> *With the blessing of Zeus and good Aeacus,*
> *Of Peleus also, and good Telamon and Achilles.*

So he closes his prayer with a childlike litany of the saints, a salute to the divine light, and a brief whimper. But it is the litany of the saintly heroes we remember most, the faltering prayer.

Death terrified him, as it terrified all Greeks. Deeply religious, he rejoiced in the holy splendors of Delphi and Olympia, but even the sacred mysteries and great processions of athletes were not proof against despair. The muscles of his mind could not grapple with death. He could bring himself to believe that the heroes and the chosen ones were granted an eternal vision of Paradise, a land where athletic contests took place very much as they did on earth, but once again when he describes the abode of the blessed we detect the faltering note, the shocked awareness of a dark river flowing endlessly into the night:

> *For them the sun shines in all its fullness*
> *Throughout our earthly night.*
> *In meadows red with roses they wander*
> *Around the city in the scented shade,*
> *Where the trees bear golden fruit.*
> *Some ride on horses, others play at wrestling,*
> *Still others play with draughts or on their lyres,*
> *While the sweet flowers of perfect joy*
> *Are heaped around them,*
> *A lovely land of perfume.*
> *Here a perpetual incense fumes*
> *With the far-shining fire on altars.*
> *On the farther shore faint rivers roam*
> *Dark as the night's eternal gloom.*

He believed, and did not believe: it could hardly be otherwise. There were darknesses in him, and his assurance masks many fears. He had been brought up in an aristocratic tradition marked by rigid observance of religious duties, and lived long enough to see the traditions questioned. In his poems he cries a little too loudly for honor and renown, and there must have been times when he saw those endless processions of sunlit athletes, however heroic and half-divine, marching irrevocably to their doom. Though he moved among the great ruling families of Rhodes, Corinth, and Athens, and was invited into the palaces of the rulers of Macedonia, Cyrene, and Syracuse, continually celebrating the heroic tradition, he was not himself heroic. When the crisis fell, and the Persians were at the gates, he was asked to compose a poem to fire the Greeks with enthusiasm. Polybius records that his answer was "a most shameful and injurious rejection." He took the easier and less dangerous way of writing a pompous ode on "the gleaming brightness of courageous Peace," of which four terrible lines survive.

In 475 Mount Etna erupted, and five years later Hiero, tyrant of Syracuse, won the chariot race at the Pythian games. Hiero had founded a colony on the slopes of Etna, and Pindar might be expected to pay a graceful tribute to the colony with some passing reflections on the eruption. What he does is something very different. Quite suddenly we find him identifying himself with the volcano. In a passage of almost incredible violence he proclaims the horror of the eruption, pounding on all the instruments of a full orchestra, and he leaves us in no doubt that the horror is his own:

The unbeloved of Zeus
Shudder when they hear
The voices of the Muses: whether on earth
Or in the unresting sea.
God's enemy sprawls in the hell-pit.
Typhon, the hundred-headed, lies
Crushed beneath the sky's pillars,
He who was once nursed in the many-named cave in Cilicia,
Though now the sea-dikes of Kyme are set over him:
All Sicily lies heavy on his shaggy breast.
The snows of Etna yearlong
Suckle the biting frost.
Then will the pure fountains, the unapproachable fires,
Erupt from the secret caves within; and in the light of day
The rivers are tossed from the mountain in floods of smoke
*   ablaze with light,*
And when the night falls the ruddy flame in its toils
Hurls the rocks headlong into the deep sea far below.
This monstrous thing flings high the terrible fountains of fire,
A presage of terrors to come, a wonder to behold,
And wondrous too to men who hear its music.
So he lies bound beneath the dark-leaved heights
Of Etna, lying on a jagged bed of stone

Which tears his outstretched limbs to ribbons.
O Zeus, give us thy grace . . .

In the dark splendor of the ode for Hiero, Pindar seems to reveal himself as never before. In much the same way, using many of the same images, Coleridge revealed himself in *Kubla Khan*. Here, briefly, the floodgates were opened, and never again shall we hear such a spate of violence from his lips. Thereafter he will present a calm mask before the world.

We might have known from the beginning that Pindar's calm was illusory, for when the Greeks are calm nightmares spring out of their silence.

Pindar's roots were in the past. He looked back to the earlier and more settled age of Peisistratus, and it seems never to have occurred to him that the poet must change with the times. He never questioned the beauty and order of the established tradition. All that concerned him was "to turn the brightness outward," and to justify the ways of tyrants and athletes. There is a dark legend that ten days before his death he sent to the oracle at Ammon to inquire what is best for man. "Death," the oracle answered. But it is unlikely that he ever asked any oracle what was best for man. He had known from the beginning that the best was the sun shining on youthful athletes and all the rest was a weariness of the flesh.

Simonides of Ceos

WHEN the Greeks won their war against Persia and looked for a poet to celebrate their triumph, they did not turn to Pindar. Instead they turned to his great rival Simonides, who was born to a family of pure Ionian stock on the island of Ceos, and already an old man when the wars broke out. Like Pindar, he traveled widely and consorted with princes and tyrants, but unlike Pindar he was able to live on terms of friendship with the Athenian democracy.

Simonides is chiefly remembered for the two lines he wrote for the Spartan dead at Thermopylae. "Stranger, tell the Spartans that we lie here obedient to their laws." That is all he says in the two lines, but there is in his manner of saying it the suggestion of a ghostly caress and a brief anguish and a desperate plea. The words are not clipped and raw, as in English. They rustle like dead leaves and ripple like water. He said once: "Painting is silent poetry; poetry is painting that speaks." But what he has painted in those two lines is a landscape of the soul.

He was a voluminous poet, but only a tiny fraction of his work has survived. He was eighty when the Athenians offered him the crown for a dithyrambic chorus; he had already carried off nearly sixty prizes. For him literature was a profession, and he insisted on being paid for his verses, acquiring an undeserved reputation for meanness. Aristophanes said he would "go to sea on a hurdle to earn a penny." He was perhaps the first of the Greeks to grow rich from his pen, and he seems to have delighted in his wealth only because it represented a tribute paid to poetry.

After the Persian Wars he was constantly chosen to write epitaphs to be inscribed in marble on the battlefield. For these he developed a style so lapidary, so succinct, so tense with emotion, that he became the model for future writers of epitaphs: no one has ever rivaled him. He was a man of action as well as a poet. Leaving Athens, he entered the court of Hiero, the tyrant of Syracuse, where he was received with extraordinary honor. His repute was so high that in 475 he was able to make peace on the field between Hiero of Syracuse and Theron of Acragas (Agrigentum) when the armies were ranged opposite one another—one of the few recorded examples of the poet as peacemaker. He died six years later, and was buried with royal honors.

During his lifetime he was given the title of *Melicertes*, meaning "the honey-tongued." The verses are sweet, but there is muscle in them. Here is part of an ode to virtue which suggests his power to force the lapidary style into a mold of sweetness:

> *They say that virtue dwells*
> *On a steep high unapproachable rock,*
> *Attended by a ring of dancing nymphs,*
> *Who never yet were seen by mortal eyes*
> *Except by men who poured their heart's sweat out*
> *To climb the heights of valor.*

So he would write with a kind of casual grandeur, closer to the earth than Pindar, never perhaps permitting himself to soar into the emptiness of the heavens for fear that he would lose himself. With the same grave music he wrote a longer epitaph on the dead at Thermopylae:

For those who fell at Thermopylae
There remain good fortune and a holy glory:
Their tombs are altars: instead of lamentation
Eternal fame is theirs. Mourning is
The praise we grant them. All-conquering Time
Shall neither bring them low nor stain them with
The ruin of decay. Within their graves
Rests the pride of Greece. The witness is
The Spartan King Leonidas whose ornaments
Are valor. Eternal glory be to him!

How truly great he was we shall never know, for there are only a few tantalizing remains from his vast opus. We have an abundance of his epitaphs for drowned sailors and doomed soldiers, but only occasional fragments of his poems. Among these is the breath-taking fragment known as *Danaë*, which tells of the princess of Argos who was visited by Zeus in a shower of gold and afterward gave birth to Perseus. When her father, King Acrisius, learned of the existence of the child, he put both Danaë and Perseus into a chest and cast them out to sea. Here she laments and prays for the help of Zeus:

When the wind blew the carven chest,
And the wild waves aroused her fears,
She with her cheeks drenched in tears
Put her arm around Perseus, saying:
"My child, my heart overflows with sorrow,
And yet thou weepest not, and thy small face
Lies peaceful in the wooden chest
Studded with bronze nails—a joyless thing.
Thou liest shining in the blue dark,
Nor dost thou fear the salt waves towering high,
Nor the chill winds sweeping,
Wrapped in thy purple robe, thy face against mine.
If agony were agony to thee,
Thou wouldst lend thy little ear to what I say.
So sleep, my babe, and let the winds sleep,
And all our dread fears be put to sleep,
And let our Father Zeus descend upon us,
And if my prayers are bold,
Have mercy on me."

In the entire range of surviving Greek poetry there is no tenderness to equal this. There are passages of Sophocles and Euripides that come close to it, but there is never that pure outpouring of affection. Shakespeare might have written those lines, but scarcely anyone else. Sometimes those who dream of recovering the lost poetry of Greece put the name of Simonides first.

Bacchylides of Cos

UNTIL recently very little was known of Bacchylides, who was the nephew of Simonides. Then in 1896 a papyrus discovered in the sands of Egypt was sent to the British Museum. Unrolled, it proved to contain a fair sampling of the lost works of Bacchylides, including three complete odes addressed to Hiero and some fragments of a verse-play about the young King Theseus.

When the Alexandrians compiled a list of the nine great lyric poets of ancient Greece, they put the name of Bacchylides last. They were inclined to grant him talent, but not genius. Longinus said that "Bacchylides and Ion are both poets of impeccable elegance, while Pindar and Sophocles, hurrying at a fiery pace, drive their genius so hard that they sometimes stumble and commit the most horrible errors." The implication was that it was far better to be a genius who occasionally stumbles than a poet who is faultless within his own narrow field. Not all critics shared this opinion, for Horace and Tibullus ranked Bacchylides among the very greatest of the Greek poets.

We know very little about his life. Like Pindar and Simonides, he received large commissions for composing poems for victorious athletes. Pindar called himself "an eagle" with some justice; Bacchylides called himself "the nightingale of Cos." He does not sing with the full voice, and he cannot soar into the heights for long, but at his best he is unforgettable. Here he is describing the Eagle in a wonderful ode on Hiero's victory at the Olympic games in 470—the same victory for which Pindar composed the most sumptuous of his odes:

> On wings of outspread bronze
> The Eagle cleaves the air
> Of the towering sky,
> Herald of the Thunderer,
> Lord of the far-reaching earth,
> Secure in the faith

Of his fierce power,
While the quaking birds
Cower in fear:
Nor can the earth's peaks
Hold and tame him,
Nor can the rough cliffs
Of the unwearying sea
Impede the flight
Of his flashing crests
Sped with the west wind's might,
Bright in the eyes of men.

Such verses testify to an astonishing power held under rigid control. Pindar flashes fire, goes off at tangents, strikes relentlessly at the unexpected, and is always headstrong. Like Shakespeare, he seems never to have scratched out a line. Bacchylides moves more heavily, more earnestly, conscious of the intractability of words. "Storming the gates of song is no small task," he wrote, implying that he composed as much with his intelligence as with poetic passion. But no one ever wrote of the coming of Theseus to Athens, and the strange dread which accompanied the visitation, so powerfully or so convincingly. The fragmentary *Theseus* is a lyric dialogue which moves like a slow and fearful march:

Who is this man who cometh?
Who are his companions?
Like a great host under arms,
Or wandering alone with slaves,
A wayfarer from far-off lands,
Mighty and valiant is he,
With strength which has slain so many!
Surely a god must speed him,
Who topples the unjust down.
No light task ever it was
To be free of all mortal ills.
All things end in the drift of time.

He marches with two companions.
Over his glistening shoulder
He swings an iron sword.

His hands grip shining spears.
A finely embroidered helmet
Encloses his red-gold hair.
He wears a purple vest
And cloak of Thessalian wool.
From his eyes spurt forth red sparks,
Color of Lemnian flame:
A boy in the flush of manhood,
Playing the game of war
With clang of bronze on bronze,
He seeks illustrious Athens.

The *Theseus* reads like an early work, the young poet stretching his wings, not yet aware of the intolerable difficulties and dangers which attend the making of poetry. Theseus was almost the patron saint of Athens, and the poem was probably written in honor of one of the special festivals celebrated in his honor. The portrait of the hero is wonderfully complete. Homer will say of Achilles that "he strode like a mountain," and in that moment we see Achilles plain. Bacchylides etches the colors on the plate and shows us the hero in human terms. Sometimes he could do things that Pindar could not do.

With Pindar we never feel that he shares the joys of common mortals. Bacchylides, being of common clay, praises peace more ardently than he praises war. In the following poem he celebrates peace with a warmth which suggests that he had seen too many wars:

To mortal man Peace bringeth good tidings,
Huge wealth and flowers of honey-throated song,
And to the gods she bringeth the yellow flames,
Burning thighs of sleek oxen,
Fat sheep on the iron altars
Leap to Olympus, while the naked boys
Play on their flutes, dance daylong in sacred chorus.

Then on the iron shield-thong the brown spider
Intricately weaves his dusky web:
Rust grows on spears and two-handed swords,
And the trumpet-blasts of bronze are no longer heard.
Eyelids at dawn
Sink into sleep,

Into the ripeness of honeyed slumber,
While the streets are thronged with revels of love,
And hymns in praise of boys ascend like flames.

Though Bacchylides may have written these verses long after the Persian invasions, he belongs, like Pindar, to an earlier age. There is a lushness in his poems which reflects the gold and white cities of Sicily and Ionia rather than the dusty alleyways of Athens. Great he is—greater than we perhaps suspect—but something is missing.

Neither Bacchylides nor Pindar is critical of his times. It never occurs to them that the values of the princely tyrants and the heroic athletes are questionable. In time there will come another music, the muscles will grow harder, and the hymns in praise of boys will be exchanged for more nervous choruses. With Aeschylus, Sophocles, and Euripides we enter a world where the inquiring mind demands more than the celebration of human splendor. It demands answers to hard questions and goes into battle stripped for the fight.

11 «« TOWARD AN INTELLIGIBLE UNIVERSE

O UT OF Miletus came the first philosophers whose speculations are recorded, but their accomplishments are oddly evanescent. Thales, Anaximander, and Anaximenes are like figures seen in the sunrise when the mist still lies on the ground. They speak, gesticulate, point to the sun and moon, and vanish in the mist before we have understood exactly what they are saying. All we know for certain is that they have thrown the mythologies away and are attempting to define the universe in the light of reason, and of reason alone.

When Thales said that all things are made out of Water, he was not implying that water could be changed into bricks. He was speaking of a continuing fluid element in nature, amorphous, transparent, invisible to the eyes of men, or visible only as water is visible. He was postulating a first principle, and describing it as briefly and succinctly as a man can. And when Anaximander defined the first principle as 'the Boundless,' he too was affirming the existence of a reality not visible to human eyes, a powerful and generating force that moved through the universe. "The Boundless," he wrote, "comprehends the whole and steers all things." These first philosophers were concerned to discover how the universe was held together, and how it acquired energy and direction. What was the ship made of, what wind blew on its sails, who steered it? Today we are still very far from knowing the answers to these questions.

Significantly Anaximander used the words "to steer," in Greek *kybernān*, from which came the Roman *gubernare* and our own *govern*. We speak of the government of the universe, and they were determined to wrest its secrets. They were deeply religious, and if they set the mythologies aside it was because they found that mythology shed little light on the divine mechanism. Many years later in a play aimed to unseat Socrates from his position of influence among the philosophers of Athens, Aristophanes proclaimed: "They have dethroned Zeus, and Vortex is King." But philosophical speculations on Water, Air, Fire, Earth, and Vortices were not designed to dethrone the gods: they were designed for the immensely difficult purpose of trying to understand the universe. Water was not water, Air was not air. The Boundless was boundless, but perhaps only in the sense that a sphere is boundless. The Vortex too had a perfectly valid philosophical meaning. The Milesian philosophers were confronted with the same difficulty that confronts philosophers today: words are inadequate tools for unlocking the secrets of Nature.

The Milesian philosophers made a start; they set the machinery in motion. The surviving works of Thales, Anaximander, and Anaximenes cover only four or five pages, but these pages stand at the beginning of all our sciences. For the first time the speculative mind, untrammeled by religious prejudices, was demanding answers to clearly defined questions. Not by prophecy nor by revealed religion nor by mythology would man attempt to unriddle the universe: he would attempt to solve the mystery with his unaided intelligence alone.

Pythagoras

IT was said of Pythagoras that when he attended the games at Olympia he stripped naked to show the people that he had a golden thigh. Both Aristotle and Diogenes Laertius tell the story, and we are left in some doubt whether we are intended to believe it, or what precise significance was attached to it. Everything we know about him suggests that there was something godlike about him. There was no need of a golden thigh.

He was born about 560, an Ionian from the island of Samos. His father, Mnesarchus, was a seal engraver, and we know nothing more about his parentage. At an early age he set out on a voyage of discovery, visiting Egypt with a letter of introduction from Polycrates, tyrant of Samos, to King Amasis. It was a time when cordial relations existed between Greeks and Egyptians, and for some years he seems to have remained in Egypt, learning the language and devoting himself to study under the Egyptian priests. Finally he returned to Samos, only to discover that Polycrates was no longer the benevolent ruler of the past, but a man given over to all the vices of tyranny. He fled to Croton in Italy, where he established a school of philosophy limited to three hundred students, and for a while he seems to have been the virtual ruler of the city. There is a tradition that he was present during the war between Croton and Sybaris, and was overthrown in a palace revolt and then burned to death when the rebels set fire to the house where he was hiding.

But if we know little about his life, there is abundant evidence of his character: remote, highhanded, aristocratic, superbly disciplined. He wore his austerity like a garment, and hinted at his divinity. He used to say that he could remember all his past lives and his past deaths: he could remember every detail of his sufferings in Hell. Once, according to Xenophanes, he saw someone beating a dog, and stopped him, saying: "You must not beat him! Just now in the dog's yelping I heard the voice of a dear friend of mine who died long ago." He forbade his pupils to eat meat, eggs, or beans, and he pointed to the temple of Apollo at Delos as being the most holy, because no victims were sacrificed there; instead there were offerings of wheat, barley and cheesecakes. He was a mystic, a pacifist, a believer in the transmigration of souls, but these were the least important things about him. His fame rests on his achievements as a geometer and mathematician, and on the marriage he contrived between speculation and number.

For Pythagoras numbers were holy. Each number possessed a character of its own, and power radiated from it. There were pure numbers, impure numbers, perfect numbers like 10, which is the sum of the first four numbers, and the father of all the numbers that come afterward. He discovered—or his pupils discovered—that the addition of odd numbers to one will give squares: $1 + 3 = 4$ or 2^2, $1 + 3 + 5 = 9$ or 3^2. In the same way odd numbers added to a square give other squares: $1^2 + 3 = 2^2$, $2^2 + 5 = 3^2$, $3^2 + 7 = 4^2$. The surprising properties of numbers, the way in which they marry and form groups, all of them in some mysterious way dancing around the number 10, seemed to suggest a universe governed by number. He believed that the universe was a mathematical design of wonderful intricacy and neatness, and a man with sufficient patience and understanding would be able to resolve all its problems numerically. Numbers were the divine bricks out of which the universe was made.

Fascinated by numbers, the Pythagoreans discovered that music too follows intricate mathematical patterns. So Philolaus wrote about musical strings held at the same tension: "From the lowest to the third string is a fourth, from the third to the highest string is a fifth. Between the middle and third strings is a tone. The major fourth has the ratio 3:4, the fifth 2:3, and the octave 1:2." Having reduced music to the simplicity of number, it was only a short jump to reducing the planets to musical instruments; and the Pythagoreans would sometimes console themselves by listening to the music of the spheres.

How deeply they worshiped numbers we know from an extraordinary passage written by Philolaus some fifty years after the death of Pythagoras, when the Pythagorean tradition was still very much alive:

Consider [he wrote] the effects and nature of Number according to the power residing in the Decad. It is great, comprehensive, all-sufficing, being the first principle of divinity and of humanity, guiding all things. Without it all things are without limit, obscure, indiscernible. For the nature of Number is to be a standard of reference, of guidance, and instruction of every doubt, throwing light on everything that is unknown. For were there no Numbers and their essences, then nothing that exists would be made clear, either in themselves or in relation to other things. . . . Therefore it follows that it is in the nature of Number to work on divine and supernatural existences as well as on human activities and thoughts everywhere, and in all handicrafts and in music.

Such claims belonged to the spirit of the times, when new techniques were emerging, all serving the science of Number. When Pythagoras discovered that the square of the hypotenuse of a right-angled triangle was equal to the squares of the other two sides, he sacrificed a hecatomb in honor of the perfect beauty of the theorem. It was in that spirit that Euclid and all subsequent Greek mathematicians explored the vast landscape of Number, plotting the shape of a universe which was abstract, pure, irremediably truthful, and strangely elegant.

"Chatworth" Apollo, from Tamassos in Cyprus.

Poseidon, found at sea off Artemision.

Apollo from west pediment of Temple of Zeus, Olympia.

Zeus and Ganymede, from Olympia.

Heracles from east pediment of Temple of Aphaia, Aegina.

Apollo of Piombino.

Ares by Alcamenes. Roman copy.

Apollo of Piraeus.

He was as elegant and austere as Number. "His dress was white, very clean," says Diogenes Laertius. "He was never known to have eaten too much, or to have drunk too much, or to have indulged in the pleasures of love. He abstained wholly from laughter, and when he was angry, he never chastised anyone, whether slave or freeman." His formidable austerity and purity became a legend. His influence was lasting, for among those who followed in his footsteps were nearly all the mathematicians of Greece, and Plato himself.

Numbers alone could not unlock the secrets of the universe, and one after another great philosophers emerged, all attempting to discover the archetypal patterns of knowledge and the shapes of power.

Heracleitus of Ephesus

HERACLEITUS was born in Ephesus about 544, being the son of the local tyrant. He inherited the title of *basileus*, but relinquished it in favor of his brother, apparently because he despised the people of a city which had grown soft with luxury. Ephesus was like another Vienna, rich, worldly, profoundly contemplative.

Like Pythagoras, he had the aristocratic temper, instinctively solitary, remote from the world as in a grave, happy only when he was walking alone in the mountains. Unlike Pythagoras, who prided himself on his calm, Heracleitus could be violently ill-tempered. Once when the Ephesians ostracized one of his friends, he told them all to go and hang themselves. "The Ephesians would do well to hang themselves," he declared, "every grown man of them, and leave the city to beardless youths, for they have cast out Hermodorus, the best man among them, saying, 'We will have none who is best among us; if there be any such let him go elsewhere and live among others.'" At another time he took his children to the temple of Artemis and amused himself by playing dice. The townspeople flocked around him, struck by the presence of the former statesman and prince playing a game of chance. "Poor fools!" he shouted at them. "What are you watching me for? Don't you know that it is better to roll dice than to meddle with your politics?"

He was a man of strong opinions which he expressed trenchantly and fiercely. He did not share the current opinion of Homer and declared that the great poet "should be thrown out of the lists and whipped." Homer should never have said: "Would that strife might perish from among gods and men!" According to Heracleitus, strife was the prerequisite of the world's existence, the substance of all movement, the fabric by which men live, and he liked to clash contraries together to show that strife made a pleasant sound. He liked doctors as little as he liked Homer. "Physicians," he wrote, "cut, burn, stab and torment the sick, and then they ask for their undeserved fee." He had the typical aristocrat's disdain for the masses, saying that "the best choose immortal glory among mortals above all other things, while the masses eat their fill like cattle."

He was not a pleasant or comfortable philosopher. He hated vigorously, despised earnestly, and seems to have despaired easily. The works of men pleased him no more than the works of the gods. The solemn rites practiced by mortals seemed inconsequential and meaningless to him; he thought all mysteries unholy, the phallic hymns were especially shameful, and acts of purification reminded him of nothing so much as a man washing his feet after deliberately stepping in the mud. His desolate observations on the mysteries probably derive from the fact that as prince and hereditary priest of the Eleusinian Demeter, he knew the inner workings of the mysteries better than most men.

Heracleitus left a prodigious impact on men's minds, notwithstanding the fact that his surviving works consist of little more than a hundred oracular statements which can be written easily on five sheets of paper. These fragments can be knit together with the help of a brief summary of his book *On Nature* written by Diogenes Laertius, who found it in the Temple of Artemis. *On Nature* was divided into three parts: one on the universe, one on politics, and one on theology: and the surviving fragments fit well enough into these contexts. Diogenes Laertius claimed that the book was written with deliberate obscurities *pour épater les bourgeois*, and he quotes a charming verse from the poet Timon to prove his case:

> *Among them came that cuckoo Heracleitus,*
> *The enigmatical obscure reviler*
> *Of all the common people.*

But the obscurities of Heracleitus are not always, or even very often, clothed in darkness. He is obscure because the light beating down on his mind is too violent, too harsh, too blinding. His apothegms give a clear, almost too clear, portrait of his intransigent and willful mind. Like Leonardo da Vinci, he had the faculty of saying brilliant and biting things memorably, and in a very short space. Here are a few of his apothegms:

The Sun is new every day.
Souls smell in Hades.
The thunderbolt drives all things in their course.
The name of the bow is life, but its work is death.
Gods are mortals, men are immortals, each living in the others' death and dying in the others' life.
We step and we do not step in the same streams; we are and we are not.
You cannot step twice in the same stream, for other and other waters are forever flowing on.
Time is a child playing draughts: the kingdom belongs to a child.
The Sun will not overstep his bounds; if he does, the Erinyes, the handmaids of Justice, will find him out.
In the night man kindles a light for himself, when he is dead but remains alive. The sleeper, whose vision has been extinguished, lights up from the dead; and his awakening is a lighting up from sleep.
The wisest man, beside god, appears like an ape, in wisdom, beauty, and all else.
The Lord who is the oracle at Delphi neither speaks nor conceals, but gives a sign. And the Sibyl with raving mouth, uttering her solemn and unadorned words with no breath of perfume on them, reaches over a thousand years with her voice because of the god in her.

Such statements suggest the temper of the man, but tell us very little of his philosophy: they are no more than sparks struck off the anvil of his mind. The words are "solemn and unadorned with no breath of perfume on them," and he wears his oracular mantle as though he were born to it, as indeed he was. Yet he was the child of his time: the making of chiseled, elegiac apothegms was characteristic of the period before the Persian invasions of Greece.

His philosophy, such as it was, seems to have derived from a concept of mystical fire in which the universe was bathed. All things took their birth from the fiery streams and were continually being changed. These streams of energy or fire obey the ineluctable laws of destiny; out of the upward and downward flow of fire comes the strange phenomenon of a universe in a continual state of becoming. He seems to have believed that at long intervals the entire universe of becoming is consumed in these mystical flames, but the conflagration is only the beginning of another cycle of change. Behind the world, behind all universes, is the deathless flame.

In all this Heracleitus is very far from believing that "man is the measure of all things." Against the eternal flames man is almost nothing, and his strivings after virtue are in vain. Virtue can have little meaning for a man who affirmed that "good and evil are the same" and that "it is all the same whether a man is quick or dead, awake or asleep, young or old, for the former change and become the latter, and the latter change back into the former." A man was simply a small spark in the torrents of flame, and there was no breath of divinity in him; and when he perished "his corpse was more fit to be thrown away than dung."

Heracleitus states his fiery nihilism with extraordinary conviction in phrases that ring like metal. He stands at the sunset, not caring whether there is a dawn, a proud, obstinate, imperious figure lit with the flaming colors of his imagination. According to Diogenes Laertius, there was nevertheless a vein of humility in him. He said once that no one, by whatever road he might travel, could ever possibly discover the boundaries of the human soul. But this was in fact the only humble saying attributed to him. There is more of the flavor of the man in the story that he was once asked why he remained silent, and answered: "So that you may talk."

Parmenides of Elea

IF Heracleitus stands at the sunset, Parmenides stands in the cool dawnlight. He too was a patrician, rich and noble, conscious of his dignity as a philosopher, but in every other respect the contrary of Heracleitus. He wrote not in metallic apothegms but in verse. He did not believe that the universe was bathed in a mysterious fire. He saw the world as Being, not as Becoming. Beyond the ever-changing evanescent world of the senses lay the realm of Immutability. What is, is. What was, is. What will be, is. What is not, cannot be thought. The One is god. In this way Parmenides asserted the undeviating and unchanging reality of Being, the vast and all-embracing substance of the world we know, where the river flows but is always the same, and there are no upward and downward streams of fire, and there is no sunset. Parmenides saw the world as though it were transformed into sudden crystal.

He begins his poem with a visionary invocation of the daughters of the Sun leading him out of darkness into an intense light. The doors of Justice are thrown open, and the goddess speaks:

> Listen and hear my words and let them be known,
> There are only two ways of understanding—
> The first is Being: impossible for Being not to be.
> This is the way of faith, for truth attends it.
> The other way is Not-Being: impossible for it to be,
> And wholly beyond understanding, beyond conceiving.
> What is not cannot be known, cannot be spoken,
> And Being and knowing are the same thing.

From this beginning Parmenides reaches out toward the nature of Being, by which he means the totality of the universe, which is uncreated and indestructible, without beginning or end, having a finite unity, "since it now is, all at once, one and continuous." From this fundamental dogma he builds up his picture of the universe as motionless and unchangeable, everywhere similar to itself, resembling in its perfection of form a rounded sphere. Our senses are aware of endless movement and distraction, creation followed by destruction and destruction in its turn followed by creation, but these sensations are no more than fictions. Being, as seen by the eyes of truth, is uncreated, permanent, and unalterable, "being immovable in the bonds of mighty chains." These chains, the laws of Being, seem to derive from the great chains with which, Homer says, Zeus upholds the world. The heroes of Parmenides' poem are not Achilles, Ajax, Agamemnon, Hector haunted by his doom, and Helen rejoicing in her beauty. Here the heroes are Being, Not-Being, the One, the Sphere, Divine Necessity. Their battleground is the walled city of the mind, and their wars are bloodless, though they involve the entire universe.

Parmenides' starting point in his description of the universe is the unity of all things. The One is all, indivisible, of the same density throughout. He adds that "it is lacking in nothing, for if it lacked anything, it would lack everything," meaning that it would enter into the realm of Not-Being, which cannot be thought. Again and again

Parmenides insists that Being is absolute, incomparable, and without contraries. It is not only that there are no upward and downward streams of Being, but there are no contraries at all, and all change is merely illusion. We speak of things coming to birth and dying, of alterations in color and position, but we are simply using conventional words to describe appearances. For the ever-changing world of Heracleitus he substitutes a world already perfect and therefore in no need of change.

The worlds of Parmenides and Heracleitus are irreconcilable: it is as though in fact two entirely different universes were being depicted by men of vastly different temperaments. The world of Heracleitus is haunted with doom and rejoices in continual turmoil; the world of Parmenides is aware of its own perfection and everlasting beauty, and is content to remain motionless.

That motion—all motion—was an illusion of the senses was an inevitable corollary of Parmenides' picture of the universe. It was left to his pupil, Zeno of Elea, to devise a series of paradoxes designed to show the impossibility of movement. He showed that if a tortoise was given a head start, even Achilles could never overtake it, for by the time Achilles has reached the place where the tortoise started, the tortoise is already ahead, and when Achilles has reached *that* point, the tortoise will have advanced still farther, and since the running track is made up of an infinite series of points, Achilles will never be able to overtake the tortoise. And if this should seem to be mathematical quibbling, Zeno points to an arrow flying through the air and shows that at any given moment the arrow must be in one and the same space: therefore the arrow is at rest in every moment of its flight. Zeno was showing that language could not embrace the paradoxical nature of motion. According to tradition, he was the lover as well as the pupil of Parmenides, and took part in a rebellion against the tyrant Nearches, who had seized power in Elea. Zeno was arrested, brought into the presence of the tyrant, and ordered to name the conspirators. Instead, he answered with a list of those who had helped the tyrant to power. "Tell me more names," said Nearches. "Then I name you, for bringing about the destruction of the city!" Zeno answered, and bit off his own tongue and spat it at the tyrant. He was sentenced to death and died heroically, being pounded to death in a mortar.

Plato in the dialogue called *Parmenides* tells a strange story of a meeting between Parmenides, Zeno, and Socrates, which took place in

Athens. Socrates was then a young man, perhaps only twenty-two or -three, but he had already elaborated his concept of the Ideas, the quintessential and heavenly form of everything that exists: a concept which derived directly from the immutable and perfect One of Parmenides. Parmenides was about sixty-five years of age, white-haired, but still virile. Zeno was a tall, handsome man, about forty, concerned only to defend the theses of his master. Soon Parmenides and Socrates are engaged in a calm discussion of the One and of the nature of the Ideas, with Socrates allowing that the Ideas may have no existence outside our minds, and Parmenides insisting that if an Idea of anything is absolute, then it cannot relate to the world of appearances, The absolute table excludes the table we take our meals on, and is wholly unrelated to it, existing in a world of its own. So they argue, Socrates defending the Ideas and Parmenides defending the One, coming to no conclusions until quite suddenly Parmenides, having opened a small breach in the argument of Socrates, summons the walls to fall down:

Then, said Parmenides, the nature of the beautiful in itself, and of the good in itself, and all the other Ideas which we suppose to exist absolutely, are unknown to us?

It would seem so, said Socrates.

I think that even stranger consequences follow?

What are they?

Would you, or would you not say, that absolute knowledge, if it exists, must be a far more exact knowledge than our knowledge; and the same of beauty, and of the rest?

Yes.

And if there is such a thing as participation in absolute knowledge, no one is more likely than God to have this most exact knowledge?

Certainly.

But then, will God, having absolute knowledge, have a knowledge of human beings?

Why not?

Because, Socrates, said Parmenides, we have admitted that the Ideas are not valid in relation to human beings; nor human beings in relation to them; for their relations are limited to their respective spheres.

Yes, we have agreed on that.

So it follows that if God possesses this perfect authority, and perfect knowledge, his authority cannot rule us, nor his knowledge know us, nor any human being; just as our authority does not extend to the gods, nor our knowledge embrace anything of the divine: whence it follows that the gods are not our masters, neither do they know the works of men.

Surely, said Socrates, it is monstrous to deprive God of knowledge!

Well, Socrates, said Parmenides, here are a few, but only a few of the difficulties we are involved in if Ideas really exist and we regard them as absolute unities.

Parmenides had provided a chilling demonstration of the danger of trafficking in absolutes, and since nearly everything that could be said about the One was equally true when said about the Ideas, he was destroying his own case as well as the case of Socrates. The One was like quicksilver slipping through the fingers. It existed, but as soon as you tried to touch it, it vanished. Words could not encompass it; it seemed to defy all human explanation. It embodied an aspect of truth, and in time it was to feed the mainstream of Greek philosophy and later of Christianity, but it was not the whole truth. Within the One there was no motion, no reason for existence: there was no place for the gods, and none for the colors of life.

> *The One remains, the many change and pass;*
> *Heaven's light forever shines, Earth's shadows fly;*
> *Life, like a dome of many-colored glass,*
> *Stains the white radiance of Eternity,*
> *Until Death tramples it in fragments—*

So Shelley wrote, giving a small place to the colors of life in the eternal scheme of things, challenging Parmenides with painted glass. But even in Shelley the One offers singularly little hope to mankind. One cannot feed one's mind for long, or even for a few hours, on the white radiance of Eternity. Because life and growth and beauty and strife and the existence of the gods had no place in the pure and motionless world of Parmenides, the philosophers who grappled with the problem began to think there might be a way of marrying the One with the Heracleitean Fire.

Empedocles of Acragas

EMPEDOCLES is one of those philosophers who almost vanish beneath the weight of their legends. It was said of him that he walked like a king, wearing a purple robe and a laurel crown on his head, and his sandals were shod with bronze. They said he was a magician who could raise the dead, a doctor who could cure diseases by uttering spells, an engineer who could divert winds and storms by strategically placing asses' skins in high places. They said, too, that although he behaved like a king, he opposed tyranny and refused the crown of his native town, but he was not above being treated as a god, an immortal among mortals. There was a vast pride in him. He believed himself to be a superior being who had progressed far beyond the usual preoccupations of mortals into a world where everything was bright and clear and where all problems were resolved. Diogenes Laertius says he died as mysteriously as he lived. He had recently brought a dead woman to life, and his friends gathered in a field to celebrate his divinity with a feast:

> *Then after the banquet they lay down, some going a little way off, and some lying under the trees nearby in the field, and some wherever they happened to choose. But Empedocles himself remained in the place where he had been sitting. But when day broke, and they arose, he alone was not found. And when he was sought for, and the servants were examined without success, at last one declared that he had heard a loud voice summoning Empedocles at midnight, and the servant said he rose up and saw a great light shining in heaven, and nothing else. As they were all amazed, Pausanias descended and sent some people to look for him, but afterward he was commanded not to busy himself about the affair, as he was informed that what had happened was deserving of gratitude, and that it behooved them to sacrifice to Empedocles as to one who has become a god.*

> (Diogenes Laertius, *Empedocles*, x)

According to another legend, Empedocles made his way to Mount Etna, which was then erupting, and hurled himself into the flames, but a few days later one of his sandals was found on the mountainside. They knew it belonged to him, for it was shod with bronze. There was still a third story that he died obscurely in the

Peloponnese. "There is no known tomb," wrote Timaeus, "but we should not regard this as extraordinary. Many men have no tombs."

What is certain is that Empedocles was already a legend in his lifetime, and that as doctor and philosopher he possessed a strange power over his patients and pupils. He was also a brilliant orator, and Aristotle claims that he "invented rhetoric, and taught it to Gorgias, who in turn peddled it in Athens." He was something of an engineer, for he drained the marshes of Selinus during a pestilence and changed the courses of rivers. But his chief claim to our attention are his two poems, *On Nature* and *On Purifications*, of which some five hundred fragmentary lines have survived.

In his stern and haughty poems—for no one could be more arrogant in poetry—Empedocles announces the marriage between the One and the Heracleitean Fire, and he accomplishes this by the simple process of introducing two matchmakers, Love and Strife, the one drawing things together, the other separating them, the one creating, the other destroying, and both having their being within the motionless circle of the One. The universe, and all within it, is held in balance by these opposite poles. Within the enclosing circle there is ceaseless movement of repulsion and attraction, but the circle itself remains whole. Empedocles solves the problem by enclosing the Heracleitean Fire within the One.

It is not, of course, quite so simple, for he goes on to describe the ceaseless flux within the One in terms of fire, air, earth and water, the ultimate elements of creation. All things are produced out of their play with one another. Love brings them together, Strife separates them. So they are born, and so they eventually die, only to be reborn in new and ever more marvelous combinations. "From these elements," he says, "there rises everything that is and everything that ever shall be—trees and men and women, wild beasts and birds and fishes that dwell in the waters, and even the gods with their long lives, living in highest honor."

As Empedocles goes about the task of drawing an intelligible picture of the universe, he sees a constant change working through creation, producing out of the same elements the reptiles and the gods. It is not only that everything is alive and in motion and being ceaselessly transformed, but everything is moved by the desire for life, for movement, and for transformation: all the elements are continually conspiring toward change. There are no moments of rest, no sheltered places where it is possible to escape from the flux. In the course of time a man goes through endless transformations. "I have been a youth and a maiden, a bush and a bird, and a fish darting in the sea." Then he remembers that he has been a god, and the gods too must suffer transformations.

For there is an ordinance of Necessity, a divine decree, ancient, eternal, and sealed by great oaths, that whenever one of the daimones, whose portion is length of days, has sinfully stained his hand with blood, or followed Strife, or perjured himself, he shall be banished from the abodes of the blessed for thrice ten thousand seasons, being born throughout this time in all manner of mortal shapes, exchanging one laborious path for another. The mighty Air will pursue him seaward, and the sea will spew him forth on the dry Earth, and the Earth will cast him to the beams of the unwearying Sun, and the Sun will hurl him back into the whirlpools of Air. One takes him from another, and all reject him. One of these now am I, a fugitive from the gods and a wanderer, for having put my trust in senseless Strife.

It is an exalted view of life, and to many it must have been very satisfying. According to this view, all creation was kin. And, seeing creation in this way, he was led to see likenesses unobserved before. "Hair and leaves and the heavy feathers of birds, all spring from the same origin, and so do the scales of reptiles." Before men were made in their present form, there must have been many-handed monsters bearing a distant likeness to men. He speaks of men with faces and breasts looking in strange directions, of the offspring of oxen with the faces of men, and the offspring of men with the faces of oxen. There was a time "when heads grew up without necks, when arms went wandering about naked and bereft of shoulders, and eyes went roaming without foreheads." These happy monsters are not so much products of his poetic vision as the inevitable consequences of his theory of creation, which demands that fire, air, earth, and water shall join in all conceivable proportions and assume all conceivable shapes.

Other consequences followed his belief in the kinship of creation. One should not eat the flesh of animals. Plants too should be regarded tenderly, for they too feel pleasure and pain and know desire. He forbade the eating of laurel leaves, and liked trees so much that he gave them the first place in creation, saying that they came long before men.

Parmenides and Heracleitus were pitiless, for they gave to humanity only a small portion of creation. Empedocles exults in humanity and in everything that is alive, however monstrous its appearance, and however dangerous. Above all the experimental creatures stood the One, which enclosed and contained all things, with no head, no branches sprouting from its shoulders, no feet, no knees, no hairy parts. The One was pure Mind, filling the universe with its own thoughts, uncreated, undying.

Above all the Greek philosophers loved the One, the single rope which held all diversity together. At various times it was Fire, Air, Earth or Water, and sometimes it was all four together. One was continually multiplying itself, with the result that it sometimes seemed to vanish in its multiplications. Then at the end of the road they would find it waiting for them again.

12 «« THE REIGN OF THE TYRANTS

IN TIME Athens was to become the center of research and free inquiry, but there was nothing in her beginnings to suggest that she would become the most powerful city in Greece and the haunt of philosophers and poets. In Athens an entire civilization was hammered out and given shape and charged with such intellectual fire that it was to become as enduring as anything in the world, but at first there were only the shadowy forms of petty kingdoms spread over the plain of Attica and ghostly peasants earning a bare living from the soil. No one would have guessed that destiny had marked the small plain of Attica.

At some unknown date, perhaps in the ninth century B.C., there arose a legendary hero called Theseus who united these petty kingdoms by force. He was so solidly fixed in Athenian tradition that he must have had a historical existence. They say he came as a youth from Troezen, fought the Marathonian bull and led the Athenians against an invasion of the Amazons, and later joined with his friend Pirithoüs to make war against the Centaurs; and no doubt the legends relate to real battles fought in the darkness of time. Thucydides says he united all the people of Attica and "compelled them to make Athens their citadel, and to inscribe their names on the Athenian muster rolls." For the first time under Theseus Athens emerged as a power in Greece. There was the Acropolis and a small town at its feet, and a handful of villages which owed allegiance to the king. But many years passed before Athens possessed a port of its own.

We know nothing with any certainty about the ancient history of Athens. The king vanishes, the nobles take charge, there are the inevitable revolts of the farmers and workmen, who find themselves reduced to slavery by the exactions of the nobility. Classes emerge, and obscure wars take place. Suddenly Eleusis falls to the Athenians, who find themselves in possession of a port. We hear of ships being outfitted, and the beginning of trade with neighboring countries, while the nobles quarrel among themselves and cause blood feuds which will continue for centuries and devise a code of laws to keep the people in permanent subjection. For stealing a cabbage or an apple a peasant might be sentenced to death. As the laws grow harsher, the revolts become bloodier. At last, about the year 600 B.C., when the Athenians were in danger of exterminating one another, a young noble called Solon appears in the market place and stills the fury of the opposing camps, reciting a poem in which he urges the rich to abandon their hope of keeping the people in subjection:

> Behold, a great grief wells up in my heart
> As I see the oldest home of the ancient Ionians
> Dismembered by the sword.

Then, although rich and descended from the ancient kings of Athens, he thunders against those who by their love of money and overweening pride have very nearly brought about the destruction of the city.

Men listened to Solon perhaps because he represented a new kind of Athenian. He was poet, merchant, dreamer, adventurer, man of affairs, and on occasion an unscrupulous conniver and rabble-rouser who would go to any extreme to promote his political beliefs. Athens had fought Megara over the island of Salamis, but so much blood had been spilled that at last the Athenians broke off the conflict and passed a law that anyone who wrote or spoke about the conquest of Salamis should be sentenced to death. Plutarch describes how Solon carefully composed some verses and arranged that his family should give out that he was mad. One day he descended upon the market place and began to utter the verses like a man divinely inspired, calling upon the Athenians to wipe out the shame of their defeat and to take the island by force. But this was only the first deception. He sent a renegade to the Megarians on the island to invite them to a festival on the mainland where only Athenian women would be present. The Megarians jumped at the bait, only to find themselves at the mercy of Athenian youths disguised as girls. "None of the

Megarians escaped," says Plutarch. "The Athenians set sail for the island and took it."

Solon had the cunning of Odysseus; and there were some who said he was never more cunning than when he strode into the market place and abused the rich for their sins of avarice and cupidity:

> *You who are stuffed to the gills with your wealth,*
> *Bloated and swollen with the taste of it,*
> *Take heed that your heads do not swell overmuch,*
> *Lest in the end we spew you out of our mouths.*

The violence of the diatribe seems to have stunned the nobles, who gave him full powers. He became both *archon* and *nomothete:* he was both head of state and chief legislator. In a series of sweeping enactments he canceled all debts, abolished most of the privileges of the nobility, limited the size of their holdings, and prohibited the mortgaging of persons. The rich acquired their wealth by shipping their grain outside of Attica: he forbade the shipment of any grain at all, while permitting the shipment of olive oil, of which there was a surplus. He freed the debt slaves and permitted men to marry women from outside of Attica. He introduced coinage. He decreed an amnesty for exiles. He enacted a law by which a man without children could leave his property to anyone he desired: previously it was inherited by the man's family. This law was especially significant because it was designed to break up the power of the clan. In Solon's view not the clan but the *polis,* the city of Athens, should receive men's chief allegiance.

But all this was only the beginning. He devised a constitution and saw that the laws were written up on wooden tablets for all to read. He gave men liberty to claim damages for injuries received. He forbade dowries, thus putting all young women on an equal status. He also passed a law forbidding men to speak evil of the dead or of the living.

Solon contrived so many healthy changes in so short a time that it was as though Athens had suffered at the hands of the most violent revolutionary; but the laws were sensible, and they were accepted peacefully as the only alternative to civil strife.

But even these laws were less important than the new dignity which Solon gave to labor. He invested craftsmanship with honor; and from being a city where a few nobles ruled over a debt-ridden peasantry, Athens became a city of craftsmen. He made a law that a son need not support his father in old age unless the father had taught him a trade. Work was no disgrace: on the contrary, the real noble-man was the skilled craftsman. In all this he was simply attempting to bring Athens up to the level of Ionia, where in the space of a few years remarkable technological advances had been made. We hear of Anacharsis the Scythian improving the anchor, and going on to invent the bellows and the potter's wheel. About this time Glaucus of Chios is said to have invented the soldering iron and Theodorus of Samos to have invented the square, the lathe, the rule, and a new method of casting bronze. The watchword was now *techn*ê, which may be translated as "skill methodically applied." Instead of feudal princes, those relics of the half-forgotten Mycenaean age, there would be skilled mechanics. The *seisachtheia*, "the unloosening of the bur-dens," had come just in time to introduce a new industrial age.

We know Solon chiefly from his surviving verses, Plutarch's essay on him, and Aristotle's *Constitution of Athens*. The figure that emerges is of a burly, vigorous, highly intelligent man, who made decisions quickly and kept to them, and reckoned every day well spent only when he had undermined an ancient stupidity and intro-duced a modern improvement. One day he standardized weights and measures. Another day he reformed the calendar. He was that kind of man, unbending in his duties toward modernity. He was one of those rare dictators who never succumbed to a love of power. When he felt harassed by people asking him to explain the laws or demanding special privileges, he simply abandoned Athens and went off to Egypt, an-nouncing that he would be gone for ten years. He had had enough of the nobles begging him to restore them to their former eminence, and he had no sympathy for the people who had hoped he would destroy and disinherit the entire nobility. "He could have made him-self a tyrant," wrote Aristotle, "but he preferred at the cost of provok-ing the enmity of both classes to be the savior of his country and the ideal lawgiver."

Such praise Aristotle gave to no other head of state. In time a legendary aura accumulated around Solon, but he was no legend: he was the first fully rounded figure to emerge in Athenian history, and one of the most charming. He had a rough, no-nonsense kind of humor. Plutarch tells the story of how Anacharsis came to call on him in the hope of making friends with him. "Home is the place for making friends," Solon said gruffly, hoping to send him off to his native Scythia. "Yes," said Anacharsis, "*your* home is a place for making friends." After that, Solon received him kindly, and he seems not to have been put out when Anacharsis told him that making laws for people was the height of folly: laws were spiderwebs to catch the poor, but the rich would burst through them. Solon replied that men keep their promises when nothing is to be gained by breaking them, and he would so arrange the laws that the people would find that nothing would be gained by breaking them. Laws, it seems, were promissory notes on the bank of the state.

Anacharsis proved in the end to be the better prophet. Though Solon brought the reign of law to Athens, he failed to bring about a lasting peace. For four years after he left Athens there was a precarious armistice. Then the fishermen of the shore, the shepherds in the hills, the peasants and landowners of the plains were at each others' throats.

When Solon returned to Athens at the end of his ten-year exile, he was out of touch with the times. He had extracted promises of peace, and he had urged the people to obey the laws for their own safety, but they wanted neither peace nor safety. His influence was waning, and he seems to have retired from politics altogether, content to watch the passing scene. For twenty long years he had either ruled Athens or he had been the *éminence grise* advising the reigning *archon;* when he stepped down he no longer had any heart for public affairs.

In his absence his young cousin Peisistratus had come into prominence among the hillmen and shepherds. Like Solon, he possessed gifts of intelligence and cunning, and in addition he was remarkable for his physical beauty. One day, shortly after Solon's return, he appeared in the market place covered with wounds, telling a story of how he and his mules had been set upon by cutthroats, and he asked for a bodyguard. Solon, too, had possessed a gift for dramatizing himself, and he recognized the family trait. He warned the Athenians against letting Peisistratus have a bodyguard. "I am wiser than half the people and braver than all the rest," Solon said. "I am wiser than those who do not realize he intends to make himself tyrant, and I am braver than those who realize it and keep silent." No one listened to him. In despair he took his armor and set it up outside his house, saying he had helped his country as far as it lay in his power, and there was nothing left for him to do. He was by now an old man, nearly eighty, but his mind was keen and his instinct for self-dramatization at least as well-developed as his cousin's. Peisistratus was given a bodyguard of fifty cudgel-bearing ruffians. With their help, and some additional forces supplied by his partisans, he seized the Acropolis and declared himself tyrant.

Happily, he had inherited the family trait of benevolence. All over Greece tyranny was in the ascendancy, but Peisistratus ruled like a constitutional monarch. He was rich, popular, and he possessed something of Solon's humanity. His country seat was at Brauron near the seacoast, five hours' steady walk from Athens, but his home was his palace on the Acropolis. During his reign scholars began those long researches which eventually produced a definitive text of Homer. Suave, elegant, with a taste for luxury, he was largely responsible for the new cult of Dionysus and the development of the theater. He presided over the strange marriage between the chaste Athena and the phallic Dionysus.

He had been in power for five or six years when the factions of the Shore and the Plain rose against him; he fled to Brauron, and for a while took no further part in politics. When he returned to power he employed a charade which would be completely incredible if we did not know the family propensity for self-dramatization. Herodotus was moved almost to tears by the absurdity of the story. "It was the silliest trick that history ever recorded," he observed. "The Greeks are not fools, and for centuries they have been distinguished from others by their superior wits; and the sharpest wits of all belong to the Athenians, who fell for the trick." It was the very absurdity of the ruse that seems to have appealed to the Athenians. In the village of Paeonia, halfway between Brauron and Mount Hymettus, he found a girl called Phyé, six feet tall and fair-haired, who agreed to impersonate the goddess Athena while she drove Peisistratus in his chariot to Athens, preceded by heralds who announced that the goddess herself had honored the King by becoming his charioteer. Herodotus casts no doubt on the tale. He is sure that it happened, but he is at his wits' end to understand how it happened, and why the Athenians permitted it.

For thirty-three years Peisistratus was in and out of power. Whenever party feelings were exasperated, he simply left Athens quietly and returned to Brauron or went traveling; and when he decided the time had come to return he would find some dramatic way to announce his arrival. He built magnificently, and set about making

Athens indistinguishable from the great Ionian cities. He enjoyed talking to peasants, and the story was told of his meeting with a peasant and asking him what profit he got from his flinty soil. "Aches and pains," the peasant replied, "and that's what Peisistratus ought to have his tenth of." He was so pleased with the reply that he exempted the peasant from paying taxes.

He built on the Acropolis a great temple to Athena which was destroyed by the Persians. Today some of the pedimental figures representing Heracles and the serpent-tailed heroes can be seen in the Acropolis Museum; the paint is still fresh on them. They have full lips, blue beards, and exquisitely patterned hair; the coiling tails are like spun candy. To this time, too, belong many of the superb black-figured vases, where archaic stiffness dissolves into subtle movement. Most beautiful of all are the marble maidens he set up on the Acropolis to guard the shrine of the goddess. Fourteen of these maidens were found in 1886 when the archaeologists were digging northwest of the Erechtheum. They are painted in delicate tints of emerald, scarlet, yellow, and bronze. Spirals and meanders run down the plaited folds of their gowns: once they were adorned with earrings and bronze coronets: and they wear their finery as though accustomed to it. Though they have the archaic smiles proper to priestesses, their young bodies are taut with a quivering vitality and a purely sensuous elegance.

During his periods of exile Peisistratus settled in Thrace, acquired land on the Hellespont, and set about building a fleet which would safeguard the corn route to Athens from the Black Sea. He set up one of his sons as despot of the important Asiatic Greek town of Sigeum, and encouraged Miltiades, an Athenian nobleman, to settle on the northern side of the strait, and that single decision may have been the most fruitful he ever made, for Miltiades learned the habits of the Persians and accompanied Xerxes in his forays against the Scythians and went on to defeat a Persian army at Marathon. Peisistratus was continually making alliances with the tyrants of Ionia. He made the first preliminary sketch for an Athenian empire, and gave to Athens the leadership of the Ionian race.

He was a tyrant, but a good one: a man with energy and compassion, generosity and cunning, fond of the pageantry of life, hating black, and enjoying the colors of the rainbow. He encouraged the arts, as Solon had encouraged the crafts, and on the least provocation he would introduce festivals. He recaptured Salamis, and insisted that on the anniversary of the capture there should be flower-decked processions of boats to the island. He was present at the birth of drama, when Thespis won a prize for tragedy in 534, being the first actor to appear in his own right divorced from the chorus, changing his roles as he changed masks, and playing in turn all the several parts of the play. He was remembered, too, for having introduced the Scythian policemen to the streets of Athens, and for seeing that the city was well supplied with fountains.

The age of Peisistratus was an age of luxury and faultless taste. In his strange dramatic way Peisistratus moved about the city as though his only purpose was to embellish it and bring delight to the people. Two centuries later Aristotle was writing: "We often speak of the tyranny of Peisistratus as the age of gold."

13 ❦ THE SOVEREIGN PEOPLE

O~~N~~ THE death of Peisistratus, power fell into the hands of his sons Hippias and Hipparchus. They were men well trained in the art of government, following in the footsteps of their father, and both were conscientious and deeply religious rulers. It was remembered of Hippias that he constantly consulted the oracles, and of Hipparchus that he was a patron of poets and scholars. Hippias assumed the larger share of government, while Hipparchus seems to have contented himself with ceremonial affairs and the cultivation of a literary salon. They were intelligent rulers, cultivated and popular, determined to elevate Athens to a position of greater power and influence in the world.

According to Thucydides, Athens under their rule achieved heights of splendor undreamed of before. It was a time of sumptuous elegance. New palaces and monuments were springing up, artists were encouraged, new colonies were being founded, and no one starved, for the corn ships arrived regularly from the Black Sea. Hipparchus invited great poets, among them Simonides and Anacreon, to attend his court, and he paid them liberally. Taxes were low, amounting to about five per cent of income, the main cost of government being borne by the tyrants themselves. At their own expense they paid for the sacrifices in the temples and carried on necessary wars. The ghost of Peisistratus still ruled: his firm and gentle hand could still be felt on Athens.

Among the contributions of the tyrants to Athens was the Altar to the Twelve Gods, which they erected in the Agora, and thereafter all distances were measured from this altar; and they built roads lead-

181

ing in all directions from the Agora. They had the tyrants' love for town planning, and some of their later unpopularity may have been caused by the inevitable destruction of the dwellings of the poor. Believing themselves to be under the special protection of Apollo, they made a sumptuous grant to his temple at Delphi for the construction of a new altar. These gifts, however, were regarded by the people with disapprobation, for they believed they could make better use of such largess. Outwardly Athens seemed calm, basking in its own splendor, but there were mutterings below the surface.

Few dynastic tyrannies endure for more than two generations, and the tyranny of the Peisistratids was no exception. And tyrannies rarely fall as the result of a frontal attack by their enemies. They usually fall as the result of curious accidents and small poisons which are introduced into their systems until the whole body is corrupted. An obscure middle-aged aristocrat called Aristogeiton delivered the blow that led to the eventual downfall of the Peisistratids.

It happened that Aristogeiton had fallen in love with a handsome boy called Harmodius. Hipparchus also saw the boy, fell in love with him, and was determined to pursue his suit in spite of Aristogeiton's prior claim. The boy, however, insisted that he was still in love with Aristogeiton. So matters rested, while the boy and the middle-aged roué debated the next movement in the game, knowing that whatever it was it could only be disastrous, for there was no limit to the powers of the tyrant. It would be a simple matter to remove the boy by force, and simpler still to order the death of Aristogeiton. Aristogeiton concluded that the only salvation lay in overthrowing the tyranny. Thucydides claims that he grossly miscalculated his own danger and that Hipparchus had no intention of taking the boy by force, but Thucydides had his own reasons for defending the actions of tyrants and it is possible that Aristogeiton had taken the measure of his enemy.

Hipparchus was a petulant man, smarting under the boy's refusal to share his bed, and he decided to insult the boy in such a way that he and his whole family would feel the weight of authority and at the same time suffer ignominy. This he did by summoning the boy's sister and informing her that she had been chosen as a basket carrier in the procession of the Great Panathenaea. It was a signal honor, reserved for well-born virgins. Hipparchus, as president of the board of rites, could choose whomever he pleased. A few days later he announced that the honor had been withdrawn. The inference, among those who did not know about his love for Harmodius, could only be that the boy's sister was not a virgin. Harmodius now joined Aristogeiton in his plotting for the downfall of the tyranny, determined to avenge the honor of his sister. It seems that there was never a large group of conspirators, and at most eight or nine men, friends of Harmodius and Aristogeiton, were involved. On the day of the Great Panathenaea they decided to kill both Hippias and Hipparchus.

This festival, founded by Peisistratus, was the most sumptuous and carefully ordered of all the festivals that took place in Athens, and the tyrants took leading roles. They were the grand marshals and superintendents of the procession which started in the Outer Cerameicus and proceeded through the Inner Cerameicus and across the Agora to the cliffs of the Acropolis, and so by a winding road to the temple of Athena. It was early in the morning. Hippias was in the Outer Cerameicus, and Hipparchus was not far from the temple of Apollo Patroüs within the gates, presumably surveying the line of march and inspecting the marshals who took up their positions along the processional way. The conspirators were with the crowds outside the gates, which were thrown open, for the procession was about to begin.

Armed with daggers, Aristogeiton and Harmodius were about to hurl themselves on Hippias when they saw the tyrant's brother standing unguarded inside the walls, and almost at the same moment they recognized one of the conspirators talking familiarly with Hippias, who was always accessible to anyone who wanted to speak with him. At the sight of Hippias talking so calmly to the conspirator, Aristogeiton and Harmodius took fright. They were sure the plot had been revealed, and in a moment they would be arrested. They decided that at least they would kill Hipparchus, and so they rushed through the gate, hurled themselves on him, and stabbed him to death. Afterward it was related that he had had a strange premonition during the previous night, dreaming that a tall and beautiful man stood over his bed and murmured mysterious words to him:

O lion, endure the unendurable with an enduring heart.
Know that he who shall harm thee shall pay the penalty.

So Herodotus records, and since he made careful inquiries about the murder, it is possible that the tyrant really did have the dream.

With the first blows, the crowd began to surge through the gates, and marshals and soldiers came hurrying up. The boy Harmodius was killed on the spot. Aristogeiton escaped in the crowd.

When Hippias heard about his brother's death a few minutes later he ordered the hoplites to move out of their ranks and lay down their arms. Then he searched them, and as many others as he could lay his hands on. Those carrying daggers were immediately arrested. Aristogeiton, too, was arrested, and under torture he gave the names of many people implicated in the plot, including many high dignitaries close to Hippias, and he seems to have done this with the deliberate intention of creating as much havoc as possible. The guilty and the guiltless were arrested, and all were put to the torture. There was a reign of terror in Athens. Hippias saw himself confronted with a vast conspiracy; he could not bring himself to believe that it was a small and ill-organized plot engineered by a middle-aged man and a boy.

Thucydides says that Aristogeiton committed in prison "an impious act" by deliberately implicating people who had nothing to do with the plot. By this he meant that Aristogeiton committed an offense against the guardian gods of the city, shaking the divine foundations of the *polis* and shattering the trust which had existed between the divinely appointed tyrants and the people; and in fact this is exactly what happened. Aristogeiton had accomplished exactly what he set out to do.

In prison he was constantly cross-examined and constantly tortured. Broken in mind and body, he was deliberately kept alive in the hope that he would reveal more names. Hippias visited the prison and offered Aristogeiton the privilege of death if he would make a complete and final list of the conspirators, and Aristogeiton pretended to agree, first demanding that Hippias would give his hand to confirm his promise. Hippias did so. Aristogeiton immediately abused him for giving his hand to the murderer of his brother, raging at the tyrant for committing this act of impiety. Hippias could no longer control himself. He whipped out his dagger and stabbed Aristogeiton to death.

The bloodbath continued long after the killing of Aristogeiton. The character of Hippias changed, and from being a generous benefactor of the city, he became a pitiless taskmaster and a murderous despot. Hundreds of innocent people were killed, thousands were banished. He had hoped to put out the fire. Instead he fanned it.

For three more years Hippias held Athens in a grip of terror, and then seeing that he would be able to hold it only a little while longer, he set about constructing a fortress at Munychia, the hill overlooking Piraeus, intending to establish himself there with his armed guards and his court; and from Munychia, if necessary, he would escape from Attica to Ionia. One of his more unpopular acts was to marry his daughter to the son of the tyrant of Lampsacus, who was known to have some influence with the Persian king. If he lost Athens, he planned to retake it with the help of the Persians.

Meanwhile the work of destroying the tyranny was continuing quietly with the help of the secret societies. Cleisthenes, who belonged to the wealthy family of the Alcmaeonids, was in Delphi. He had considerable influence with the Pythian priestess, who now warned all Spartans visiting the shrine "to free the Athenians from tyranny" if they wanted their wishes fulfilled, and by constant reiteration of the message she so worked on the minds and imaginations of the Spartans that they began seriously to plan an invasion of Attica, although they had a treaty of alliance with the Peisistratids. A small invasion force landed at Phaleron, but Hippias had his own agents in Sparta, and learning that they intended to land on a wooded part of the coast, he cut down the trees and prepared an ambush with the help of a thousand Thessalian cavalrymen. The invaders were driven back into the sea.

Later, as the cries and warnings of the Pythian priestess became more urgent, still another expeditionary force marched out of Sparta, this time under the leadership of Cleomenes, the Spartan king. Once again the Thessalian cavalry fought the invaders, but they were hurled back and Cleomenes marched on to take Athens, while Hippias took refuge in the Acropolis. He had food and water, and could have resisted a long siege, but when his sons secretly escaped from the citadel, and were captured on their way to the coast, he was forced to surrender. The Spartans, remembering the long alliance with the Peisistratids, gave them five days grace in which to remove all their possessions from Athens; and their heavily loaded ships sailed off from Piraeus to Ionia. For nearly fifty years the Peisistratids had been absolute rulers of Athens. They never ruled again.

When Hippias left the Acropolis, the Spartans took possession of the citadel, garrisoned it, and regarded themselves as conquerors of Athens. They were the first foreigners to establish themselves on the citadel, and the Athenians were in no mood to exchange the tyranny

of Hippias for the tyranny of Cleomenes. Cleisthenes called the people
to arms, and for two days and two nights the armed people watched
all the exits, standing seventeen deep at the gates, preparing to starve
the Spartans into surrender. Finally Cleomenes surrendered. He was
forced to leave all his armor and equipment in the hands of the
Athenians, and to abandon the city with only the clothes he was wearing. A century later the chorus of old men in Aristophanes' play
Lysistrata fondly recalled the humbling of the king as he came down
from the Acropolis with an unkempt beard, ragged, and smeared with
dirt. They forgot that Cleomenes had helped them to overthrow the
tyranny, while they enjoyed the exquisite triumph of watching him
depart.

Cleisthenes was the hero of the hour. He, too, had contributed
to the downfall of the tyranny, placing the wealth of the Alcmaeonids
at the service of the people. Earlier, he had attempted an armed uprising, constructing a fortified post at Lipsydrion above Mount Parnes,
within the borders of Attica, organizing a small army and summoning
partisans from Athens. Lipsydrion means "dry fountain," and proved
to be a trap; Hippias was able to reduce the fortress without any great
difficulty. Soon men were singing a drinking song:

> *The faithless old fountain is dry,*
> *Where men were sent to die!*
> *They showed themselves to be*
> *True sons of liberty.*

About this time many political songs were being sung, and the
best of them was a drinking song in honor of Harmodius and Aristogeiton, the lovers who had precipitated the revolution:

> *I will wear my sword on a myrtle bough*
> *Like Harmodius and Aristogeiton,*
> *Who slashed the tyrant to death*
> *And set Athens free.*

> *O most dear Harmodius, surely you are not dead,*
> *But you are living still in the islands of the Blessed*
> *Together with Achilles, the swift runner,*
> *And Diomedes, son of Tydeus,*

I will wear my sword on a myrtle bough
Like Harmodius and Aristogeiton
Who at the procession for Athena
Killed Hipparchus, the tyrant lord.

Everlasting shall be your fame,
O most dear Harmodius and Aristogeiton,
Who slashed the tyrant to death
And set Athens free.

Even greater posthumous honors were accorded them, for they were painted on Panathenaic vases within the shield of the goddess and on *lekythoi*, which were placed with the dead in their tombs. There seem to have been many statues of the heroes, and the most celebrated was a bronze set up in the Agora, showing the two heroes naked, advancing with daggers drawn, the one young and beardless, the other with a heavy pointed beard, and for many years it was decreed that no other statues should be set beside them. Thirty years later Xerxes, plundering the city, removed the bronze to his palace at Susa, and there, long afterward, Alexander the Great discovered it. He ordered it returned to Athens.

With the victory over Hippias and Cleomenes, Athens could rejoice in its new-found freedom. But if Cleisthenes was the hero of the hour, he was not yet in complete command of the city, for there were still remnants of the party of Hippias in positions of power. Among them was the resourceful Isagoras son of Tisander, who revived an old charge against the Alcmaeonids that they were "the accursed ones," corrupters of the sacred soil of Athens, to such an effect that Cleisthenes was forced to leave the city, and to quell the resulting turmoil Cleomenes was once more invited to bring an army into Attica. With the help of Cleomenes, Isagoras dissolved the council and prepared to set himself up as an absolute dictator. He had not counted on the people of Athens, weary beyond endurance of the continuing tyranny and of the presence of the Spartans. They came out on the streets. Isagoras and Cleomenes were forced to take refuge in the Acropolis, while the people guarded the gates for the second time in the same year. Cleomenes' second intervention in the affairs of Athens was no more successful than the first, and he made his way back to Sparta with a safe-conduct issued by an Athenian mob. Isagoras was arrested and put to death. The mob sent for Cleisthenes, and entrusted him with full powers. He at once set about the entire political reorganization of the state, bringing about a democratic form of government.

In this way, following a tyranny which had endured for half a century, three invasions of Spartans, and a reign of terror, liberty came to Athens.

DEMOCRACY, as we know it today, came to birth on a winter day in 507 B.C. on the Acropolis at Athens, when Cleisthenes issued the decrees which brought about a revolution in the art of government. There, for the first time, he announced the concept of the sovereign people, and so arranged the forms of government that they were able to rule freely.

An observer visiting Athens that winter might have been justified in believing that the victory of Cleisthenes would lead to still another dictatorship. He was a man with a quick and supple mind, he was the possessor of vast wealth and rejoiced in the exercise of power. The people had surrendered their powers to him, and there was nothing in his character to suggest that he would surrender his powers back to the people. But that is precisely what he did. The "accursed" Cleisthenes became the first democrat.

What he did was to cut through the traditional power groups and refashion them in such a way that none could use power effectively to dominate the rest; in so doing he neutralized the special interests. Power interests in Attica were centered on three groups, called the Plain, the Shore, and the Mountains. In the Plain lived the Athenians and the neighboring farmers, all deeply concerned with the prestige and wealth of the city. The Shore included all the villagers of southeastern Attica from Mount Hymettus to Sunium together with the sailors and fishermen, traditional enemies of Athens. The Mountains included the villagers of the hill country, the peasants, shepherds, woodcutters, and charcoal burners of northern Attica. All had special privileges and loyalties, and voted for their special interests. Cleisthenes made it impossible for them to vote selfishly by reapportioning the political districts into *trittyes,* each consisting of thirty parishes, of which ten came from the Plain, ten from the Shore, ten from the Mountains. In this way he succeeded in producing political units representative of all the interests of the country. Athens was forced to share her power with mountaineers and fishermen.

The *trittyes* were a purely artificial creation designed for a very real purpose: the spreading of power over the largest possible area. Each constituency consisted of three areas, which were rarely contiguous. It is as though in New York State a constituency might consist of a small area of Manhattan, several farming towns in upper New York State, together with one or two towns on Lake Erie. These areas might have little in common, but this was precisely the reason they were brought together.

The *trittyes* were only one of a series of bold innovations. He completely overhauled the local government of the parishes, previously called *naucraries* because each had to produce its appropriate contribution to the navy. These were now called *demes*, meaning "the people." The *demes* were self-governing units with their mayors, town councilors, treasurers, priests and priestesses to attend to the local gods, and they passed laws which were binding so long as they did not conflict with the laws of the state. They formed the basic political units, and to make them more effective Cleisthenes ordered that all those who resided in the *deme* at the time of its institution were automatically enfranchised. Even resident aliens and emancipated slaves were included. Once enrolled, a family remained a member of the *deme*, and even when the members of the family traveled to other regions they carried the name of the *deme* with them. So Socrates was known as Socrates of the *deme* Alopece to distinguish him from many others who bore the same name. It was almost as though the *deme* became a kind of surname. In this way he would be introduced, and in this way his name would appear on his tombstone.

Cleisthenes refashioned and regrouped the political units, and went on to refashion and regroup the tribal or clan units which had existed ever since men could remember. There had been four tribes in Attica. They bore archaic names—Hopletes, Geleontes, Argadeis, and Aigikoreis—and no one any longer could remember whether there was any meaning attached to the names. He increased the number of tribes to ten, and named them after local heroes. He seems to have had an affection for the number 10, for about the same time he introduced a solar calendar based on ten months of thirty-six or thirty-seven days instead of the lunar calendar based on twelve months, which was in use up to his time. The Council of Four Hundred became the Council of Five Hundred—fifty men from each of the ten tribes. They were elected by lot. A few years later the same method was extended to the highest officers of state, the *archons*.

The declared aim of the new constitution was *isonomia*—equal rights for all before the law. By a system of built-in safeguards, by appointing men to high office by drawing lots, by choosing out of the Council of Five Hundred fifty men each month to carry out the ordinary business of government, and by submitting all important laws to a popular referendum at the Assembly, where the entire body of citizens could attend, Cleisthenes had brought about a working democracy. In such a democracy a poor man had very nearly the same chance of obtaining high office as a rich man. Aristocratic connections still carried weight, and so did riches, but government was largely tamed in obedience to the popular will.

Among the innovations introduced by Cleisthenes—one more of the many safeguards—was ostracism. Once a year, at a meeting of the Assembly, the citizens voted against any of their number judged to be dangerous to the state. Each voter wrote on a potsherd (*ostrakon*) the name of the person he thought deserving of banishment. In theory, and perhaps in practice, no one could be ostracized unless a minimum of six thousand votes was cast against him. Ostracism, therefore, was a means to rid the state of dangerous and brilliant men who by their personal popularity had gathered strong factions around themselves and might be expected to stage a *coup d'état*. By this system the strong could be laid low, and the cruel could be dispossessed of the power to inflict cruelty, and the proud could be humbled. Through ostracism Cleisthenes put a brake on civil disorders. Most of those who were ostracized took comfort from the fact that banishment was a tribute to their strength.

In this mathematical way Cleisthenes remodeled the state. All existing political boundaries were reshuffled at his bidding; all former loyalties were canceled; all former totems were taken down and replaced by new ones. By introducing democracy he had ensured that a revival of tyranny was virtually impossible. He built so well that the democratic forms he had invented survived with little change for more than a hundred years. Without democracy there might have been no successful war against the Persians, and it is certain that there would have been no Golden Age.

Democracy was heady wine, and people got drunk on it. For the first time in human history power had passed into the hands of the people. In other countries priest-kings, tyrants, and dictators were continually coming into existence, asserting their right to command and dominate the people, as they still do, but the reforms of Cleisthenes showed convincingly that the people acting in concert could manage their own affairs and accomplish more by their own exertions than they accomplished when they were unwilling slaves. They thought more keenly and fought more ferociously when the yoke was removed from them. "As long as they were held down by authority," wrote Herodotus, "they shirked their duty on the battlefield, as slaves always shirk their duty, but when they won their freedom, every man longed to distinguish himself."

Under Cleisthenes the Assembly of citizens became the sovereign voice of the state, and no laws could be passed without its assent. The checks and balances of democracy introduced a state viable to human needs: and only the constant emergence of demagogues made the way hard and the outcome dubious when confronted by tyrannies. Now the people had the power in their hands. Now, as free men, they could face the armed might of Persia.

14 « THE COMING OF THE PERSIANS

UNDER the Achaemenid emperors Persia had become the greatest power in the known world, her influence extending far into Central Asia and across the deserts of North Africa. Egypt and all of Palestine were in her possession, ruled by satraps who obeyed the orders of the emperor in his place at Susa. Cyrus, the founder of the empire, had called himself "king of the universe, great king, mighty king, king of Babylon, Sumer and Akkad, king of the four quarters of the world," and few were prepared to dispute his claim. His descendants made the same claim, but with less conviction.

The sudden emergence of Persia as a world power was reflected in events taking place far beyond the limits of her empire. Its effects could be felt in Carthage and Rome, and they were especially visible in Greece, where the threat of a Persian invasion became increasingly real as Cyrus in his westward advance captured the Greek cities of Ionia, enslaving the population and sometimes killing off all the men old enough to bear arms. Miletus alone escaped the wrath of the Persian king, having offered to pay tribute and to swear loyalty to the king even before he had started his campaign to subdue the Asiatic Greeks. The Phocaeans escaped from the Persian Empire by abandoning their city and sailing off in a body to found a colony in Corsica, not far from the daughter-city of Massilia. In the same way the people of Teos abandoned their city and founded a new one at Abdera in Thrace. Ionia became a Persian colony under the heel of satraps who minted coins with their own portraits taking the place of the Greek goddesses formerly stamped on them.

In later years the historian Xenophon would say that Cyrus was the noblest, the most generous, and the most civilized of all the kings who ever ruled, but that was not the opinion of the conquered Ionians who saw their cities razed and their temples desecrated. For the Greeks Persia was an enemy all the more to be feared because her tyrannical rule was sometimes clothed in benevolence. The empire was ruled by a vast civil service and an inspectorate responsible only to the emperor. A splendid system of roads with posthorses stationed every few miles enabled the imperial couriers to take messages from one corner of the empire to another in a few days. In refinement and delicacy Persian art knew no rivals: every engraved gem, every gold beaker, every sword hilt was fashioned with uncompromising good taste. But even the Spartans, tyrannically ruling over their helots, complained bitterly against the authoritarian rule of the emperor, the absolute dictator who regarded Persians and non-Persians alike as puppets subject to his will.

Herodotus tells the story of two Spartans, Sperchias and Bulis, men of good families and great wealth, who came to Persia to offer themselves as sacrifices in exchange for two Persian ambassadors murdered by the Spartans. On their way to Susa they visited Hydarnes, the Persian commander of the entire Asiatic seaboard, who gave them a hospitable reception and invited them to dinner. During the meal Hydarnes asked them why they refused to be friends with a great king who knew how to honor the brave. "Believe me," said Hydarnes, "the great king rewards all those who merit his generosity. Should you find it in your hearts to submit to him, I am sure he would give you lands in Greece and put you in authority over them."

"Hydarnes," came the answer, "you do not properly understand the problem. You have experience of one kind of life, but not of the other. You know what it is to be a slave, but not having tasted liberty, you do not know whether it is sweet or not. If you had known freedom you would urge us to fight for it, not from afar with spears, but with axes at close quarters!"

The two Spartans went on to Susa, where they were received by the emperor. They refused to prostrate themselves, and declared proudly that they had come freely to atone for the deaths of the Persian ambassadors. The emperor, impressed by their bearing, told them he would not take their lives. The Spartans had broken the laws which all men held in common, and he was not disposed to commit the same crime. "Besides," he added, "if I kill you, I would be freeing the Spartans from the burden of their guilt."

Herodotus admired the nobility and generosity of the Persians, but he had no illusions about their tyranny. As he depicts them, they were worthy opponents of the Greeks. In many ways they were more civilized, more refined, and more artistic. They were even more moral; and Herodotus noted as especially remarkable their hatred of telling lies and the absence of any statues or idols in their temples: they worshiped from the hilltops. Yet they were cruel, vindictive, and absolutely merciless in war, and so powerful that no one except the Scythian tribesmen had yet effectively opposed them, and even the tribesmen had not met them in pitched battle.

By the late summer of 490 the Persians were ready for their long-promised occupation of Greece to punish the Athenians for supporting the Ionian revolt. A fleet of 600 galleys was assembled off the island of Samos, its first task being to dominate and crush the islands of the Cyclades. A landing was made on the island of Naxos, where the population fled to the hills as soon as the Persian fleet came in sight. The Persians destroyed the temples and burned the city. It was a foretaste of what was to come.

Instead of sailing straight for Athens, the Persians sailed up the channel between Attica and Euboea and invested the important city of Eretria, in alliance with Athens. The Eretrians fought with desperate courage for six days before the city was betrayed to the enemy; the entire population was expelled and sent into captivity near the Persian capital of Susa. The Athenians realized that what had happened to the people of Eretria could equally well happen to them, and an army, 9,000 strong, was hurriedly dispatched to prevent a Persian landing on the coast of Attica. A runner, sent to Sparta to demand help, learned that help would be forthcoming after the full moon. When at last the Spartans arrived on the battlefield, it was too late.

The banished Hippias accompanied the Persian forces as an adviser. He had spies in Athens, and the promise of Persian assistance in setting up a government. The Athenians, however, were in no mood for resuming a tyranny. The small army was nominally under the command of the *polemarch* Callimachus, who included Miltiades among his staff. Miltiades had every reason to fight against the Persians and to destroy any hopes that Hippias might have of returning to power. His father had been murdered at the orders of Hippias, and after accompanying the Persian expedition against the Scythians as a volunteer, he had deliberately burned the bridges over the Danube to cut off the retreat of Darius. While Callimachus wavered, uncertain whether to give battle to the Persians who were landing on the plain of Marathon, Miltiades insisted that they should be fought and pushed back into the sea. The Greeks were on the hills overlooking a crescent-shaped plain bounded by marshes and swamps fed by underground springs. It was necessary to fight the Persians while they were still hemmed in by the marshes. Athens was only a day's march away.

The Athenian force was pathetically small and ill-equipped: there were no cavalry, no bowmen, no baggage trains. A thousand men from Plataea came to join them, but they were still hopelessly outnumbered by the enemy encamped on the shore. Four or five days passed. The Persians knew they could not advance on Athens until they had dealt with the Greeks in the hills, but they were in no hurry. They were waiting for news of an uprising in Athens. Strategical command of the Greek army was held by the ten tribal *strategoi* in rotation, and all offered to surrender their commands to Miltiades, who had considerably more experience of Persians than anyone else. He refused their offers, waited patiently for the day when it became his turn to command, and then led the attack. The Greeks advanced at the run, forming a long wavering line across the plain. "All along the line," says Herodotus, "they grappled with the Persians, and fought in a way not to be forgotten. They were the first Greeks, as far as I know, to charge at a run, and the first who dared to look without flinching at the Persian dress and the men who wore it. Until this time no Greek could hear the word Persian without terror."

The Greek line broke in the center, but the wings held firm. The Greek center was weak, being only four men deep, while the wings were eight men deep; it is therefore a reasonable assumption that the Greek strategy was to envelop the Persians by two simultaneous flanking movements while deliberately sacrificing the center. While the Persians were busily following the remnants of the center, now hurrying toward the hills, the Greek flanks drew in for the kill. There was a massive slaughter, for at close quarters the Greeks, heavily armored, had advantages over the lightly armored Persians, whose cavalry proved ineffective on the marshy ground and whose archers had little training for fighting at close quarters. The Greeks claimed

6,400 Persians killed for a loss of 192 of their own men.

The Persian fleet sailed toward Athens, but the expected news of an uprising failed to come, and the attack was called off, perhaps because the Spartan army, 2,000 strong, was already drawing close to the city.

Marathon made the Greeks drunk with victory. They had driven an overwhelmingly superior force into the sea and the marshes, and emerged almost unscathed. But no one had any illusions that this was a final victory.

Darius, the Persian emperor, died five years later, and the task of subjugating the Greeks was left to his son Xerxes, who proceeded to accumulate an army so vast that no serious opposition could be expected. "What nation of Asia did not Xerxes lead against Hellas?" asks Herodotus, and he proceeds to enumerate some forty-six nations. The entire Persian navy—Phoenician, Egyptian, and Ionian Greek— was to be thrown into the adventure. Herodotus claimed that the Persian forces altogether numbered 2,641,610 men, and although this figure has been questioned, and by some authorities pared down to a more manageable fraction, there is no doubt that the Persians assembled troops from all over their far-flung empire. To avenge the disaster at Marathon nothing less than the complete subjection of Greece was demanded.

By the winter of 481 all preparations for the invasion were completed. Xerxes established his headquarters at Sardis and sent heralds to all the Greek states except Athens and Sparta, demanding earth and water—the symbols of subjection. In the spring the enormous army set out for Abydos where 1,207 warships and 3,000 transports were assembled. Two bridges made of ships anchored stem to stern and held together by huge cables had been thrown across the Hellespont; for seven days and seven nights the army crossed over, and began the long march down the coast of Greece.

Against a land attack the Greeks had three lines of defense. The first was in the Vale of Tempe below Mount Olympus, where a narrow pass opens into Thessaly. The second was at Thermopylae, where the mountains shut off northern from central Greece, leaving another narrow pass only a few feet wide. The third was the Isthmus of Corinth, where the Spartans were strengthening the defensive wall which had probably stood there since Mycenaean times.

A small token force was sent to the Vale of Tempe; it fled before the Persians came in sight. Thessaly surrendered, and the Thessalian cavalry went over to the Persians. The Spartans and Athenians decided to hold Thermopylae, and accordingly some 8,000 hoplites and light-armed troops under the Spartan King Leonidas were dispatched to the pass, while a Greek fleet numbering some 333 ships sailed up the strait between Euboea and the mainland and anchored off Thermopylae, to prevent the Persians from landing troops in the rear.

The battle lasted for three days. Wave upon wave of Persians was flung at the pass, but they were all beaten off. On the third night a traitor led a Persian column over a mountain path to take the army of Leonidas in the rear. Only 300 of his soldiers were Spartan, belonging to the royal guard. Leonidas knew the position was now untenable. He sent home his allies, and threw his men at the Persian hosts. All perished. Many years later there was erected over their graves a memorial stone with the famous inscription:

"Stranger, tell the Spartans that we lie here obedient to their laws."

But while the Spartans were dying at Thermopylae the Persians were dying at sea. A storm sprang up off Cape Artemisium, and some 400 ships were dashed against the coast or sunk at sea. The Greek ships had ridden out the storm, and retired to Salamis to protect Athens, but not before attacking the Persian fleet and capturing thirty vessels which could now be added to their own. The margin between Persian and Greek ships was narrowing.

Thermopylae was a massacre; the naval battle indecisive; and there was nothing to prevent Xerxes from continuing his march on Athens and later on the isthmus. Themistocles, the Athenian commander, realized that only luck and extraordinary boldness stood between the Greeks and defeat. Of boldness he had plenty. Half-Thracian, with a quick and agile mind, capable of forming precise judgments on matters he knew little or nothing about, he was planning by a single bold stroke to destroy the vast remnant of the Persian fleet.

Earlier an Athenian deputation had consulted the oracle at Delphi with disastrous effect, for the oracle had answered with a categorical prophecy of defeat. According to the oracle, the blood was already dripping from the roof-beams and the shrines of the gods were sweating in the expectation of fire. "Save yourselves," said the oracle, "and bow your heads in grief!"

The deputation emerged from the conference with the oracle like men sentenced to death. An onlooker suggested that oracles sometimes changed their minds, and something might be gained by returning to the shrine as suppliants with olive branches in their hands. They found olive branches, but refused in their desperation to act as suppliants. Instead they warned the oracle they would remain until they received a more favorable reply. Previously the priestess had said the Persians would destroy everything in their path; now she spoke mysteriously of a safety that lay behind wooden walls and of a battle that would take place, apparently near Salamis. "Do not wait for the coming of the horsemen, and the mighty army of foot soldiers," declared the oracle, "but turn your backs and run. At some other time you will meet them face to face. Holy Salamis shall destroy the sons of women, either when Demeter is being scattered or when there is a coming together of the harvest."

What this meant the messengers did not profess to know, though they recognized that it was a less disastrous prophecy than the first. In Athens there was, as always when the oracles were delivered, much debate upon the interpretation, some believing that the "wooden walls" referred to the wooden fence around the Acropolis, others that it referred to the Athenian ships. But if the oracle was pointing to salvation on the sea, why did she speak of Salamis destroying the sons of women? Themistocles argued that everything depended upon the adjective applied to Salamis—"Luckless Salamis" would have boded disaster for the Greeks, but "Holy Salamis" clearly threatened the enemy more than the Athenians and their allies; he advised his countrymen to meet the invader at sea. His advice was that Athens should be abandoned, that the women and children should take refuge in Aegina, Salamis, and Troezen, and that all the able-bodied men should take to the ships. He made the announcement in the Assembly to general agreement: an Athenian who counseled surrender was put to death on the spot, and a crowd of women went to his house and stoned his wife and children to death. The mood of the citizens was harsh, determined, completely resolved. Only by sea could the Persians be stopped, and only by abandoning Athens could they hope to return to their city.

The order for the evacuation of Athens has survived by an odd chance. In 1932 a Greek peasant, Anargyras Titires, living in Troezen, decided that he needed a stone step for his garden and searched among the tombs of an abandoned graveyard. From a child's grave he found a stone which suited his purpose. It remained in his garden until 1958 when a local high school teacher interested in antiquities called upon the villagers to collect all the stones they possessed which bore inscriptions. Titires remembered the inscribed stone and carried it to the local one-room museum, where it was seen in the following year by Professor Michael Jameson of the University of Pennsylvania, who took squeezes and photographs and over the following months made a careful translation:

The Gods.

Resolved by the Council and the Assembly on the motion of Themistocles son of Neocles of the deme Phrearrhoi: To entrust the city to Athena the Mistress of Athens and to all the other gods to defend and to ward the barbarian off the land. The Athenians themselves and the foreigners who live in Athens are to remove their women and children to Troezen. . . . The old men and the movable possessions are to be removed to Salamis. The treasurers and the priestesses are to remain on the Acropolis protecting the possessions of the gods.

All the other Athenians and foreigners of military age are to embark on the 200 ships that lie ready, to defend themselves against the barbarian for the sake of their own freedom and that of the rest of the Greeks along with the Lacedaemonians, the Corinthians, the Aeginetans, and all others who wish to share the danger.

The generals are to appoint, starting tomorrow, 200 trierarchs, one to a ship, from among those who have ancestral land in Athens and legitimate children and who are not older than fifty; to these men the ships are to be assigned by lot. They are also to enlist marines 10 to a ship, from men between the ages of twenty and thirty, and four archers to a ship. They are also to assign the petty officers to the ships at the same time that they allot the trierarchs. The generals are also to write the names of the crews on white tablets, taking the names of the Athenians from the lexiarchic registers, the foreigners from those registered with the polemach. They are to write the names, assigning the whole number to 200 equal divisions and to write above each division the name of the trireme and trierarch and the names of the petty officers so that each division may know on which trireme to embark. When all the divisions have been composed and allotted to the triremes, the Council and the generals are to complete the manning of the 200 ships after sacrificing a placatory offering to Zeus the Almighty and to Athena and to Victory and to Poseidon the Securer.

When the manning of the ships has been completed with one hundred of them, they are to meet the enemy at Artemisium in Euboea, and with the other hundred of them they are to lie off Salamis and the rest of Attica and keep guard over the land.

In order that all Athenians may be united in their defence against the barbarian, those who have been sent into exile for ten years are to go to Salamis and to stay there until the Assembly come to some decision about them, while those who have been deprived of citizen rights . . .[1]

This document, so strangely brought to light after so many centuries, deserves to be quoted in full because it is far more than an order for the evacuation of Athens. It is in fact the order for mobilizing all the human resources of Athens and her allies, and it is remarkable as much for what it includes as for what it leaves out. The exact number of men on each ship, exactly how the muster rolls should be prepared, what gods should receive placatory offerings, and exactly what positions should be taken up, all these are stated in a spare, concise prose which suggests the rigorous mind of Themistocles, of whom Thucydides said that he possessed "a quick natural intelligence which permitted him to be the best judge of those sudden crises which permit of little or no deliberation, and the best prophet of the future, even the remote future." Since no one else had the power or the ability to draw up the document, we can safely conclude that the words were delivered by Themistocles from his general headquarters on the Agora about September 15, 480. Within a week the issue had been decided.

The orders of Themistocles were obeyed. The people of Athens abandoned the city to the enemy. The women, children, and the old who made their way to Troezen were well cared for, according to Plutarch, who tells us that all of them received a daily payment of two

[1] M. H. Jameson, "A Decree of Themistokles from Troizen," in *Hesperia*, XXIX (1960), 198–223. The missing last words are provided in Plutarch's *Themistocles:* "Themistocles proposed a decree by which those who were banished for a time might return to give assistance by word and deed to the Greek cause."

obols, while arrangements were made for the children to continue their schooling; they were also given permission to gather fruit wherever they pleased in the orchards. The statue of Athena from her temple on the Acropolis was removed to a safe hiding place, and Themistocles let it be known that the goddess had left the city and taken flight toward the sea. On the journey to Piraeus it was discovered that her great shield with the ferocious Gorgon head was missing. The Gorgon head represented the indomitable powers of the goddess, and the loss was serious, but Themistocles characteristically put it to good purpose and on the excuse that he had to search Athens for the shield, he sent men into the houses of the rich to ransack them for buried treasure: many hidden valuables were found, and these were used to pay the soldiers and sailors. Meanwhile the priests on the Acropolis reported that the sacred serpents had not eaten the food set out for them, and they too must be presumed to have followed Athena out to sea. In Athens a few old men, unable to travel, were left behind, and it was remembered that the city was given over to donkeys and stray dogs wandering forlornly through the deserted streets. Xerxes was only a few miles away.

With the over-all strategy worked out to the last detail, the task of Themistocles was to see that there was no wavering. It was a dangerous strategy, not calculated to please those with unsteady nerves, and when Xerxes advanced on Athens, broke through its outer defenses, and proceeded to put the city to the flames, massacring all those who remained behind including the priests guarding the temple on the Acropolis, some of the captains of the ships in the bay of Salamis took fright and hoisted their sails, threatening to run to the ports of the Peloponnese, where with luck they would be safe for a little while longer behind the strong defensive wall on the isthmus, or to the Greek colonies in Italy or North Africa.

The admiral in command of the allied fleet was the Spartan Eurybiades. His nerve had failed him, and he was about to give orders for a general withdrawal when Themistocles pointed out that the 200 Athenian ships formed a floating city which could be anchored anywhere, off the coast of Italy or elsewhere, but they had chosen to fight where they had the greatest advantage over the enemy—here in the narrow straits, not in the open sea—and reason demanded that they should pursue the most reasonable course, "for when men abandon reason, the gods do not choose to follow the blind wanderings of men's minds." The commander of the Corinthian fleet pointed out bitterly that a man with no city behind him could have no vote and should not be permitted to take part in the deliberations. Sharp taunts were exchanged. Quietly Themistocles sent off a message to Xerxes through one of his slaves, a Persian captured in the wars, saying that the Greek navy was about to sail out of the bay of Salamis, and suggesting that Persian ships should be brought up to block the exit from the bay. Xerxes fell into the trap, and the news that the Persian fleet would shortly be attempting to bottle up the Greek navy was spread among all the captains of the ships in the bay.

Everything happened exactly as Themistocles intended it to happen. During the night 200 Egyptian ships rounded the island of Salamis and blockaded the western channel of the bay, while the rest of the Persian fleet, composed of ships manned by Persians, Phoenicians, and Ionian Greeks anchored off the eastern approaches. During the night, too, Xerxes pitched his camp on a site overlooking the bay below Mount Aegaleos, and there, sitting on a gold chair with a gold umbrella over his head, he remained through the greater part of the next day.

When morning came most of the Greeks ships were anchored behind the long headland called Cynosura which points across the bay, and were therefore hidden from the Persian fleet. Soon the entire Persian fleet wheeled toward the outlets of the straits like sledge hammers hoping to crush the Greeks between them. In those crowded narrows there was no room for technical skill. The Greek ships, low in the water, were more maneuverable than the heavy Persian galleys with their high poops and their innumerable banks of oars. Too late the Persians realized they were caught in a trap. They could not move out of the straits; they could only sail frantically from one side to the other. The fast, light Greek ships swarmed round them like a cloud of hornets. The Persian ships, colliding with one another, stung to fury by the accuracy of the Aeginetan archers, and by the Athenian skill in slicing off banks of oars by driving through them at full speed with the bronze beak acting as an ax, fell into inextricable confusion. Twelve hundred Persian triremes were jammed together in a narrow space, offering perfect targets for the Greeks, who surrendered to an orgy of slaughter. The poet Aeschylus, who fought in the battle, described it a few years later in his play *The Persians:*

The sea vanished
Under a clogged carpet of shipwrecks, limbs, torsos,
No sea, and the beaches were cluttered with the dead,
And the rocks in the bay were cluttered,
The Asian ships whirling about in an insane rout,
While with snapped oars, balks of timber from wreckage,
The Greeks stoved and hammered and slew, as though the enemy
Were no more than mackerel swept up in a net, or any kind of fish.
Weeping and moaning, and also triumphant songs,
Hovered over the sea until nightfall.

That night the remnants of the Persian fleet withdrew, too mauled to continue the fight, though the Greeks feared they would regroup and attack a second or a third time, for even the remnants of the fleet heavily outnumbered the allies. The Persians had lost 200 ships, the Greeks lost 40, and no one was able to count the number of the Persian dead. The victory was complete, and for many days afterward Persian sailors were cast up on the shores of Salamis.

Themistocles, quietly proud of his accomplishment, declared that the war could be ended immediately by sending a small flotilla to the Hellespont to cut off the Persian line of supply. The advice was sound, but the allies were in no mood for further adventures: they wanted time to lick their small wounds. There were celebrations in Sparta, with Themistocles receiving the crown of olives for his wisdom in ordering the campaign, and Eurybiades receiving the palms for valor. Themistocles was also given a superb chariot, and 300 youths accompanied him to the frontier when he returned to Athens, which he immediately rebuilt in spite of a general agreement among the allies that all the cities sacked by the Persians should be left untouched as a memorial to the tyranny of the enemy.

The battle of Salamis was a crushing blow to the pride of Xerxes, who by assuming direct command of the fleet and ordering the action in the narrow straits, was alone responsible for the debacle. By maintaining a blockade, even a blockade lasting only a few days, he could have starved out the Greek ships and brought about so many dissensions among their captains that any concerted action by them would have been impossible. He had acted in hot blood, quickly and impulsively. Themistocles had acted throughout with logic and incomparable coolness. The Athenians rewarded him by removing him from power.

Too crippled to renew the fight, the Persian fleet withdrew to Asia, while the greater part of the army made the long journey along the coastal plains to the Hellespont, still in Persian hands, though Themistocles thundered that there was nothing to prevent the capture of the narrow straits between Europe and Asia, and all through the winter he kept insisting that a Greek fleet should sail north and wreak damage on the enemy. In Athens there was as yet no rejoicing. The best of the Persian soldiers, comprising the Immortals of the imperial guard together with picked contingents of Medes, Sacae, and Bactrians were now bivouacked in Thessaly under the command of Mardonius, the brother-in-law of Xerxes. Having failed to conquer Greece by an overwhelming army trained in the tactics of a steam roller, he had decided that the second act of the drama should be played by an élite corps of highly trained soldiers of proved loyalty. Most of the Ionian Greeks, Egyptians, and Phoenicians left Greece. Now for the first time it became possible for Persians and Greeks to meet head on.

With Themistocles no longer in command in Athens, Mardonius decided to win the war by intrigue, calculating rightly that Aristides would prefer an accommodation with Persia to an enforced alliance with Sparta. In the early summer of 479 he sent Alexander, King of Macedonia, to the Athenians with an offer of a free pardon for the crimes they had committed in the past and an alliance with Persia on equal terms. The Athenians rejected the offer, but not before the Spartans took alarm at the calculated attempt to isolate them. They offered an alliance with Athens on equal terms and offered to replenish the Athenian granaries and in other ways make good the damage done by Persian arms. The intrigues failed, and Mardonius saw himself compelled to fight to the bitter end. Only one advantage remained to him: he could choose his own battleground.

All through the summer the Athenians and Spartans sparred among themselves, nervously debating the course they would pursue, each distrustful of the other, but circumstances demanded that they should present a united front to the enemy. There was a continual exchange of envoys. Tempers flared. Almost to the last moment their habits of intrigue took precedence over the need for unity. At last, in July, Pausanias, regent of Sparta, passed over to Eleusis with a field army of 5,000 Spartan hoplites and 35,000 armed helots to join the 8,000 Athenian hoplites under Aristides. For some reason the Greeks lacked cavalry, with the result that they suffered incessant cavalry raids from the enemy and many of their supply trains were captured. They were in a desperate plight; food was scarce; the wells and fountains on their path were choked with rubble, and they suffered from thirst; everything pointed to a Persian victory. If they could have chosen their own battleground, they might hope to destroy a large part of the Persian army, but they were in no position to make any demands on the enemy, who had pitched camp at Plataea on the Boeotian Plain. There they remained behind their stockades. The Greeks brought up reinforcements until they amounted altogether to about 100,000 men, and they pitched camp on the plain in sight of the enemy, and they too built up stockades. The two armies watched each other warily. According to Herodotus, they remained in this strange watching posture for eight days before they finally came to grips with one another.

At last on the eighth day the Persians made a sortie into one of the passes of Cithaeron and destroyed a Greek provision train amounting to 500 pack animals; all the animals and the men were destroyed. The raid showed only that the Greek position was untenable because they could no longer protect their lines of supply and because all their escape routes through the Cithaeron passes could easily be cut off. What Mardonius did not know was that the Greeks had no intention of retreating and no longer depended on their supplies. They realized only too well that they would stand or fall at Plataea, on this battleground of the enemy's choosing.

For two days there were skirmishes as each side attempted to probe the defenses of the other. The Greek archers were heavily outnumbered, and were driven back. Provisions were running low, the water supply was short, and there was always the danger of an encircling movement by Persian cavalry. Accordingly, the Greeks decided to withdraw during the night until they had their backs to the wall of Mount Cithaeron. In this way they would prevent any possibility of an encircling movement by the enemy, and with any reasonable luck they might be able to retain their escape routes through the passes. The withdrawal, however, was carried out haphazardly, while ferocious arguments broke out between the leaders, and when morning came the Spartans and the Athenians were widely separated, while a third line composed of recruits from some twenty Greek cities was wandering around the ruins of the ancient city of Plataea. The Greeks seemed to have no co-ordinated plan and to be inviting disaster.

To make matters worse the Spartans had been offering sacrifices and examining the auguries, and it was evident that the gods regarded the outcome of the battle unfavorably. With three separated armies among the foothills of Mount Cithaeron, the Greeks were in no position to put up a determined fight, and it must have seemed to the Persians an easy matter to pick off these armies one by one. Mardonius therefore sent the bulk of the Persian army against the Spartans, with his cavalry in the van and the bowmen coming up behind. Riding a white horse, he fought with the Immortals. The Spartans were on high ground with the mountains behind them, and stood firm, calling upon the Athenians for support. Happily or unhappily the Athenians were unable to move, for the full force of the Persian right wing was marching on them. The Spartans therefore had no recourse except to remain in their untenable position until the Persians either drew back or massacred them to the last man.

Once more the Persians made the mistake of underestimating Greek determination. "The barbarians," wrote Herodotus, "were able to take hold of the Greek spears and break them off, for in boldness and warlike spirit they were in no way inferior to the Greeks." But except for the Immortals most of the enemy consisted of inexperienced and untrained troops, and boldness in this strange battle was no substitute for Spartan discipline. The waves of Persians hurled themselves against the Spartans and were thrown back. An attack by Mardonius also was thrown back, and in this engagement Mardonius was killed. The loss of the general had the effect of paralyzing the Persian will to fight, and soon the Persians, still vastly outnumbering the Greeks, were fleeing demoralized in the direction of Thebes. A single Spartan, whose name was Aeimnestus, had by killing Mardonius altered the course of the battle, and in so doing decisively affected the history of Europe.

With the Persians in Thebes, Pausanias seems to have believed that it was only a matter of a few days before they could be reduced by assault. The Spartans, however, had little experience and less skill at assaulting fortresses, and the task was left to the Athenians, who had no share in the victory on the battlefield. They scaled the walls and massacred the defenders at their leisure. With that massacre, which

Aeschylus likened to an offering of a bloody cake on the altar of a god, Persian power on the Greek mainland came to an end.

About the same time that Pausanias was organizing his forces on the foothills of Mount Cithaeron the Persian fleet was lying at anchor off the island of Samos. Here a small Greek fleet found them, and the Persians, fearing a revolt by the Samians, withdrew to Cape Mycale on the Asiatic mainland, where they beached their ships and built a stockade of stones and tree trunks surrounded by a deep trench. The Greeks fought their way into the stockade, killed all the native Persians they could find, and set fire to the stockade and the ships. Once more the Greeks won a complete victory over the Persians. According to tradition, the victory of Mycale took place on the evening of the same day which saw the victory at Plataea, and in some mysterious fashion news of the Persian rout on the mainland gave strength to the men fighting in the burning stockade. The date is believed to have been August 27, 479.

Mycale was the final blow, from which the Persians never recovered. Henceforward power passed to the Greeks, who believed that the gods who had fought for them at Salamis, Plataea, and Mycale would continue to fight at their side. In celebration of their victories they endowed the Temple of Apollo at Delphi with one tenth of the treasure captured from the Persians. Among the offerings to Apollo was a gold tripod on a pillar of three brazen serpents. The serpent pillar, bearing the names of the thirty-one Greek states which took part in the campaign, was later removed by the Emperor Constantine to the Hippodrome of Constantinople, where it remains to this day.

From Delphi the oracle announced that the victory was owed to Zeus, and accordingly an altar was erected to him under the name of the Zeus of Freedom. It was decreed that in Plataea the games of Eleutheria, or Freedom, should be celebrated every fifth year, while the Plataeans themselves offered to perform an annual sacrifice on the anniversary of the battle, with the sacrifice of a black bull and libations of wine and milk to the army of Greek dead. For at least five hundred years these sacrifices were continued with the same toast spoken gravely by the chief magistrate of the town: "I drink to those who lost their lives for the freedom of Hellas."

Freedom was in the air, so palpable a thing that men believed it could be touched and caressed, and they sang songs to it as to the gods. Freedom made them drunk with their new-found powers. This sudden exaltation swept across the Greek mainland and fired the imaginations of the Ionians. There could be no turning back to the days of tyranny: the armed people demanded a proper share in government and once more insisted on a democracy, with the archons chosen from the whole body of Athenians. But it is well to remember that the flowering of the Golden Age turned on a single event. One man, one moment, changed the course of history, and we may well wonder what might have happened if the Spartan Aeimnestus had not crushed the skull of Mardonius with a stone.

15 ≪ THE TRAGIC TRIUMPH

W E MAY never know where the Greeks came from, or what roads they traveled on their long journey from Asia, or what destiny was ordained for them, but in almost the first words of the first tragedy known to have been composed on European soil we have a hint of both the roads they traveled and the destiny in store for them. "We are fugitives fled from the divine land bordering on Syria," announces the chorus of *The Suppliant Maidens*. It is a theme which will continually be repeated in the long aftermath of the Persian Wars. Aeschylus, the great granite figure who stands at the beginning of all our drama, evidently felt deeply on the subject of exile. There is a sense in which all his dramas are variations on the same theme: the tragedy of man living in exile from the gods, the angel who has fallen from heaven and bitterly remembers his former glory. In the foreground the heroes struggle, while far away in the distance we see very faintly the colors of the lost paradise.

This sense of exile, the brooding knowledge of former glory, haunts his characters almost to the exclusion of any other perturbations. From the moment when the chorus of the Danaïds enters the stage with a frightened prayer to Zeus to afford them the protection due to defenseless strangers, we enter a world where exile is the customary condition of the human creature. The weapons of exiles are few. They may, like the Danaïds, threaten to kill themselves and so bring evil down upon the city where they have taken refuge and where they are unwanted. They may revile the gods in the hope that the gods will see the error of their ways and relent and return them to their proper homes. They may throw themselves on the mercy of the gods or, like Prometheus, they may engage in unscrupulous bargaining. The weapons of exiles are cunning, intimidation, and terror. They are, as it happens, the same weapons which are used by the gods.

Those somber plays of Aeschylus have a curiously modern air, and Aeschylus himself seems to have possessed a curiously modern temper. He was, as Milton said of Spenser, "a sage and serious poet," determined to get to the heart of things, to batter his way to ultimate truth. Longinus, who praised him for the audacity of his imagination and the heroic grandeur of his ideas, rebuked him for writing verses which were frequently rough, unpolished and unrefined, but it was that very roughness which permitted him to take Heaven by storm. Only a man who had Prometheus in him could have written *Prometheus Bound*, and only a man who had known exile in his heart and nerves could have written *The Suppliant Maidens*. He must have been a man of demoniac energy, for the energy pours out of his rock-hewn verses, and it is not surprising that later generations of Athenians edited his plays, smoothing out the roughnesses to make them more agreeable in much the same way as Dryden smoothed out the roughnesses of Shakespeare. But that roughness, the hard-packed metallic hammer blows, gave his poetry a resonance and power unequaled by any Greek poet who came after him.

Pausanias tells a pleasant story of Aeschylus' early vocation for poetic drama. "When he was a boy he was set to watch grapes in the country and fell asleep. In his slumber Dionysus appeared to him, and ordered him to apply himself to tragedy. At daybreak he made the attempt, and succeeded very easily." It was the general opinion of antiquity that he was a man possessed, drunk with poetic vision, drawing strength out of his unconsciousness. Sophocles said of him: "He did what had to be done, but he did it unconsciously," and Aristophanes put in the mouth of Euripides the summary judgment that there was little of Aphrodite in him, and both statements have the ring of truth. Several writers report that he wrote in a state of drunkenness, depicting him as a perennial toper: but it is more likely that he was drunk with divine frenzy than with wine.

He belonged to the generation which grew up before the Persian Wars. His father, Euphorion, was a member of the old nobility. Born about 525, he was already thirty-five when he fought at the battle of Marathon, and he went on to fight at Artemisium, Salamis, and Plataea. According to Herodotus, his brother Cynegirus was one of the heroes of the battle, losing his hand from a blow with an ax when trying to climb up the stern of a Persian ship. At Marathon Aeschylus and his two brothers performed so brilliantly that Athens ordered a painting to commemorate their feats. He enjoyed his military career, and when he died at Gela in Sicily, the inscription on his tomb made no mention of his dramas:

> Aeschylus, son of Euphorion, the Athenian,
> Lies under this tomb in wheat-bearing Gela.
> The grove at Marathon speaks of his proved valor,
> The long-haired Persians knew it all too well.

Though only seven of his plays out of the ninety he has known to have written have survived, we know him nearly as well as we know Euripides, who left nearly three times as many. That abrupt, hard-bitten, tormented man dominates the Greek stage, and sometimes his harsh voice can be heard echoing in the plays of other dramatists. He left his stamp on the theater. It was not only that he was the great innovator, but his innovations were such as to endow drama with a continuing vitality. He was the first to represent the Furies with snakes in their hair—at the sight boys fainted and women miscarried—but this was the least of his inventions. He was the first dramatist to take full charge of the production of his plays, even to the extent of devising the choreography, designing the costumes and the masks, and inventing the buskins which gave the characters the stature to dominate the audience. Before his time the actors died on stage: Aeschylus deliberately arranged that they should die off stage, thereby giving their deaths an imaginative dimension far more terrible. But all these innovations pale before his supreme achievement: dialogue. Before Aeschylus there was only one actor who delivered himself of soliloquies, while the chorus recounted the development of the drama. By introducing the second actor and curtailing the functions of the chorus, he led the way to the stage as we know it today with the actors continually debating with each other and working out their fate in dramatic confrontations.

These innovations were as much the product of the times as of the feverish imagination of the poet. Previously there had been exposition, the slow unrolling of a panoramic legend, with the dramatist playing a role hardly distinguishable from that of a storyteller.

With the introduction of the second actor the story is divorced from the storyteller and there is a violent leap into a world of actuality, of clashing wills and conflicting purposes. For the first time the hero springs forth fully armed against his adversary.

We do not know exactly when the second actor emerged, but it must have been about the same time as the first Persian invasion of Greece. It was the time when sculpture too was changing its form, no longer concerned with static representation but with light and shade, with movement, with the sense of continuing action, with portraits which seem to have the breath of life in them. Action had become the watchword. The contemplative hero, half embedded in rock, smiling his archaic smile, steps out freely to take possession of his inheritance. It was a world where ancient tyrannies were crumbling before the advance of the awakened and aroused populace. In such a world there was no place for the tyranny of the storyteller's art. What was needed was the freedom to debate, the freedom to grapple with the adversary. So for the first time we confront the hero in command of his own destiny.

The singular achievement of Aeschylus was that he invented the individual, and he did this very simply by giving him an accomplice in misfortune. Sophocles was to introduce the third actor, but the third was little more than a shadow of the second. Significantly Sophocles was also credited with the invention of white buskins which somehow conveyed the proper respect due to heroic nobility. It was not perhaps a very useful invention.

The discoveries and inventions of Aeschylus might, as Philostratus remarked in his *Life of Apollonius of Tyana*, have been suggested by an inferior dramatist. What was remarkable was not so much that the discoveries were made, but that there existed one man with sufficient authority and practical experience to put them into operation and to establish a tradition. He was also quite evidently a man of forceful temperament who would insist on his orders being carried out to the letter, and being a poet with an immense range of imagery and emotional power he was able to shape his theater according to his desires and produce plays which could bear the weight of his poetic ideas.

His earliest drama is probably *The Suppliant Maidens*, which must have been written before the Persian invasion, since it deals sympathetically with Argos, which refused to come to the help of the

Athenians and was therefore regarded by them with little sympathy in the following years. To the seacoast of Argos come the fifty daughters of Danaüs, fleeing from Egypt to escape marriage with their cousins, the fifty sons of Aegyptus, twin brother to Danaüs. Like a rainbow-colored wave thrown up on the shore, they perform their stately dances of supplication on the stage, demanding the hereditary right of asylum. The King of Argos listens attentively to their pleas, but knows that if he submits to their demands he will be compelled to fight the Egyptians. He can do nothing but wait on events, while the dancers whirl round him. At last the herald of the Egyptians arrives, threatening war. The king of Argos defies the Egyptians and allows the suppliant maidens to live within the city walls.

That is all, but it is more than enough to permit Aeschylus to demonstrate his powers. We may not believe that Danaüs had fifty daughters or that they made the dangerous journey across the seas, but our disbelief would be unintelligible to the Greeks, for the legend was well known. The play dealt with high moral principles involving the sanctity of asylum, unnatural marriage, and the just powers of a king: implicit in the argument was the relationship between the divine laws and the civic virtues. The maidens formed the chorus and dominated the stage. These maidens were dressed in bright barbaric garments, as the king observed when he first set eyes on them in fear and trepidation, hoping against hope that the mirage would vanish at the touch of his wand. But the mirage refused to vanish: as suppliants they had the legal right to stay, but he is only too well aware that their staying must inevitably lead to tragedy. *The Suppliant Maidens* was the opening play of a trilogy: the two remaining plays were *The Egyptians* and *The Daughters of Danaüs*, of which only fragments survive. But from these fragments and from other sources we learn that the maidens were eventually compelled to marry their suitors, and on the wedding night each maiden took a long pin to bed with her. Only Hypermnestra refused to kill her husband, being moved to spare him because Aphrodite had blessed their love for one another. So much we learn from *Prometheus Bound*, and there is a surviving fragment of *The Daughters of Danaüs* which would seem to be her blessing:

> *Love from the holy heavens must wound the earth,*
> *While earth demands of heaven its many bridals,*

And from the heavenly bridegroom showers descend
Upon the bride, who bringeth forth for men
The wheat of Demeter and all the flocks and herds.
Even the forest flowers are touched by dewy bridals.
Over all these things am I acknowledged Queen.

But while Aphrodite claims possession of Hypermnestra, other gods and other laws will claim possession of the murderous maidens, judging them and consigning them to Hades. All through this sunlit play, like thunder heard in clear skies, there is the brooding presence of Zeus, lord of the universe and stern arbiter of human destinies.

Some twenty years after writing *The Suppliant Maidens*, Aeschylus wrote *The Persians*. Two Persian invasions had been thrown back, and the archaic mood has been exchanged for a new vigor, a new sense of purpose. Themistocles had been banished, Cimon was laying the foundations for the Athenian empire by his naval operations in Ionia, and the young Pericles was beginning to be known as the defender of a more liberal policy than Cimon would ever tolerate. Aeschylus, writing a play to explain God's purpose in giving victory to the Greeks, was inevitably caught up in the politics of the time. He invited Pericles to act as *choregos*, or chorus master, thus making clear where his sympathies lay. And just as in *The Suppliant Maidens* he filled the stage with the wild and colorful dresses of the suppliants, so now he filled it with the jewel-encrusted robes of Persian courtiers in the great palace at Susa as they wait for news from Xerxes, the king whose absolute power could once bend all mankind to its will.

Xerxes, though scarcely visible, dominates the play. His power, his majestic presence, his armies, his errors and defeats—these are the subject matter of the play. The action throughout is seen through Persian eyes, and Aeschylus performs the considerable feat of describing the invasion of Greece without mentioning a single Greek name. Such an omission could only be deliberate. Quite clearly the aim was not to boast of a great victory but to understand the workings of the divine economy: for what crimes, what sins against the spirit, had the gods punished the Persian hosts? Out of what beginnings came that vast catastrophe?

There is almost no action in the sense that the modern stage presents action. Dreams, auguries, presentiments and premonitions, the ghost of a dead king, the voices of messengers: out of these Aeschylus constructs a play which seems to go unerringly to the heart of the mystery. There is no heroic conflict: only the long waiting, the sense of doom, of hope betrayed and human lives uselessly squandered, as the Persian elders are gradually confronted with the knowledge of an empire in ruins. But while there is almost no outward action, the inner turmoil rages unceasingly. It is a play of fierce ambitions and tumultuous defeats, and is all the more effective for being concentrated among a small group of people at the Persian court. Dominating them all is Queen Mother Atossa, whose courage recoils before a nightmarish vision of the coming disaster. She relates her dream to the elders:

> *Then saw I two women gloriously arrayed,*
> *One wearing Persian raiment, the other Dorian.*
> *They stood before my eyes. O, they moved*
> *In mortal majesty beyond all knowing,*
> *Like sisters of a perfect beauty, glowing*
> *With supernatural fire; and they did dwell*
> *In lands apart, one on the barbaric coasts,*
> *The other in Hellas. Then it seemed*
> *Dissension sprang among them, and my son*
> *Striving to restrain them, yoked them both*
> *And reined their harnessed necks upon a chariot.*
> *Exulting in her rich array, the Persian gave*
> *Obedience to the reins, and she smiled proudly.*
> *The other with indignant fury spurned*
> *The curb. She rent the harness with her hands*
> *And tore the yoke to pieces . . .*

The violent rending of the chariot of Xerxes becomes the theme of the play, and the classic situation is already stated with the confrontation of those two superb sculptural figures. Implicit in the argument is that Greek simplicity and rigor have overcome Persian luxury and ostentation. These are the essential elements of victory, but they do not tell the whole story. Simplicity and rigor alone would prove ineffective unless some crime had been committed against the gods. In despair the queen mother returns to the past and to her husband's ghost for an answer. Characteristically Aeschylus paints her journey to the tomb in sunlit colors:

> *Without my former splendor, without my chariot,*
> *I walk from the palace now, bearing my gifts,*

Peace offerings for the father of my child
Such as will give some comfort to the dead.
I bring white milk from an unblemished cow,
Milk that is sweet to drink, and from the shining
Bees I bring bright honey torn from flowers,
And holy water from the virgin springs,
And living juices from an ungrafted vine,
Old Mother of the fields, and from the gray-green olive trees
That wear their clouds of ever-youthful leaves
Sweet oil to pour on tombs: and wreaths of flowers,
Those children of the teeming countryside . . .

If Atossa hoped to find some blessing at the tomb, she was soon to learn that even the ghost of a king—for Darius rose out of the tomb—could bring no comfort. Darius has known the curse that lay upon the Persians. "When men are bent on ruin, God helps them to fall." By a stroke of genius, Aeschylus makes Darius the judge who examines the causes of the Persian defeat. From him she learns the name of the crime, which was *hubris*, the overweening pride leading inevitably to destruction. Xerxes had committed many follies, but the most disastrous was the building of the bridge over the Bosporus to carry his armies from Asia into Europe. The gods had appointed that there should be a barrier between the two continents, and Xerxes had plunged blindly into impiety. By building the bridge he had in effect polluted the holy waters. Other crimes, too, were committed. He had burned down the temples of the Greeks, forgetting that all temples are holy, even those of his enemies. He had been too daring, too impetuous. After listing his son's crimes and urging the elders to enjoy the little time they have left on earth, Darius vanishes, and soon Xerxes himself appears on the stage. The ghost wore the majestic garments of a Persian king. Xerxes appears in rags, so weighed down by grief that he can do little more than murmur the names of his lost generals. So the play ends in lamentation with a dazed king wandering aimlessly across the stage.

Scholars have been puzzled by the appearance of the pathetic king trailing his rags at the end of the play, imagining that it takes from the greatness of the theme, but in fact no other ending was possible. Seen on a spring day in 472, when the memory of Salamis was still fresh, and the Acropolis was still in ruins, that sudden and long-awaited appearance had in it something of a *theoria*, a visitation by a god. Not that Xerxes was godlike, but that his humbling by the gods had given him a strange and terrible stature. Those rags are like the empty eyes of Oedipus. Almost there was no need for him to speak: it was enough to see him in his agony. The queen mother was given nobility and poetry, Darius appeared as a judge robed in majesty, Xerxes was a hero destroyed by his crimes. As Aeschylus has written it, there can be no jubilation when he comes on the stage, only the silence of a molten horror, a breathless pause of wonder.

Among all the characters produced by ancient drama, there is nothing to equal the towering figure of Prometheus as he lies shackled to a rock in the northern wastes of Scythia, with an iron stake driven through his chest, the blood pouring out of him. It is the first portrait of a god in agony, silent and brooding in some lost region of the earth. He, too, had committed the sin of pride, but on a scale so immeasurably greater than Xerxes' that they seem to be different sins. He had stolen fire from Heaven and given it into the hands of men, and for this defiance of a divine law he is punished by Zeus with a superb punishment. Prometheus is perfectly aware that he has been chosen for a punishment which exceeds that received by any other gods, as his crime exceeds any crime committed by them. He boasts of his crime, while addressing the universe:

> *O dazzling heavens, O ye swift-feathered winds,*
> *O springs of rivers, and the waves'*
> *Multitudinous laughter, O Mother Earth,*
> *O Thou all-seeing Sun, to Thee I pray.*
> *Behold a god who suffers at the hands of gods!*

> *Behold I am racked with torment:*
> *Ten thousand years shall pass*
> *Of timeless agony*
> *In this imprisonment*
> *Where the Prince of the Blessed has set me.*
> *I groan for my present sorrow,*
> *I groan for the sorrow to come.*
> *Who knows the end of woe?*

> *What words are these I say?*
> *I have known all before:*

No agony comes unknown.
I must accept my fate
As lightly as I may,
Knowing that as men say
None can ever claim
To break Necessity.
Shall I be silent now?
Such is beyond my power:
But why should I not speak?
I suffer this for men,
My feet and hands are bound.
I found the fennel stalk
With its secret heart of fire,
Which when revealed became
Teacher of craft to men,
Of marvelous use to all.
This was my only crime
For which I stand accused,
Riven and fettered here,
Spreadeagled under the heavens.

Listen, a murmur comes,
A scent upon the winds
Rising from unseen springs—
From heaven or earth, who knows,
Some curious thing advances
To look upon my sufferings:
What else could summon it?
I, chained and wretched god,
Enemy of Zeus, most hated
Of all who entered into his holy courts—
I loved mankind too well!
What is this I hear?
Whistle of bird-wings near,
Air murmuring with the murmuring wings,
Catching my heart with fear!

That tremendous speech is more than a cry of defiance hurled
at the new gods who dispossessed the Titans, and far more than an

agonized cry. Prometheus is providing a portrait of himself, sketching in the features of his divine humanity, giving weight and purpose to his sufferings, and for the first time introducing a note of music which will be heard throughout the play. The music is strangely lyrical, almost gay. He rejoices in his sufferings, and he is proud of them. There is agony and defiance, but there is also irony in the description of the usurper as "the Prince of the Blessed," and there is gaiety in the prayer to the heavens and the waves' multitudinous laughter. This is a god who talks in the recognizable accents of a man.

The soft whistling sounds he heard came from the daughters of Oceanus, who form the chorus, flocking around him with their brilliantly colored wings. They, too, belong to an older dispensation, for Homer called Oceanus "the father of the gods," and he belongs to a time before Cronus usurped the throne. Oceanus is old with the wisdom of the ages, and like the chorus he sympathizes with the plight of Prometheus, only warning him against the sin of pride. But Prometheus is weary of warnings. "It was not pride that drove me to this fate," he proclaims. Zeus has punished him for one reason only: he gave civilization to men.

> *It was not pride that drove me to this fate,*
> *Nor willfulness that makes me silent here.*
> *Agonized thoughts devour my vitals.*
> *The rebel gods derived their powers from me:*
> *I shall not speak of this now. Other thoughts*
> *Burn within me. Besides, these things are known to you.*
> *I shall speak of the miseries that beset mankind;*
> *Once they were witless and I gave them sense,*
> *I gave them reason and the power of thought.*
> *I say this now for no unruly purpose.*
> *Simply: I gave them gifts.*
> *First, they had eyes, but saw with little purpose.*
> *They had ears, but could not hear with them.*
> *They thought in shapes of dream, and their long lives*
> *Were lived in vast confusion. They did not know*
> *How to make homes of brick facing the sun,*
> *Nor how to work in wood. In sunless caves*
> *They dwelt beneath the earth like swarming ants.*
> *When winter came they had no way of knowing it,*

Nor flowering spring, nor summer full of crops.
Their acts were reckless till I came
To teach them of the stars, their rising and their setting,
A difficult art. Then I taught them numbers, chief of sciences,
And putting letters together—this too I taught them,
Since letters are a help to memory, mother of many arts.
I was the first to harness beasts to the yoke
With trace and saddle, making them men's slaves,
Bearers of many burdens. I harnessed the horse to the chariot,
I made it obey the rein, and be an ornament
To luxury-loving princes. Who else but I
Discovered the flaxen sails that bend the seagoing ships
Over the turbulent waves. Such arts I made for men.
Alas, I have no art to free me of my agony!

The catalogue of Prometheus' gifts to men is not yet over: there remained the occult arts of medicine and prophecy, divination and the mining of copper, iron, silver, and gold—all these Prometheus had recklessly placed within men's grasp. The chorus approves and mourns Prometheus' fate, cursing Zeus for all the harm he has brought upon the world of the gods and men; and when Io enters, a maiden wearing the horns of an ox, driven to madness by a pursuing gadfly, Prometheus rejoices to be in the presence of a mortal, one moreover who is predestined to be the ancestor of his own deliverer. His far-ranging mind soars through time and space as he predicts the journeys and travails of this maiden who, like him, suffers from the vengeance of Zeus. She has refused the god and undertaken a long voyage to escape from him. It is all in vain, for Zeus will catch up with her. She will bear a son, and after many ages pass Heracles will be born from her descendant. Prometheus is more defiant than ever now that he has set eyes on the woman who bears within herself the seeds of his deliverance, for Heracles will be the chosen vehicle to free him from the tyrant's chains. Thirteen generations will have to pass before he achieves his freedom, but he exults as though freedom were close at hand. And then more quietly he tells her about the lonely voyages she must undertake through legendary lands, luxuriating in the recital, for long ago he bade farewell to legends of this kind. He is the god who brought the arts to men: he has cut himself off from those visionary places, yet they still haunt him. He has rolled up the map, but he still murmurs the names of the ancient places:

When you have crossed the stream between two continents,
Turn to the rising sun, to the burned Gorgonian plains,
Crossing by the edge of the fuming seas, by Cisthene,
Where dwell the ancient maids, daughters of Phorcys,
Three swan-shaped hags, with one eye and one tooth between them,
On whom no ray of sun looks down, nor the nightly moon
Sheds any light. Three more winged sisters dwell near,
The snake-haired Gorgons, enemies of humankind—
No mortal ever looked on them and lived.
These are the perils that I guard you from:
But this is not all, for other dangers there are—
Beware the hounds of Zeus whose teeth are sharp.
They are griffins: no one has heard them bark.
Then too the one-eyed Arimaspians
Who ride on horseback and live on the flooded banks
Of the Plutonian river whose waters wash down gold.
Do not go near them. Then go to the remote region
Where live the dark-skinned men, living
Near the fountains of the sun, and there also
You will find a river called Ethiopian.
Follow the river till you reach the cataract,
Where from the Bybline hills there gushes forth
The holy stream of the Nile to quench men's thirst.
The river will lead the way to the Nile delta.
There you will found your distant colony
Which is ordained by fate for you and for your children.

So Prometheus dreams; and as he says himself, he has time on his hands for dreaming. He is in no hurry, for he possesses foresight and surveys the far-distant future as easily as he surveys the distant past. He knows that in the future Zeus will send an eagle to gnaw at his liver and that Heracles, with the permission of Zeus, will set him free by shooting the eagle with his bow, and that the wise old Centaur Chiron will be wounded by a poisoned arrow from the same bow, to go down into an eternal agony in Hades, "taking upon himself the pains of Prometheus" in fulfillment of the prophecy. He knows all this, and recites it as though it were accomplished fact instead of actions destined to take place in a remote and almost unthinkable future. What he does not know is that the trap has already been sprung.

For with the swift coming of Hermes, messenger of the gods and

angel of doom, Prometheus learns that the time of boasting is over.
Like Lear on the blasted heath he cries out to summon the storm of
Heaven:

> *Now let there fall upon me the curling fire*
> *Of lightning; let the air scream with thunder*
> *And fierce convulsion of the savage winds.*
> *Let the earth be pulled up by its roots*
> *In the teeth of the whirlwinds, and the wild seas*
> *Confound the courses of the heavenly stars,*
> *And let me be raised on high and dashed down*
> *Into the black depths of Tartarus—*
> *Let the ineluctable rigors of doom be upon me—*
> *Still, still they cannot kill me!*

But if he cannot be killed, at least he can go down into Hell,
there to live out the punishment which is reserved for great sinners,
and the play ends in fire and brimstone, the rock with the impaled
Prometheus shuddering violently and then collapsing, leaving nothing
behind.

Prometheus Bound was the first part of a trilogy, which included
Prometheus Unbound and *Prometheus the Torch-Bearer*. The opening speech of the second has been preserved in a Latin translation by
Cicero, showing us little more than a subdued Prometheus complaining against his fate. We know that Heracles was one of the leading
characters of *Prometheus Unbound*, but we do not know the precise
working out of the drama, and no synopses survive. *Prometheus the
Torch-Bearer* no doubt recounts the adventures of the god as he descends into the world of men, bringing order and science into their
chaotic lives. Prometheus has preserved men from the vengeance of
Zeus, and his reward is to be regarded as the greatest benefactor of
mankind. All arts, all sciences spring from him, and just as Oceanus
was the father of the gods, so Prometheus became the father of men.

After Prometheus, Agamemnon is the most impressive of the
characters invented by Aeschylus, who followed the existing legends
but so shaped and colored him that he becomes a new creation. He
returns victorious from the Trojan War, only too well aware that
victory has a price which must be paid in suffering. He is haunted by
his own pride, and when Queen Clytemnestra lays a purple carpet for
him, he gazes at it sadly: not that the carpet in itself is dangerous,

but that it represents a triumph for which he has only contempt now that the long wars are over. The queen tells him how she has waited ardently for this reunion. She stands at the foot of the palace steps, gazing up at the conqueror in his chariot, tempting him. Cassandra, the prophetess, sits beside him: she has the gift of warning, and the grief of knowing that her warnings will be unheard. And still Agamemnon gazes at the carpet, which is like the carpet strewn upon the altar of the gods. As a conqueror he has a perfect right to step on it; as a man he knows that he must avoid the temptations of pride:

> O treat me not like a soft and delicate woman,
> Or gazing open-mouthed, give me acclaim,
> As though I were barbarian. This carpet here
> Will draw the envy of wide heaven should I touch it.
> So are the gods worshiped.
> No mortal ever walks on rich embroideries.
> Treat me as a man, with a man's honoring,
> Not as a god. The voice of rumor takes
> These gifts and spreads them wide.
> To be of humble mind is God's best gift.
>
> (*Agamemnon*, 918–929)

Agamemnon is a careful man, determined to act justly, aware that he has reached that pinnacle of existence where the gods can observe him minutely; and therefore he deliberately abases himself by removing his sandals when he steps on the carpet. He could not, even if he wanted to, destroy his victory over Troy. He comes in triumph to his palace, and even as he steps barefoot on the carpet he knows that a terrible fate is in store for him.

The heroes of Aeschylus always have foreknowledge of their doom. They do not know how or when they will die, but they know that "the gray ones" are waiting for them at every turning of the road, and yet even with this knowledge they must go forward, because to go backward is to admit an even greater defeat. "If disaster must come," said Eteocles, "let it be disaster without shame. A man's honor is the only thing that remains to him after death." So Agamemnon steps on the carpet and suffers his punishment, not because he has entered his palace barefoot but because "the wild and bloody lions who swarmed above the towers of Troy" must be punished in a fatal ceremony of expiation in the place most dear to him and by the person

Young Citharoedus singing. Detail from amphora.

Heracles at war with Birds. Detail from amphora.

Women at the Well, between Dionysus and Satyr.
Detail from amphora.

Young nobleman on horseback. Detail from vase.

Young peasant on horseback. Detail from vase.

Women putting away clothes. Attic kylix, by Douris.

Dancers—boy with double flute, girl with castanets.

Horse's head in collar of acanthus.

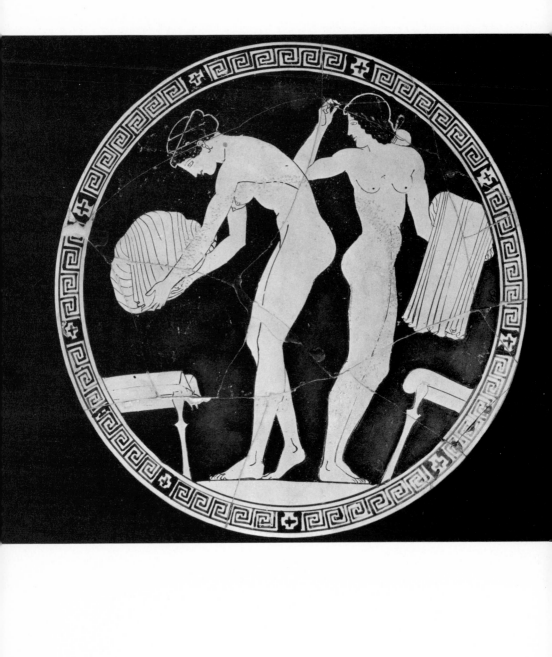

closest to him. To demand less from him would be to defraud the gods of some part of their own glory.

The irony of Agamemnon's fate is underscored throughout the drama, for Aeschylus, like his audience, is perfectly aware that the carpet—the very vivid carpet which remains relentlessly on stage like a stream of blood—is the least important element in the unfolding chronicle of a war between man and his fate. There were many compelling reasons for his death, and many ways in which it could be brought about. He could have tripped over a stone and broken his head; he could have killed himself with his own sword; instead Aeschylus chooses that he should be killed by the carpet.

The beauty of *Agamemnon* lies in the subtle exploration of the hero's death. Never for a moment does Aeschylus lift his eyes away from his main purpose: the weaving of all the strands which go to explain a hero's fate. The divine decisions clash; there is war in Heaven as on earth; there are many powerful forces pulling the hero to his death, and these forces sometimes quarrel among themselves; but in the end the ultimate decision is made known in a manner which is as simple as the truth is complex. Clytemnestra takes the burden of guilt upon herself, though in fact she is scarcely more than the purple carpet in one of its many disguises:

> *I stand here where I struck him. I did it.*
> *I will not deny what I have done. It's over now.*
> *I left no loophole, no escape from death.*
> *I threw around him like a vast fishing net*
> *A fatal wealth of purple, which by my cunning*
> *Caused him to be gathered in my power:*
> *Twice I struck him. Twice yelling in his agony,*
> *His knees buckled under him; and then he fell;*
> *And then I struck again, this time in honor*
> *Of Zeus, the lord of Hell, while he lay prostrate,*
> *Gasping his life away. He spattered me*
> *With a river of his blood—*
> *On me there fell a dark refreshing flood*
> *Of deathly dew, as on the cornfields*
> *The buds burst forth beneath the showers of heaven.*
>
> (*Agamemnon*, 1379–1392)

Clytemnestra, of course, claims to be the sole agent of the murder, but this is to misunderstand the nature of her crime. Not Clytemnestra but the gods have brought about his punishment; and not the gods only. Dark and mysterious forces have assembled in the heavens, while even darker forces have assembled in the heart of Agamemnon. The drama ends with Clytemnestra's observing to her lover that all accounts are now settled, and "the time has come to bring good order to our house." Irony, too, in the hands of Aeschylus becomes one of the dark forces which rule the universe.

The Libation Bearers, the second work of the trilogy, deals with a time ten years later. Orestes and Electra, the children of Agamemnon and Clytemnestra, plot to bring about the downfall of their mother, and they go about it with the quiet, deliberate cunning of people who have been reduced almost to madness by despair and by their horror of the act they must perform. No more than Clytemnestra herself are they the sole agents of their crimes. Out of the skies, the earth, and the underworld come the anarchic promptings of violence:

> *Innumerable are the dread*
> *Dangers the earth breeds;*
> *The land-locked seas enclose*
> *Undreamed-of savage beasts,*
> *While between earth and sky*
> *The fiery torches blaze;*
> *All birds and creeping things,*
> *All, all are in the throes*
> *Of violent winds.*
>
> (*The Libation Bearers*, 585–592)

So sings the chorus, and we are never for a moment left in doubt of the violence of those winds. Terror rides rampant over an oppressive landscape, but the second play of a trilogy can never have the impact of the first. Something is missing. Perhaps it is the purple carpet which mysteriously came to represent by an abstraction of color all the mysterious forces playing on a doomed king. Clytemnestra is no heroine; she says she is a woman who took a lover out of loneliness, and her children despise her, as Clytemnestra herself never despised Agamemnon. The great cry "The dead are slaying them that live" echoes through the play, and when she dies she has been dead so long that she must be accounted one of her own slayers, not at the moment of her physical death—for she is made to slay herself —but at some remote period in the past.

The Eumenides, the concluding drama of the trilogy, takes its euphemistic title from the terrible daemonic beings called "the kindly ones," who are the agents of Zeus' vengeance. They pursue Orestes to avenge his mother's murder, but they are halted as a result of the clash of wills in Heaven, for Apollo protects tyrannicides, while Zeus must punish them. Orestes takes refuge in Athens, where the goddess Athena takes pity on him. When a trial is held, "the kindly ones" thirst for vengeance, while Apollo defends the crime, being himself deeply implicated, for the chorus points to him and openly accuses him. "The kindly ones" threaten to let loose anarchy upon the world unless the criminal is punished. They will banish justice, and destroy all trust between men. They will cast the spells which bring back the ancient nightmares. So they rant dreadfully, until Athena intervenes, stepping down from her high throne into the world of men.

The intervention of Athena is by its very nature lacking in drama. She puts an end to the clashing of wills, and she does this quietly, almost methodically. Her mere presence stills the tempest, as she proclaims the coming of a new dispensation, the new world lit by the radiance of her intelligence. She judges the past and finds it wanting. Those waves of madness and doom which ran like raging lions through the age of the heroes cannot touch her:

> *I bid my people honor and uphold*
> *The state made free of anarchy,*
> *Nor shall the tyrants have their grip upon her.*
> *I say we should not banish terror utterly,*
> *For who, unless he fears, lives righteously?*
> *Let there be just terrors. May you find*
> *Salvation in your citadel, your country's walls,*
> *Such strength as nowhere else is ever found,*
> *Whether in Scythia or in the Peloponnese.*
> *So I establish my court to protect the people,*
> *Grave, quick to anger, incorruptible,*
> *A watching sentinel, guardian of those who sleep.*
>
> (*Eumenides*, 696–706)

With these words Athena inaugurates a new dispensation of time, a new justice, a new man. The tragedy of Agamemnon is resolved into an allegory on the birth of a new civilization. Not the doomed hero but the *polis* becomes the special subject of divinity. And in blessing the *polis* Athena emerges as the enemy of all tyrannies, even the tyranny of mythology. Henceforward the true heroes are the people of Athens.

In this way Aeschylus concluded his long epical tragedy which began when a watchman in the house of Atreus saw the beacon light announcing the home-coming of Agamemnon. The play ends with the vision of the shining city. But Aeschylus knew, as we know, that like the heroes the city is doomed.

THIS IS the setting forth of the researches of Herodotus of Halicarnassus, in the hope of preserving from decay the memory of what men have done, and of preventing the wonderful deeds of the Greeks and the Asiatic people from passing into oblivion; and more especially to show how they came to make war on one another."

In this all-encompassing way Herodotus begins his history of the world, and in fact he offers more than he promises. He was not a historian only. His concern was with the living flesh of the past, the colors and shapes of things, the voices and intonations of people, the way they held themselves, and their most intimate beliefs. His main concern was to tell how the Greeks were able to throw off the yoke of Persia, but in order to do this he must study events which happened long before, and peoples who were so far away from the centers of Greek and Persian power that they might seem to be unaffected by the war. In his eyes all things that happened in the world were related. Some Scythians in central Russia, disputing over hides, might cause a sandstorm in the Sahara. Every piece of the mosaic affected every other piece, and he must know all of them and set them in their proper place in the grand design.

Herodotus is "the father of history," but only in the sense that he towered over his predecessors. He shames his successors by his unfailing generosity and humanity. Gibbon said that Herodotus "sometimes writes for children and sometimes for philosophers." Instead, he wrote for all men, and especially for the crowds that gathered at his public recitations. It was for them that he told so many "cliff-hanging stories" and for them that he added so much local color. The commentators argue about the accuracy of his details, forgetting that the only accuracy worth bothering about is the accuracy of the whole. Herodotus presents us with the whole, telling us everything he knows, cutting through vast segments of time and space, going as far back into legendary ages as any man may decently dare to go, pulling his highly colored villains and heroes out of his sack and displaying them—even the most villainous—for our admiration. His characters stand before us a little larger than life, unlike the characters of Thucydides who sometimes resemble points of force, throwing no shadows. He revels in life. We can almost hear him hooting with joy whenever he discovers a new color among the unending colors of the human spectrum.

We know almost nothing about his life. He was born about 485 in Halicarnassus in the lull between the Persian storms, and according to Suidas, his family belonged to "the better class." When Lygdamis, the tyrant of Halicarnassus, seized power, Herodotus went into exile on the island of Samos, where he began writing his history. Suidas also says that "he drove out the tyrant on his return to Halicarnassus, but later when he found himself in disfavor with the citizens, he became one of the original settlers of Thurii, then being colonized by the Athenians, and there he died and was buried in the market place." That the historian should himself have made history is not surprising, nor is it surprising to learn that he was a failure as a politician.

We do not know when he set out on his travels, and we can be sure of only a few of the countries he traveled in. He evidently knew Samos well, and had a great affection for the island. He certainly visited Egypt, but we have no means of telling how long he spent there or whether he went up the Nile to Assuan. He seems to have known the coast of the Black Sea and to have been in Arabia, and he knew the various kingdoms and principalities of Asia Minor well. He talks at considerable length about Cyrene without ever quite convincing us that he knew the city at first hand. Of India, Persia, and Scythia he speaks as a stranger possessing a rare collection of travelers' tales, and even when he describes the battles fought against the Persians on the Greek mainland he never quite convinces us that he had visited the battlefields. There is nothing in his *History* to prove that he was a great traveler. He may have amassed most of his knowledge by talking with Samian sailors, and by consulting the books in the Athenian libraries. We rarely know where he derived his knowledge. All we know is that he imposed his own vision on the stories he collected and sifted, and that he wrote about the far places of the world with unfailing grace and deceptive ease.

His theme was the greatness of man and the glory of human endeavor, and he was therefore studiously impartial, weighing the Greeks against the barbarians and holding the balance even, believing that there is greatness and accomplishment in all nations under the sun. His method derived from the Homeric epic: he would tell the story in a series of episodes each with its appropriate hero and cast of subsidiary characters, but where Homer saw the downfall of men as due to the intervention of the gods, Herodotus clearly ascribed their downfall to their pride and the errors they were continually making in their search for power.

There are intervals when Herodotus seems to abandon his grand design, and like a magpie he will go running after ill-considered trifles. Long stories are inserted for no better reason than that he enjoyed the telling of them. He has been listening eagerly to some stories told in the market place; he knits them together, breathes his own life into them, and inserts them in a section of the *History* where they will do no harm. His aim was not to produce an account of the Persian Wars in logical and chronological order: the illogical, the absurd, the indefinable must also have their place. The patchwork quilt was sewn together unself-consciously. He tells the story at a leisurely pace, and he likes to pause for refreshment.

The pauses make the book. In those pauses the windows are flung wide open and life comes pouring in. At such moments he will tell how the Danubians get drunk on smells, how the Arabians cut their hair, how the Scythians use human scalps for napkins, and how the Indians follow the trails of fox-sized ants when they burrow in the sand and bring out gold, and he will tell with relish the various kinds of kisses practiced by the Persians. He has a great store of marvelous tales which he relates slyly, not always letting us know whether he believed them. He was fascinated by the spices of Arabia and went to some pains to discover how they were collected. He learned that frankincense was especially difficult to collect, for it grew on trees guarded by swarms of small, brightly colored, winged serpents. Cassia, too, was difficult to procure, for it grew in shallow lakes guarded by multitudes of fierce batlike creatures which shrieked shrilly and swooped down on anyone attempting to invade the lakes, so that the cassia seekers had to cover their bodies with oxhides and other skins. The gathering of cinnamon was even more remarkable: even the Arabs did not know where it came from, though they supposed it must be India:

They say there are great birds which carry the dry sticks of cinnamon—we have derived the word from the Phoenicians—into their nests built of mud on the precipitous cliffs, where no man can follow them. Then, to get the sticks, the Arabs cut up the carcasses of oxen or donkeys or other animals with very large joints, and these are laid on the ground at the bottom of the cliffs, while they withdraw to a safe distance. Soon the birds fly down and carry off the joints of meat to their nests, which are not strong enough to bear so great a weight and they come tumbling to the ground. The Arabs thereupon come running out to pick up the cinnamon, which is afterwards exported to foreign lands.

(Histories, III, 111)

We can only guess what Herodotus himself made of this fable of the cinnamon sticks. He may very well have believed the story on the ground that Arabia was so strange a country that anything was possible there. His credulity varies according to geography. The winged serpents of Arabia, as he describes them, are matters of fact, while the holy serpents guarding the shrine of Athena on the Acropolis at Athens are considerably more dubious. "The Athenians," he wrote, "say that a great serpent lives in the shrine as guardian of the citadel, and they present a honey cake every month as to a creature existing." This smacks of impiety, and one wonders whether he lowered his voice at the end of the sentence when he was reciting to the Athenians.

Herodotus told many other fables equally unbelievable. He tells a wildly improbable story of some Phoenicians sailing out of the Red Sea and making the circumnavigation of Africa. It took them three years before they rounded the Pillars of Hercules and returned to Egypt, a slow journey, and made all the slower by their habit of settling on the land every autumn and waiting for their seeds to grow. Herodotus cannot quite bring himself to believe the story, but he adds the one providential detail which makes it certain that the story is true —they said they found the sun on their right hand when they were sailing west around the bottom of Africa. Because Herodotus is so often right, we cannot afford to dismiss even his story about the winged, brightly colored serpents guarding the incense-bearing trees.

He believed what he wanted to believe. He denied the existence of goat-footed men in Central Asia, but he was prepared to believe there were headless creatures in Libya with eyes in their breasts. He declared that a ravine in Thessaly had been deliberately made by Poseidon: there was nothing strange in a god fashioning a deep gorge for his own pleasure. But when he was told by the Babylonians that a god slept in the topmost chamber of a high tower, he permitted himself the observation that "he simply did not believe it."

For two thirds of his immense *History* Herodotus is concerned to paint the background of the Persian war. He roams all over the known world in order to set the stage in a proper perspective. Asia Minor, Greece, Egypt, and Scythia are discussed at length because all of them fell within the Persian orbit. The most affectionate descriptions are of Egypt, which he admired unreservedly. He especially admired the imperturbable decorum of the Egyptians, their habit of stepping aside for their elders and bowing gravely to one another when they passed in the street. They treated their women as equals, were always washing themselves, and were scrupulous in the observance of their religion. He thought they were the wisest of mortals, and after the Libyans the healthiest. "The names of nearly all the gods came to Greece from Egypt," he wrote, and he believed that the entire Pantheon of Greek gods except Poseidon and Hera could be traced back to Egyptian originals.

He had affection for the Egyptians; for the Persians he had abiding respect. He evidently sympathized with their religious observances. "It is not in their law," he wrote, "to set up images and temples and altars, and they count those who do as fools: the Persian gods are not man-shaped like the Greek. Their habit is to sacrifice to Zeus, going to the tops of the highest mountains, believing him to be the whole circle of the heavens. They worship sun, moon, earth, fire, water, and the winds. Having no altars, they kindle no fires; there are no libations, flute players, garlands, nor sprinkled meal; they have no use for any of these things, so familiar to us." There is no doubt where his sympathies lie. If he did not approve of putting out the dead to be eaten by birds, he admired their joyful acceptance of customs learned from other nations; there was nothing parochial about them, and they took what pleased them, even pederasty, which they learned from the Greeks. And when Herodotus comes to describe the war between Greece and Persia, he makes a serious attempt to be the dispassionate observer, balancing his sympathies. If the Persians are not as wise as the Egyptians, nor as audacious and enterprising as the Greeks, they have virtues of nobility, generosity, and humanity which are not to be despised. Indeed Plutarch called him *philobarbaros*, meaning that he loved the Persians too well, in an essay unequivocally called *De Malignitate Herodoti*. But Herodotus was never malignant, although by granting the Persians a certain grandeur he gave dignity to the eventual triumph of the Greeks.

What is clear is that Herodotus knew the Persians, talked to them in their own language, and genuinely liked them. As he describes the advance of the huge armada against Greece, he seems to be perpetually at Xerxes' elbows, seeing him in a series of close-ups. Since the stories he relates are not likely to have been those recorded in the court chronicles, it is fairly certain that he drew his information from people close to the emperor. And when he tells, for example, the story of the two Spartans who came to Xerxes to offer themselves up as sacrifices in exchange for the murder of two Persian ambassadors only to be given their freedom, he is equally fair to Spartans and to Persians, but it is the generosity of Xerxes that we remember. Similarly, when he tells how Xerxes wept at the thought of all the millions of his soldiers passing before him because they would all be dead in a hundred years' time, Herodotus is not pointing to his weakness but to his humanity.

It is this humanness, this sense of the appropriate human gesture, which makes Herodotus so eminently readable. He tells a serious history with the artifices of a novelist, while inventing nothing. Strabo, a superb collator, lacks this gift completely: he cannot breathe life into the dead facts. "Herodotus has given us a good deal of nonsense," he wrote. But there is surprisingly little nonsense in Herodotus, and very often Strabo's careful detail is no more illuminating than a list of statistics.

Herodotus knew what he knew, and he was sometimes exceedingly cautious about things he did not know. The one-eyed Arimaspi on the borders of China, who stole their gold from the watchful griffins and marched with goat-footed men and Hyperboreans to the sea, are dismissed out of hand. He had heard reports that there was a sea in Northern Europe, but this too seemed unlikely and incredible.

Stories about the Tin Islands left him unmoved, and so too did accounts of a great river flowing into the northern sea. He had not seen them, knew no one who had visited them, and was content to believe they did not exist. He was right about the Arimaspi, but wrong about the Tin Islands and the river. Whether right or wrong, he was always very human in making his judgments.

One of the indirect causes of the Persian invasion of Greece was a revolt by the Scythians on the western shores of the Black Sea. A Persian army was sent against them, but they proved to be masters of guerrilla warfare and were so contemptuous of the armed might of Persia that they amused themselves by sending scurrilous messages to the Persian king. On one occasion they sent Darius a bird, a mouse, a frog, and five arrows. This was rightly interpreted as meaning: "Unless you turn into birds and fly in the air, or into mice and burrow underground, or into frogs and jump into the lakes, you will never reach home, for you will be shot to death by Scythian arrows." Darius found it impossible to engage them in battle, and he was afraid of having his supply lines cut off. Weary of being harassed by them, he withdrew to the Hellespont, but left a large army in Thrace to recoup his lost fortunes. With a Persian army installed in European Greece from the Propontis to the Strymon River, the Greeks knew that a further attack on the mainland would not be long in coming.

Herodotus gives a lengthy account of the Scythians, and he is in fact our chief authority for their habits and customs. He knew them well, or rather he knew the sedentary Scythians who lived on the shores of the Black Sea and traded with the Greek colonists in Olbia, Tanais, and Panticapaeum. From them he learned about the Scythians in the interior—the head-hunting Tauri, the Neuroi who became wolves once a year, the Boudini with their bright red hair and startling blue eyes, who lived (according to Herodotus) in wooden towns and ate lice. He knew all about their gods and goddesses, their methods of sacrifice, and their burial customs. Surprisingly, he never mentions their most important contribution to the arts—a wild, yet wonderfully controlled way of depicting animals in gold, ivory, and bronze. No other race ever carved animals with such abundant vigor. Stags, reindeer, horses, and lions are shown struggling together or at full gallop. Scythian art subtly and deeply influenced Chinese artists, and left indelible traces in far-off Scandinavia, while even in England and Ireland motifs which originally sprang up in the Asiatic steppes are clearly visible. The energy of Scythian art leaped across the boundaries of time and space. The tormented animals which peer out of the pages of the *Book of Kells* derive from the Scythians, and so do the animals which gaze down at us from the capitals of Romanesque churches.

But though Herodotus tells us nothing about Scythian art, he tells us in a few close-knit pages nearly everything else about them that we might want to know. Here he describes the burial of a king:

> *When a king dies, they dig a square pit of great size, and when it is ready they take up the body, slit open the belly, clean it, fill it with various aromatic substances, crushed cypress, frankincense, parsley seed, and anise, and then it is sewn up again and the whole body is coated with wax. Then it is placed in a wagon and borne through all the neighboring tribes, and in the course of its progress, following the custom of the Royal Scythians, every man cuts off a piece of his ear, shaves his hair, makes a cut all round his arm, gashes his forehead and nose, and thrusts an arrow through his left hand.*
>
> *When all the tribes have been visited, then at last the funeral cortege makes its way to the country of the Gerrhi, who are the most northerly and remote of all the Scythian tribesmen. Here the body is laid in its grave, stretched out on a mattress, and spears are fixed in the ground on either side to support a roof of withies laid on wooden poles, while in the open space around the body of the king they bury one of his concubines, first killing her by strangling, and also his cupbearer, his cook, his groom, his steward, and his chamberlain, and some of his horses and gold cups and other treasures of gold, for they do not use silver or bronze. Afterwards they raise a vast mound above the grave, all of them vying enthusiastically with each other to make it as big as possible.*

(Histories, IV, 71)

To the medieval commentators, and even to the Greeks, such descriptions seemed to be little more than barbaric fantasy. The lurid and savage account of the burial rites of the Scythian kings, with their wives and servants and horses killed in order to accompany them to the shades reads like fiction, but every word is true, as the archaeologists discovered when they explored the Scythian tombs in Russia. Today, from the excavations at Pazyryk in the Altai Mountains, we know that Herodotus was describing precisely and accurately what happened at the burial of a great Scythian chieftain. In 1948 a chieftain was found in a tumulus which had flooded with water immediately after the burial, and the water had turned into ice. Thousands of years had passed, but nothing had changed. The colors were fresh, the horses' reins were still in place, the dead concubines and stewards and chamberlains still lay where they had fallen, and in addition there was a carpet with lustrous scarlet colors lying on the floor of the chariot. The carpet was clearly of Persian manufacture.

Herodotus knew the Scythians almost as well as he knew the Persians. He knew the names of their gods, remarking pleasantly on the justice of the Scythian name for Zeus—*Pappaeus*. He had evidently pored over the maps showing the boundaries of the Scythian tribes, for he describes the position of each tribe minutely. Hearing that "feathers fill the air in the remote regions of Scythia, making the land impenetrable to travelers," he very sensibly comes to the conclusion that the feathers are snow and that the northern regions are uninhabitable by reason of the severity of the winter. There is no nonsense about him. He will tell a story—even a very long story—and at the end he will quietly give his verdict of the truth of it.

In his day the world was wide open. A Greek could travel unhindered from the Rhône valley to the remote regions of Persia, and from the second cataract of the Nile to the Central Asiatic plains, and he could do this without benefit of passport. Suddenly, miraculously, the world had opened like a flower to show itself in all its glory. Herodotus rejoiced.

He did, of course, do a good deal more than rejoice. However gaily he wrote, he was aware of a solemn purpose. His theme was as solemn as any theme can be, for it was nothing less than the survival of freedom under the divine law. Aristotle called him *mythologus*, not as an insult but as a compliment and at the same time as a precise description of his uncanny power to relate the works of men to the works of God. For him the coming of the Persians was a divine visitation which could be thwarted only by the intervention of divine forces. Over his entire history there broods the presence of the immortal gods.

This gaiety, this solemnity, are the essential characteristics of the Periclean age. Though Herodotus wrote about the wars as though he were an eyewitness, he belonged to the generation of the sons of the men who fought at Marathon: he belonged to the generation of

Sophocles, who was his friend. He was the first to relate tragedy to the entire body of a people. The fate of Prometheus, Agamemnon, and all the other heroes is little enough compared with the fate of the Greek people. The god-given prize was freedom, to live as free men in a barren land.

So he ends his story on a note of triumph and a note of warning. He tells how at the conclusion of the war the Athenian general sailed to the Hellespont and rolled up the cable which Xerxes had flung between Asia and Europe, taking it to Athens as a trophy of victory. The general was Xanthippus, the father of Pericles. Then, looking backward, he tells of a remark made by Cyrus, the founder of the Persian Empire. It is a remark worth remembering in our own time. "Soft countries," said the king, "breed soft men. You will never find in one soil luxurious fruits and fine soldiers, too."

17 ≪ PERICLES

WHEN old men who could re-
member Peisistratus looked at Pericles they would sometimes draw
back in alarm, for they saw in the young defender of Athenian democracy the exact facsimile of the features of the long-dead tyrant. It
was not only that they had the same face, the same build, and walked
with the same air of solemn distinction, but they shared the same
voice, very low and sweet, the sentences being spoken rapidly and
precisely, but becoming more and more complicated as they went
on. Like Peisistratus, Pericles had a full, rather feminine face with a
broad forehead, small deep-set eyes, a fine nose, and quick lips, and
while the forehead was broad, it was also very high. If there was any
difference, it seems to have been that Pericles had the higher forehead,
and to this there was added an extraordinary pointedness of the whole
head, for which he was nicknamed "squill-head," and people would
make jokes about how that vast forehead threatened to capsize, taking
the rest of his body with it.

Pericles was perfectly aware of his resemblance to Peisistratus.
This resemblance made him a marked man, and very early in life he
realized that he would have little chance of advancement in government circles. It was ironical that he should resemble the tyrant, for
he was in fact descended on his mother's side from Cleisthenes, the
revolutionary who overthrew the Peisistratids. His father, Xanthippus,
was the admiral in command of the Athenian forces at Mycale, the
strange battle on the Ionian coast which was perhaps the decisive
victory in the Persian Wars. Xanthippus was a man of wealth and
taste, a friend of the poet Anacreon, a convivial host to the Spartan

kings who stayed in his house when they came to Athens, and he was able to give his son the best education available. Pericles attended the lectures of Zeno of Elea, who had his own school in Athens. The most famous tutors were invited to teach him. Among them were Damon, the most celebrated musician of his time—he liked to introduce philosophy into his discussions of music, and was eventually banished for his philosophical opinions—and Anaxagoras, the philosopher, who was nearly put to death for insisting after the discovery of a meteoric stone which fell at Aegospotami that the sun must be a stone like this, only white-hot. For the Greeks the sun was a god, and to say that it was nothing more than a stone was blasphemy. The young and noble Anaxagoras, not many years older than Pericles himself, had an enduring influence on him. Anaxagoras was one of those dedicated scholars who are prepared to follow knowledge wherever it leads, even into the most dangerous places, and in the end the pursuit of knowledge led him to madness. But in those early years, while he was teaching Pericles, he was a brilliant and wayward philosopher with a passion for discussing the most abstruse subjects vigorously and cleanly, even though in the end he would usually introduce his conception of *Nous*, or "the World-Mind," by which all problems were ultimately resolved.

Anaxagoras was a force, a power to be reckoned with. He was stubborn, intransigent, and completely fearless. Children might cry: "*Nous! Nous!*" after him in the streets, and philosophers might say that *Nous* was no more than the Heraclitean Fire or the Strife of Empedocles under another name, but Anaxagoras knew better. He had a vision of the universe that was clear and curiously satisfying: a universe in which nothing perished and nothing was born, where all things interpenetrated each other and all life was one life. Over this universe *Nous* reigned supreme, "being the thinnest of all things, and the purest, possessing perfect knowledge about all things and the greatest power, and therefore powerfully maintaining all things that are living, both great and small." Anaxagoras could also be down to earth, as when he said that man is the wisest of all animals, but only because he has hands. It was said that he was the first to study eclipses, and he was the first to declare that the Nile floods came from the melting of the distant snows. It was from him, according to Plato, that Pericles derived his elevation of mind and scientific temper, and it is possible that he was also indebted to Anaxagoras for his dry humor.

Pericles, then, grew up in a house of wealth and traditions and strenuous intellectual activity. He was a reserved, studious, handsome man who enjoyed playing on the lyre and entering into philosophical debates, and he might have been only one more of the young aristocrats of Athens if it had not been that Anaxagoras fired him with a vision of the world ruled by the pure intelligence. From this came his unruffled serenity, his sense of mission, and his desire to re-create Athens until it resembled the heavenly city of his imagination. How unruffled he could be we learn from the story told by Plutarch of how he was doing some urgent business in the Agora when a heckler accosted him, cursing him roundly, and kept on cursing him until Pericles went home in the evening with the heckler hard on his heels, and still there was that flood of vile language. All the time Pericles said nothing. When he reached his house he ordered a servant to light a torch and see the man safely home.

In the days when Pericles was young there were still many old men walking the streets of Athens wearing long flowing Ionic tunics, their long hair done up in a bun fastened by a golden "grasshopper." Though the elegance of the age of tyrants had not entirely vanished, and there were still women who wore heavily embroidered costumes of the thinnest cloth and with the delicate pleats which we see in the statues in the Acropolis Museum, the fashions were already changing. Women were wearing the austere *peplos*, which was like the *sari* worn by Indian women today, but simpler, while men had taken to wearing a short tunic with an oblong *himation* draped over one shoulder. Ornamentation was frowned upon by the generation which had fought through the Persian Wars. The mood was sober, even austere. It was a mood which agreed well enough with the temper of Pericles, who was habitually grave. Once when someone declared that Pericles was making an affectation of gravity and was therefore no better than a charlatan, Zeno the philosopher replied that others might well learn to imitate that gravity if in the end they came to imitate his nobility of mind.

At the festival of 472 Aeschylus entered four plays, of which only *The Persians* survives, and the young Pericles was asked to take over the duties of *choregos*. He paid all the expenses of the musicians and singers of the chorus, trained and fed them, and superintended the rehearsals. Such duties were not assumed lightly, and were sometimes prohibitively costly. When the play was finally performed the *chore-*

gos sat in a chair of honor, wearing sacred raiment from the temple of Dionysus, and like the actors he received the applause of the audience. When Pericles first stepped on the stage of history he wore the raiment of a god and leaned on the arm of Aeschylus.

He was twenty-two or twenty-three when he appeared as *choregos*. Three years later he was already being regarded as a rising power in politics, walking warily for fear of being ostracized, always aware that his resemblance to Peisistratus counted against him. Traditionally the Alcmaeonids had sided with the people against the aristocracy, and Pericles followed the established tradition, serving under Ephialtes, "the sea-green incorruptible," a man of the people who had risen to eminence by sheer force of character. Ephialtes had inherited from Themistocles the conviction that the Spartans were a continuing threat to Athenian power and must somehow be put into quarantine. Against the aristocracy, which traditionally favored the Spartans, Ephialtes thundered continually. The chief object of his hatred was Cimon, the son of Miltiades, whose vast wealth and increasing fame as a military leader threatened the popular party, for no one was more popular in Athens and no one was so generous. Cimon was supported by the sailors, for he had led them into victorious battle. He was supported by the tradesmen and artisans employed in his great campaign for rebuilding Athens and furnishing it with beautiful buildings. He was a jovial sailor, tall and thickset, with curly hair flowing down to his shoulders; he had a good singing voice, and he could drink as well as the next man, and he liked to walk through the streets accompanied by two or three young well-dressed companions, and if he saw an elderly man in rags, he would tell one of his companions to slip out of his clothes and present them to the man who needed them; and they said that he kept his orchards unfenced, so that anyone who wanted the fruit could pluck them.

Cimon had power, money, fame, and the common touch. He also possessed something of considerably more value than any of these, for he was a legend of towering eminence. An oracle had commanded the Athenians to bring home the relics of Theseus, king of Athens, the young hero who in the legendary and distant past had defeated the Amazons, the Centaurs, and the Minotaur, and who more recently had appeared in shining armor to aid the hard-pressed Athenians at the battle of Marathon. Theseus had become the national hero, the focus of men's dreams and aspirations as they watched the city being reborn after the Persian Wars. He was the hero of Athens, as Athena was the goddess of Athens; and whoever found his relics and brought them to Athens was assured of a share in the heroic legend. And when Cimon claimed to have found the bones on the island of Scyros during a raid against a nest of pirates, he very sensibly arranged that the translation of the relics to Athens should be accompanied by great festivities and parades in which he took the central place. The bones were buried in the heart of the city, and the cult of the hero was formally inaugurated.

Against Cimon, Pericles and Ephialtes waged their political warfare at a disadvantage. It was not only that Cimon was the high priest of the cult of Theseus, and the victor at the battle of Eurymedon where he destroyed the Phoenician fleet and routed a Persian army, and the most liberal, generous, and quick-witted of politicians, but the temper of the times demanded adventurous policies of a kind more easily identified with Cimon's aristocratic and conservative beliefs than with the democratic beliefs of Ephialtes. Expeditions were still being sent overseas to plunder and sack the cities occupied by Persian armies on the coast of Asia Minor. Naxos revolted against Athens, and the Athenians put down the revolt with complete ruthlessness, dismantled the walls of the city, confiscated her fleet, imposed an annual tribute, and deprived her of freedom. A few years later a revolt in the island of Thasos off the Thracian coast was similarly quelled. Cimon was in charge of the siege of Thasos, feeling powerful enough to leave Athens in the hands of his lieutenants.

Gradually the popular party was gaining ground, with Ephialtes leading the attack against entrenched privilege, with Pericles beside him or hovering in the background. Already Pericles had adopted the fashion of life which would continue until his death. There was always a reserve about him. He never walked abroad like Cimon, exchanging banter with the people he met on the street. He was never seen to walk anywhere except along the road which led from his house to the Agora; he would return as quickly as possible, the gates would close, and then there would be silence again. Even with his relatives he maintained his distance, and it is related that when his kinsman Euryptolemus married, he stayed only long enough to drink the health of the bride and bridegroom and then quietly rose and went home.

Pericles gave the appearance of doing nothing, but in fact he was already a powerful force in Athens. Messengers were continually arriving at his house with reports, and leaving with his orders. Politicians flocked to see him. He was not wealthy as Cimon was wealthy, but considerable funds were at his disposal, and very soon there would be more. His silence and remoteness gave him authority, and the time to study. While some accused him of pride, others said he was conserving his forces and like the ship of state, the Salaminian galley, he would always appear on grave and important occasions. He was for the people, but not of them, and all his life he had an aristocratic disdain for the rough-and-tumble of the market place.

He came to power as the result of an earthquake, and fell from power as the result of a plague.

The earthquake occurred in Sparta in 464. It was so violent that only five houses were left standing in the Spartan capital, and perhaps a quarter of the people were buried in the convulsions. The helots took this opportunity to rise in revolt, establishing themselves in the steep, heavily wooded mountains of Ithome. The Spartans called for help to put down the revolt, and troops came from Aegina, Plataea, and Mantinea. When the Athenians were asked to send troops, Cimon, always friendly toward Sparta, passionately espoused the cause of the Spartans. "Will you stand by and see Greece lamed of a leg," he declared, "and our own city deprived of a yokefellow?" He won the day. Four thousand armored men, about a third of the Athenian field army, went off to fight against the rebellious helots.

Ephialtes had protested against sending an army to help Athens' rival; it would be better if Sparta sank into the earth, leaving no trace. He hinted that Cimon preferred the safety of Sparta to the safety of his own country, and he took advantage of Cimon's absence to press through the Assembly a series of laws which effectively clipped the power of the archons, leaving them with only a few ornamental powers. The archons were survivors of a long aristocratic tradition. They were still permitted to adjudicate at trials for homicide, but for the rest they were limited to superintending the sacred olive tree and supervising the property of the Eleusinian gods. When Cimon returned from Sparta after a few months of ineffective campaigning in the mountains of Ithome, the damage had been done.

There was worse to come, for when the soldiers returned the Athenians learned that the expedition had been a fiasco. The Spartans themselves had ordered the Athenian army home. "The Spartans were afraid of the daring and revolutionary spirit of the Athenians," wrote Thucydides, "and fearing that they might be won over by the enemy, they ordered them off the field, the only allies to be so treated, without cause rendered, but with the words that they were no longer required." No doubt the Athenian infantry had been expressing themselves freely about the social and political conditions they found in Sparta, and perhaps—for nothing is more likely—the army was infiltrated with agents of the popular party of Ephialtes, who now took the opportunity to impeach Cimon, accusing him of being the servant of the Spartan king. Cimon was on trial for his life. There was a clamor for his execution, for the Athenians were merciless toward those they regarded as traitors, while the shock of the Spartan affront hurt keenly. And while Cimon pointed to the great victories he had won for Athens, Ephialtes pointed to the danger of letting a man who was such a close friend of the Spartan king live. The story is told that Cimon sent his sister Elpinice to plead with Pericles for his life. Pericles heard her out, and then said: "Elpinice, you are too old to meddle with these affairs." Then he took his place as one of the accusers at the trial, speaking carefully and moderately, and Plutarch says that "of all the accusers Pericles did least harm to Cimon."

Instead of being sentenced to death Cimon was banished for ten years. His banishment was an unprecedented victory for the popular party. But Ephialtes did not live to enjoy his triumph; he was murdered a few weeks later. Some said he was killed by a hired Boeotian bravo in the pay of Cimon's party, and there were others who said he was killed by members of his own party who were jealous of his fame and growing power. Today no one knows who killed him.

Pericles stepped into power like a man who had been preparing himself for it all his life. He seemed to know at every instant exactly what was needed to increase the splendor and glory of Athens. Almost his first act was to order the construction of a powerful navy to give Athens dominion over the seas. The alliance with Sparta was abandoned, and new alliances were formed with Argos and Thessaly, both inveterate enemies of Sparta. At all costs he was determined to safeguard the empire that Athens had won in the Aegean, and not to attempt further conquests unless he was sure of the superiority of his own forces.

He held the leading strings, but he was never in sole charge, never the dictator. In theory he exercised only the power given to a *strategos,* but in fact he dominated Athens during the next thirty years by his gift of persuasion, his manipulation of political forces, and his visionary desire to see Athens towering in splendor over all the neighboring states; and in a speech delivered to the Athenians he said quietly and confidently that he was moved by only one impulse: his determination to build a state in which the people would be able to live forever. He meant what he said. In the state he desired the people would be like gods: death and suffering would not touch them: they would live in eternal peace, and their whole lives would be dedicated to noble ends.

He did not, of course, bring about such a state, but we would be underestimating the force of his character and his vision if we failed to realize that his underlying intention was to bring into existence a divine state in which the people were the supreme masters of their environment and were themselves touched with divinity. He brought Athens to the greatest heights it had known, or was ever to know, and during all the years in which he was the dominant power in the state we are made aware of a mind working on two levels: he was the visionary who saw Athens as though it existed outside of time altogether, lit with the radiance of eternity, and at the same time he was the cautious legislator, the intricate manipulator, the student of political forces, taking great chances only when they were absolutely necessary, and even then he would have in reserve a series of plans to offset any disasters that might occur. His daring was always calculated, but his vision sprang from roots so deep in himself that he could hardly have known their origin.

The popular party had brought him to power, and to this party he remained faithful throughout his life. The people wanted a more democratic, a more representative government. Pericles therefore abolished the restrictions on voting for the Council of Five Hundred, and threw it open to all eligible citizens. Cleisthenes had introduced a form of democratic government which established equality by making all, or nearly all, the offices of state open to the people chosen by lot, thus ensuring that everyone had an opportunity to serve the state and no one would be able to entrench himself in a position of power. Pericles observed the flaw in the argument. The shoemaker, the ship chandler, and the schoolteacher could serve the state only if they had private incomes or could somehow arrange for others to take over their duties while they were serving on the state boards. The rich could afford to serve the state; the poor could not. Pericles therefore instituted a system of payment from the state treasury for all government servants. The poorest citizens were now able to serve, without the fear of living in official poverty. First it was arranged that the councilors who took part in the Council of Five Hundred should be paid. The plan was later extended to judges and jurors, and still later it was extended to military service, while at a much later date the poorer citizens were supplied from the public treasury with the price of admission to the theater: and this was not done in the spirit of *panem et circenses,* because it was felt that the poor should be entertained at public expense, but because the theater in Athens was a sacred festival, and it was intolerable that the poor should be excluded from it.

According to Plato, it was a common saying that Pericles corrupted the Athenians by this system of payments, which rendered them "idle, cowardly, babbling, and avaricious." Pericles would have answered that a true democracy is an expensive enterprise, and only the state treasury had the resources to pay for it. If there were abuses, he could answer truthfully that they were inevitably less than the abuse of the entire people which took place under a tyranny.

Pericles' first task was to safeguard Athens from any possible combination of enemies. With Thessaly and Argos as allies, and Sparta still exhausting her energies fighting the helots in the mountains, he determined to open up the road to the Peloponnese to Athenian power, and since Megara was at that time quarreling bitterly with Corinth, he was able to bring her into the alliance. The greatest immediate threat now came from the rich and powerful island of Aegina, which had contributed more ships in the Persian Wars than any state except Athens. The Aeginetans realized only too well that if Corinth fell their own fate was sealed, while the Athenians realized that there must inevitably be war with Aegina if they were to remain masters of the Saronic Gulf. Pericles had no illusions about the need to subdue Aegina. He thundered that Aegina had become "the eyesore of the Piraeus"—it is one of the few authentic phrases known to have been spoken by him—and set about the destruction of the island with a ruthlessness rarely employed subsequently. After a siege of two years the island surrendered, the walls of the chief city were dismantled, and the Aeginetans were compelled to enter the Delian League, which had been founded to promote the interests of the Athenian Empire, and to pay an annual tribute of thirty talents, while the large estates were sequestered and given to Athenian settlers. Among those who were given grants of land from the conquered territory were the families of Plato and Aristophanes.

Not all the adventures of the Athenians were so successful. In 459 a fleet of some two hundred ships belonging to the League set sail for Cyprus to destroy the Phoenician cities and the Phoenician garrisons which were spread out over the island. About the same time Inaros, a Libyan chieftain, raised the Egyptian Delta country in revolt against the Persian king. He sent an appeal for help to the battle fleet coasting off the shores of Cyprus, and soon the entire fleet was being diverted to the Nile on instructions from Athens. The move was made against the express wishes and desires of Pericles, who could see no advantage to be gained in an adventure so far from home, in unknown waters, against enemies never met in battle before. The fleet sailed up the Nile, made contact with Inaros, helped him to capture Memphis, the capital, near the modern Cairo, and they might have gone on to capture the whole of Egypt if it had not been for the stubborn and unexpected resistance of the Persian garrison in the fortress called the White Castle. The siege went on interminably. The Greeks seem to have divided their forces, sending part of the fleet to raid the Phoenician coast and another part back to Athens where it was sorely needed, with the result that the Persians were able to raise a large army at their leisure. Sweeping through Egypt, they drove the Greeks out of Memphis, finally blockading them on the island of Prosopotis in the Delta. There the Greeks were besieged for eighteen months while water engineers were summoned to divert the channel to enable the Persians to cross the riverbed and take the Greek fortifications by storm. Inaros was captured and impaled, and only a small remnant of the Greek forces survived to make the long journey to Cyrene. For six years they had wasted their strength in Egypt, and there was nothing to show for it.

There exists no surviving account of how many Athenians took part in the Egyptian campaign, but it cannot have been less than a quarter of the standing army. The Athenians were learning to their cost the danger of fighting on too many fronts. In 459 the Erechtheid tribe erected in Athens a monument of stone which bore the names of 177 men belonging to the tribe who had died in battle. The inscription above the names reads:

Of Erechtheis
These died in the war in Cyprus, in Egypt, in Phoenicia,
At Haleis, in Aegina, at Megara, in the same year.

Pericles desired peace, but was confronted with war. There were continual skirmishes wth the Corinthians. Thebes, too, was always a danger especially now that the oligarchs of the city were in league with the Spartans, determined to build up a Boeotian Confederacy north of Athens as a counterpoise to Spartan power in the south. Between those two millstones Athens might yet be crushed. Pericles saw the danger and marched an army up to Tanagra, the nearest Boeotian city to Athens, and there while he was encamped Cimon came secretly from exile to ask permission to fight as an ordinary citizen soldier in the ranks of his tribe. He had already sent his offer to the Council in Athens; they had refused; and Cimon was in danger of his life once again. He sent a message to the men of his tribe to fight well for their city, and then departed. It was counted in his favor that he had made this secret journey, and it was remembered afterward when there was a debate on whether he should be recalled from exile.

The battle fought at Tanagra in the summer of 457 was no more decisive than many other battles fought during that century of wars. The Peloponnesian forces won the day, probably because the Thessalian cavalry deserted to the enemy. Pericles fought well, throwing himself into the forefront of the battle and acquiring a well-earned reputation for gallantry; but as dusk came down, and the Athenians saw that the mule train bringing up their supplies had been cut off by the Thessalians who were nominally their allies, the issue was no longer in doubt. The massacre went on through the night and was still going on the next morning, when Pericles ordered a general retreat. The Spartans claimed the victory, but were too exhausted to follow it up by an attack on Athens. In honor of their victory they set up a gold shield over the gable of the Temple of Zeus at Olympia. Two months later the Athenians sent another army to Boeotia, and this time they were more successful. All of Boeotia except Thebes fell under their sway, and the danger from the north was held in abeyance.

The Athenians set about building the Great Wall, joining Athens to Piraeus. It was more than a wall; it was in fact a fortress five and a half miles long, roofed with tiles, constructed of stone, and surmounted by a crenelated gallery of brick. Spartan armies would hurl themselves in vain against this fortress which had the shape of an armored tunnel. We hear of another wall of the same kind joining Phaleron to Athens, but this seems never to have been completed.

With Boeotia, Megara, and Argos under her sway, and Aegina destroyed, with all the Aeginetan navy in her hands, Athens in the autumn of 457 could look back on a series of campaigns which offered hope of a settled peace. Almost the Saronic Gulf had been converted into an Athenian lake. Not Sparta, but Corinth, seemed to be the most dangerous of her remaining enemies, and accordingly Pericles planned a series of lightning raids on Corinthian possessions. Chalcis was captured, and soon Pericles himself was leading an Athenian squadron against Sicyon, where he defeated an army sent against him; then, taking with him a body of Achaeans, he crossed to Acarnania and besieged the town of Oeniadae, which he failed to capture though he laid waste all the surrounding country. In these campaigns few Athenians were lost. The reputation of Pericles as a military leader was enhanced because he had shown himself as a terror to the enemies of Athens and because he had acted so cautiously that few families suffered any bereavement.

More and more Pericles found himself thinking of peace—peace with Sparta, peace with Persia. In the hope of arranging a treaty with Sparta, he asked that Cimon be recalled from exile, and about this time he seems to have sent secret envoys to the Persian king at Susa. Only one great obstacle remained to the safety of Athens: this was the control of the Dardanelles to ensure safe passage for the corn ships from the Black Sea, since corn ships from Egypt could no longer be relied upon. Accordingly he conducted an expedition to the Thracian Chersonese, where he strengthened the Greek cities by settling a thousand Athenian colonists, and he fortified the isthmus for defense against the warlike tribes. About the same time he established colonies in Naxos, Andros, Lemnos, and Sinope on the Black Sea. "In this way," says Plutarch, "he was able to relieve the state of many idle agitators, and to give aid to the poor, and to overawe the allies by placing his colonists near them to watch over their behavior." Some ten thousand Athenians became colonists. To the allies and to the enemies of Athens they were the visible sign that imperial Athens, still ruled by the majority and therefore a democracy, was determined to safeguard her far-flung frontiers.

About the year 454—the exact date is unknown—Pericles embarked on a *coup de main* which had the effect of placing the allies still more within the power of Athens. At a meeting of the Assembly he proposed that the treasure of the Confederacy, which had been kept on the island of Delos, be transferred to Athens. He claimed that Athens had a right to the treasure, for had not Athenian ships swept the seas clear of pirates and were not the Athenians the acknowledged leaders of the alliance? To leave it in Delos was to invite the attention of the Phoenicians, who still maintained a large fleet in the eastern Mediterranean. The treasure was in fact already in Athenian hands, for all the "Stewards of the Greeks," the elected officials responsible for the treasure, were Athenians. There was therefore nothing to prevent the transfer of the treasure from Apollo's island to Athena's Acropolis. Athenian power now extended across the Aegean, and even farther afield. "Now all the best things of Sicily and Italy, Cyprus, Egypt, and Lydia, of Pontus and the Peloponnese, and any other place you care to name, are swept, as it were, into one single center, and all this has come about through the establishment of a maritime empire." So wrote "the Old Oligarch" in his *Constitution of the Athenians* a few years later. Athens with her colonies and great battlemented walls was now at the height of her power, with vast wealth at her command, her battle fleets patrolling the seas from the Crimea to the Egyptian Delta, from Asia Minor to the coasts of Italy. There was time now for the Athenians to contemplate their own city and rebuild it so that it would endure for eternity.

One suspects that "eternity" and "freedom" were the words most often on Pericles' lips. That passionate and impassive democrat was the most tyrannical of men, but he was a tyrant only for the sake of Athenian democracy. He moved mysteriously, appearing only at infrequent intervals on the rostrum and speaking in a quick low voice with scarcely a gesture ruffling the folds of his gown, and before he spoke he would offer up a prayer to the goddess that no unbecoming words should come from him. It was remembered that sometimes, but very rarely, lightning would shoot from his eyes and thunder from his tongue. And sometimes he was heard to whisper to himself: "Remember, Pericles, you are in command of free men, Greeks, Athenians."

His statue by Cresilas has come down to us only in Roman copies.

Bare-chested, helmeted, with thick curls escaping from under the helmet and a curling beard, he peers at us even now with an expression of intellectual superiority and extraordinary calm. It is the face of a man who knows where he is going, because he has made his peace with the gods: a man who never doubted for an instant that he had chosen the right path. But these portraits, as they are usually photographed, are misleading. Turn the face around until you see the sharp profile, and you see another aspect of the man. The strong nose and heavy chin stand out, to reveal stubborn determination and remorseless courage in the service of an ideal, and there is more than a hint of brutality.

The contemplative and the man of action were evenly matched in him. Descendant of the "accursed" line of the Alcmaeonids, he could scarcely escape a heavy burden of responsibility: what was remarkable in him was that he embraced responsibility for thirty years, and in all that time he seems never to have slept. He watched over the destiny of Athens like a nurse watching over a child. Athens was his continual study, and its very existence his continual reward.

"His temper was so dispassionate, his life so pure and unblemished, that he may well be called Olympian," said Plutarch, and it was no more than the truth.

18 « THE GOLDEN AGE

IN THE year 452 Athens was a poor town crowding the foot of the Acropolis, the huddled lanes of small, squat mud-brick houses forming a wheel around the great rock. The houses were like caves, dark, windowless, and unsanitary, and the narrow winding roads crawled up the side of the rock or vanished in the surrounding plain. Athens resembled an Oriental slum, evil-smelling and strangely somber, as though a curse had been laid upon it. A visitor from Persia or from the Ionian cities in Asia Minor would have wondered how this shanty town could possibly exert so much influence in the world.

In those days it was still a city without elegance, with no marble buildings, no traces of its former grandeur under the Peisistratids. The Persians had methodically destroyed the temples, and just as methodically set fire to the city. Nothing remained of the temples and palaces on the Acropolis except blackened rubble and the stumps of pillars. A makeshift temple had been erected to house the *xoanon* of Athena, the wooden image of the goddess which had been sent down from heaven in some remote and legendary age, but there were no other buildings on the rock. Cimon had constructed a wall around the Acropolis and built a small gateway, and Themistocles had built a wall around the city: these massive walls had the effect of making Athens resemble an armed camp. An armed camp it was, for the Athenians had been fighting uninterruptedly for nearly forty years.

Almost there was no city: it resembled a few villages at the foot of a rock. There were no ornamental gateways inlaid with painted tiles, as in Persia; no great processional roads guarded by stone beasts, as at Memphis; no monuments or statues of any size.

Even a hundred years later, when Athens had risen from the ruins and become the most beautiful city in the world, there was little to be said for its streets, which still wandered in the most haphazard way imaginable. Dicaearchus, a disciple of Aristotle, described it as "dusty and ill-supplied with water, wretchedly laid out on account of its antiquity, while the majority of its houses are mean and very few good. A stranger at first sight may well doubt that this is Athens."

The Athenians, endlessly discussing the nature of the *polis*, never succeeded in building a city where men could live comfortably, and indeed they attached very little significance to comfort. They were to build glorious palaces for their gods, but in the Golden Age it never occurred to them to build palaces for themselves.

The rich lived on their country estates outside the walls; the poor lived in their desolate hovels. Only their native health and the strong sun kept them from dying off like flies. Here and there the huddled lanes opened out on fields of olive trees or pasture lands where the sheep grazed, but already the city was expanding and these small acres were fast vanishing. Everywhere there was poverty, beggary, and slavery. Half-wild dogs roamed about. They were useful scavengers, for the streets were used as latrines, and the refuse was simply thrown out the windows. In every backyard, and sometimes in the houses, there were pigpens, and the filth from the pens would make its way into those narrow lanes, where the doors opened outward and there was scarcely room for two donkeys to walk abreast. Pestilences came from the malaria-ridden marshes to the south of the town; and the hot winds of summer brought dust storms, so that people walked about veiled. The wounded hobbled on their crutches, wearing their bloodstained rags, and the rich wore their Ionian finery and rode on caparisoned horses.

What the visitor to Athens would notice above everything else was the astonishing uproar which went on all day and most of the night. There was the continual neighing of horses and donkeys, the squealing of pigs, the chirping of song birds, and the deafening chorus of cicadas, and there was also the incessant, high-pitched, nervous shouting of the Athenians themselves. They were forever shouting and quarreling and carrying on conversations at a distance. They loved the sound of their own voices, and they deplored all silences. To these sounds there was added in the years following the Persian Wars the characteristic hammering noises of the new factories. Swordsmiths and ironsmiths, stonemasons, armorers, wheelwrights, carriage makers, carpenters, all were contributing their proper share to the pandemonium.

By common consent there was one place louder than all the rest. This was the Agora, where every morning until midday the Athenians did their marketing. Here, beside their small stalls and booths constructed out of matting, wickerwork, and a few boards, the merchants vied with one another in producing the largest volume of sound. We are told that the fishmongers were the loudest, the most obscene, the most quarrelsome, and the most adept at giving short weight, but the shrill voices of the myrtle sellers were nearly as loud. Sprays of myrtle were plaited into wreaths and coronets, to be laid on graves or presented to the gods. Pricked out with flowers they were worn on the brow or hung on the doors of houses. The myrtle sellers were the loudest and coarsest of the women in the market place, and for a suitable fee they could be induced to serve as flute girls or prostitutes. Even louder than the fishmongers and the myrtle sellers was the terrible voice of the herald who would order the market place cleared so that everyone could attend the Assembly. Then the great rope painted with fresh scarlet paint would be swept across the market place, and anyone seen wandering around the streets of Athens with a smear of red paint on him would be fined, for not being in attendance at the Assembly.

The ugly voice of the herald was deliberately cultivated: it was intended to have an explosive, frightening effect, sending people scurrying away to listen to the orators. But the Athenians liked their own voices best. Long after the herald had uttered his bloodcurdling cries, there would be knots of people arguing and shouting themselves hoarse in the market place. Then the Scythian police would be summoned, and they would herd the people away with their staves.

The orators at the Assembly cultivated voices which were loud and piercing, capable of drowning out all opposition. Though one observer speaks of the people "listening open-mouthed and gaping like roasting shellfish on the coals," there is a good deal of evidence to show that the people were rarely spellbound, but continually muttered, shouted, cursed, and roared their approval or disapproval of the orators. Even when Socrates was on trial for his life and making his last appeal for justice, he was constantly interrupted. Heckling was

Head of Zeus by Phidias, from coin of Elis.

Head of Apollo from Leontini tetradrachm.

Head of Apollo from Catana tetradrachm.

Head of Arethusa from Syracuse tetradrachm.

Silver decadrachm of Syracuse, with head of
Persephone.

Spartan soldier wearing Corinthian helmet.
Height 4¼ inches.

Veiled dancer from Alexandria.

Jockey.

developed as a fine art among the Athenians: interruptions were carefully stage-managed on behalf of one or other of the political parties;
and the paid claque often interfered with the processes of democracy.

The Athenians were connoisseurs of voices, endlessly comparing
them and remarking their finer points, debating eagerly on their
qualities of resonance and subtlety and musicality, as though the human voice possessed a life of its own, dissociated from what it conveyed; and they especially respected men like Pericles who carried
"a thunderbolt in the tongue." Cleon, a fiery and effective speaker,
complained that the Athenians were "helplessly at the mercy of the
pleasures of the ear, and they attend political meetings as though
attending a performance by Sophists, and in this respect they are far
from being councilors of the state." A comic poet called the Athenians
"eared owls, they alone among the Greeks." In this matter of the voice
every Athenian claimed to be a professional.

For the Athenians the human voice acted as a kind of drug, and
they were only too easily seduced by it. A fine presence counted less
than oratorical skill. If the speaker was honest, so much the better.
If he was dishonest but presented a clever case, so much the worse
for his opponent; the Athenians preferred cleverness to honesty,
subtlety to forthrightness. Odysseus was a man after their own hearts.
He was a sly, treacherous, and persuasive speaker, and could talk himself out of any difficulty.

Nowhere else in the ancient world did there exist this cult of the
human voice and of the arts of persuasion. Almost the Greeks invented argument. When Aristotle gathered together a library of these
books in preparation for writing his own *Rhetoric*, he was amused
or appalled to discover how many of them were concerned with the
specious tricks of oratory and the art of playing on the weakness of the
human heart, and how little they were concerned with the logical
presentation of a case. They codified fraud, down to its last minute
particulars. Sophistry was the invention not of the Sophists, who were
usually philosophers eagerly debating the nature of the universe, but
of the rhetoricians and especially the teachers of rhetoric.

In speech the Athenians found themselves as individuals; in their
religion they found themselves as a community.

They were devout believers, devoted to their gods. They could
not have told where the lives of the gods ended and their own lives
began. They worshiped feverishly, with intense devotion and con-

viction, and it could scarcely be otherwise since they believed the gods walked by their side. The chief responsibility of an Athenian citizen was the worship of the gods: all other responsibilities—making speeches, earning a living, marriage, rearing children, paying taxes, serving as a soldier in wartime, attending the Assembly and electing officials—all these derived their sanction from the gods, and in the eyes of the Athenians they would have been meaningless without divine sanction. Every law began with a tribute to the gods, every public meeting began with a prayer.

In the divine economy power flowed from the gods, whose mysteries were continually being celebrated. The gods had their rites and liturgies, demanded sacrifices, and rewarded those who served them. Each of the Olympian gods had his college of priests conducting and observing the appropriate rites and services, with the acolytes and temple servants in attendance on them. The crowded calendars were filled with religious feasts.

In Athens Zeus was worshiped as the god of winter storms in November and as a god of graceful ease in February, when the storms had passed. Apollo was the god of spring, when he received the first fruits at the Thargelia, and of summer, when he received the sacrifice of a hundred white bulls in the first month of the year, and of autumn, when he received the gift of olive branches adorned with purple and white wool and autumn fruits. The great festival for Athena took place in July, and was followed in August by another festival for Apollo, the Metageitnion, in honor of his prowess in compelling people to live in good-fellowship. Demeter and Persephone were worshiped at the Eleusinian Mysteries in September, and in the following month Demeter was again worshiped in the Thesmophoria, a fertility rite at which the women prayed for fertility not only for the fields but also for themselves. In the winter months came the Lenaea, the Anthesteria, and the Great Dionysia, at all of which Dionysus was worshiped with drunken revels, stage plays, and processions of people carrying flowers. There were more festivals associated with Dionysus than with any of the other gods, but this did not mean that he was more honored than the rest. It was simply that Dionysus was the most human of the gods and the one whose services were most enjoyable. It was scarcely necessary to worship Zeus, Athena, or Apollo. They were everywhere, penetrating the air and the stone from which Athens was made. They were the superb rulers who had long ago gathered to themselves the greatest accumulations of power.

All these feasts were organized by the state and superintended by state officials. These feasts were held to honor the public gods, but even more honor was paid to the private gods of the hearth and home. In every house there were statues of Hecate, goddess of the night, and Hermes, the messenger of death. There were gods of the tribe and the clan, and the strange gods who had entered Athens from abroad and were not wholly naturalized. Wherever a man looked he would find a god waiting to protect or thwart him.

The Athenians of the classical age were as superstitious as peasants. Necromancers and sorcerers abounded, soothsayers sang in the streets, witches promised to draw down the moon for a fee, and omens were regarded with wide-eyed credulity, so that if a drop of rain fell on the Assembly it was thought to be a sign of the displeasure of Zeus, and if a mouse gnawed through a bag or if a cock crowed late in the evening, disasters were portended. And when they went to war, the seers always accompanied them, to make the proper sacrifices before a battle and to examine the entrails where some message of the gods was mysteriously written. There is scarcely a page of Xenophon's *Anabasis* in which he is not offering sacrifices to learn the will of the gods.

The weight of superstition hung heavy over the Athenians, but it was no heavier than the weight of superstition that hung over the Elizabethans two thousand years later; and, like the Elizabethans, the Athenians practiced their vices wholeheartedly. They frequented the boys' brothels on the slopes of Mount Lycabettus as often as the prostitutes' quarters in the Cerameicus. They had no shame, shame of the body being unthinkable in a people who delighted in the flesh and were continually bathing naked in the gymnasia, believing that all evil was washed away by water. Women were not held in subjection, but openly took part in the life of the city, attending the theaters and taking part in all the religious ceremonies. They were the equals of men in everything except political power, and if we can trust Aristophanes and the *Menexenus* of Plato, which describes how Aspasia wrote the funeral speeches of Pericles, they wielded as much political power as they desired.

Such were the people, cruel, gentle, beautiful, intelligent, devout, and wildly superstitious, who in the space of a few short years transformed a ruined town into a place of splendor.

The Parthenon

WHEN about the year 452 Pericles began to plan the rebuilding of the temples destroyed by the Persians, he had at his command the wealth of the Delian treasury, removed to Athens for safekeeping only two years before, and the services of the greatest sculptors and architects of Greece, but this was only the beginning. What was needed was that the entire community should take part in building the temples. So it came about that there was scarcely anyone in Athens who did not have a share in bringing those temples to life.

Nothing quite like this dedication to divinity had occurred before, and we shall not see its like again until we come to twelfth-century France, when whole populations were engaged in building cathedrals. Quite suddenly all the ordinary purposes of life went into abeyance, while the people set about making a temple worthy to be inhabited by Athena and all the other temples on which she shed her divine benediction. "The people of Chartres harnessed themselves to the carts laden with stone, or wood, or grain," wrote Robert de Torigny in 1144. "Everywhere penance and humility prevailed, and everyone forgave his enemies. Singing in triumph beneath the lash and thong, they praised the miracles performed by God before their eyes." An Athenian, seeing the Parthenon coming to birth, might have written in very much the same vein.

Every trade and skill, every science and art was employed in the building of the temples. Centuries after they were built Plutarch gave an account of the various occupations directly employed. "The materials were marble, bronze, ivory, gold, ebony, and cypresswood," he wrote, "and the arts or trades which wrought and fashioned them included smiths, carpenters, masons, braziers, goldsmiths, painters, embroiderers, and turners. The conveyance of them by sea involved merchants, sailors, and ships' masters, and by land cartwrights, cattle breeders, wagoners, ropemakers, flax spinners, leather cutters, paviors, iron founders, and miners. Every trade was, as it were, commanded by a general with the lower ranks arranged in an orderly fashion under him, these consisting of journeymen and laborers who acted as the instrument and body for the performance of the service. And because all the trades were represented, wealth was distributed among people of every class and condition."

Pericles himself was responsible for the general plan, and together with the architects Ictinus and Callicrates and the sculptor Phidias he formed a governing committee to organize its execution. Phidias had already carved the great figure of Zeus at Olympia, and being a genius of sculpture and a man of great force of character and ferocious pride, he took upon himself the carving of the immense figures of the two pediments, and it is possible that he sketched out every single figure of the frieze. A Michelangelo does not permit others to do his work for him, and Phidias was another Michelangelo, using students and lesser sculptors to do the journeyman work while reserving for himself the design and finish of every sculpture. "Everything," says Plutarch, "was virtually under his control, for he took charge of all the workmen, and this came about as a result of his close friendship with Pericles."

Despite differences in treatment, the pedimental compositions and the frieze have enough in common to suggest that they come from a single mind. In the pediments a soaring boldness of conception; in the frieze a sustained delicacy of arrested movement. The gods depicted on the pediments, even those who are resting and calmly observing the scene, are all figures of towering energy. There is defiance in them, as they proclaim the victory of Athena and Poseidon, the sea-god, whose presence can be explained by the destruction of the Persian fleet, although he had long ago had his habitation on the Acropolis, leaving the mark of his trident on the rock and a salt well which mysteriously connected the Acropolis with the sea. Still, it is Athena's temple, and Poseidon is present only by her favor.

We know the original appearance of the pediments from drawings made by Jacques Carrey of Troyes, an artist in the service of the Marquis de Nointel, French ambassador to Turkey, who visited Athens in 1674. Carrey's drawing of the west pediment gives a very nearly complete representation of the original design. We see Poseidon leaning back and aiming his trident at the unseen enemies of Athens, while Athena holds her sacred olive branch in one hand and with the other checks two splendid, unruly horses who represent the wild and chaotic powers of nature now tamed by her divine energy and spirit. Athena and Poseidon are represented in violent movement, and their motion surges in turbulent waves across the whole length of the pediment, breaking like foam at the angles. The theme of the checking of the wild horses will be repeated on the frieze, but without this explosion of energy: quietly, with no violence to disturb the calm and orderly progress of the procession.

The presence of the two gods creates a wave of divine terror among the other crowded figures of the pediment. All huddle together, some leaning backward in fear, others gazing forward impetuously, dazzled by an event whose significance is beyond their understanding, while one, a maiden, simply gazes into space as though unaffected by the tumult and another leaps to her feet as though she would hurl herself upon the horses. Her vigorous torso now stands among the treasures of the Lord Elgin Room in the British Museum, together with the river-god, now headless, who can be seen on the left of Carrey's drawing, as he raises himself on his left arm and swings round to watch the miraculous apparition of the gods.

Figure 6. Pediment of the Temple of Athena in the Acropolis. Drawing by Carrey.

We can scarcely guess the names of all the figures. The leaping girl may be Iris, the angelic messenger, for there are slots in her shoulders indicating wings, and the crouched and huddled figures may represent the ancient gods and goddesses who ruled over Athens before Athena seized power. Beside the angelic Iris stands a figure who looks back over his shoulder, and this may be Hermes, the messenger of the gods. The river-god may be named after the Ilissus or the Cephissus, both rivers flowing through Athens.

The east pediment, the one seen first by the worshiper as he climbed up the steep slope leading onto the Acropolis, was already severely damaged in Carrey's time, and he could draw only the figures at the angles. Pausanias says the pediment showed the birth of Athena. It was an easy birth, for she sprang fully formed from the

head of Zeus. The surviving sculptures show the gods at ease, luxuriating in the presence of the newborn goddess. Dionysus rests languidly on a panther skin, beside Demeter and Persephone who are
seated together, while at the other end of the pediment a sumptuous
Aphrodite reposes on the lap of her mother Dione. It is the moment
of calm that follows a birth. All the world is new and fresh, and the
gentle winds scarcely ripple the luxurious garments.

Though only the ruins of the pedimental sculptures remain—
there is a small scattering in the Acropolis Museum with the more
massive works in the British Museum—we see them today perhaps at
greater advantage than the Greeks ever saw them, for we see them
as sculpture, while they saw them like painted dolls embellished with
golden hair, pink faces, and garments painted in vivid scarlet and
emerald. Gold shields, gold tridents, gold sandals and crowns were
everywhere.

So, too, with the great frieze that stood forty feet above floor
level, like a ribbon running round the temple, half-hidden by the
columns. This solid band of reliefs, originally more than five hundred
feet long, celebrated the people of Athens, who were thereby raised
to the level of the goddess. Because it could be seen so dimly, the
brightest colors were employed to give sharpness and distinction to
the individual figures, while the background was painted in a glowing blue. The west frieze, probably the first to be carved, showed the
young horsemen and their attendants preparing to take part in the
Panathenaic procession; we see them fastening their boots, grooming
their horses, or merely standing in attitudes of quiet self-absorption.
They are all amazingly self-conscious, aware of their beauty within
the greater beauty of the procession. Then they move off slowly, the
horses high-stepping to music, until at a turning of the road they are
met by a steward who checks their impatience with an upraised arm,
echoing the gesture of Athena on the pediment.

Some youths wear wreaths, some wear cloaks which fall loosely
from their shoulders, others wear crested helmets and leather cuirasses
over their short tunics, while still others wear heavy cloaks which
wave like scarves behind them. There are no stirrups, no saddlecloths.
The bridles and reins of hammered gold have vanished. The effect is
of a display of massive youthful energy, of controlled and irresistible
power, and of great calm. Chariots follow: they are ceremonial
chariots, for in classical Athens no one any longer drove a chariot

to war. Then come the elders, the lyre players and the flautists, the boys carrying jars of wine to be thrown on the flames of sacrifice, and the pure-white heifers and sheep which will be offered up on Athena's altar. On the south frieze we see the cavalry again, and once more there are musicians and youths bearing offerings and the beasts of sacrifice. In the southeast corner a heifer is seen making a sudden lunge at a youth, almost knocking him off his feet, and next to it another heifer nuzzles pathetically against a youth in a work of supreme beauty.

On the east frieze walk the girls carrying wine jars and bowls for pouring libations. Here, too, are the gods who have come to attend the ceremonies of Athena: Poseidon whispers to Apollo, Artemis smiles at Aphrodite, lame Hephaestus, leaning on his stick, engages in conversation with Athena, while Zeus looks on and all the other gods cluster around. There is a sense of trembling calm, of almost casual wonder, such as one might find among people sitting down to a wedding feast. But there is no feast, and the climax of the action is the simple folding by the maidens of the *peplos*, the sacred robe presented by the people of Athens to their adored goddess. It is the simplest gesture imaginable, and like the presentation of the ear of corn at the Eleusinian mystery it has the power to rejoice the heart.

Within the Parthenon stood the immense gold-and-ivory figure of the virgin goddess, Athena in majesty, with all her instruments of royalty about her. Her shield, her spear, her gown, were all plated with gold. Gold, too, were her sandals and her helmet. She stood there in the darkness of the *cella*, illuminated only by the light filtering through the shadowed doorway or perhaps by the pale glow of sunlight pouring through a sheet of alabaster in the wooden roof, gleaming among shadows, too large and too awesome to be fully comprehended. There were a few minutes at dawn when she became a blaze of gold, for the temple faced the east and she caught the sunrise. Then for the rest of the day she stood in a mysterious darkness.

The actual work on the Parthenon was begun in 447 and completed in 432. Such speed could be brought about only by a highly organized and disciplined community. There was no carelessness in the execution. In nine years the entire Parthenon with its fifty-eight columns and more than five hundred sculptured figures rose from the ground. "It rarely happens," commented Plutarch, "that ease and speed result in a work of enduring power or perfection of beauty, and for this reason the works of Pericles are all the more marvelous, for they were made in a short space of time to last for a very long time. As soon as they were erected, they had the venerable air of antiquity, and now that they are very old they have the vigor and freshness of buildings erected yesterday."

The Parthenon was scarcely finished when it was decided to build a palatial gateway, to serve as a kind of prelude to the Parthenon. It was to be far more than a gateway. There were to be reception rooms and galleries filled with paintings, but although the main gateway and one picture gallery were completed, this extravagantly costly refinement was abandoned in 432, at the beginning of the Peloponnesian War.

Eleven years later, during a lull in the war, work was begun on the Erechtheum, a strange and exquisitely beautiful palace intended to house the sacred relics, which included not only the *xoanon* of Athena but images of Erechtheus, the king with the serpent tail who had ruled over Athens in legendary times, and of his twin brother Butes, both sons of Poseidon, and of Cecrops, a later king, and his daughter Pandrosus, which means "sprinkled with dew." This small Ionic temple was built close to the edge of the northern cliff of the Acropolis. The site was holy ground, for here according to tradition Athena had wrestled with Poseidon for possession of Attica, and here was Poseidon's salt well which gave a murmuring sound when the wind was blowing from the south, and the mark of his trident could be seen on the rock. Here, too, was the sacred olive tree, and somewhere within these precincts lived the sacred snakes.

The Erechtheum served many purposes, and not the least of them was to give an effect of lightness and delicacy to a temple complex grown heavy with the sheer weight of the Parthenon, the massive gateway, and the other buildings which had grown up between them. The small temple to Athena-Victory, a larger temple to Brauronian Artemis, and a long colonnaded building called the Repository of Bronze, which may have been an armory, crowded the southwestern approaches to the Parthenon. The Erechtheum, all blue and white, resembled a wing lifting men's thoughts lightly above the weight of monuments.

It was a temple, a prison, a graveyard, a reliquary. Here Athena kept watch over the ancient gods, to prevent them from rising again. Here she was robed with the sacred *peplos*, and a golden lamp was kept burning continually, and there was a hollowed-out bronze palm tree through which the smoke was led through the roof. Close by was the grave of Cecrops, and since no rain was permitted to fall on it, a small porch was thrown out from the palace to enclose it. This was the Porch of the Maidens, where instead of columns stood Athena's priestesses, richly robed and wearing the sacred baskets on their heads: their purpose was to protect the grave, but also to demonstrate the power of the goddess over the ancient legends.

The Porch of the Maidens faces south. On the north side another porch gave entrance to the small chambers reserved for Erechtheus, Butes, and Poseidon. Here, too, there seems to have been an altar to Hephaestus, who was associated with Athena because he had wielded the ax that split open the head of Zeus, so giving her birth. To the west was an enclosure sacred to Pandrosus.

All these purposes were served in a building of remarkable complexity, delicacy, and power, shaped like a cross and build on different levels of rock. Athena's chamber was especially holy. Facing it stood the altar of Zeus on which the white heifers were sacrificed on the day of her festival.

The Parthenon is wholly masculine, the Erechtheum wholly feminine. It has the waywardness, the faintly sinister gracefulness, the delight in adorning herself of a truly beautiful woman. There is no hint of severity. Here Athena wears her robes, having put her armor away, and settles down to sumptuous domesticity, playing with her serpents, cultivating her olive tree, and watching over the dead and dying gods of the past.

The great complex of buildings on the Acropolis was only part of an extensive and carefully planned program. All through this period new buildings were going up in the Agora. The civic offices were rebuilt, and the two great colonnades with their shops and offices, called the Painted Stoa and the Stoa of Zeus, gave shelter and entertainment to the passers-by. On a hill overlooking the Agora was built the temple to Athena and Hephaestus, the only temple in Athens which has been preserved undamaged to this day. Across the Agora marched the new processional way to the Parthenon. All this area was new and gleaming, glinting with Pentelic marble. "What I desire," said Pericles, "is that you should fix your eyes every day on the greatness of Athens as she really is, and that you should fall in love with her."

The Panathenaea

IT was not difficult to fall in love with the magnificence of Athens. She shone in calm splendor in the radiance of a youthful goddess. Athena was a goddess of formidable persuasions and daemonic energy, but when it suited her purpose she could be gently beneficent, and it was that beneficence, flowing from the Acropolis, that was felt by the Athenians, while her thunder was reserved for their enemies. Athens in its glory reflected her smiling presence.

On her birthday in summer a great procession was held, and every four years there was a still greater procession. At the Great Panathenaea Athens paid supreme honor to her goddess, but also to herself. On that day prisoners were set free and slaves were permitted to feast with their masters. But, while there was much gaiety, the main procession took place in an atmosphere of high seriousness, for at heart Athena was an austere goddess, possessing unimaginably vast powers, and she was far from being solely the divine protectress of Athens, for her authority extended throughout the Greek community and the Greek colonies overseas. No one forgot that when she was born Olympus reeled, the earth cried out in alarm, the seas raged, and the sun was stopped in its course.

Like all ceremonies, the Panathenaea developed gradually. At first Athena's birthday was celebrated by horse and chariot races, and the original procession consisted only of her priests, her ministrants, and young horsemen and charioteers: this is the procession portrayed on the Parthenon frieze. Peisistratus enlarged the traditional ceremonies by athletic contests and competitions at which rhapsodists were invited to declaim their poems to the goddess. The stark and simple ceremonies of an earlier age were abandoned, for it was his intention to present her as the rival of Olympian Zeus with Athens as the sacred site of her mystery. Instead of the simple woolen robe woven for her in antiquity, he presented her with a robe sumptuously embroidered with representations of her battles against the Giants. In time the robe would become as large as a ship's sail.

During the Periclean age the Panathenaea was celebrated with a pomp and splendor never equaled before or since. For nine months Athenian matrons and maidens of good families wove and embroidered the immense robe of saffron wool which during the procession would be hung from the yard and mast of a wheeled ship for all to see. The ship provided the frame for the holy robe, but it was also the proclamation of Athenian mastery over the sea.

At dawn the celebrants gathered in the Outer Cerameicus. Then in the half-light the nine archons made their way into the Acropolis to await the coming of the procession. When the sun rose the great concourse of people began to move slowly and reverently through the city along the Sacred Way. They were led by musicians playing lyres and flutes. First came the foot soldiers and cavalry, then the victors in the games, followed by the priests wearing their golden crowns and garlands of flowers, then the sheep and white bulls which would be offered up in sacrifice, and these were followed by old bearded men of distinguished presence waving olive branches. Then came the ship of Athena manned by priests and priestesses wearing their crowns and garlands, with noble Athenian maidens walking by its side, very solemn, keeping time to the music. Other maidens followed them, some holding olive sprays, others with baskets of wine and oil and wheaten cakes and meal for the meal offerings, and some carried the long curving knives of sacrifice. Behind them came youths carrying gold and silver plates, followed by matrons and maidens from the colonies carrying baskets of wine and oil on their heads, and after them came foreigners distinguished by their bright red cloaks and by the oak branches they carried in honor of Zeus Xenios, the protector of strangers. At the end of the procession came the ambassadors from foreign states.

Every detail of the procession followed an elaborate protocol. At intervals marshals were stationed to see that the procession was orderly and moving at the proper tempo. From the Outer Cerameicus the procession moved to the Eleusinion, which it circled, and then made its way past the Pelargicon and the Pythion to the western entrance of the Acropolis. At the great gateway, the Propylaea, the procession seems to have divided, with the women going straight to the Erechtheum while the youths and men rode and marched around the Parthenon. The sacrifices were made on the altar of Zeus outside the Erechtheum. In honor of Athena the soldiers stripped and danced the Pyrrhic dance with much clashing of swords and shields. Hymns were sung. The embroidered robe was carefully folded and offered to the goddess, and the meats from the sacrificial altar were divided among the priests and the celebrants.

Such was the procession which moved across Athens in a rainbow-colored wave to offer a robe to the goddess, but nearly every week other processions formed to pay tribute to one or other of the lesser gods. Within Athens herself only one other procession rivaled it for pageantry and splendor. This took place on the first day of the Great Dionysia toward the end of March when spring was in the air and the sea was subsiding after the winter storms and the multitudes came in from the surrounding countryside. That was the day when the *xoanon* of Dionysus was removed from his temple in the marshy land south of the Acropolis and carried off beyond the Dipylon Gate to a shrine not far from the Academy. In his attempted flight to Eleutherae Dionysus was escorted by a solemn procession of youths singing dithyrambs, some in armor, others naked, and all wreathed with flowers. There followed the bulls and sheep to be sacrificed, and the priests of Dionysus, and the unmarried girls with baskets on their heads holding the sacrificial implements, and behind them came the entire population of Athens and of half the country villages, all gaily attired, wearing crowns of flowers or masks, all singing the wild songs in praise of the new wine. They paused briefly in the Agora while a chorus performed before the statues of the gods. Then they were off again, dancing and singing, through the Dipylon Gate and out into the open fields.

At the small shrine of Dionysus more dithyrambs were sung, the bulls and sheep were sacrificed, and the wine was poured out and distributed. When the feast was over, the revelers reclined on ivy leaves, drinking and making merry. In the afternoon there were choral contests, and at nightfall the revelers formed a drunken procession back to the city, singing and dancing by torchlight. This was the *komos*, the triumphal return of the god to his home. But his home was no longer the temple. Instead, garlanded youths placed the wooden figure on an altar in the theater, where he remained for the five remaining days of the festival, gazing down and blessing the tragedies and comedies performed in his honor. During those five days the theater became his temple, and the dramas were his sacred mysteries.

19 «« SOPHOCLES

IT WAS in the nature of things that after Aeschylus the form of tragedy should change, becoming more human, more sensuous, more lyrical. Aeschylus depicted the world of the gods and the great warrior kings, gaunt creatures whose voices rang out across the stage like the hammering of metal. Sophocles, too, described the gods and the warrior kings, but he made them human and recognizable, and he gave them tenderness. In all his seven surviving plays there is an air of stately quiet. The most terrible things happen—Antigone starves to death in her tomb, Hercules writhes in a poisoned robe, Oedipus tears out his eyes with the brooch taken from his dead wife, who has hanged herself—and yet, though the terror is only too manifest, we remember chiefly the nobility and courage of the characters. They move to their deaths in a strange quietness.

As Sophocles conceived the characters of his heroes and heroines, they were only a little larger than life. They breathed the same air that men breathed in the market place, and they were seen walking against the familiar luminous landscape of Attica, amid the temples and the barren rocks. They differed from ordinary mortals only in being more daring, more urgent, more desperate, more determined to defy their fates. There is nothing gaunt or ghostly about them; they are full-fleshed, with red cheeks and clean limbs. In the appearance they present to us they are in fact very much like Sophocles himself, who was renowned for his physical beauty, his grace of manner, and his skill in dancing. Aristophanes describes him as a man "contented in the world above and in the world below," and that sovereign contentment, which is not acquiescence, is characteristic of his heroes. Aeschylus was a hardy soldier who fought at Marathon. Sophocles saw little fighting, but at the age of sixteen he appeared in celebrations following the victory at Salamis as the leader of the processions, naked, crowned, and holding in his hand a lyre.

He was born in Colonus, a little more than a mile northwest of Athens, the son of a master swordsmith, who reaped a fortune during the Persian Wars and was able to give his son all the advantages of wealth. He won prizes in wrestling and music. He was twenty-seven when he came forward as the rival of the aging Aeschylus, and won the prize. It was the year when Cimon returned from his expedition to Scyros, bringing with him the bones of Theseus, and the judges were still deliberating whether to give the prize to Aeschylus or Sophocles when Cimon accompanied by his generals entered the theater in triumph. Because the judges were deadlocked, Cimon and nine of his generals were asked to make the judgment, and they unanimously gave the victory to Sophocles. According to tradition, Aeschylus fell ill of shock and in a towering rage sailed off to spend the rest of his life in Sicily.

The story may well be true: it fits in with what we know of Sophocles' happy capacity to achieve with ease and authority whatever he attempted. A kind of blessedness attended him throughout his life. In 440 he was appointed one of the ten *strategoi* who accompanied Pericles in an effort to reduce the aristocrats' revolt in Samos. He was later given the post of president of the Imperial Treasurers of the Tribute, and after the Sicilian disaster of 413 he became a member of the governing body known as the Committee of Public Safety. Deeply religious, he founded a shrine to Heracles, and became a priest of one of the gods of healing. He was a friend of Herodotus, and wrote an ode in his honor; and when Euripides died, he showed his grief by bringing his actors and chorus uncrowned on the stage. Plutarch says he wrote with greater ease and simplicity as he grew older, and this too is what we might expect in a man who developed quietly, in an untroubled progress to maturity. The story that his son Iophon brought him to court in his old age and demanded to be appointed administrator of the poet's estate on the ground that he was senile may be an unpleasant fiction, but that Sophocles should stand up in court and read to the jury an ode from *Oedipus at Colonus* to prove that he was in complete command of his faculties is a pleasant conceit. He died in 406, a few months after Euripides, and according to Phrynichus "his life ended without any blemish whatsoever." He was ninety years old at the time of his death, and he had lived through the most glorious period of Greek history. He died only just in time. In the course of the following year Athens lost the last remnant of her fleet at Aegospotami and lay at the mercy of her enemies.

Of the living and breathing Sophocles only a few rare glimpses have come down to us. Plato in *The Republic* tells how Sophocles was asked in his old age whether he was still capable of making love. He replied: "Hush, if you please! It gives me the greatest pleasure to have escaped from these pleasures, as from a furious and savage master." Whether or not he abandoned love-making, he seems to have taken a young courtesan called Archippe into his house when he was very old. Her former lover Smicrides, when asked what Archippe was doing, replied: "She sits there as the owls sit among the tombs." There are many allusions to his love of boys. The best and the longest, from the poet Ion, describes a meeting with him:

I met Sophocles the poet at Chios when he was sailing as general to Lesbos; he was playful in his cups, and cunning. Hermesilaus was a Chian, a friend of his, and consul for Athens, and he was entertaining his guest when there appeared standing beside the fire a handsome, blushing boy. The boy was the wine-server. Sophocles was plainly attracted to the boy and said: "Do you want me to drink with pleasure?" and when the boy answered: "Yes, indeed," then Sophocles said: "Then don't be too quick in handing me the cup and taking it away." There was a straw on the cup, and when the boy tried to remove it with his little finger, Sophocles asked him whether he could see the straw clearly. The boy said he could see it very well. Sophocles said: "Then blow it away—I wouldn't want you to get your finger wet." So the boy brought his face close to the cup, while Sophocles drew the cup nearer to his own lips in such a way that their two heads drew together; and then when the boy was very close Sophocles embraced and kissed him. Everyone applauded, and there was much laughter and shouting, because Sophocles had pulled such a neat trick. Sophocles said: "You see, I have been practicing strategy, for Pericles told me I was not much of a general, though I could write poetry. Don't you think my strategy has been very successful?"

(Athenaeus, *The Deipnosophists*, XIII, 603)

Such, then, was the occasional behavior of a man who in his writings displayed a breath-taking serenity and composure, which was perhaps only a mask for a feverish sensitivity.

Of his seven surviving plays there are three, forming the Oedipus cycle, which are regarded by universal consent as his masterpieces. These are *Oedipus the King, Oedipus at Colonus*, and *Antigone*, and of these it can be said that none excels another, for all of them move along a high majestic plane without faltering, without the least falling from grace, and with a miraculous charity and understanding. When we see a play by Aeschylus, there is the roar of thunder in our ears, the voices echo and re-echo against the darkening cliffs, and eagles wheel in the lightning-lit skies: all nature is implicated in the doom falling about the hero. In the plays of Sophocles all events take place in the quiet sunlight, and the doom confronting the godlike heroes arises solely from themselves. The Aeschylean heroes are always a little like somnambulists wandering through the dark night of the soul. Oedipus and Antigone are wide awake, and they wander through the earth we know.

Although these three plays form a cycle, they were not written consecutively, and there was an interval of forty years between the production of the first and the last. *Antigone* was composed about the year 441, when Sophocles was already in his fifties. Twenty years later came *Oedipus the King*, and *Oedipus at Colonus* was not produced until 401, after the poet's death.

In *Antigone* (to take them in the order of the poet's thought) we are presented with a simple conflict of divided loyalties raised to a pitch of horror by the determination of both Antigone and her adversary to pursue their loyalties beyond human reason. By order of King Creon the body of Polynices, killed while attempting to seize the kingdom, must be left unburied: this is the ultimate punishment for traitors and usurpers, and those who disobey the decree must be stoned to death. Antigone, the sister of Polynices, revolts against the decree and secretly pours earth on the body in sacramental burial of her brother. She is arrested, but proclaims her innocence. True, she has disobeyed the king's law, for which she expects to die, but there is a higher law which derives from the gods demanding love and sympathy for the dead, and this she has obeyed. Creon condemns her to death, not without some trepidation, for his own son Haemon rebukes him. In the end Antigone hangs herself, Haemon attacks his father with his sword and then turns it upon himself, and Cleon's queen stabs herself in sorrow over the death of her son. Cleon is last seen standing alone amid the holocaust he has brought down upon himself. "Take me away," he cries. "All things I touched are ruined, and my head is bowed by a fate too heavy."

The slow accumulation of disasters takes place in the daylight, quietly, in an orderly fashion. There is no alleviation. Step by step the characters advance boldly to their doom. Cleon is no villain. He is simply a man upholding the civic law, weak-willed in everything except his desire to keep the civic peace, tempering justice with some mercy, knowing that there is no solution to the conflict except the destruction of the principals: yet almost to the very end he is determined to uphold the law as he knows it. Too late he relents, but by that time Antigone is dead, and his son has become a madman. The death of the sorrowing queen is the last shattering blow which brings the play to a conclusion.

The role of the chorus is curiously ambivalent, but only in the sense that a pair of scales is ambivalent. Its function is to keep the balance even, to ward off the inevitable tragedy, and to safeguard the working of the heavenly laws. The chorus is therefore both actor and spectator, being the link between the audience and the actions on stage. It warns, pleads, and extols, and it is continually asking questions of the characters while raising more questions in the minds of the audience. Repeatedly the chorus reproves Antigone for going "beyond the uttermost bounds of daring and stumbling against the enthroned laws," and at such moments seems to be fighting on the side of Creon, but in fact the chorus is neither for Creon nor for Antigone. Against the choruses warning Antigone of inordinate disobedience must be set the choruses extolling the inordinate power of human love:

> *Love, the unconquerable,*
> *Spender of rich men's wealth,*
> *Keeper of all night vigils*
> *Beside the sweet faces of girls,*
> *Roamer of seas and country haunts,*
> *Not even the Immortals can escape from you,*
> *Nor any man who lives for the day.*
> *All are drunk with your splendor.*

Even the righteous men
Are cast into ruin and strife:
A house is divided against itself:
Love bears the victory away,
Shining in the kindling eyes
Of the bride, and the greatest gods
Bow before Aphrodite
Who works her will upon all.

The still more famous chorus on the splendor of man is introduced after Creon has given orders for the arrest of Antigone who has dared to throw earth on the polluted body of Polynices. In a moment she will appear, head bowed but unrepentant. There are subtleties in this chorus which praises the subtle daring of men, but it is important to observe that the chorus praises her action; and the casting of earth upon a corpse is likened to the casting of seed into the ground and the taming of animals, acts which are against the natural order though necessary to man. The chorus is saying that man's disobedience has led him to violate the earth and to place the animal kingdom in bondage, but who shall say that he has committed a crime? It is a long chorus, but it must be quoted in full because it is one of the central documents of the Greek ethos. Here Sophocles is proclaiming the rights of man in the face of the gods:

Many marvels there are,
But none so marvelous as Man.
Over the dark sea he rides
In the teeth of the winter storm,
Driving through towering spray,
While the oldest of gods, the Earth,
The hoary, the indomitable one,
He wearieth year by year
With the turning of the plowshare
Drawn by the patient mules
Over the endless furrows.

The lighthearted birds of the air,
Beasts of the field and forest,
He traps in his loaded snare:
The fish in the depths of the sea

Are caught in the woven nets
Of his intricate mind.
He binds to himself the beasts
Who roam the mountainside:
Horses with windy manes,
Bulls plunging wild in the grass,
All are enslaved by him.

He is learned in speech and thought;
Ideas rise swift as the wind.
Statecraft, too, he knows,
And the mind of the market place.
He has learned to deflect the snows
And the spears of the winter rain,
He has made himself secure
From all the winds that blow.
He has made himself immune:
Only one thing stands in his way—
For death he has no cure.

Skillful beyond belief
Is man's intelligence
Which guides him now to the heights,
Now to the darkest depths.
If he honors the laws of the state
And reveres the gods of the earth,
How proudly the city stands!
But should he break the laws
In his outrageous pride,
Then cityless is he,
Adrift in the world of men.

Though the last verse of the chorus is loaded in favor of Creon, the representative of the state laws, all that has gone before is a triumphant cry in favor of the dignity of man. There is exaltation in the very sound of the opening lines. It is not that men are wonderful, but that they are marvelous almost beyond belief, and it is not only that they can tame the wild beasts and plow the earth and protect themselves from the elements, but they possess prodigious powers for good and evil and there are no heights which they cannot achieve, no depths which they cannot sink into. By proclaiming the dignity and the rights of man Sophocles is proclaiming that the gods are dependent upon men just as men are dependent upon the gods. Man is no fallen angel; man is divine.

The unique splendor of the Greeks lay in the fact that they were perfectly prepared to accept this verdict on man. It was not a new verdict, for it was inherent in the Homeric heroes and in Pindar's glorification of the athlete, and indeed there is scarcely a poet or philosopher who did not share the belief that men were in some way touched with divinity. Plato puts into the mouth of Protagoras words which may very well be his own. Describing how men came to live on earth, Protagoras is made to say: "Since men partake of the divine and have a special relationship with the godhead, they were the first to believe in the gods and to erect altars and statues to them." So the Greeks would sometimes speak of distinguished poets and philosophers as *theoi*, meaning that they were "godlike" or at the very least "touched with divinity."

The *Antigone*, however, is not a play where the gods are abundantly present. Apart from the great choruses and the superb speech in which Antigone confesses her guilt and glories in it, there is a certain bleakness in the stately development of the drama as it moves toward final ruin and catastrophe. We sympathize with Antigone, for she is all too human, but we should remember that the ancient Greeks also sympathized with Creon, who loses both wife and son, confronting defeat without whimpering. There was something heroic in him at the end, but it is not the fiery heroism of a great man. He, too, is all too human.

With Oedipus we enter another dimension altogether. There is heroic fire in this man who is both cursed and blessed, belonging to the earth and to Heaven, being more than man because he is a King touched with divine madness and at the mercy of mysterious prophecies. For him there is reserved an extraordinary end, and the place of his death is to be blessed forever.

At the beginning of the play Oedipus is the great king who has destroyed the Sphinx and saved Thebes: no one can compare with him in reading the dark secrets of the soul. He has the prophetic instinct of kingship; he wears his robes royally. By the end of the play he is an outcast, a cursed wanderer and beggar let loose upon a world which distrusts and fears him.

What was his crime? The chorus continually warns us that his sufferings were brought about through his insolence: but it was not his fault that Apollo had prophesied before his birth that he would murder his father and marry his mother. His real crime was nothing less than his greatness, his high intelligence, his heroic nature. For this insolence, which is wholly unconscious, he must be destroyed and be himself the agent of his own destruction.

Sophocles plays an extraordinary war on the nerves. The ominous prophecies, the threats, the tensions are carefully spaced, so that we have no sooner overcome our terror than we are confronted with something still worse. It is the technique of the murder mystery raised to the level of supreme art. As in the *Antigone*, there is an atmosphere of high solemnity which makes the unfolding of these horrors almost too great to be borne. The terror is not of the earth only; it is a metaphysical terror, a sudden flash of lightning coloring the whole universe. What is at stake is far more than the life of a king: the greatness and nobility of all men are being questioned. Apollo, lord of the intelligence, noblest but least august of the gods, holds the fate of the king in his hands. The lightning strikes when he discovers that Jocasta, his wife and mother, has hanged herself. The Messenger tells the story:

> *The King came bursting in, shouting so violently,*
> *And while we gazed at him, he paced*
> *Frantically across the chamber, crying:*
> *"Give me a sword, a sword! Where is my wife?*
> *This wife who is no wife—this field, this mother's womb,*
> *Where I was sown, and where I sprang,*
> *And where I reaped my harvest!"*
> *As he raved, some demon seemed to guide him—*
> *Not us—we had no power—and so he was led—*
> *Roaring he rushed upon the doors*
> *And bent the bolts out of their sockets,*
> *Went stumbling into the room, and saw his wife*
> *Hanging with a twisted rope around her neck,*
> *Went roaring up to her and cut the rope.*
> *Then when he laid her on the ground, there came the worst.*
> *Her dress was pinned with golden brooches.*

These he tore from her, then lifted them high up
And drove them against his eyeballs, shouting:
"No more, no more shall my eyes see the crime!
The thing that now confronts me I have done!
Henceforth I shall go my way unseeing,
And what I see shall be in utter darkness:
Dark faces of those I love—" So he cried,
And struck his eyes again and yet again
With the gold brooches. From broken eyes
And from the bleeding sockets came the blood
To dew his beard, not oozing drop by drop
But flowing in black rivers thick as rain.

It is of course the supreme moment of the tragedy, and nothing that happens afterward can alleviate the horror of the scene where he stands with the body of Jocasta lying at his feet and his hands clutching the golden brooches and lifted high in the air, and soon the brooches will descend like the points of swords. The horror is not in the blood pouring out of his eyes "in black rivers thick as rain" so much as in the figure of the hero about to destroy himself: the lifted hands alone have power to chill the blood. As we shall see, the same posture is employed, but with a totally different meaning, in the final scene of *Oedipus in Colonus* when the king goes to meet his mysterious death.

Oedipus the King relates the punishment that fell upon Oedipus as the result of the working out of ancestral forces. As in the *Antigone*, there is the stately progress toward unalterable doom. The end is torture, the bodies broken, courage annihilated. There is a sense in which everything has been said, and out of the broken presence of the king no further adventures can be extracted. What else is there to say when the fates have taken their revenge?

There is a good deal to say, as the Greeks well knew. In Sophocles' *Ajax* the hero kills himself halfway through the play: there follows a long and complicated debate about the disposal of his corpse. This debate takes the form of a patient inquiry into the honor of the dead prince, with a court composed of his peers pronouncing judgment. The death is incidental; the judgment is all. So in *Oedipus in Colonus* Sophocles is concerned with the final judgment upon the king, the ultimate disposal of the living corpse and of the legend surrounding his life. It is not enough that a hero should be doomed, for in a sense all heroes are doomed, since doom is the air they breathe and all their postures invite the retribution of the gods. What is important—and for the Greeks nothing could be more important—is the continuing life of the hero long after he is dead. *Oedipus in Colonus* recounts the adventures of Oedipus in the strange borderland world which Coleridge called Life-in-death.

As the play opens, Oedipus is not dead, nor is he living. He has come out of nowhere, a blind white-haired old wanderer, dressed in rags, bent beneath the weight of curses, knowing himself the object of the world's horror. He does not know where he has come from or where he is going: only that the end is near, for Apollo has warned him that in the Grove of the Dread Goddesses he will enter into Hades, and it has come to his knowledge that he has already entered the fearful grove. Leaning on the arm of his daughter Antigone he asks for pity, some place to rest in quietness, but the country folk refuse his request. Instead of leaving the place, he wanders deeper and deeper into the grove, the enchanted forest. He will not emerge until he has the assurance that he can stay there. The chorus pleads with him to go, but he prays to the Dread Goddesses for mercy and makes offerings to them of pure water, honey, and olive sprays. His prayers are answered, and he remains, an old man waiting for the end.

It is not enough that he should die quietly in a holy place: there must be a judgment, the discovery of the meaning of his death. So one by one the witnesses crowd round him, as though he had summoned them for this very purpose. First his daughter Ismene comes riding across the plain. Then comes Theseus, King of Athens, who has also known obloquy and exile, and who offers his protection. Theseus vanishes, and his place is taken by Creon, who has usurped the throne and demands that Oedipus should return to Thebes so that his disembodied ghost shall lay the ghosts of those he has killed. Creon is severely practical. He wants the corpse of Oedipus, and will do everything in his power to get it. Polynices, the son of Oedipus, arrives to join the debate: he too is in exile. They are still debating and unraveling the mystery of Oedipus and his tragic passion when a shattering peal of thunder is heard, and then at last we hear the verdict as Oedipus goes down to his death. The verdict is a very simple one: nothing less than his benediction by the gods. From the world of suffering he enters the world of an eternal blessedness, becoming himself a kind of guardian angel ruling over Athens, guiding its destiny from some hidden chamber in the rocks.

The final scene in *Oedipus in Colonus* may have been the last scene that Sophocles ever wrote. Though written in old age, it has a power and amplitude which no other poet has excelled. Somehow Sophocles succeeded in describing what one would have thought to be impossible—how a man becomes a god. The description of the last earthly moments of Oedipus is put into the mouth of the Messenger:

His going was a marvelous thing to see—
You saw him go, for you were witnesses and know
No helping hand accompanied him. He went alone,
Leading the way to the very brink of the Abyss,
To the Bronze Stairs which plunge to the roots of the earth,
And past the stone bowl carved in memory
Of the solemn covenant between Theseus and Pirithoüs,
Not far from the Rock of Thoricus, and beside
The Hollow Pear-tree and the Marble Tomb,
And there he sat and loosed his beggar's clothes,
Calling his daughters to him, asking for water,
Water from the fountain to cleanse his limbs
And pour libations to the dead.
Then they climbed the hill of Demeter,
Who waters all green things, and soon returned
With water for their father, whom they bathed
And clothed in the proper fashion for a dying man.
When all was done according to his pleasure,
All his desires fulfilled, then—then—
They heard the roar of thunder in the underworld.
The daughters trembled at their father's knees,
Wept, and beat their breasts, fiercely lamenting:
And hearing them, he held them in his arms, saying:
"My children, the day of my death has come.
The end has come, the end of all your caring,
The long and bitter caring, and yet one word—
The word of love—frees us from the pains of living.
I loved you more than anyone has loved you.
The end has come, and you must live without me."
They clung to one another weeping,

The father and his daughters, till there came
A time when no tears flowed: then silence fell,
And then a Voice was heard, so terrible
It made their hairs stand up on end.
Again and again the Voice was heard, crying:
"Oedipus, why delay? Your time has come!
Too long, too long this waiting! Why delay?"
Then knowing that the spirit summoned him,
He asked that Theseus come, and then he said:
"Dear friend, give me your hand, protect
My children, and my children, give
Your hands to Theseus. Let this binding pledge
Testify to your enduring care for them,
Being kind to them at all times."
Theseus obeyed, and uncomplaining
He swore on oath to do as he was bidden.
When this was done, then Oedipus
Laid his blind hands upon his daughters, saying:
"My children, show your nobleness of heart,
And have the courage now to leave this place.
You must not ask to see what is forbidden,
Or hear those things which no man dares to hear.
Go—go quickly! Only King Theseus
May see me at the end!" All this we heard him say,
And then we led the sobbing girls away.
Then, having gone a little space, we turned,
And saw no sign of Oedipus—only the King,
His hands before his face, shielding his sight
From some dreadful thing he dared not look at,
And afterwards he bowed to the goddess Earth
And to the Powers of Heaven, all in a single prayer.
No one knows by what death Oedipus perished—
Only Theseus knows. Only we know
There was no blaze of fire from Heaven,
No sea-wave rose. He vanished;
And whether there came a messenger from the gods,
Or whether he entered gently the dark world
Of Hades, this too remains unknown.
Not with lamentations did he die,

No grief nor agony attended him in his going.
Most marvelous was his dying.

Beyond this it would seem impossible for any dramatic poet to go, for here poetry has become vision. The hero dies, and in some mysterious way passes into godhead. Over this scene, as over some scenes in the New Testament, there hovers a blaze of calm fire.

The three Theban plays of Sophocles tower over his remaining works as the *Prometheus Bound* and the *Agamemnon* tower over the works of Aeschylus. They move slowly to a stately music, like hymns, and there is never a moment of faltering. The steady flow of the imagination is not so evident in the other plays: the fire glows, and goes out, and glows again.

Here and there in *The Maidens of Trachis* the fire burns brightly. He depicts Deianira, the wife of Heracles, with charm and gentleness. Her love for the hero is wholly innocent, and even when he proves unfaithful to her and sends into his own house the beautiful captive Iole, for whose sake he sacked a city, she has only pity and understanding. She studies the girl and decides that it would be a simple matter to win back her husband's love. She remembers that many years before the long-haired Centaur Nessus, "a monstrous creature of untold age," had while carrying her across a river attempted to molest her. Then Heracles shot him with an arrow poisoned with the Lernean Hydra's blood, and the dying Centaur told her that if she gathered the blood around the wound, it would be a charm to prevent her husband from loving any other woman. She had kept the blood carefully hidden away in a bronze vessel, away from fire and heat, for these, according to the Centaur, would weaken the power of the love potion.

The innocence of Deianira is her undoing. Strange things happen when she smears the love potion on a robe she has woven with her own hands. A tuft of wool dipped in the love potion shrivels into powder when she tosses it away, and where the powder falls the earth oozes like fermenting grapes. All this she sees as she prepares the robe and sends it to Heracles, who has remained in Euboea to offer sacrifices for his victories, yet the full significance of the powder and the earth's ferment does not dawn on her until too late. Her son tells her how his father put on the robe smeared with a burning poison, and in his agony killed the young herald Lichas:

He threw the robe around him, and then began
To sacrifice those twelve unblemished bulls,
The first fruits of the spoils; in all there were
A hundred beasts laid out upon his altars.
So praying with serene unclouded countenance,
Proud of his robe, my wretched father watched
The scarlet flames feeding upon the blood
Of oxen and the juices of the pinewood.
Then sweat broke from him, and the robe
Clung tightly to his side, sticking to every limb,
Glued as though a workman glued it there.
This was the beginning. A prickling pain
Racked and gnawed at his bones, while the poison,
As though from serpent's venom, devoured him.
He called to Lichas—the poor innocent,
Who had no part or parcel of this crime—
Accusing him of having instigated
Some treacherous plot against him
By bringing him the robe, while he, poor youth,
Replied: "It was a gift, O Heracles, sent by your wife,
Placed in my hands and so delivered to you."
Hearing this, my father cried aloud,
Roared at the top of his lungs, seized the boy's ankles,
Dashed him on a rock which rose
Out of the sea's foam. The skull of Lichas
Was broken into fragments, and his hair
Was spattered with the dew of brains and blood.
And all who watched were crying out in horror
To see my father mad, his herald dead.
None dared to face him. An agony
Flung him to the earth, and then he leaped
High in the air, while from the Locrian headlands
To the Euboean shores his cries resounded:
Yet when the agony had spent itself,
Now writhing on the earth and now lamenting,
He shrieked his curses on the marriage bed.

(*The Maidens of Trachis*, 759–791)

When she hears these words from the lips of her son, Deianira
goes quietly into her house and kills herself.

The play does not end there, for the resolution of the drama demands that Heracles should be brought on the stage in his agony, cursing the innocent wife who is the cause of his death. No man had ever made him moan before. In his anguish he can only remember that he is the hero who wrestled with the Nemean lion, slew the hundred-headed Hydra, the three-headed hound of Hell, and the Erymanthian boar, and held the sky upon his shoulders. Told that Deianira has died by her own hand, he rages on as unforgiving as ever, and when he learns she has used what she thought to be a love potion given to her by the Centaur Nessus, he starts up in alarm, for now at last he knows that his wounds are mortal, for there was a prophecy that he would die at the hands of one "who has passed the border between life and death." Once again we hear the ancient cry that "death comes to the living from the dead." The hero dying calls upon his son to build a funeral pyre for him on the summit of Mount Oeta sacred to Zeus, and then utters one last command—his son must marry Iole, who has brought disaster on the entire family. The prophecies are now fulfilled, innocence has accomplished terrible destinies, and there is no place for tears, for as the chorus sings in the last words of the play: "Nothing is here but Zeus."

The Maidens of Trachis is a disturbing play, because the focus continually shifts from the innocents caught in the web of their undoing and the ferocious rage of the hero trapped in his poisoned robe. Heracles in his fury is not a pleasant spectacle, and he is all the more unpleasant in contrast to Deianira who goes about her tasks—even the task of poisoning him—with infinite gentleness. She has no hatred for Iole. As she says:

> The flower of her age is in its spring,
> But mine in autumn. And the eyes of men
> Pluck the fresh petals, and throw the old away.

With that compassion and forgiveness Sophocles is at home; it is the world he knows. Heracles, the unheroic hero, belongs to a world almost outside the scope of drama. He rants uproariously like any *miles gloriosus*, and we hardly care whether he lives or dies.

There is little compassion or forgiveness in the *Electra*, which follows the same story as Aeschylus' *Libation Bearers*, but with important differences. Once more we are in the house of Agamemnon, waiting for Orestes and his sister to murder Clytemnestra and Aegisthus. The years have passed, and Electra, hollow-eyed and broken by what seems to her an eternity of grief, dreams of the day when punishment will be visited upon her mother and her mother's lover. She is an unwelcome guest in the house. Sometimes her mother visits her, and then they argue bitterly, Clytemnestra defending herself by claiming that she had done no more than punish Agamemnon for offering his own daughter Iphigenia as a sacrifice, Electra maintaining that Clytemnestra is no more than a common murderer. Orestes enters the house in disguise, carrying the urn which he says contains the ashes of Orestes. Clytemnestra welcomes him, sighs with pleasure at the thought of Orestes' death, and is stabbed to death. Then Aegisthus enters, having heard in the market place that the body of Orestes has been brought to the house. He is invited to see the body, and calls out to the servants to fetch Clytemnestra, who would also want to see the body. "She is very close to you," says the disguised Orestes. "Do not look far away."

This is the moment toward which the entire play has been working. At this moment the play jerks to a sudden halt in an explosion of unalloyed horror, while the air trembles and a kingdom falls.

Aegisthus pulls up the cloth that has covered the body of his wife, and starts back in terror.

"Are you afraid?" Orestes asks quietly. "Is the face strange?"

Strange it is; stranger than anything Aegisthus had thought to see; and as it dawns on him that he is in mortal danger he asks into whose hands he has fallen, and Orestes says: "Have you not learned yet that the dead have come to life?"

Dragged off in an inner room to be butchered, he makes one last cry:

> *Why drive me into the house?*
> *Must this good deed be hidden from the sunlight?*
> *Strike, and have done with it!*

In that wonderful cry he almost redeems himself. This love of the light floods up from the depths of the Greek soul, never more fiercely than at moments of great danger. For Electra there can be no more terrible punishment than to be cast into a dungeon, to live out her life in darkness and silence—the punishment which Clytemnestra has promised her. When she first appears she sings a mourning song for her lost father:

O holy light!
O air spread evenly
Over the whole earth!
And now so much despair,
My heart breaks in my breast . . .

For Electra, and for the Greeks, there was always the harrowing
inconsistency between the sun's brightness and the darkness in the
human heart, between the *evenness* of the sunlit air and the jagged
pathways of human desires. For them the heavens were constant, and
man's inconstancy led him to despair, even to madness.

In the *Ajax* Sophocles tells a pitiless story of a man who has been
one of the great heroes of the Trojan War brought to madness and
death by his arrogance, for when he fought against the Trojans and
Athena offered her aid, he bade her help others less fortunate than himself. "I shall win honor and glory on my own" was his boast, and for
his overweening pride the goddess punished him with a strange blindness and a stranger rage. One night he stole away from his tent,
rounded up all the cattle and sheep he could find, drove them back
to the tent, and there butchered them, believing he had slaughtered
the enemy. The story of the great slaughter is told four times—by
Athena, by Odysseus, by the chorus, and by Tecmessa, the captive
wife of Ajax. There are subtle differences in their telling of the story,
but there is no doubt that Ajax has been overcome with madness.
Why? No one knows. The Salaminian sailors, faithful followers of
Ajax, ask whether it was because some spoils were withheld from the
gods, a gift not made, a victory unblessed by the gods. Only gradually
does it appear that Ajax has brought defeat upon himself. After
Achilles he was the most brilliant of the warriors in the Greek camp;
now he sits amid the murdered sheep and cattle, wondering what
crime he has committed, while Tecmessa tries to warm him back to
life.

Tecmessa is one of those heroines who are all sweetness and
gentleness. She cannot fathom why the gods should punish a husband
who has been good to her and to her son. "Love is the eternal genera-
tor of love," she says, and the words are torn out of her in despair
against the laws of Heaven. Her role is to mourn the lost splendor;
and though she plays little part in the drama, she is central to it. When,
in a greater despair, Ajax falls on his sword in a deserted place along

the shore, there is still no resolution of the conflict: only the knowledge that the heavens must be obeyed, and love is powerless against the anger of the gods.

On another deserted shore Sophocles sets the scene for another play in which one of the great heroes of the Trojan War is compelled against his will to obey the dictates of the gods. The *Philoctetes* was written during the last years of his life, when he was eighty-seven, but there is no failure of genius. The poetry flows with the same strenuous speed, and tragic events follow one another with the same orderly progress toward the inevitable climax. Only one thing is missing—the terror that lies at the heart of the other tragedies. For ten years Philoctetes has been abandoned on the island of Lemnos because he suffers an offensive sore in his leg, where he was bitten by a serpent. He had lit the funeral pyre of Heracles, and in reward he received a bow and arrows which infallibly reached their mark. Now he waits for death, knowing that men will come and try to wrest from him the divine bow and arrows which will give victory to whoever owns them. Odysseus and Neoptolemus, the son of the dead Achilles, come to the island and attempt to carry him back to Troy so that he can preside over the final defeat of the Trojans, but Philoctetes has no heart for it, remembering how his companions left him to die on the island.

The drama, then, recounts the play of wills between two heroes and a sick and dying man. All are cunning; all are determined to achieve their own victories; the prize is Troy. But, strangely, we have no feeling that the outcome is of any great concern. We do not believe that Troy will fall to Philoctetes' bows and arrows. Odysseus is a ranting bully, like the Heracles of *The Maidens of Trachis*, and we find ourselves wondering whether he has strayed from another play. There is, somewhere, a failure of intensity. Longinus compared Homer's *Odyssey* with the setting sun, saying that the grandeur remained but not the intensity; and so it is in the *Philoctetes*.

Perhaps, in old age, Sophocles no longer possessed the same affection for the heroes and the gods. He worshiped Apollo, but the other gods seemed to fall away into a remote Olympus of their own, while the heroes vanished in the dust of battle. There was no failure of nerve, but there was a failure of energy. The most beautiful of the lyrics in the *Philoctetes* is a plea for a calm death addressed to Apollo, the god of the divine light:

O Sleep without a care,
Come upon my prayer,
Breathe with softest air
Upon my eyelids.
Come, my lord, and spread
Over me the splendor
Of thy blessed peace.

Characteristically Sophocles used the word *"aiglê,"* sacred to Apollo and the Muses, for it means splendor, glory, daylight, and the gleam of all sunlit things.

In the British Museum there is a bronze portrait of Sophocles which may have been made about the time he wrote the *Philoctetes.* Age has withered him, but there are still remnants of his youthful beauty. The sparse beard is neatly curled, and there is a ribbon round his head to keep his hair in order. He is lost in meditation, and his lips are pursed together as though he were about to speak the verses dawning in his brain; and there is about that bronze, now black with age, the sense of the presence of a long-dead poet still singing.

20 «« EURIPIDES

AESCHYLUS was obsessed by the power and greatness of the gods and the half-divine heroes, Sophocles by the nobility of man, and it was left to Euripides to proclaim men's griefs. There is a sense in which he is the greatest of the Greek dramatic poets because his range is incomparably wider than any other, enclosing the entire realm of human suffering. Aeschylus speaks heroically, as befits a hero; Sophocles speaks in the accents of the aristocracy; Euripides speaks to the people. For the first time on the European stage we are aware of ordinary suffering humanity.

Euripides had the gift, very rare among the Greeks, of being able to sustain his sorrow over the catastrophes that afflict individual men and women; and sometimes when he writes he seems to be blinded by tears. He has no resources against the baffling decrees of fate; he will simply describe what he has seen without recrimination or special pleading, knowing that there is no medicine for the lacerated human heart and no cure for the murders that are committed every day. The characters of Sophocles stalk the stage with magnificent youthful effrontery, even when they are doomed. The characters of Euripides tremble, shuffle their feet, and plead for mercy; they are creatures like us, and there is a limit to their endurance. His continuing theme is man's frailty before the ineluctable decrees of Heaven.

He could not, and perhaps did not want to, make his characters larger than life: they are earth-bound and live out their tumultuous lives in settings which were familiar to his audiences, and no other Greek dramatist so delights in scenery. Just as in the thirteenth century the paintings of Giotto show the gradual emergence of a sense of space and *paysage* at the same time that there emerges a sense of man's full individuality, so in Euripides we see the characters emerging into the sunlight against landscapes which are almost extensions of themselves. Euripides will paint in a scene at length, glorying in his descriptive powers. His choruses are full of the flashing streams and shining hillsides of his beloved Attica.

The surviving portraits show a man with a high forehead, beaked nose, and heavy curling beard, with an expression of settled melancholy; it is the face of a man given to nightmares, obsessed by the suffering of others, possessing a strange tenderness toward women and children. He was a realist, but sometimes his lonely fantasies and dreams gripped him. Once he dreamed of a marble column which rose slowly out of the earth and suddenly from the top of the column there grew long golden hairs, which spoke.

He was born, according to tradition, on the island of Salamis in the same year and on the same day as the battle. His father, Mnesarchides, was a man of property in the town of Phlya about six miles northeast of Athens. His mother, Clito, was of noble family, though it amused Aristophanes to say that she kept a grocer's shop and hawked fruit and flowers on the street. As a boy he took part in a festival in honor of Delian Apollo, pouring wine for the dancers, and his biographers say that he possessed a small fame as an athlete in his youth. He was well-schooled after the fashion of his time. Strabo says he took "the entire course of Anaxagoras," and the great Sophists Prodicus and Protagoras were his teachers. He was a close friend of Socrates, and there is a pleasant story that Socrates always attended a new play by Euripides even if it meant traveling to Piraeus to see it.

Though famous and successful in his lifetime, Euripides was constantly under attack. He was parodied and ridiculed by the comic poets, and usually regarded unfavorably by the aristocratic judges at the theater, who seldom awarded him the prize, preferring to give it to obscure competitors whose names are now forgotten. He rarely occupied any official position, but it is related that after the great disaster in 413 he was sent as an ambassador to Syracuse. According to Plutarch, his plays were so popular among the Sicilians that captured Athenians who could recite passages of his work were pardoned and sent back to Athens.

Euripides, then, was a man who embodied in himself the human aspects of the Greeks. Not that he was a typical Athenian: he was altogether too somber to be typical of these people, who were given to astonishing displays of gaiety. It was said of him that he was "gloomy, thoughtful and austere," that he avoided the society of men, and did not know how to jest in his cups. The legend that he avoided the company of men may have derived from his habit of retreating to a cave on the island of Salamis. Modern authors who bury themselves in their seaside retreats are rarely accused of being hermits.

Of his private life we know little except that he was the father of three sons and enjoyed watching them grow up. One, the eldest, became a merchant, the second became an actor, and the youngest became a tragic poet.

Euripides' fame increased as he grew older; so, too, did the attacks upon him. Aristophanes, though privately friendly, attacked him publicly in verses of quite extraordinary venom. A certain Hygiaenon accused him of impiety for the famous line in the *Hippolytus:* "My tongue has sworn, my mind remains unsworn." Euripides answered in court that the proper venue for the trial was the floor of the theater, and he earned acquittal by the keenness of his retort. According to the recently discovered biography of Euripides by Satyrus, he finally left Athens because he was plagued unmercifully by the lampoons of minor poets. He took refuge in the court of King Archelaus of Macedon, who had gathered around him a group of great artists, all refugees from Athens. Zeuxis, the painter, and Agathon, the dramatist, and many others lived under the king's protection.

In exile Euripides was treated with great distinction, and lived on terms of intimacy with the king. Plutarch tells a pleasant story of a courtier who asked for a gold cup from the king's hands. "I shall not give it to you, because you are the kind of man who asks for things," said King Archelaus. "I shall give it to Euripides who never asks for anything." Aristotle tells an unpleasant story of a courtier who made a remark about the foulness of Euripides' breath and was immediately arrested and given over to the poet to be scourged. Both stories may be true, for the savagery of Macedonian kings was equaled only by their generosity.

In that savage land jealousies and intrigues flourished, and those who were close to the king were sometimes in greater danger than the king himself. One day the poet was walking alone in the woods near the palace when a hunting party set out, accompanied by huge

Molossian hunting dogs. They found Euripides and tore him to pieces. It was generally believed that this was a deliberate murder, perhaps organized by the slave Lysimachus who was in charge of the dogs. The king cut off his hair in sorrow, and some time later the Athenians asked for the body to be returned to Athens. The king refused, perhaps because there was no body to return.

So died Euripides, who more than any other man founded the drama as we know it today, a friend of Socrates and author of a hundred plays. When Aeschylus and Sophocles were half forgotten, the plays of Euripides were still being performed. He wrote of gods and heroes, but he gave them the preoccupations of the people of Athens. He took the drama out of the skies and placed it solidly on the earth.

Long before he died he had acquired the reputation of hating women. How this arose is something of a mystery, for no one, not even Shakespeare, wrote about them so tenderly. His women are more real, more powerful, and altogether more appealing than his men. From the *Alcestis*, the first play to come down to us, to the *Iphigenia at Aulis*, which he left unfinished at his death, his plays are dominated by women. From the proud and murderous queen to the humble handmaiden, from the nymphomaniac to the dedicated virgin, from the virago to the gentle-tempered shepherdess, he knew them well, too well for comfort. The great gallery of his women has never been excelled.

The *Alcestis* sets the mood. When Apollo was punished by Zeus for killing the Cyclops, he was made to take service as a herdman under King Admetus, who treated him with so much gentleness that in return Apollo offered him immortal life if he could find someone who would die for him. Alcestis, the king's wife, leaped at the opportunity of dying for her husband, and as the play opens she is on her deathbed with her children around her. There are moments when she bitterly repents, thinking of those others who might have died instead of her, and she is troubled at the thought of Admetus' taking another wife. She sings of the sun and the light of day and the eddying, hurrying clouds, and she prays that her children will look long on the sun. Then she dies and is received into the hands of Hades, "the dark-haired god," and Admetus gives way to his grief. He promises to make an image of her, which he will place on the bed and worship for the rest of his life, and he is still raging in his grief when Heracles comes and begs for shelter. The king offers it willingly, for it is a sacred thing to welcome a guest. "Take him," says the king, "to a wing of the house, so that he will not hear our weeping." And Heracles, who does not know who has died, amuses himself by drinking and crowning his head with myrtles and singing lustily.

At last Heracles comes to his senses, and since Admetus is his friend and kind to him, he vows to wrestle with Death and bring Alcestis back to life. The king is still grieving when Heracles returns with a veiled woman. "Take her," he says. "You will not regret it." The king upbraids him, saying he has suffered enough without being taunted in his grief. Heracles says he has won the woman in a wrestling match; he must leave her somewhere; the king should have pity on him, and at least offer her some shelter. "Look upon her, and be happy," Heracles says, and then the king lifts the veil and sees his wife standing before him. The tragedy ends in a moment of piercing joy.

We hear that note of piercing joy again in *Iphigenia at Aulis*, when Iphigenia comes to the sacred grove of Artemis and offers her life for the sake of calm seas, for the goddess Artemis has summoned a storm to prevent the fleet of Agamemnon from sailing to Troy and can only be appeased by her sacrifice:

> *Then Iphigenia stood beside her father, saying:*
> *"Father, I have come, as you desired,*
> *And willingly I give myself for Hellas,*
> *And for my country I desire my sacrifice.*
> *If this is heaven's decree, then lead me on,*
> *And you shall prosper and attain the prize,*
> *Returning safely to the fatherland.*
> *But let no Argive lay his hands on me—*
> *I yield myself in silence without fear!"*
> *All heard her, marveling at the virgin's strength,*
> *And then Talthybius proclaimed long silence:*
> *A reverent hush ensued, while the seer Calchas*
> *Drew from the scabbard within the golden basket*
> *His sharp-edged knife, and placed a crown*
> *Upon her head, and then Achilles*
> *Ran round the altar, bearing in his hands*
> *The basket and a bowl of holy water, shouting:*

"Daughter of Zeus, O slayer of wild beasts,
Whose wheeling light gives splendor to the dark,
Accept the offering which is rendered now,
The pure blood falling from a virgin's throat,
And grant safe landfall to our ships,
And may our spears destroy the Trojan walls."
And then the priest upheld the knife and prayed,
And sought to find the place where he would strike,
While we in anguish prayed, our heads downcast.
And then—O miracle! We heard the stroke,
And yet the virgin maid had gone, astounding all
By her strange vanishing. The priest cried out.
The army shouted in amazement. An augury
As though a god unseen had stepped among us
Happened before our eyes. Where the virgin lay
Lay now a huge and lovely hind instead.

(*Iphigenia at Aulis*, 1551–1583)

Euripides has this magic, this power of making us see things which never took place on land or sea. "Look upon her, and be happy," says Heracles, and we fall into the enchantment of seeing whatever he wishes us to see. He has an astonishing narrative power, telling his stories as artfully as Herodotus or Plato, who were both experts in elaborating significant detail. He does not tell us how the long knife flashed in the air, nor are we told the expression on Agamemnon's face. With unerring instinct Euripides tells us only one thing about the physical appearance of the sacrifice—"We heard the stroke." It is enough. The stroke comes like a thunderclap, and when Iphigenia vanishes and the lovely hind appears in her stead we are prepared for it, because after the thunderclap we are prepared for anything.

Again and again Euripides demonstrates this enchanting power to tell a story so convincingly that we become the willing victims of his imagination.

In the *Medea* he paints the portrait of a woman of supreme vengefulness. She had once killed her brother and strewn the pieces on the road so that her father will delay his pursuit of Jason and the Golden Fleece. She is a woman who will stop at nothing, with an appalling power for evil. When she learns that Jason is preparing to abandon her and the two sons she has given him so that he can marry a princess of Corinth, her mind is made up. She will destroy the princess and her own sons. To accomplish the destruction of the princess, Medea summons her sons and gives them an embroidered robe and a gold diadem to present to the princess. The robe is poisoned.

Poisoned gowns were the commonplaces of Greek mythology, and we have already seen how Sophocles dealt with the gown which Deianira presented to Heracles. He roared and ranted, fell unconscious, awoke in intolerable pain, writhed, screamed, cursed, and uttered furious maledictions upon his wife. He never convinces us that he is anything but an actor pretending to be Heracles. But when Euripides describes the princess putting on the gown and dying in a nest of poison, with one striking image he brings us into her presence, and we believe everything he tells us to the very last word.

It is a triumph of *grand guignol*, but it is also a triumph of dramatic art, and Euripides prepares us for it with exquisite cunning. He tells how the children arrived at the palace and were greeted with joy, because everyone had heard that Medea had given her consent to the marriage. Then they are led into the bridal chamber of the princess. Jason is there, and at first the princess is disturbed by the presence of the two boys bearing gifts, as well she might be, and it is Jason himself who convinces her that no harm and much good will come from accepting them. From shuddering fear she moves quickly to acquiescence and then to delight. Jason and the boys are dismissed from the chamber, while she puts on the robe:

> *She took the embroidered robe and put it on,*
> *Then with the gold diadem she crowned her head*
> *And in the shining mirror arranged her hair,*
> *Smiling back at her lifeless image there.*
> *Then rising from her chair, around the room*
> *She walked with white feet treading luxuriously,*
> *Rejoicing in the gift. Often and often*
> *She would stretch her foot out straight and look along it.*
> *But afterwards a fearful change occurred.*
> *Suddenly she turned pale, and reeling back,*
> *Her legs all trembling, she was near*
> *Falling on the ground, but reached a chair*
> *In time, and there an old and wizened servant saw her,*

And thought her seized by Pan or one of the other gods,
Whispered a little prayer, but that was before
She saw the white foam drip from her mouth and the eyes
Rolling and the face all bloodless. Then she raised
A different kind of noise—a wild screaming . . .
The princess lay in torment. The gold diadem
Spewed out a marvelous stream of fire,
The gold-embroidered robe the children gave her
Gnawed at her lovely flesh and sent her leaping,
Shaking her hair in all directions, trying
To shake the crown away, but still the diadem
Sat tight upon her brows, and twice as fiercely
The flames came blazing out. Spent,
She fell upon the ground, unrecognizable
Save by a parent. Where her eyes had been
No one could tell, her face being shapeless.
Fire and blood oozed from the top of her head
Like the drops on pine-bark. The flesh
Fell from her bones. Terror held us back.
We dared not look at the corpse.

(*Medea*, 1159–1177, 1186–1202)

Nothing spoken by Medea reaches these heights of terror, and indeed there is scarcely any other passage in the works of Euripides which achieves the sheer crystalline accuracy of this visionary narrative. There are marvelous terrors in Euripides. He can tell nightmares better than any man. There is, for example, a scene in *Heracles* where Heracles goes completely mad. He sits on the floor and in silence gives himself up to a grotesque imitation of a man enjoying a Gargantuan feast. Then he strips naked, wrestles with no one, crowns himself with an invisible crown like the winner at the athletic contests, and then with a murderous light in his eyes he goes hunting after his children, thinking they are the children of his enemy, stabbing one to death and smashing the skull of the other with his club. To stop his murderous rage Athena hurls a rock at him, and then the old man is lashed down with ropes and kept from further harm. It is a powerful scene, but we do not feel that we are at the heart of the mystery. But in *Medea*, as we watch the princess dying, we are held magically at the burning center, and there is no faltering. "Where her eyes had

been no one could tell." We know this is true, because he has prepared us for it; and when the princess puts on the robe and steps lightly
over the carpet, admiring herself, we hear the note of doom when we
encounter her "lifeless image" in the mirror. When the poet says:
"She would stretch her foot out straight and look along it," he has
made us his prisoners. There, finally, unalterably, exquisitely, he lays
the trap and we fall into it willingly. The mad Heracles is horror; the
dying princess is the purest terror.

Euripides does not always reach these heights, but whenever he
speaks of women we are aware of the depth of his understanding of
them. He knows their motives, their secret springs of action, and
what they see when they look into the dark recesses of their souls,
and he knows their sufferings. Here Medea tells of the fate of all
women:

> *Of all that is living and has intelligence*
> *We women are the unhappiest of all creatures.*
> *Firstly, we must buy our husbands with*
> *Dowries of hoarded gold, and so provide*
> *Ourselves with masters of our flesh:*
> *And it is even worse to have no master.*
> *Then it is a question whether we find*
> *A good or bad one; for there is no easy way*
> *For a woman to divorce her husband,*
> *Or in some other way disown her master.*
> *So she inherits new ways and customs,*
> *And by prophetic instinct must arouse*
> *The secret of commanding him who shares her bed.*
> *Then if this task succeeds, the husband lives*
> *In quietness with her, bearing the gentle yoke,*
> *And enviably they live together. If the task fails,*
> *It would be better a thousand times to die!*
> *And if he wearies of his life indoors, a man*
> *Can have the solace of companionship abroad*
> *With his own sex, while wives*
> *Must look for solace to their husbands only.*
> *They say we live our safe and sheltered lives,*
> *Protected by our lords, while they go fighting.*
> *False! False! For I would rather be*

Three times in line of battle, shield in hand,
Than bear one child.

(Medea, 230–251)

The *Hippolytus* is a quieter play than the *Medea*, though Phaedra hangs herself and the virginal Hippolytus is destroyed by the gods for loving his virginity too much. Phaedra is consumed with lovesickness for her stepson, the son of Theseus by the Queen of the Amazons. Euripides knows how lovesickness feeds on itself, how it throws out poisoned shoots which then come and curl round itself, touching the wounds and inflaming them still more with its poisons. Phaedra rings true, but it is in the portrait of the nurse that Euripides excels himself. At first the nurse is shocked when Phaedra vows that she is helplessly in love with Hippolytus, who is completely indifferent to her. "It is all a mischievous madness," she says. "Put such thoughts away." When she realizes they cannot be put away, she suddenly veers to the other extreme and urges Phaedra to give way to her desires, cajoling her, swearing that we are all creatures of Aphrodite and to refuse the goddess is to show an insolent pride. "Be bold in your love!" she cries. "The gods have willed it so."

It is one of the greatest moments in Greek tragedy. In the cry— *Tolma d'erosa!*—we are brought close to the secret of the tragic Muse. So had Prometheus dared, and so had Xerxes, and so had Oedipus; all were bold in their loves, and all had perished, never quite knowing why they had brought such terrible punishments on themselves. The nurse pleads for a daring escape from the coils of love, and goes in search of Hippolytus, hoping against hope that the youth will submit to his stepmother's desires, for only in this way can the nurse save her mistress from disaster. Hippolytus, however, is dedicated to Artemis, the chaste huntress, and scornfully refuses his stepmother's bed in a speech which is like the masculine response to Medea's lament on the sorrows inflicted on women:

Why hast thou, Zeus, put women in the world
To live in the sun? They are a curse on men!
For if we wished to propagate the race,
There should have been a better way to do it
Without the use of women. In thy temples
Men could have put up money—gold, iron, or bronze—
And bought their children in a simple way,

Then taken them to their womanless homes.
But that's not the way it is! Today our daughters
Drain the wealth from a house with all their dowries.
There's proof enough that women are a curse!
And then the man who takes this cursed creature,
If he thinks highly of her, wastes his own substance
In giving her dresses and a wealth of jewels,
Poor fool that he is, accomplishing his own ruin!
The luckiest husband has a stupid wife,
One whose mind's a blank. The clever wife—
There's trouble for you! God forbid
I'd ever have a wife who has a mind!
Lust brings evil to the clever ones.
As for the silly mindless drones they have
Not wit enough for lecherous delights.

(Hippolytus, 616–644)

In his cold rage of chastity Hippolytus brings about his own downfall, for while he taunts Phaedra in her torment he is also taunting Aphrodite, and this is an even more serious matter. He is riding in his chariot by the seashore when a great bull-headed wave rises and destroys him. The crime was not that he vowed himself to chastity. The crime was to have been intolerant of her anguish, setting himself up so high that he could give her no word of sympathy, and by the wantonness of his chastity he brought about her destruction.

The play is not concerned with lechery and chastity only, any more than the *Medea* is concerned with a woman's vengefulness or *Prometheus Bound* is concerned with stealing fire from Heaven. Vast and intricate forces are let loose on the stage. The characters come sharply into focus under the magnifying glass, and they are revealed to be far more complex than we ever suspected. Phaedra is not simply a woman surrendering to despair; there are gleams of cold logic, sudden acts of generosity, moments of candor. We see her in three dimensions, in all her moods. Hippolytus, too, is capable of tenderness, and he is never more tender than when he offers a garland of flowers to the goddess:

For thee, O Queen, I twined this wreath of flowers
Plucked from a virgin meadow to be an offering:
From that inviolate place where shepherds never

> *Fed their flocks, nor was there ever heard*
> *The ringing of a scythe. There only bees*
> *Come in the haunted springtime to the meadow.*
> *The gardener is Reverence. He waters it*
> *With river-dews, and from his garden*
> *None may pluck the flowers but those who are pure*
> *In all things, having learned*
> *From wisdom all the arts of purity.*
> *Therefore, O Queen, receive this wreath of flowers*
> *From reverent hands to bind thy golden hair.*
>
> (*Hippolytus*, 73–83)

Such quiet lyrics are to be found everywhere in the work of Euripides. For no reason at all he will pause to describe in song some real or imagined scene of natural beauty, the flight of birds over water meadows, the blue shadows waving over mountains, a girl washing clothes in a stream. So it is at the beginning of the *Hippolytus* when the chorus enters and announces that it has learned of Phaedra's lovesickness:

> *There is a rock flowing with water*
> *Whose source, men say, is Ocean.*
> *There flows from the rock a stream*
> *Where pitchers may dip deep,*
> *And there was one I knew*
> *Dipping red robes in the river dew,*
> *Then spreading them out to dry*
> *On shoulders of sun-warmed rock.*
> *From her we learned the news*
> *That the Queen was wasting away,*
> *Hiding her golden head*
> *In the shade of fine-spun veils.*
>
> (*Hippolytus*, 121–134)

We never learn the name of the maiden washing the red robes, and we never see her again. She plays no part in the unfolding of the drama, but her radiance lingers over the opening scenes, which are flooded in sunlight. Then the black storm clouds come racing in.

There is no sunlight in *The Trojan Women*, which was produced in 415 in the interval between the massacre at Melos and the departure of the Sicilian expedition. It is a play of unrelieved darkness and horror, with not one single moment when the mind is permitted to relax. Beneath the walls of ruined Troy the princesses of the House of Priam wait to learn their fate. All night Queen Hecuba has been lying on the earth, too stunned to move. Now in the early dawnlight a herald enters to summon Cassandra, who is to be given as a concubine to Agamemnon, and he explains the fate reserved for the other prisoners. Polyxena will be made a handmaiden at the tomb of Achilles—we learn later that her throat will be cut and the blood will be poured as a libation to his shade. Andromache, the beautiful wife of Hector, will be given to Achilles' son, and Hecuba herself, once Queen of Troy, will become the slave of Odysseus, the man she hates most among the Greeks. So the muster roll continues, and suddenly Cassandra whirls out of the darkness in the white veils of a bride and waving a torch:

> *I light the fiery torch*
> *On my own wedding day.*
> *Behold the splendid flame,*
> *This offering I have made*
> *To Hymen and to Hecate.*
> *Lords of the marriage bed,*
> *I wave the fiery torch*
> *According to the law.*
> *O dancers, leap and whirl,*
> *As once in days gone by*
> *Fortune blessed our father.*
> *Holy is the dance.*
> *Come, Phoebus, now*
> *Perform the sacred rites*
> *Within the leafy shrine.*
> *Hymen! Hymen! Hymen!*

The appearance of Cassandra at this moment is a stroke of the highest dramatic art. She is completely mad, and drunk with prophecies. As she dances wildly against the ruins of Troy, swinging her torch around her head and throwing its light on the grief-stricken prisoners, she seems to have come from another planet, where there is no grief. She knows that the victory belongs to Troy, and that the Greeks will perish on their return to Greece. She knows that she has been given to Agamemnon, but he will perish. She knows that she too will perish, but this knowledge, instead of causing her grief, makes her all the more jubilant. So she dances and sings her spine-chilling songs of victory on the ruins of Troy, and no one who has ever seen this apparition on the stage can forget the impact of this girl dancing so lightheartedly among the dead and dying. This is the pure terror, comparable to the terror in the recital of the death of the princess in the *Medea*.

Cassandra vanishes, never to return, leaving the air luminous. Soon Andromache learns that her son will be hurled from the topmost tower of Troy. She cannot hide her son; she can only lament. Suddenly Menelaus appears, demanding that Helen present herself. He is determined to murder her on the spot, but when at last his wife appears—she who is the cause of the Trojan War—he cannot withhold his admiration of her beauty. Dressed in all her finery, she comes upon the stage with something of the power of Cassandra. Her beauty is like a knife twisting in a wound. Almost she dares Menelaus to kill her. She lies in her teeth. She tells how she has been wronged by the Trojans, and how often she has tried to escape from Troy with a rope thrown over the walls. Her words are never convincing, but her beauty convinces; and Hecuba, who has seen her sons destroyed and her city at the mercy of the enemy, reviles her bitterly. "I deserve to be pardoned," says Helen. "It is all the fault of Aphrodite. Myself, I had no part in this affair." We know she will not die, for no man could bring himself to extinguish such beauty; and she goes to his bed.

In *The Trojan Women*, grief flows in waves from a dark center, horror is piled on horror, but the nerves of Euripides are steady. It would seem that the play was written in deep-felt protest against the massacre at Melos which had taken place only a few months before. Andromache, holding her baby son in her arms, speaks of "the foulscheming of the barbarous Greeks," and in the flow of these words there is a stinging reproach, a jolt of hatred directed at the politicians in the audience.

Almost nothing happens in the play, but everything happens. To read it is to be saddened, for it seems formless with grief continually pivoting around itself, and one shape of grief is very much like another. On the stage it is a different story. Cassandra, crowned with flowers, sings her marriage song, and the play is at once elevated into another order of things. Helen enters, and once again the play spins out of orbit and acquires new meanings, more remorseless than ever because beauty defies all terrors. And when Andromache's baby boy is brought in on his father's shield, crushed after being thrown from the tower—the beautiful bronze shield and the splash of red at the heart of it—then Euripides has us wholly at his mercy, for he sets the women to examining the baby's wounds.

When at last the city is set on fire and the captives are driven down to the sea, it is almost an anticlimax.

Euripides never wrote with more assurance. One has the feeling that the whole man poured himself into the play, holding nothing back. It is a play about women, for the men who appear in it are no more than masklike engines of destruction. Here he proved, if any proof was needed, the depth of his despairing love for women.

Helen in *The Trojan Women* plays a role that is wholly evil. Three years later, in 412, Euripides wrote another play in which she appears: this time she is gay, innocent, and charming.

As a dramatist he could, of course, portray her exactly as he chose: he was not expected to be consistent. In the *Helen* he chose to depict her according to the tradition deriving from Stesichorus, who tells us that she spent the years of the Trojan War not in Troy but in the palace of King Proteus on the banks of the Nile. When the Greeks reached Troy, they could find no trace of her. She had vanished—vanished as though she had never existed:

MENELAUS
She never came to Troy. The gods deceived us!
MESSENGER
What did you say? And all that suffering for nothing?
For a wisp of cloud?

(*Helen*, 704–706)

So Euripides wrote his play about a Helen never seen on earth or in the heavens, the purely imaginary Helen who remained constant through all her tribulations and who regarded the ten-year war as an event taking place in a far-off country, having little to do with her. We are not expected to believe in the characters, any more than we are expected to believe in the characters of *The Tempest*. Here, too, there are shipwrecked sailors, magic spells, enchanted landscapes, actions of exquisite nobility and of astonishing vulgarity. As the play opens, Helen is standing beside the tomb of Proteus, commiserating with herself because she is the cause of the Trojan War, though Hermes wrapped her in a cloud and flew with her to Egypt. Theoclymenus, the son of Proteus, is determined to marry her, but she desires only to be united with Menelaus. Seven years have passed since the end of the war, and all she knows is that the Greeks destroyed Troy for her sake. She is praying by the tomb when Teucer, one of the Greek heroes, comes to shore saying that he is searching for Theonoë, the prophetess, sister of Theoclymenus, who will tell him where to found a colony, and soon her husband Menelaus arrives wearing the picturesque rags appropriate to a shipwrecked sailor, and Helen confronts him with her beauty:

HELEN
Look at me. Surely I resemble your wife!
MENELAUS
The features are the same, but you couldn't possibly—
HELEN
Look again! What more assurance do you need?
MENELAUS
Well, you're like her. I won't deny that.
HELEN
Surely you can trust your eyes!
MENELAUS
My eyes deceive me. Besides, I have another wife.
HELEN
I never went to Troy. Only a phantom was there.

(*Helen*, 576–582)

There must be an end, of course, to this delicious fooling, and so the play becomes a struggle between Helen and Menelaus, as they attempt to flee from Egypt together, and Theoclymenus, who is determined to make Helen his bride. Helen manages the escape with the most charming effrontery by telling the king that Menelaus is a shipwrecked sailor who has brought news of Menelaus drowned at sea, and she is in duty bound to offer the proper funeral rites for her dead husband over the place where he may be presumed to have died—far out to sea. Theoclymenus agrees to give her a ship, fifty rowers, and a sacred bull. He also promises to let Menelaus take complete charge of the ship, which is joined by a small complement of shipwrecked Greek sailors disguised as mourners. Soon the ship is sailing off the shores of Egypt, and the mourners are bringing out the swords they have hidden in their clothes. The bull is sacrificed, the fifty rowers are slaughtered, and the ship sails off to Greece.

The play is scarcely a play. It is as gentle and sweet-tempered as *The Tempest* and has the same ominous overtones; and like *The Tempest* it is a divertissement rather than a well-constructed play with well-developed characters. It is intended to amuse, and occasionally to frighten. There is a lovely song to Demeter which has nothing whatsoever to do with the play, and there is an enchanting chorus which is like a distant echo of a chorus in the *Hippolytus:*

> *By a blue and shining lake*
> *And a grassy bank,*
> *I washed my purple robe*
> *And laid it on the reeds to dry*
> *On a golden day,*
> *And then I heard a sudden cry,*
> *A wailing in the shuddering air—*
> *As though a nymph were crying there,*
> *A Naiad screaming in despair,*
> *Seeking for a place to hide,*
> *Or else great Pan had stolen her*
> *And laid her down within a cave,*
> *And made of her a ravished bride.*

(Helen, 179–190)

So it is throughout the play—the calm sunlight of a summer day, and then suddenly there is the whistling of the wind and the screaming of the nymphs.

No one ever wrote poetry as Euripides wrote it, so gaily, so humanly, with such a vast imaginative range and with such depths of feeling. They accused him of atheism because he sometimes permitted his characters to shake their fists at the gods, but that is to misunderstand his essential humanity. He believed, and did not believe. There were times when he was appalled by the human condition, and other times when he was so delighted with it that he was drunk with the sight of every face he saw; and his faith was all the stronger for having doubted. He had Shakespeare's gift of tears and wild hilarity, and indeed they might have been brothers under the sun.

When he died, the Athenians put on their robes of mourning for him. It was a tribute they paid to no other poet.

21 ⫷ ARISTOPHANES

T̲HE OLD curmudgeon still leers across the centuries, the wicked eyes lighting up with savage joy. He bellows and roars and rants, and nothing can stop him. He shouts all the four-letter words he knows, and for good measure invents a dozen more. He will scream with hatred at the sight of a man delicately lifting the skirts of his gown from the mud, and he will go into paroxysms of laughter when he encounters men who wander about the world with expressions of settled gravity. He cared not a fig for Pericles, Socrates, and Euripides; if he could, he would have laughed them out of existence. He was a dirty old man. Sometimes he was venomous, with the pure distilled venom of a viper, and on occasion he could whip himself into an ugly ranting rage scarcely distinguishable from madness. Yet this impudent old man has a certain claim to our affections. He was the sweetest clown who ever lived. He was the spirit of anarchic comedy let loose upon the world.

What Aristophanes wanted above all was a life given over to the joys of the flesh and a world at peace; what he found was a city fatally involved in ambitious wars which inevitably led to the sacrifice of human joys. He had no patience with politicians. Once when he wrote a play lampooning the most powerful political figure in Athens he could find no one who dared act the part, so he played it himself, painting his face with wine lees. When, ten years after the outbreak of the Peloponnesian War, there was a faint glimmering of peace, a sudden hope in the air, he wrote a play called *Peace* in which an old peasant soars to Heaven on the back of a gigantic dung beetle and triumphantly succeeds in rescuing Peace from her grave, and in almost

307

the last words of the play he permits the chorus to celebrate the coming of peace with words like a benediction:

Joy! oh joy! No more helmet, no more cheese nor onions! I have no pleasure in battles. What I want is to drink with my good companions by the fireside, when good dry wood, cut in the height of summer, is crackling, roasting chick pease on the coals and acorns among the embers, and kissing the pretty Thracian maid while my wife is washing herself. There is nothing more pleasant when the rain is falling and the seeds are sprouting than to turn to a friend and say, "Well, Comarchides, what's for today? I've a mind to drink, while the heavens are watering our fields. Come, wife, roast some kidney beans, and mix a little wheat with them, and bring some figs, too. Syra, tell Manes to come off the fields—the ground is too wet for stripping the vine leaves or grubbing around the roots. Someone bring me the thrush and the two chaffinches, and there are some curds too, and four pieces of hare, unless the cat stole them last night—I never knew what that damned noise was! Serve up three pieces, boy, and give one to my father, and ask Aeschinades for some myrtles with berries on them, and then, since you'll be going that way, tell Charinades to come and drink with me to the honor of the gods who are watching over our crops!

That was the life he wanted, but there was little of it in Athens at the time of the Peloponnesian War, when men went hurrying to battle with tears in their eyes, and the scarlet-coated captains with three feathers in their helmets paraded like fighting cocks until they reached the battlefield, when they were likely to leave the poor soldiers to fend for themselves. "A curse on captains!" says the chorus, and goes on to utter the immemorial cry: "Wait till I get my hands on them—"

Aristophanes was in a subdued mood when he wrote the chorus. Usually he is more violent, more impudent, more obscene. The meal he describes is tame indeed compared with the Gargantuan feasts, with the names of the dishes seven feet long, which he likes to present to the audience. What he especially enjoyed in a play was to pit one farcical character against another and to prod them into a whirlwind knockabout fight while they shout themselves hoarse and flail their arms and accomplish nothing at all, and just at the moment when they are hoarse with exchanging happy obscenities, he will give them a new

excuse for going at each other's throat. His plays explode like a pro-
liferation of firecrackers. He had a sense of the life roaring through
human veins, a fierce excitement in living, and an overwhelming
affection for the creatures of his imagination, who were also the common people of Athens, with the result that he, more than anyone else,
has given us the entry into the ancient city. We know the faces of
those people because he has written about them. We know the sights
and smells and colors, and how they went about their affairs, and
how they amused themselves and made love. He threw the doors wide
open, as Shakespeare threw the doors wide open on Elizabethan England, and such events are sufficiently rare to make us pause.

In *The Acharnians*, the first of his comedies that has come down
to us, he pits a simple-minded Athenian against all the horrors and
absurdities of the Peloponnesian War. Dikaiopolis goes off and makes
a separate peace with the Spartans, lambasting Pericles, Euripides,
and everyone else who is stupid enough to prefer war to drinking
and wenching. "If the Spartans stole a little dog from you, you would
be off on the instant with three hundred warships to avenge the
crime!" One after another he knocks off the preposterous wooden
heads of his private enemies. The great general advances to war and
immediately falls headlong into a ditch. The public informer of Athens
finds himself sold off to the Boeotians. A wretched Megarian, starving
as a result of the blockade of Megara, wraps up his daughters in sow
skins and sells them to Dikaiopolis, who is a little shaken to find them
so hungry and talkative. The play ends with the hero reeling happily
on the arm of a flute girl, having made his private peace with Athens
as well as with Sparta.

The Acharnians was written when Aristophanes was only twenty,
but already in full command of his art. The speed is prodigious, one
scene following so fast on the heels of the other that they are in danger
of colliding. What is astonishing, and revealing, is that the play was
performed in the midst of a war. Aristophanes showed not the slightest
fear and was awarded the first prize. The sweet temper of the Athenians was abundantly proved by the award.

The Knights, which was produced in the following year, was
sterner stuff altogether. Cleon, a merchant of hides, had become the
most powerful political figure in Athens, and Aristophanes shared
Thucydides' intense dislike of him. He invents a sausage seller who
has been told by the oracle that he must assume power. "The long

dragon drinker of blood will triumph over the eagle with hooked claws," says the oracle, and it is a matter of only a few moments to show that "the long dragon drinker of blood" is a sausage and that "the eagle with hooked claws" is Cleon. A dazed sausage seller orders Cleon to surrender his powers. Cleon refuses. A slanging match, which continues for almost the entire length of the play, shows the two contestants at their vitriolic worst and at their wildly humorous best. They give no quarter. They roar themselves hoarse. They accuse one another of all the abominable crimes they can think of and implore Athena and her city to decide between them:

CLEON

O Athena, if I am not ready to fight in your defense alone and against all your enemies, may I perish, may I be sawn to bits alive and my skin be cut up into ribbons.

SAUSAGE SELLER

O Demos, if I do not love and cherish you, may I be grated with cheese and made into mincemeat, and may a hook be passed through my testicles and may I be dragged to the boneyard.

So, in great glee, reviling one another roundly, they debate the cause of Athens until the sausage seller emerges victorious.

With *The Wasps* Aristophanes lambasts the Athenian jury system with the same venomous and gleeful attention to ridicule. There was nothing in itself wrong with the jury system, under which citizens serving on juries received three obols a day, or about half the wage of a skilled artisan, but by insisting on its abuses and reducing it to farce Aristophanes is able to suggest that it is wholly unworkable and might as well be abandoned. There are only two main characters, Philocleon (Bless Cleon) and Bdelycleon (To Hell with Cleon), his son. Philocleon is an indefatigable juryman, his son is opposed to the whole system. They are both clowns, in love with the ridiculous. Under the promptings of his son, Philocleon offers to stay at home and preside over trials in the privacy of his own home, and immediately sets about trying the house dog for the theft of a Sicilian cheese. The house dog is duly arraigned, witnesses are examined, legal arguments are brought forward, and Philocleon accidentally acquits the dog, a thing he has never done before. Thereupon, realizing the enormity of his error, he faints.

At this point Aristophanes, having bludgeoned the jury system, puts into the mouth of the chorus an extraordinary speech in which he celebrates "the men of Marathon," and bitterly attacks their descendants—the useless stinging wasps who make life miserable for the comic poets. He summons Marathon and Salamis and Athena herself to witness that he has deserved well of Athens. Through the chorus the poet himself steps onto the stage, tears off his mask, and roundly abuses his audience with a shrill bitterness and vehemence which even now, twenty-five centuries later, can make us catch our breath.

The Wasps is intended to sting, but after stinging his audience Aristophanes is prepared to make amends. Having broken the play in the middle with a long and passionate speech in which the Athenian mob is described as having "the stench of a sea-calf, the unwashed testicles of a Lamia, and the rump of a camel" he must think up some farcial situation to bring it to a conclusion and decides to introduce Philocleon to high society, where he is grotesquely out of his depth. When we see him last he is drunk and staggering along some Athenian street at night, accompanied by a flute girl with a torch to light the way. There follows a scene of exquisite bawdry, which should be included here because it represents Aristophanes in one of his happiest moods. They are climbing a street, and Philocleon holds a rope to her.

PHILOCLEON

Up, up, my little golden cockchafer,
Take the rope in your hand, but have a care—
The thing is worn to shreds, but rubbing pleases it.
Wasn't I clever to steal you away from the guests?
So in return you should be kind to my rope, eh?
But of course you won't pay up! I know you well:
You'll tease me a bit, as you've teased so many others.
Listen, my dear, if you'll go along with me,
I'll keep you when my son dies. You'll be my little pumpkin.
Not that I have any money in the bank. The truth is
I'm very young still, my son looks after me.
Dear boy, he never lets me out of his sight—
The little cummin-chewing thick-pated swine!
He thinks I'm going to hell, and yet I am
His only father. That's him! He's coming after me!
Stand by me, girl, and hold the torch.

I'll have a bit of fun with him, as once before
During the Mysteries he had his joke on me.

BDELYCLEON

There you are, you puffed-up old lecher.
What are you whoring after? Nails in your coffin!
By Apollo, I'll see you don't get away with it!

PHILOCLEON

You and your pickled lawsuits—

BDELYCLEON

None of your stupid nonsense any more!
You took the flute girl away from the party, didn't you?

PHILOCLEON

Flute girl? What flute girl? You're out of your mind,
Or else you've been spewed out of Hell!

BDELYCLEON

Lord, there's the girl from Dardanis herself!

PHILOCLEON

There's no girl—only a torch
Lighting the market place to honor the gods.

BDELYCLEON

Is this a torch?

PHILOCLEON

Of course it is!

BDELYCLEON

Then what's the black part in the middle?

PHILOCLEON

That's the pitch running out while it burns.

BDELYCLEON

If you look on the other side, there's a girl's behind.

PHILOCLEON

Nonsense, dear boy. It's a bit of the torch sticking out.

Aristophanes is clearly enjoying himself, one happy invention following fast on another, though he will show his teeth again before the play is over. Philocleon blundering with the flute girl is the proper stuff of comedy, being improper, ludicrous, and entirely memorable.

During the following year, with preparations for the Peace of Nicias well advanced, and his inveterate enemy Cleon no longer alive, Aristophanes produced *Peace* to celebrate the end of the wars, little knowing that they would continue for seventeen long years. It is a happy play; for once his malice is held in check. Trygaeus—the name means Vintager—flies to Heaven on a dung beetle's back. There he meets Hermes, relegated to be nothing more than a caretaker of the Olympian furniture now that the gods have moved to the farthermost reaches of Heaven, leaving War in possession of Olympus. Hermes tells Trygaeus that War has buried Peace in a deep pit, whereupon Trygaeus has the happy thought of bribing Hermes with a gold cup in the hope that he will be allowed to rescue her. Then before setting to work, he offers a libation to the gods in the presence of the chorus which shares his enthusiasm:

TRYGAEUS

May this day be remembered as one when the blessings
Of peace were showered down on Greece, and may those
Who haul on the ropes never go into battle again.

CHORUS

May we pass our lives peacefully, caressing
Our mistresses, and poking the fire.

TRYGAEUS

If there are any here who delight in war,
O Dionysus, may they never cease
To draw barbed arrows out of their elbows.

CHORUS

If there are any, ambitious to be generals,
Who hate to see Peace return, may they
Quake with fear on the battlefield.

TRYGAEUS

May all spear makers and sellers of shields,
Desiring war for the sake of advancing trade—
May they be taken by pirates and fed on raw barley.

CHORUS

May all those who desire to be generals,
And all slaves plotting to go over to the enemy,
Come over to us, or may they be broken on the wheel!

When Peace is rescued at last, Trygaeus, Hermes, and the chorus vie with one another in extolling her blessings. She is like the gleaming of iron mattocks in the sunlit fields, and the bleating of the ewes. She is all the tipsy slave girls and overturned wine jars and grapes hanging on the vines and violets growing on the banks of streams. Dazed with their good fortune, they praise her and revile her enemies, among whom Aristophanes includes Pericles for having issued a decree prohibiting trade with Megara, and then they bustle about to find some way of bringing her to earth until it occurs to them that Peace is large enough to reach from Heaven to earth, and so they simply climb down her.

With the coming of peace, the armament manufacturers are understandably disturbed, but Trygaeus points out that all is not lost. Breastplates, suitably propped up on three stones, can be transformed into chamber pots, helmet crests into mops for dusting tables, helmets into wine jars. Trygaeus goes off to marry Fruitfulness, one of the handmaidens of Peace, and the play ends in preparations for the marriage feast.

Peace is a gentle play, with no wasps to sting the audience into fury. Aristophanes is in a mood to let bygones be bygones, and he even has a good word to say for Cleon, whose death that year at Amphipolis gave him a popularity he never possessed in life.

The Birds was produced in 414, during the days when ominous rumors were reaching Athens about the Sicilian expedition. But there is nothing in the least ominous about the play, which takes the form of another gaily nonsensical adventure against the powers of Heaven. Two Athenian adventurers, Peisthetaerus (Plausible) and Euelpides (Hopeful), grown weary of city life, decide to abandon the earth altogether. They meet an intelligent hoopoe and suggest that the time has come for the birds, the rightful rulers of the skies, to enter into their inheritance, a heavenly country of their own—Cloud-cuckoo-land. Haven't they suffered long enough? Isn't it time there was an end to the continual murders in frying pans "with sweet and greasy sauce poured scalding over your backs." So the parliament of birds assembles, and all enthusiastically agree to build Cloud-cuckoo-land. They come flocking in their thousands from all over the world—thirty thousand cranes from Libya bring stones for the foundations of the city, the storks bring bricks, the swallows bring mortar, the pelicans square up the gates with their beaks. In no time the city comes into existence. Soon there appears a melancholy procession of men from earth to examine and offer their unconsidered tidbits of advice—a poet, an inspector, a decree-merchant, a town planner who is clearly modeled on Hippodamus, the town planner of Piraeus. "It's very simple," he says. "All you have to do is to inscribe a square within a circle, and in the middle there will be the market place, and all the streets will converge on it in the form of a star." Prometheus arrives: he tells them that the gods are in great difficulties, for lacking the savor of the sacrifices they are almost driven out of their wits. Three ambassadors arrive. They are Poseidon, Heracles, and poor Triballus, a Thracian god of dubious ancestry, who utters pure nonsense. Triballus is a mistake, since the play has already arrived at the stage of pure nonsense and can absorb no more. Cloud-cuckoo-land has proclaimed its independence. "The gods are hereby forbidden to pass through our city, and mortals are hereby informed that they may no longer send the smoke of their sacrifices through it." But Peisthetaerus is prepared to make an accommodation provided the gods surrender their power to him; and when we last see him he is being assisted by his winged cohorts, while the thunder and the lightning play around him, into the palace of Zeus. He has demanded Basileia, who is clearly Athena, as his bride, and as the play ends he is on his way to the bridal couch.

The Birds is a dazzling play, for never before had an Athenian dramatist devised such an irreverent game with the gods, reducing them to the dimensions of farce, accomplishing his purpose with kindness and wit until with the last trumpet chords he utterly demolishes them. The spectacle of Peisthetaerus entering into possession of his heavenly kingdom is a *tour de force* of quite astonishing amplitude. The besotted old Athenian, who is first seen wandering across a barren wasteland with a crow perched on his shoulders, reels into Heaven at last with all the panoply of the gods. He dances a jig with Basileia. He preens himself and ogles the audience, and with his stentorian voice he demands that the lightning shall play for him and the thunderbolts drip from his hands, while his own angelic messenger intones a welcoming chant:

> *See, see, he comes*
> *More brilliant than the brightest star of heaven;*
> *He strides toward his golden gleaming mansion.*
> *The shining of the sun's rays blazing forth*
> *Were not more dazzling than his glory*
> *As now he comes with his attendant bride,*
> *More beautiful than any earthly queen:*

While round his head the lightning flames
And thunderbolts of Zeus pour from his hands.
The sweetest perfume known pervades the heavens . . .

The audience, of course, is perfectly aware that "the sweetest perfume known" contains some earthly elements, for Aristophanes is a master cataloguer of smells, enumerating them with the same careful passion with which he enumerates pimps and vegetables. He knows his way around smells, and is not in the least ashamed of them. But what is chiefly astonishing about this scene is the delirious irreverence, an irreverence so vast and so impudent that it becomes almost pardonable. Peisthetaerus is not one of those men who steal fire from Heaven; he simply takes over the whole of Heaven, chases the gods out of it, and then makes a beeline for the nuptial couch.

Why Aristophanes was never arrested for corrupting the young and causing untold damage to the gods is one of the minor mysteries of fifth-century Athens. The proper function of the comic genius is to shake the pillars of society until everyone is covered with the white plaster falling from the ceiling; it is not the function of comedy to make war on Heaven. Aristophanes, however, feels no need to set limits to his imagination. He seems to have been arrested only once, and this at the very beginning of his career, when Cleon objected to something he said in a play called *The Babylonians*. He says in *The Acharnians* that his enemies slandered him by accusing him of scoffing at Athens and the Athenians, and they gave him such a drubbing that it almost killed him. His wounds healed quickly, and he continued to scoff at anything that took his fancy for the rest of his life.

In *Lysistrata* he scoffs at women, but reserves his keenest barbs for men. To put an end to the wars Lysistrata and the women of Athens meet in solemn conclave to swear that they will refuse all sexual favors until men have come to reason and put up their shields. They are perfectly conscious of their powers, and debate the matter with the utmost seriousness. The oath, to be effective, must be accompanied by the proper sacrifices, and Lysistrata immediately thinks of sacrificing a sheep over a buckler, according to the manner of the heroes in Aeschylus' *Seven against Thebes*, but Calonicê, rolling her eyes, suggests there would be advantages in sacrificing "something we can ride," like a white horse. "Where," asks Lysistrata sensibly, "do you think we will get a white horse?" Finally—for Aristophanes has taken the measure of Athenian women—it is decided to swear the oath over a bowl of wine from Thasos. It is a good oath, and they sing it with the appropriate unction:

> *Let me not lie down with any man,*
> *Even though he is swollen with passion.*
> *I will remain at home in perfect chastity,*
> *Beautiful in my saffron-colored gown,*
> *Inspiring him with the utmost desire,*
> *Never surrendering myself voluntarily,*
> *And if he should force his way upon me*
> *I shall be cold as ice, unmoving.*
> *In no way shall I comfort him.*
> *I shall not crouch bottom-up like a lion.*
> *If I keep this oath, may I drink the wine;*
> *Otherwise may I be swollen with water.*

Such an oath can be kept only if the women carefully remove themselves from men's company. Accordingly, Lysistrata leads them to the Acropolis, where they place themselves under the protection of Athena and suffer nightmares, or pretend to suffer nightmares, from the hooting of her owl and the presence of her sacred snake. The "men of Marathon," the hoary wiseacres, decide to take the Acropolis by storm, but they are soon repulsed by "the monstrous regiment of women." A more serious danger comes from subversion. Cinesias slips into the Acropolis. He protests his love for his beloved Myrrhine, and tempts her home by weeping over his loneliness, the disorder in the house, and the sufferings of their motherless child, but though he comes within an inch of arousing her desire, she is too strong for him and skips laughing away at the precise moment when he hopes she will melt in his arms. Such tactics inevitably lead to the discomfiture of the male population to the extent that they are willing to make any sacrifices to have their women back again: they are even willing to give up war.

The *Lysistrata* is a political tract disguised as a farce, and Aristophanes hugely enjoys himself as he explores the implications of enforced chastity among men and women. The invention never flags, there is no straining for effect, no attempt to give the story a greater weight of meaning than it can bear. Lysistrata and her cohorts of chaste women are completely credible, and their adventures follow

naturally from the original premiss that a chaste womanhood will
shock the males into submission. Aristophanes was never more serious,
never more concerned with the public well-being of Athens, than
when he wrote this gay and lighthearted play. In the two following
plays, the *Thesmophoriazusae* and *The Frogs*, the gaiety remains, but
there are shrill overtones of anger and resentment. Both plays are
bludgeoning attacks on Euripides.

At this late date no one knows why Aristophanes hated Euripides
with such self-righteous fury. At the time of the production of the
Thesmophoriazusae Euripides was still alive; when *The Frogs* was produced, he was dead; but living or dead Aristophanes attacks him with
unconcealed venom, hoping to annihilate him by laughter.

The *Thesmophoriazusae* tells how the women of Athens revolted
against Euripides. They claim that Euripides is unjust to them, and
what is still more serious, he has failed to understand them. A widow
left with five children complains that she has scarcely sold a myrtle
chaplet since he proved in one of his plays that there were no gods.
Euripides disapproved of young women marrying much older men,
and Aristophanes introduces the haunting cry: "Shall no maidens
marry rich, old husbands?" Evidently Euripides knows nothing about
the real lives of women: how they trick their husbands, and take
lovers, and pretend to be suffering the pangs of labor while babies
are brought to them in stewpots with their mouths full of honey to
prevent them from crying: then the foundling is presented to the
husband with the cry: "Look at the young lion! The spitting image
of you!" Euripides has maligned women with his atrocious ignorance
of them, and so they set about arresting him, but instead arrest his
beardless secretary, who has dressed himself up as a woman. The
secretary pleads for Euripides, to no avail. Scenting a plot, the women
suddenly converge on the witless secretary and forcibly undress him.
Then for a moment Aristophanes floods the stage with his happy improprieties, and all bitterness is forgotten.

Women in Parliament and *Wealth* are both allegories of communism, and it is possible that they were written after a reading of
Plato's *Republic*, which advocated the equality of the sexes and community of property.

One night the women of Athens slip out of their houses, and
while their menfolk are ludicrously running round the bedchambers
searching for them, they take power. Among their most advanced

laws is one decreeing that old and ugly women are equal to the young and beautiful, and no man may have a girl before he has first satisfied some ancient crone. Aristophanes plays with the idea as though warming his hands over a distant fire; he cannot quite bring himself to believe that the fire is anything but a mirage. *Women in Parliament* is a comedy written in a tragic mode.

Wealth is even sadder, for the mirage is more splendid. It recounts how a good and just man Chremylus was told by the oracle to befriend the first person he met when he left the temple, and since he is obedient to the oracle he befriends an old blind beggar, little knowing that this is Plutus, the god of wealth in disguise, who has lost his sight because Zeus wishes him to be impartial, rewarding the just and the unjust alike. Faithful to his vow, Chremylus leads the old beggar to the temple of Asclepius, the god of medicine, where he regains his sight, and thereafter he rewards only the just. Aristophanes has some fun describing a world where only the just are wealthy, but it is almost too serious a matter for jest. Cario, the servant of Chremylus, dreams of wealth as in an earlier age a character in *Peace* dreamed of food:

How pleasant it is, friends, to live well, especially when it costs nothing! What a deluge of blessings fall upon our house, and that too without our having wronged a single soul! Ah, what a sweet and pleasant thing is wealth! The bin is full of white flour, and our casks are running over with fragrant wine, and every vessel in the house is crammed with gold and silver, a wonderful thing to see, and the oil jars are full to overflowing, and the oil flasks are filled to bursting with unguents, and the attic with figs. And every cruet, pitcher, stewpot and pannikin are turned to bronze, and the old rotting wooden pails for fish are turned to silver, and the box for the night soil is turned to ivory. The slaves among us play tiddlywinks with gold coins, and we use no stones, but garlic leaves, when we wash ourselves. Just now my master has crowned himself with flowers and is busy sacrificing a pig, a goat, and a ram; but I was driven out of the room by the smoke which hurt my eyes.

The last line provides the clue, for the slave knows he will awaken from his dream of luxury, to find himself once more lying on a flea-bitten pallet with a stone for his pillow in one of those crowded bathhouses where the poor of Athens congregated in winter. It is beyond belief that Plutus will ever regain his sight. The vision fades, but Aristophanes goes dancing to the end.

He was the true comedian, *filius terrae*, the son of earth kicking up his heels in derision of death and bureaucracy, which is the brother of death, in love with life and laughter under the sun. Bitterness sometimes crept in, and he had the inexhaustible melancholy of all true comedians, who laugh only because laughter is an alleviation for tears. He hated as violently as he loved, and most of all he loved the common people of Athens. Moon-struck, he loved them almost to lunacy, and we know them best through reading him.

He had no successors. The world of comedy which he invented died with him. Other comedians would arise, new worlds of comedy would come into existence, but never again was there to be that full-throated, rasping voice cutting clear through all our imbecilities. He is still the best comedian of them all.

22 ❊ THE RISE OF SPARTA

ARISTOPHANES represented all that was joyous, carefree, and human in the society of his time; he loved the world of laughter, delighted in the fecundity of human desires, and never for a moment permitted himself to believe that man was created to serve the purposes of the state. His plays could never have been performed in Sparta, and in fact they would have seemed incomprehensible. The harsh, puritanical, and intolerant civilization that had developed in Sparta was designed to destroy all the normal expansive joys of men, and to reduce men to the status of obedient machines serving a mechanical state.

How it could have happened that two closely related peoples speaking the same language and living only a few miles apart could have created such totally dissimilar civilizations is a question which neither Thucydides nor Aristotle, who were both deeply immersed in the problem, was able to answer. Sparta had not always been a mechanical state. In the seventh and eighth centuries B.C. the Spartans rejoiced in Ionian luxuries. The nobles lived in ornate idleness, and the individual was free to live as he chose. Poets thronged to the court, sculptors celebrated the gods, and potters and craftsmen plied their trades. The poet Alcman came from Lydian Sardis and settled in Sparta, and there was an extensive trade in gold and rich embroideries with Asia Minor. Sumptuous shrines, including one to Athena, the guardian of the city, were erected on the small acropolis, while below, on the banks of the Eurotas River, stood the curious shrine of Artemis Orthia—Artemis the Upright—whose altars were stained with human blood. The great market place was filled with temples and the tombs of heroes; and the tomb of Alcman, who had celebrated the beauty and elegance of the Spartan girls, was especially venerated. Spartan sculptors carved with a clean-cut precision, and Spartan songs were famous for their elegance.

Early in the sixth century B.C. a sudden change came over Sparta. Culture and luxury were banished, strangers were expelled, xenophobia was encouraged and artificially stimulated, and the entire population was compelled to submit to iron laws which defined the rights and duties of citizens at all moments of their lives. There were few rights, the duties were innumerable, exhausting, and often fatal. There are times when it seems that the only freedom permitted to the Spartan was the freedom to choose his mode of suicide. The stern Spartan lawgiver Lycurgus chose to starve himself to death.

Everything in this civilization was subordinated to the art of war; the sole aim of the state was to create a race of invincible warriors. At birth the child was examined by a state official to see whether it appeared strong enough to stand the rigors of Spartan life when it grew up, and if it was weak or deformed in some way it was ordered to be exposed in one of the rifts or glens on somber Mount Taygetus overlooking the city. At seven boys were removed from their mothers and given over to state institutions. At the age of ten they began their training as soldiers and were taught to live stealthily, harshly, with barely enough food to keep alive. They were encouraged to become thieves, but woe betide those who were caught. They cooked their own meals and slept on rushes gathered from the banks of the Eurotas. The boys had no family life. Their affections were centered on the young men who ruled over them and who punished them severely for the slightest acts of indiscipline. Once a year came the supreme test of endurance, when the boys submitted to a flogging before the altar of Artemis Orthia, while a priestess watched them with the image of the goddess, bound with willow twigs, in her hands, and she would remonstrate with the scourgers if they did not work with all their strength, saying the goddess grew too heavy to hold unless the blood spurted. The image had come originally from the Tauric Chersonese, and the practice of sacrificial flogging may have derived from that barbarian land. Boys sometimes died under the flogging.

The result of this training was to produce a race of hardened soldiers who regarded their elders with awe. Xenophon, who wrote a short account of the constitution of the Spartans, spoke with admiration of the young Spartans who walked the streets with their hands hidden in the folds of their gowns, their gaze fixed on the ground before them. They spoke in low voices and were excessively polite. "They had the natural modesty of brides entering the bridal chamber," he wrote, and it pleased him that they limited their speech to only the most necessary words. They walked barefoot, and never smiled. They took their meals at a communal table and slept in communal barracks.

Spartan civilization was a form of communism, sterile, mechanical, and oddly antiquated: it was as though the world had stood still and some ascetic mythology was being worked out. Elsewhere the Greeks rewarded victors in the games with wreaths of flowers or leaves. Spartans were rewarded with iron sickles, which were then dedicated to the goddess.

Men married at thirty, women at twenty. They did not live together, for the men spent their lives in the communal barracks. The women made homes for themselves, and in time, through dowries and inheritances, they accumulated so much property and land that they became the real rulers of the state; and the luxury enjoyed by the women was oddly at variance with the stern regimen endured by the men, dedicated to absolute obedience and skill in war.

Sparta's cultural sterility was the inevitable result of her social and political structure. A small martial élite, which cannot have numbered much more than 10,000 men, women, and children, was supported by the labor of four or five times as many serfs, who were called "helots" after the town where they were first enslaved. These helots, the original owners of the land, were ruled by terror. A secret police force, called the *krypteia*, recruited from among the ranks of the young Spartans in training, ranged through the countryside by night and pounced on unsuspecting helots on whom there had fallen any suspicion of subversion. The offenders were stabbed to death and their bodies left on the road as a warning to others. Aristotle notes that these murders were accepted as part of the orderly processes of government, and to avoid the guilt of murder the chief officers of state on entering office every year proclaimed war on the helots.

The Spartans despised the neighboring states, even those like Corinth and Megara which were of Dorian descent. Corinth and Megara were given over to trade, which the Spartans were inclined to regard as a luxury leading to degeneration and corruption. With trade

came new ideas; and they dreaded new ideas. With trade, too, came
the emergence of free institutions, the contagion of freedom itself,
and these were even more to be dreaded. They despised the Athenians,
but they also feared them, for Athenian naval power was the greatest
in the Mediterranean, and they had few ships. They were soldiers,
not seamen; and they knew that if they fought the Athenians they
were in danger of winning every battle except the last, which would
be fought at sea.

Sparta and Athens had fought together against the Persians: desperation made them bedfellows. With peace and the gradual extension
of the Athenian empire, the Spartans realized that their way of life
was doomed unless Athens was destroyed. A head-on conflict became inevitable, but neither side wanted to begin the inevitable war.

The Peloponnesian War, which continued for twenty-seven
years except for a four-year truce, began in a fashion which no one
could have foreseen, far from Athens and Sparta, at a place outside
their conflicting spheres of interest. The small town of Epidamnus,
the modern Durazzo, faces the Adriatic on the Macedonian coast. A
revolution broke out in the town, one party being supported by
Corinth, a Spartan ally, the other by Corcyra, which naturally appealed to Athens for aid. The Athenians had no sooner won this
vicarious struggle than a second similar battle broke out, this time
over Potidaea in the peninsula of Chalcidice. Again the Athenians
won, routing a Corinthian army; and the enraged Corinthians appealed to Sparta for help. A conference was called, and the allies of
Sparta debated whether the time had come for a full-scale war with
Athens. Archidamus, a Spartan, urged them to abandon all thoughts
of war. "Let no one hope the war will soon be over," he said. "I fear
that if we embark on it, we may find ourselves leaving it as a legacy
for our children."

The Athenians had no large standing army and could not hope
to make a successful invasion of Sparta. Before the outbreak of the
war Pericles had announced the strategy the Athenians would follow.
"If the enemy attacks us by land, we shall attack him by sea," he
declared. "The devastation of only a part of the Peloponnese will be
a very different thing to the devastation of Attica. If they want fresh
land, they will have to take it by force of arms, while we have an
abundance of land both on the islands and on the mainland, all this
being the result of our sea power" (Thucydides, I, 143). Against

such a strategy the Spartans possessed two powerful strategies of their own: they could build a fleet, and with the help of their allies they could assemble an army so overwhelming that the Athenians would be compelled to surrender.

In the spring of 431 the Spartans invaded Attica, destroyed the crops, and sent the farmers hurrying for shelter behind the walls of Athens. Pericles dispatched 100 ships to ravage the coast of Sparta. For many years the war was to follow this pattern.

The Athenians early recognized the seriousness of the war and showed a guarded optimism concerning its outcome. It is in this light that the Funeral Speech of Pericles should be read. He celebrated the glory of Athens and of those who had died in that first year of the war, but he gave no promise of victory; and there hovers over this speech, the greatest ever made, a strange presentiment, not of defeat but of the possibility of defeat, of some eventual shattering tragedy which would lead to the dissolution of a way of life embarked upon with such high courage.

Throughout the speech Pericles compares the living force of Athenian freedom with the dead hand of Spartan tyranny. Death is everywhere in the speech. "The whole earth is a sepulcher of famous men." He implies that Athens, too, may become a sepulcher unless, by some miracle, the courage of a few may exorcise the tyranny of the many who are armed not so much by courage as by the impulse to destroy. There are only two subjects in the speech: Athens and the dead. Sometimes he seems to be weighing them in the balance.

Thucydides seems to have recorded this speech with quite unusual accuracy, only here and there interspersing ideas which are peculiarly his own. According to Plutarch, there was a typical Periclean cadence, and he had a characteristic way of expounding his ideas. A fragment of another funeral speech, quoted by Plutarch on the unimpeachable authority of the historian Stesimbrotus, has survived. Speaking over the Athenian dead who fell in the Samian War of 339, Pericles said: "They are become immortal like the gods, who remain invisible to us. From the honors they receive and the benefits they shower down on us we conclude that the gods are immortal, and so it is with those who die for their country."

In the speech delivered by Pericles at the beginning of the Peloponnesian War there is no mention of the gods. Not that Pericles did not reverence the gods, but the purpose of the speech demanded that on this occasion he should speak only of the purely human values at stake; and the goddess Athena was only too evidently present whenever he spoke of Athens; and when he spoke of freedom she was also present, and again when he spoke of education. As Pericles describes the government of Athens and the dignity of its citizens, he is so certain of the divinity moving through them that he has no need to declare it. He said:

Our constitution is called a democracy, because the government is in the hands not of the few but of the many. Our laws secure equal justice for all in their private disputes, and our public opinion welcomes and honors talent in every field of achievement, and a man is not honored because he belongs to a particular class, but on grounds of excellence alone; and on grounds of poverty no man is barred from a public career by obscurity of rank if he has it in him to do the state a service. And as we give free play to all in our public life, so we are free from suspicion in our private dealings, and we have no black looks or angry words for our neighbors if they enjoy themselves in their own way, nor do we give affront in ways which, though they may leave no mark, cause pain. Open and friendly in our private intercourse, a spirit of reverence pervades our public acts, and we are restrained from lawlessness by respect for authority and for the laws, most especially those which offer protection to the oppressed as well as those unwritten laws which bring upon the transgressors the knowledge of their shamefulness. . . .

We are lovers of beauty without extravagance, and lovers of wisdom without unmanliness. Wealth for us is not a vainglorious display, but a means of making achievement possible; and we think it no disgrace to acknowledge poverty, but it is disgraceful not to try to overcome it. Our citizens are engrossed in both their private and public affairs, and those who attend to business have no little insight into political matters. We alone regard a man who takes no interest in public affairs, not as a harmless drone, but as utterly useless; and we decide public matters for ourselves, or at least we endeavor to arrive at a sound understanding of them, holding that our discussions are no impediment to action, while all actions are foredoomed to failure unless they are first openly discussed. For we have this superiority over other men: we are the most daring of men, and at the same time we are the most given to reflection before the action. Other men are bold in ignorance, and reflection makes them hesitant. But the bravest are surely those with the clearest sense of the pleasures and dangers of life, and who nevertheless do not shrink from whatever lies before them. . . .

Those who died for Athens resigned themselves to Hope, the uncertain goddess, and in the face of death they resolved to rely upon themselves alone, in the strength of their own manhood; and when the shock of battle came, they chose rather to suffer the uttermost than to save their lives; they fled, indeed, from the shameful word of dishonor, but bore instead on their bodies the marks of men's hands, and in a moment of time, at the climax of their lives, were rapt away from a world filled, for their dying eyes, not with terror but with glory.

(*History*, II, XXXVII, XL, XLII)

Too often the Funeral Speech has been read as a statement of noble intentions, as an encomium divorced from the hard realities of Athenian life. Set it against its own time, and then we recognize the barbs directed against the Spartans, the cry of defiance directed against the savageries of dogma and brute force, and the shuddering knowledge that Athens, "the school of Hellas," may not survive the uncertainties of war. There is a deep sadness and a violent joy in the speech.

Pericles was about sixty when he delivered the speech: he had only two more years to live. In the following year came the Great Plague, which decimated the population and so shattered the morale of the Athenians that a generation passed before they fully recovered from it. Thucydides, who was stricken by it, gives a terrible account of its ravages, the temples crowded with the dead and the dying, the smoke rising from the funeral pyres all over the city, while the inevitable lawlessness which accompanies all plagues made a mockery of democracy.

Pericles himself was stricken in the plague, in which he lost two of his sons. When he recovered he went to Epidaurus to discuss terms for ending the war, but the Spartans were in no mood to be lenient now that the plague had brought Athens to her knees. So the war went on, and suddenly the Athenians turned the full weight of their fury against him. He was brought to trial and found guilty of misappropriating public funds. Then his closest friends and intimates were attacked: Phidias, Anaxagoras, and Aspasia, the brilliant mistress who had given him an illegitimate son. He was able to defend them and to see that no great harm came to them, but his small reserves of strength were soon exhausted. Having cast him down, the people then raised him up again, gave him full command, legitimized his son, and in other ways sought to make amends; but it was already too late, and he died in the autumn of 429. As he lay dying his friends gathered around his bed. They were discussing his victories and the great things he had accomplished, thinking he was asleep or had fallen unconscious, but he was wide awake, listening to them. "Strange that you should have left out the best thing," he said. "For no act of mine have any Athenians put on mourning."

He left Athens rudderless. For another quarter of a century the war continued, with occasional intervals of precarious peace. Athens survived the expedition to Sicily, where her best soldiers perished. The Athenians were carried away by visions of an empire in the West which would support them in a war against Sparta, and gambled on a quick victory. The gamble failed, all the ships and men falling into the hands of the enemy.

The last act, like the first, took place far from Athens. In the narrows of the Hellespont, off Aegospotami, the Athenian fleet perished. By an odd coincidence Alcibiades, exiled from Athens and living in a castle set high above the shore, watched the tragedy as though he were a spectator in the theater, and was unable to avert it.

For months the Athenian fleet, now numbering 180 ships, had been attempting to do battle with the Spartan navy under Lysander. Finally they discovered that the Spartans had slipped into the Hellespont. They pursued the Spartans, and at last dropped anchor below Alcibiades' castle, preparing to provoke the enemy into battle the next morning. Though Lysander's ships were completely manned and ready for action, they ignored the challenge. For four successive mornings the challenge was repeated, and always ignored. Each day, upon returning, the Athenians left their ships to forage through the countryside for provisions, each day growing more careless. From his castle Alcibiades saw the danger and sent a warning. Distrusting him, the Athenians greeted his message with contempt. On the fifth morning, when the Athenians had left their ships, Lysander threw his whole armada against them. In the slaughter that followed only nine ships escaped, among them the sacred galley *Paralus*.

"It was night," wrote Xenophon, "when the *Paralus* reached

Athens with her evil tidings, and a bitter wail of woe broke forth. From Piraeus, following the line of the long walls up to the heart of the city, it swept and swelled, as each man passed on the news to his neighbor. On that night no man slept."

The long war was over.

23 ≪ THUCYDIDES

AT NAPLES there can be seen a double bust of Herodotus and Thucydides: a single head with the two faces gazing in opposite directions. Herodotus has the kindly air of an old peasant, Thucydides might be taken for the peasant's severely aristocratic master. Herodotus is vulgar and earthy, Thucydides looks pensive and chaste, lost in the realms of pure thought. Such was the stereotype which has largely survived down to our own day, but it has little basis in truth. The two historians were dealing with different aspects of history, and both brought to their tasks a superb intelligence.

Of the historians who came to maturity during the classical age in Greece only Herodotus and Thucydides have survived out of the thirteen or fourteen known to have existed. Herodotus was famous in his own lifetime: his vast history of the Persian Wars answered the needs of his age. Of Thucydides we hear far less. He was never mentioned by the orators, never quoted by Plato or Aristotle. Xenophon undertook to complete his history, which was evidently regarded as sufficiently important to be worth completing, but it inspired no affection. It was not only that Thucydides dealt with a subject not calculated to stir the passions of the Athenians, for his *History of the Peloponnesian War* is a study in the decline and fall of the Athenian empire, but his manner and attitude toward the combatants are based on aristocratic prejudices which were very largely foreign to the Greeks. He wrote, as he said, for the ages—"My works have not been designed to meet the tastes of an immediate public, but were made to last forever." He was determined, in effect, to create an immortal masterpiece, and the Greeks who had fought through the interminable campaigns of that tragic war seem from the very beginning to have distrusted his motives. Their silence was less a mark of indifference than of disapproval.

Thucydides was a historian of towering eminence, equipped with an almost painfully precise philosophy of history. He knew what history was about—or he thought he knew. He saw with astonishing clarity the causes of human behavior and the springs of action, and he possessed an unerring instinct for tracing the intricate lines of force between the opposing armies. He saw the war as though it were an immense chess game played for the highest stakes, and continually gives the impression of a man so far above the conflict that his very detachment breeds a kind of indifference. There was something cold and inhuman in him. Even the Romans, who appreciated him highly for his exactness and his formidable narrative powers, were constrained to observe that some important elements were missing. All the gifts were present in him except an essential humanity.

When we read Thucydides we are confronted with an intelligence that cuts through all obstacles, that strips passions bare, and demonstrates an uncanny facility for going to the heart of a problem. He has read everything that has been written about the battles and has seen everyone of importance who took part in them. Of even the most minor engagements he speaks with the authority which can come only from careful study and prolonged absorption in the background and the ultimate causes which brought the engagement about. He is one of those who wrestle with problems until they are finally compelled to surrender a solution, but we are never certain whether he has wrestled with the right problem. He traces the lines of force, but sometimes he seems to forget the happy confusions of men and the multiplicity of their ambitions. When he says that a man acted for such-and-such reason, we wonder whether it was so. And sometimes we find ourselves wondering whether this historian, who seems so resolute in the pursuit of the truth, so totally above the conflict, is not in fact intimately involved in it to the extent of working out some terrible tragedy in his own life.

As we might expect, the English philosopher Thomas Hobbes, who also possessed an unerring understanding of the sources of power, saw part of the truth. "For his opinion touching the government of the State," Hobbes wrote of Thucydides, "it is manifest that he least of all liked the Democracy. It seemeth to me that as he was of Regal Descent, so he best approved of the *Regal Government*." He was in fact of royal descent connected with the reigning princes of Thrace. He was also connected, on his father's side, with the great Athenian house which produced Miltiades and Cimon, and was therefore on terms of intimacy with all the most aristocratic Athenians. He owned gold mines in Thrace, and was therefore independently wealthy. Living in Athens he had the advantage of a source of income unaffected by the fluctuations of Athenian power politics. By the nature of things his loyalties were sharply divided between Athens and Thrace, belonging to both and to neither, living in that strange no man's land which comes from having roots in two countries with widely different traditions, for Thrace belonged to the half-barbaric hinterland. Such a man might well possess intense feelings with complete absence of partisanship, and while being deeply moved by tragedies taking place before his eyes, he would feel himself in some way remote from the conflict, even from the conflicts in which he was himself involved.

It happened that in 424 Thucydides was placed second-in-command of a fleet dispatched to Thrace against the Spartan general Brasidas, then attempting the conquest of the Athenian dependencies in the north. Thucydides was then about forty-six years old, and he had already begun to write his *History of the Peloponnesian War*, foreseeing a long and perhaps inconclusive war which, whatever the issue, would shake the Greek states to their foundations. He was an obvious choice as a commander, for his connections with Thrace were well known and it was clearly hoped that he would be able to raise the Thracian tribes against the Spartan invaders. There was a lull in the war. Only in southern Thrace and in neighboring Macedonia were the armies on the march. Brasidas had chosen to invade places close to Thucydides' estates. He was universally admitted to be the most skillful and resolute of the Spartan generals, and his defeat might effectively change the entire course of the war.

Thucydides knew—he must have known—that great and decisive opportunities had been given to him. No one else possessed his influence among the Thracian tribes, and there were no other Athenian commanders who knew the land so intimately. He arrived off the island of Thasos, and there he seems to have suffered a crisis of indecision, or perhaps he merely waited to receive reports from the mainland. Eucles, the commander in chief of the Athenian expedition, had already made his way to Amphipolis, a large town nearly encircled by the river Strymon, inhabited by tribesmen and Athenian colonists. It was the administrative center of the Athenian dependencies north of the Aegean, and if it fell, all the tribesmen in the hinterland might be expected to go over to the Spartans. Eucles put the town in a state of defense, and waited for Thucydides to appear with his small but well-equipped forces. The mere appearance of Thucydides in this town where he was known to everyone would hearten the defenders.

Brasidas possessed an excellent secret service. He had his own agents inside the town, and he was carefully watching for movements of the small fleet anchored off Thasos. He knew that Thucydides owned the nearby gold mines and possessed the loyalty of the tribesmen, and it would be necessary to act quickly. Thucydides remained on his flagship. The weather was atrocious, and perhaps the messengers he sent had not returned, but it is more likely that he was waiting on events, unable to make up his mind. Brasidas saw his opportunity. He decided abruptly to make a forced march against Amphipolis, marching his men all day and all night through the driving snow, storming the bridge over the Strymon in the cold dawn, and immediately inviting the defenders to a parley in which he offered terms so unlike those which had been expected that Eucles, who had given up hope of seeing Thucydides, was compelled to surrender, though he could easily have held the town a few days longer.

Thucydides never explained the reasons for his delay. Better than anyone he knew the importance of Amphipolis, which supplied vast revenues to Athens from the export of furs, gold, and timber used in the construction of Athenian ships. As soon as he heard that Brasidas was outside the walls of the town he raced his seven ships from Thasos to Eion at the mouth of the river Strymon, arriving there at dusk. In his strange way he congratulated himself on having stolen a victory from the Spartans, who, if he had not arrived in the nick of time, would inevitably have taken the small coastal port the next morning.

The damage had been done, however, and Thucydides' responsibility for it was plain for all to see. He occupied the following days in supervising the defenses of the port, and presumably, though he does not say so, in ineffectual contacts with Thracian tribesmen who, having witnessed the fall of Amphipolis and seen the might of the Spartan army with their own eyes, were disinclined to rise in revolt against their new masters at the summons of a prince who had arrived too late on the scene. Thucydides noted, purely as a matter of fact, that the tribesmen were hurriedly going over to the Spartans. He mentions the names of the chieftains, and it seems likely that some of them were connected to him by ties of blood.

Brasidas meanwhile had not been resting on his laurels. At Amphipolis he fitted out ships and prepared to sail downriver and storm Eion. Thucydides had the barren satisfaction of fighting off two determined attacks, one against the jetty and the other against the walls, and thereafter quietly disappeared from his own history. All he tells us, all he is willing to tell us, is that "for twenty years I was in exile from my country after I held the command at Amphipolis." It was an odd and revealing statement, for he had never held the command at Amphipolis.

Of his subsequent life we know very little. It would appear that he was recalled to Athens and placed on trial, with Cleon, then at the height of his power, acting as the chief prosecutor. We do not know how he escaped the death penalty. He had influential friends and great wealth, and it is possible that he bribed the jurors or the jailers. He liked to call himself "Thucydides the Athenian," but during those twenty years he could live neither in Athens nor in any of the territories under Athenian dominion. An ancient Life recounts that he fled to his estate in Thrace, but the estate seems to have remained in Athenian hands until the end of the war. He tells us that he was often the guest of Spartan commanders who gave him the information on which he constructed his history. He may have been present at the battle of Mantinea in 418, which he describes with an unusual richness of detail, and he was almost certainly in Syracuse at the time of the ill-fated Athenian invasion, for he speaks of those events with the assurance of an eyewitness. He says of himself that he was in exile, but it is more likely that he was a fugitive from Athenian justice, living continually in fear of capture or assassination. At last, in 404, either because he was pardoned or in reward for services to the Athenian state, he returned to Athens. He was already an old man, and had only a few more years to live. He died about 396. There is a persistent tradition that he was assassinated.

From all we know about him, he seems to have been a man who tortured himself willingly, and carried a load of guilt through twenty years of exile. Far from being the detached observer studiously avoiding taking sides, he was intimately involved in the war and deeply implicated in its horrors. Only a man who has known guilt, terror, anguish, remorse, and humiliation could have written with such nervous calm and such an assumption of icy detachment.

In ancient times there existed a pleasant parlor game which consisted of comparing Herodotus with Thucydides. It was a game played by Lucian, Plutarch, and many others, with lengthy dissertations and quotations, and it was oddly ineffective because the two historians cannot be usefully compared. They differed in personal temperament, in their concepts of the function of the historian, and in their ideas of the nature of history itself. Most of all they differed in their understanding of men. Herodotus saw men whole, in three dimensions, fathers of families, with wives and children about them, and he accepted and delighted in the multiplicity and confusion of their ambitions. He was interested in landscapes, and how men wrest a living from the soil, and what food they ate, and how they worshiped their gods, and one feels that he would cheerfully sit down to a meal with them and worship their gods with them. There was no single thread which would lead a man through the labyrinth to the truth; he must understand all the affairs that interest them. One cannot imagine Thucydides sitting down with soldiers and peasants, though he might be induced to share a meal with the commander of an army or the head of its military intelligence. He was a lonely and fastidious man, only too well aware of his royal and aristocratic connections. He saw men in the mass, and no one has ever studied mass emotions with more scrupulous care. Men were lines of force, integers, pinpoints. He did not love them, and he regarded most of them as expendable.

But if it is impossible to feel any friendship for Thucydides, as one feels an abiding friendship for Herodotus, there is no denying his superb mastery of his material, his way of hammering it into its proper place in a narrative intended to disclose the entire machinery of the war. He has invented a form of history, and mastered his craft. He has made it all the more difficult for himself by deliberately keeping to a calendrical pattern—"Thucydides the Athenian," he writes, "describes the events as they happened, by summers and winters . . ." The calendar can be a tyrant, but he obeys it nevertheless, with the result that his account of a campaign on one front must grind to a standstill while he takes up another campaign on another front. We are continually being confronted with sudden changes of direction. His opinion that the history of nations is continually repeating itself because human nature does not change leads him to search for parallels where none may exist. He worships accuracy, and is continually repeating for our benefit that he has gone to great pains to discover the precise number of combatants, the exact order of attack. His opinion of human nature and his worship of precision derive from his aristocratic character, and so too does his style based on old Attic, which must have read to the Athenians of the fourth century B.C. very much as the tortured prose of Donne reads to us today.

It is not, however, for his mastery of detail and for his passionate recital of the shifting lines of force that we admire him. What is admirable is his psychological penetration, his profound gift of analysis. In the occasional portraits which appear at intervals in his work he shows an extraordinary grasp of the mechanics of the human mind, often at cross-purposes with itself. How brilliantly, how deftly, he can sum up an entire nation we learn very early in his work when, in a few lines, he sums up the characteristics of the Athenians:

They use their bodies in the service of their country as though their bodies belonged to other men, but their minds are completely their own, all the more their own when employed in their country's service. When they have conceived a plan but fail to carry it to fulfillment, they seem to themselves to have suffered a personal bereavement, and when they succeed in an enterprise, they consider they have gained only a mere installment of what the future may bring. When they fail, they devise new hopes and so make up for the loss. For them alone to have and to hope are the same thing, for as soon as they have an idea they execute it. In this way they toil, with hardships and dangers, all their life long; and least of all men do they enjoy what they have, because they are always going on to seek something else. Their only holiday is to do their duty, and they regard untroubled peace as far more disagreeable than the most tiresome labor. In a word, if a man should say of them that they were born neither to have peace themselves nor to let other men enjoy it, he would be saying no more than the truth.

(*History*, I, LXX.)

This is clearly Thucydides' considered verdict on the Athenians, and he will repeat it again with subtle variations in his account of

Pericles' Funeral Speech. Characteristically it has been put into the mouth of a Corinthian ambassador addressing the Spartans, and both Corinthians and Spartans were enemies of the Athenians. It is therefore presented as an opinion so completely remote from Thucydides' own thinking that we are not expected to believe that he could have shared it. But we should be on our guard. We learn soon enough that he speaks his own thoughts most directly when he has hidden them in a cocoon of historical records and relevant details. Accurate in military descriptions, he surrenders all accuracy in his set speeches. "My method," he declares in a famous passage, "is to keep as close as possible to the general sense of the words that were actually spoken, and to make the speakers say what, in my opinion, was called for by each situation." But "what, in my opinion, was called for" was not necessarily history. It was often an excuse for airing his own independent views and his personal preoccupations and deeply held beliefs.

Just as we can sometimes recognize the authentic voice of Socrates in the works of Plato, so we can recognize the voice of Thucydides when he is putting his own views into other people's mouths. It is a grave, urgent, faintly menacing voice: there is always the sense that strange and terrible crises are about to take place. He is at his best when he writes about desperate affairs, of plagues and surrenders and abysmal defeats. When he describes the Sicilian expedition, we are made aware of a doom hanging over the affairs of Greece: the Athenians seem to be wandering mindlessly from one blind, untenable position to the next, until their final collapse and their imprisonment in the quarry comes almost as a relief, to them and to us. The *relentlessness* of Thucydides is a thing to wonder at. He was one of those men who were happy only in the midst of the storm.

He prided himself on his clean-cut analytic understanding of affairs, but, as we have seen, it is precisely these qualities which are lacking. He is a surgeon probing a wound, fascinated by the mingled veins and torn sinews, not caring whether the body is that of a youth or an old man or a fish or an elephant.

It is precisely because he is so disenchanted that he speaks to us with such authority. Occasionally he will pause as it were on the wing and deliver himself of stark apothegms which have unerring force; and sometimes these apothegms are buried in the speeches of his characters, as though he were deliberately attempting to conceal them. A small anthology could be made of these apothegms which seem always to have been written at midnight:

In the hour of triumph, when fortune presents herself unexpectedly at a man's side, then the conqueror is in deadly peril.

It is a common mistake on going to war to begin at the wrong end, to act first and wait for disaster before deliberating on the matter.

Concessions to adversaries only end in self-reproach, and the more strictly they are avoided the greater will be the chance of security.

The wise ensure their own safety by not making too sure of their gains, and when disasters come they can then meet them more intelligently.

Great enmities cannot be ended so long as one side goes from one victory to another and then enforces peace on disastrous terms. They can be ended only when the victor, though capable of exacting these terms, offers an honorable and generous settlement.

It is human nature to yield gracefully to one who has himself yielded, and to fight on against an imperious enemy at insensate risks.

So he goes on in that lean and hungry style, devoid of ornament except the sinewy ornament of his involved sentences, looking down at the wars from the heights of his despair. He rarely employs images, unlike Pericles, who endeared himself to the Athenians by using them frequently, saying, for example, that when men died in war it was as though spring had been taken from the year, and when the Boeotians quarreled they resembled old oaks battering their limbs against one another, and that he could see war sweeping forward from the Peloponnese. Such things were memorable, but what one remembers in Thucydides is not the striking image: one remembers the set pieces, those deliberate and carefully contrived accounts of catastrophes.

Pericles and Thucydides stand at poles apart. They were both aristocrats by temperament as well as by birth, but they saw the world under different suns. There is a sense in which the *History of the Peloponnesian War* can be read as a long-fought struggle between Thucydides and Pericles, and how in the end there was wrung out of Thucydides an unwilling admiration for his enemy.

24 ≪ SOCRATES

I T SOMETIMES happens that a whole age may be represented by a single man of extraordinary attainments. Quite suddenly, and for no apparent reason, a man will emerge who wears the face of his century, and whenever we attempt to understand his century we find ourselves asking questions of this man. Very rarely do such men emerge. In all of Western history there are perhaps no more than eight or nine men of this kind.

Of such men was Socrates, son of Sophroniscus, a sculptor, and of Phaenarete, a midwife. He was born in 469, ten years after Salamis, in a family living in comfortable circumstances. Sophroniscus was a friend of Aristides the Just and was able to give his son the recognized education in gymnastics and music. Socrates seems to have worked at his father's trade, and Pausanias records that he carved three Graces which in his time could still be seen near the entrance to the Acropolis, and he adds the curious information that mysteries were celebrated beside the statues of the three Graces which were kept secret from the multitude. Only statues of very fine workmanship would have been placed in such a dominating position. That Socrates was a talented and indeed very gifted sculptor is eminently possible, and it is equally possible that he abandoned sculpture for the even more strenuous exercise of philosophy as soon as he realized the limitations of the sculptor's art. According to Diogenes Laertius, he said once that sculptors strove to make speaking likenesses of their models, but soon enough they became like stone themselves. What he wanted, what he lived for, was the life of the spirit. When he was still a very young man he met Parmenides and Zeno, and he may have met Anaxagoras, whose doctrine of mind captivated him, until he discovered that Anaxagoras had simply announced the doctrine without pursuing its consequences. What is certain is that Socrates was saturated with the learning of his time and from an early age consorted with the most distinguished circles in Athens.

We know his face well. That fiercely independent spirit was housed in an ungainly and ugly frame of great charm. He had a high broad forehead, a snub nose, thick lips, and a thick curling beard, so that he resembled the satyr masks used in plays. He had an odd walk which Aristophanes compared with the strut of a waterfowl, and he had a habit of rolling his eyes. He was quick and vigorous in his movements, but sometimes he would fall into fits of abstraction in which he stood quite still, sometimes for long periods of time. One summer day, while he was campaigning with the army, he fell into a fit of abstraction which lasted a whole day and night, and some Ionians were so startled to see him standing there lost in thought that they brought out their mats and watched him through his long night vigil until the dawn arose when he saluted the sun and went on his way. But it would be a mistake to regard him as a man devoted solely to philosophy: he lived hard and well, and there was scarcely any aspect of life which he did not embrace with open arms. The picture of Socrates that has inevitably dominated the imagination of all later ages is that drawn by Plato in the dialogues dealing with his trial and death when he was over seventy and his physical strength was waning, but for the greater part of his life he was a man of immense vigor, capable of enduring almost unlimited hardships uncomplainingly, with a mind like quicksilver charged with electric energy. He habitually went barefoot, and wore the same single garment winter and summer, but not because of poverty. It was simply that he had no use for possessions. When Alcibiades offered him a large piece of land to build a house on, he answered: "If I wanted shoes and you offered me an enormous strip of leather, wouldn't I be laughed at if I took it?" One of his friends said he was "born to spite the shoemakers." Deliberately he went about stripping himself of all the heavy baggage that men accumulate during their lives. It amused him to see the heaped merchandise in the market place—there was so little of it that he wanted. At all costs he wanted to be free, in order to understand, in order that there should be nothing between himself and his understanding.

There was nothing of the pedant in him. That strange, squat, burly man wandered the streets of Athens, continually asking the same insidious questions. What is love? What is justice? What is virtue? What is the state? How should men live their lives? They were severely practical questions, and he would buttonhole anyone who thought he had found the answers, submitting him to the dialectic process. Now dialectic means nothing more than conversation. There was nothing in the least new in conversation as a means to elucidate philosophical problems. What was new was Socrates' strenuous method of conversing, his ruthless determination to get to the heart of a problem, his ironic detachment, his sudden devastating sallies into the precarious defenses of his opponent. With Socrates conversation became a hard-fought wrestling match, a long-drawn rigorous cross-examination on the nature of things and ideas, a game played by an athlete striving for the highest stakes. All words, all ideas were suspect until they had proved themselves, until the sense had been wrung out of them. No half measures, no easy answers: he would cut through flesh and muscle until he reached the bone.

As a conversationalist he had certain advantages over his contemporaries. There was, first, his immense charm and attractiveness, especially among the young aristocrats who saw aristocratic qualities in his pursuit of the strenuous life of the mind. There was his legend, which had already reached towering proportions when he was still a comparatively young man. At some time before the outbreak of the Peloponnesian War one of his pupils, the dark-skinned Chaerophon, made a special journey to the oracle at Delphi to ask the question: "Is there anyone alive wiser than Socrates?" The priestess answered with a resounding: "No." Socrates seems not to have been unduly impressed by the oracle, which he interpreted as recognition of the fact that he was one of the few men who dared to admit his own ignorance, and he set about to prove Apollo a liar by attempting to find someone wiser than himself. According to his statement in the *Symposium*, he found only one person who excelled him in wisdom, and this was Diotima of Mantinea, a learned woman who once discoursed with him on the nature of love. Ignorance was one of his most potent weapons; humor was another. Philosophers are rarely humorous, but Socrates shed the light of his humor and wit on most of the arguments he engaged in. He was of a sweet, unruly temper.

While his authority derived from the charm of his physical presence, the cutting edge of his brain, and the legends that accumulated around him, there was another element in him which goes far to explain his extraordinary ascendancy over those around him. He possessed visionary powers. "Divine voices" spoke to him, warning him of dangers and foretelling the future. At his trial he spoke about these things as though they were matters of fact, and widely known. He was the prisoner of his *daemon*, that strange power which very occasionally gripped him and translated him into a world where the voices of the gods could be heard. These divine voices attended him from the days of his childhood, and according to Plato they manifested themselves when least expected, often on very trivial occasions and when he had no especial desire to hear them. They came unannounced, and vanished as quickly as they came. Of their existence—of the existence of these entirely unreasonable and sudden voices—there can be no reasonable doubt. Socrates was a mystic, whose mysticism was held in check by good humor and a razor-sharp intelligence: he would never surrender wholly to his mysticism, nor would he surrender wholly to his intelligence. The *amor mysticus* haunted him, and he clearly derived strength from his ecstasies. He was one of those rare beings, like St. Paul and Pascal, who were at home in both worlds.

As far as we know, Socrates never wrote a line of prose, and the few poems he is said to have written only prove that he did not have the makings of a poet. Our knowledge of him is derived largely from an enormous collection of Socratic dialogues recorded by Plato, from the rather dull and uninspired *Memorabilia* composed by Xenophon, and a few pages of Socratic dialogue written by Aeschines of Sphettus. Plato, more than forty years younger than Socrates, reports conversations which he could not possibly have heard, because they took place about the time of his own birth. Xenophon and Aeschines were contemporaries of Plato, and they could have known Socrates only during the last ten years of his life. What then do we know of the real words spoken by Socrates?

For a long time it has been held that the Socratic dialogues composed by Plato were the inspired tributes of a gifted pupil with no pretensions to historical accuracy. They were believed to be imaginative reconstructions of conversations spoken by Socrates, rarely if ever developed according to verbatim records. Diogenes Laertius in his brief life of Plato relates that when Socrates heard Plato reading the *Lysis*, he exclaimed: "O Hercules! what a number of lies the young man has written about me!" The story may be true, but does not necessarily impute inaccuracy to Plato, who may have embroidered the conversation a little or given to Socrates more brilliance than Socrates felt he deserved. Socrates may have been joking. The sentence can be read in four or five different ways, and we cannot fathom it unless we know the tone in which it was spoken. The possibility remains that the Socratic dialogues are reasonably accurate renderings of conversations which actually took place.

Just as scholars have sometimes attempted to dispose of the *Iliad* by dividing it among ten or twenty putative authors, so they have worked valiantly to prove that Socrates as we know him is largely a figment of Plato's imagination. Yet it is a matter of record that the ancient Greeks possessed phenomenal memories, and it was not unusual for men to be able to recite the entire *Iliad*. Shorthand was well known and was constantly employed in the law courts. Copies of the Socratic dialogues did exist, for we hear of Aeschines procuring them from the wife of Socrates. Diogenes Laertius tells us that Xenophon used "signs" to note down the conversations of Socrates. Accurate or edited texts of the dialogues may very well have been in existence in Socrates' lifetime, and it is not unreasonable to conclude that a considerable library of them was already in existence when Plato set out to produce a definitive edition. Plato's task may have been little more than that of an inspired editor, an editor with genius.

This is not to say that Plato did not frequently embellish a dialogue or juxtapose a section of one dialogue with a section from another. The *Republic*, which forms a long inquiry on the nature of justice and the state, may have been composed from many dialogues which took place at widely different times and in different places. Plato has set his stamp on all of them by giving them an artistic form of his own choosing, but the authentic voice of Socrates rings too clearly and too frequently to admit of any dispute.

So we may imagine the dialogues to be substantially accurate reproductions of conversations as filtered through the mind of Plato, who took part in many of them and knew most of the participants. Those who argued with Socrates formed a motley crew, ranging from millionaires to slaves. There was Cephalus, a wealthy merchant from Syracuse. There was the enormously wealthy Callias, son of Hipponicus. There was Crito, another rich Athenian, who on the authority of the third-century scholar Demetrius of Phaleron is supposed to have endowed Socrates with a sum of seventy minae, corresponding to about $1,400. At the other end of the scale there was the young Phaedo, a former slave, whom Socrates loved and "made into a philosopher." There was Chaerophon, with his dark skin, sallow complexion, and half-starved appearance, who returned from Delphi with the news that the oracle had declared Socrates the wisest of men. There was Lysias, the famous speech-writer, whose father was Cephalus. There was Aristippus of Cyrene, the gentle hedonist, who was first attracted to Athens by the fame of Socrates and remained by his side almost to the day of his death. There was Charmides, the beautiful boy of the *Symposium*, who grew up to become one of the Thirty Tyrants, murderous and vengeful, and Critias, also one of the Thirty and perhaps the most infamous of all, who died fighting to uphold his tyranny. Both Charmides and Critias were close relatives of the young Plato who at the age of twenty abandoned the career of tragic poet to become the most influential of Socrates' pupils. There was the young and noble Alcibiades, who behaved all his life like a corrupt and luxurious prince, but was occasionally tamed into startled humility by the presence of Socrates. Such were the men who gathered round Socrates, becoming his companions in philosophy, listening and arguing, counting the day well lost if it was spent in rigorous conversation. For the most part they were men of acute intelligence, among the flower of Athens.

In time many of them became philosophers; others continued their professional careers; a few obtained prominent positions in government. The subsequent careers of Charmides, Critias, and Alcibiades were scarcely an advertisement for the Socratic method. In the end Socrates paid with his life for the political insanity of some of his pupils.

Alcibiades was perhaps the most puzzling of the pupils. That tall, graceful, and elegant young man who spoke with a charming lisp and squandered his intelligence and his wealth as though he possessed untold credit, was sometimes moved to tears by a word from Socrates. The beautiful youth and the satyrlike philosopher were foils for one another, and they slept together in the same tent at Potidaea in Macedonia, when the Athenians were fighting the battle that was the curtain-raiser of the Peloponnesian War. During a sharp skirmish they fought side by side, and when Alcibiades was wounded Socrates threw himself in front of his friend and saved his life, performing the day's most signal act of courage; and when the generals were giving out rewards, Socrates insisted that the crown for valor should go to Alcibiades together with the complete suit of armor which was offered only to those who had fought far beyond the call of duty. Some time later, at Delium, when the Athenians were being routed, Alcibiades in turn saved the life of Socrates. Alcibiades was on horseback, Socrates on foot. A group of hard-pressed foot soldiers was in danger of being cut off, when Alcibiades saw them, swung his horse round, and went to their rescue. Although many were cut down, Alcibiades was able to shelter Socrates and lead him to safety.

Alcibiades had all the advantages of noble birth, riches, personal courage, a multitude of friends. He was famous for his eloquence, and generous to excess. He danced wonderfully, and played on the lute and the harp, and it amused him to say that only fools play on the flute, "because the flute blocks the mouth and stops up the voice." His beauty was not the ephemeral beauty of youth, but something which remained with him all his life; and people would stop to watch him passing down the street simply to gaze on that god-given beauty. He had only one fault—pride. It was a fault which was to tear him to pieces. In the end he came to commit almost every imaginable act of treachery, corruption and murder for the sake of glory. In his youth, when Socrates knew him best, there were few signs of the heaven-vaulting pride that was to destroy him. "Socrates," says Plutarch, "observed the noble qualities and fine disposition in and under his youthful beauty, and realizing his wealth and high position, and seeing that strangers and Athenians flattered and caressed him, and might corrupt him, he deliberately set himself to act as a moderator, to prevent the flower from perishing before it bore fruit." Not even Socrates could prevent Alcibiades from going down to his damnation.

Even when Alcibiades was quite young, when he was living as an orphan in the house of Pericles, who was his uncle, there were intimations of the corruption to come. Once when he was wrestling and found himself hard pressed, he bit the hand of his opponent deliberately and against all the rules. "You bite, Alcibiades, like a woman," the other wrestler said. "No, like a lion!" said Alcibiades. His desire to become a lion was an overwhelming desire, driving him to madness. He had a lion's daring, a lion's complete indifference to danger. For no reason at all except that he thought it might delight his friends, he once slapped the immensely wealthy and powerful Hipponicus across the face. The next morning he appeared in the house of the terrified Hipponicus naked and begging to be scourged in punishment. The old man not only pardoned him, but gave him his daughter Hipparete in marriage with a dowry of ten talents, an enormous sum in those days. He received another ten talents after the birth of his first child, and squandered the money as it had never been squandered in living memory. In his princely fashion he fitted out triremes and gave them to the state, paid the expenses of the chorus, contributed heavily to the war chest, and accumulated a score of mistresses. Once, while still a private citizen, he entered seven chariots in the Olympic games at an expense which might have crippled even the rich and luxury-loving tyrants of Sicily.

In nearly every respect Socrates and Alcibiades were opposites. Though they were held together by a deep affection, there was also on Alcibiades' part a residue of hate. He admitted as much at the famous banquet in the house of Agathon when he said: "Socrates has brought me to such a pass that there are times when I can scarcely endure my life, for he alone has the power to make me ashamed of myself. I clap my hands to my ears and flee from him, *and there are times when I wish he was dead!*" It was not entirely persiflage. Men who stood in awe of his demonstrable virtue would suddenly become aware of their own inadequacies, and they too would clap their hands to their ears and run from him, unable any longer to listen to his taunts. Socrates was a dangerous gadfly, and he seems to have known very early that he was playing into the hands of enemies.

The first forty years of his life were spent in the high noon of Athenian power and glory, the last thirty coincided with the gradual decline and disintegration of Athens under the impact of the Peloponnesian War. The dividing line was the Great Plague of 430, which he survived unharmed, being one of the few Athenians who seem to have taken no special precautions, relying on his astonishing physical stamina. He fought in the wars, being present during the engagements at Delium in 424 and Amphipolis in 422. About this time he may have married Xanthippe, who gained the reputation of being a shrew, though it is likely enough that her reputation stemmed from youthful possessiveness and anger over his poverty. He had become a familiar figure in Athens: his empire over men's minds was never greater than during the years when Alcibiades was rising to eminence. He was constantly to be seen in the gymnasia, and he had his own stamping ground near the bankers' tables in the Agora. Here, leaning on his staff, he would talk all morning, and in the afternoons he would wander wherever he pleased with his chosen companions. There was some talk of a school, and no doubt the young men who congregated around him regarded themselves as his scholars, but he always denied that he was any kind of schoolmaster and insisted that he never took fees for his teaching. If there was a school, it was a very odd one, for while most of his pupils were poverty-stricken boys living off a common table, there were frequent descents by rich and garlanded young aristocrats. With his accustomed generosity Socrates welcomed into his circle anyone who would give straight answers to straight questions.

Aristophanes was his friend—a dubious friend. In 423 he produced his play, *The Clouds*, in which Socrates is depicted as a monster of egotism, an impostor, a worshiper of strange gods, the owner of a Thought Factory where the pupils bend down as though searching for truffles, attempting to unravel the secrets of the universe with their noses. Socrates is caricatured unmercifully, but there is a disturbing resemblance to the real Socrates whose personal mannerisms are reproduced with sufficient accuracy to dispel any doubt that Aristophanes is deliberately attempting to laugh his friend out of existence. So we find references to his poverty, his ugliness, his trances, his cross-examinations, and his belief that his proper role was that of midwife for other people's thoughts. Alcibiades is introduced under the name of Pheidippides, a young fop busily spending his patrimony in a rage to acquire the greatest number of horses in the shortest possible time. His father, Strepsiades, comes to consult Socrates, who plays with him like a cat playing with a mouse. Strepsiades swears by Zeus, and immediately Socrates pounces on him:

SOCRATES
Zeus? What is all this nonsense about Zeus? He doesn't exist!
STREPSIADES
Oh, doesn't he? Then what makes the rain, if you please?
SOCRATES
The clouds, of course! Have you ever seen rain without clouds? Can you imagine Zeus causing rain from a clear sky, without their help?

STREPSIADES

*By Apollo, that's well spoken! I always thought the rain was
Zeus pissing through a sieve. Who makes the thunder then? Thunder
is the thing I dread!*

SOCRATES

When the clouds roll over one another—that's thunder.

STREPSIADES

That's a bold idea, but how do you explain it?

SOCRATES

*Being saturated with water, and bumping together, they burst
with furious energy and produce a vast uproar.*

STREPSIADES

But the power that makes them bump—isn't that Zeus?

SOCRATES

No, of course not. The airy Whirlwind does that!

STREPSIADES

*Airy Whirlwind, eh? I didn't know about that! So Zeus has no
existence, and the Whirlwind reigns in his stead? But you haven't yet
told me what makes the thunder roar?*

SOCRATES

*Then you didn't follow me! Didn't you hear me say that when
the clouds are waterlogged and bump against one another, then they
burst with a vast uproar?*

STREPSIADES

How can I be expected to believe that?

SOCRATES

*Take yourself then. When you have gorged on stew at the
Panathenaea, don't you get a bellyache, and isn't there a great deal of
rumbling?*

STREPSIADES

*By Apollo! So there is! I get colic, and the stew growls like
thunder and bursts forth with a tremendous noise. At first it makes a
little gurgling pappax-pappax noise, and then it grows louder, papapappax! and when I seek relief, why, then the real thunder comes,
papapappax! pappax!! papapapax!!! It thunders just like your clouds!*

There is no delicacy in Aristophanes' attack on Socrates: he
wields a heavy two-handed sword like a man in hot rage after years
of smoldering resentment. In scene after scene he bludgeons Socrates

unmercifully, accusing him precisely of those crimes for which he was later sentenced to death—disbelief in the gods and corruption of the young by teaching them a system of verbal tricks enabling them to prove that evil is good and that all laws, human and divine, may be broken with impunity. At the end of the play the outraged Strepsiades puts a torch to the Thought Factory, explaining that he is merely pursuing a subtle argument with the beams of the house. As the house disappears in the flames and Socrates and his disciples emerge suffocated by the smoke, Strepsiades shouts after them: "Chase them! Beat them! Strike them down! There are many reasons, but the chief reason is that they have insulted the gods!"

At his trial twenty-four years later Socrates claimed that the play had done more than anything else to damage his reputation and to make him hated by a good part of the population of Athens. They saw him through the eyes of Aristophanes; and the real man vanished in the savage caricature. Characteristically, when he attended a performance of the play, Socrates rose in his seat so that the audience could compare his own satyrlike mask with the mask worn by the actor. It is the only pleasant story told about the play.

Socrates spent the last years of his life under the shadow of the Peloponnesian War and the fierce rebellions that followed disaster and defeat, but these years were sweetened by the presence of young scholars who admired him this side of idolatry. And what scholars they were! The young Xenophon was wandering down a lane when he encountered Socrates, who raised his staff horizontally to form a barrier and then engaged him in conversation about where merchandise could be bought, and when Xenophon answered satisfactorily, Socrates went on to ask him where goodness and virtue could be found, and it was clear that Xenophon knew merchandise better than goodness. "Then follow me, and you shall learn where goodness is found," Socrates said. Then there was the much younger Plato, rich and aristocratic, descended on his mother's side from Solon and on his father's side from the early kings of Athens. His real name was Aristocles, meaning "best and honored." All the talents had been given to him. He was a mathematician, a love poet, a wrestler in the Isthmian games, a brilliant soldier, a formidable debater. Plato means "broad," and the name was given to him to describe his broad brow or his broad shoulders, or perhaps both together. They said of him that he was strangely quiet, never laughed outright, and often frowned "with eyebrows lifted high like a snail." He had a weak voice, but otherwise gave an impression of extraordinary strength and energy. Diogenes Laertius tells the story that Socrates dreamed one night of a cygnet resting on his knees, which immediately put forth feathers, and flew high in the air uttering a sweet note; and on the next day Plato came to visit him. Socrates remembered the cygnet and pronounced that the dream foretold the coming of his new pupil. At this time Plato was twenty years old. He was then considering a career in politics or as a playwright, but he was so moved by the teaching of Socrates that he burned his plays and abandoned his political prospects to devote himself to philosophy.

Xenophon and Plato were well-born, and so too was Critobulus, the son of Crito, who was so handsome that his relations with Socrates aroused suspicion, but Aeschines was the son of a sausage maker, and Antisthenes too had a lowly origin and rejoiced in his poverty, deliberately going about in a torn gown, so that Socrates once laughed and said: "I see your vanity through the hole in your gown." Antisthenes is almost forgotten now, but in his own day he was regarded as the most brilliant of Socrates' followers, a man with a biting wit and a fierce love of virtue. If we can believe Diogenes Laertius, he played an important role in the downfall of his master's persecutors, being in some unexplained way responsible for the banishment of Anytus and the death of Meletus, the tragic poet, whose accusations led to the trial and death of Socrates.

In the stormy years of the Peloponnesian War Socrates seems to have spent the greater part of his time in Athens. He loved the city and hated to be away from it. His mind was as swift and subtle as ever. His deftness indeed only increased with age, and with increasing insight went a deeper understanding of the mysteries that defy logic. There had been a mystical strain in him from the very beginning. Now, in those last years, he seemed sometimes like a storyteller content to relate the adventures of the soul rather than to expound the soul's meaning.

In the *Symposium* Plato describes a banquet held in the house of Agathon in 415, only a few weeks before the sailing of the ill-fated armada to Sicily, with Alcibiades as its principal commander. Alcibiades himself was one of the six speakers at the banquet, arriving late, "flown with insolence and wine," staggering a little so that he had to be supported by his companions. Earlier, Socrates had launched into an extraordinary description of the ladder of love in its joyful ascent toward perfect beauty. Just before entering the banqueting hall he had been struck by one of those queer trances which left him speechless and motionless, sunk deep within himself. When at last he spoke among the banqueters, it was as though the trance were speaking, as he relates the words he claimed to have heard from the lips of a prophetess:

So now let me tell you the proper way of proceeding to the doctrine of love, or of being conducted there by another. First then you should begin with beautiful objects here below, and from these you should mount higher toward the other beauty in view, using them as steps of a ladder, mounting from the love of one fair person to the love of two, and from the love of two to the love of all, and from the love of beautiful persons to the love of beautiful employments, and from the love of beautiful employments to the love of beautiful forms of knowledge, till you pass from degrees of knowledge to that knowledge which is concerned only with the Perfect Beauty.

This, my dear Socrates, is the life above all others that men should live, meditating on the Perfect Beauty. Once you have beheld that beauty, you will know that it cannot be measured against gold or costly raiment or beautiful youths. What if men had eyes to see this Perfect Beauty—I speak of the divinely beautiful, which is pure and clear and undefiled, untouched by the corruptions of mortality and the colors and vanities of human life—what if a man should hold that purest beauty in his gaze?

Therefore I say that when he beholds this beauty with the eyes of the mind, he will be able to create the reality of perfect beauty, not the mere image only, and having created it and nourished true virtue, he becomes the friend of God and is as close to immortality as any can be.

(Symposium, 210)

Once long before he had said: "I am a poor creature with only one talent: I can immediately recognize the lover and the beloved." Now, at the banquet, he translated lover and beloved into the transcendent world of the spirit, where they were still recognizable. Never again would he speak with such passion on the subject of love. And when finally with a kind of exquisite bathos Alcibiades interrupts the banquet with an account of how he once slept with Socrates under

Homer.

Pericles.

Socrates.

Aristotle.

Plato.

Euripides.

Sophocles in old age.

Alexander the Great.

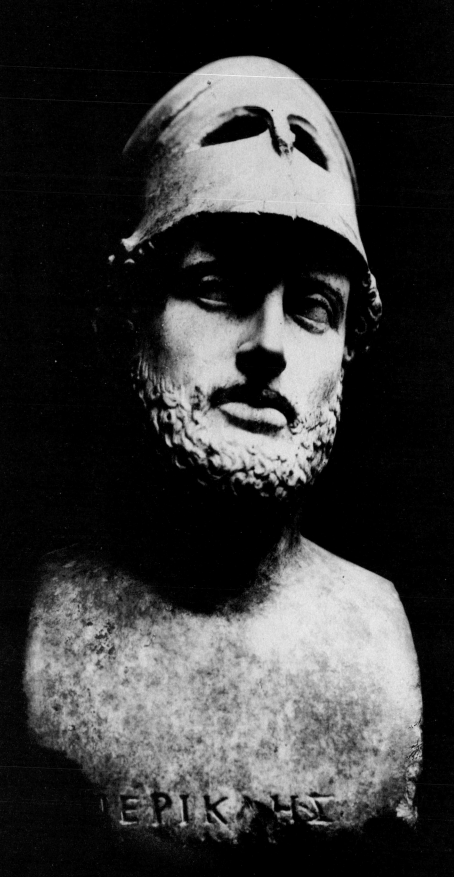

ΓΕΡΙΚΛΗΣ

ΕΥΡΙΠΙΔΗΣ

the same blanket "as innocently as with a father or an elder brother," we do not necessarily have to believe him, but his description of these encounters seems to be curiously irrelevant. All pales before the vision of Perfect Beauty spoken with such quiet assurance.

Within a few weeks of the banquet Athens, always elaborately concerned with the laws of worship, was convulsed with a series of grave religious scandals. On the eve of the Sicilian campaign the Athenians discovered that the erect phalluses of the Herms standing in the market places and outside houses had been mutilated during the night. Suspicion fell on Alcibiades, the only man believed to have sufficient daring to commit such a crime against the state. He demanded the right of a public hearing to clear himself of the charge, but he was thought too valuable to the expedition, and the hearing was postponed until after his return. Rumors about the profanations committed by him and by his friends continued in his absence until Thessalus, the son of Cimon and inveterate enemy of Alcibiades, accused him of taking part in sacrilegious burlesques of the Eleusinian Mysteries, "at which he mimicked the mysteries of the goddesses Demeter and Korê, and displayed them to his friends in his own house, while wearing a garment like that worn by a hierophant and calling himself hierophant." This was an even more serious crime than the mutilation of the Herms, and Alcibiades was immediately recalled, and those of his close friends who were in reach, including Phaedrus and Eryximachus, both of whom belonged to the Socratic circle, were arrested. Alcibiades escaped and made his way to Sparta, where he became the formidable enemy of the Athenians who had once worshiped him and given him the highest positions in the land. There he remained, putting all his abilities at the service of the Spartan king and relentlessly plotting against Athens. Four years later a *coup d'état* in Athens restored him to favor and he was able to return in triumph in 407. His triumph was short-lived, and he soon vanished into obscurity, a refugee in the courts of the minor princes of Asia Minor and the Thracian Chersonese. One day in 404, when he was about to proceed to the court of Artaxerxes, his house was surrounded by armed men and set on fire. He rushed out and was immediately shot down by the archers waiting for him.

The mutilation of the Herms, the mysterious sacrileges performed by Alcibiades followed by his wayward progress when in exile— all these things threw their shadow on Socrates. He was never implicated in the crimes of his strange pupil, and it was utterly inconceivable that he should ever partake in a travesty of the Eleusinian Mysteries, but he was sufficiently close to Alcibiades to be in danger. He was in more danger still in the autumn of 406, when singlehanded he faced the councilors of Athens and charged them with disobeying the law.

In the summer the Athenian fleet won a great naval victory over the Spartans off the Arginusae islands between Lesbos and the Asiatic mainland. Seventy Spartan ships were sunk or captured against twenty-five lost by the Athenians. Some 4,000 Athenians floating about in the wreckage also were lost: they might have been rescued if the sea had been calmer or if the naval officers had issued the orders in time. Of the ten senior officers eight returned to Athens, among them Pericles the son of Pericles, and they were promptly charged with culpable negligence by the Assembly; and this year it happened that Socrates was one of the Five Hundred. The crime was serious: the officers had failed to recover their dead after battle, and in the eyes of pious Athenians such behavior constituted a *skandalon*, an act of such gross impiety toward the dead that in comparison the victory counted for nothing. After violent debates, it was decided to try the accused en bloc, although by law they should have been tried separately. Socrates objected vehemently—so vehemently that he was denounced and threatened with arrest. The crowd protested that it was "monstrous to deprive the people of its power to do as it pleased." They sentenced the naval officers to the death reserved for traitors: they were hurled off the edge of the Acropolis. Some weeks later the Athenians repented of their deed and an order was sent out to arrest the five men who were chiefly responsible for the condemnation. All were arrested, but all escaped from prison.

Two years later, when Athens capitulated to the Spartan general Lysander, Socrates showed that he could no more be intimidated by the oligarchs who took command of Athens from the Spartans than by a bloodthirsty mob. The oligarchs, who were known as "the Thirty," hoped to sweep away the entire fabric of democratic government by the arrest and execution of all the prominent democratic leaders, and many who were not prominent. The master spirit of the Thirty was Critias, the cousin of Plato's mother, and one of his principal assistants was the handsome and brilliant Charmides, who was Plato's uncle: both had been pupils of Socrates. It was Socrates who suggested that Charmides should take up a political career, but he had never guessed that this career would be accompanied by mass executions. Socrates remained in Athens: he knew these new rulers too well to have any fear of them.

He went on talking in his customary fashion. He spoke caustically about the new leaders, saying: "I am puzzled when I find a herdsman pluming himself on diminishing the number of his cattle and worsening their condition. Should he not confess that he is a bad herdsman? I am still more puzzled when I find the governor of a state pluming himself on diminishing the number of the people and worsening their condition. Should he not confess he is a bad governor?"

Such rebukes were not taken lightly by the new rulers of the city. Socrates was ordered to appear before the Thirty and told that he must no longer have any conversations with the young. He asked at what age a man might be considered to be no longer young, and was told: "You must not talk to anyone under thirty years of age."

"But if I want to buy something from a youth, may I ask the price?"

"Certainly, but you may not ask any other questions."

"And if a youth asks me 'where does Critias live?' may I answer him?"

"Yes, you may, but there must be no speaking with shoemakers, carpenters and ironsmiths, who must by now be worn out with your questioning—"

"Do you mean that I must also abstain from the lessons in justice and piety which I learn from them?"

"Yes, you must, and also the lessons you have learned from herdsmen!"

Thereupon Socrates was dismissed from the court, knowing that his small sermon on the herdsman with the diminishing flock had struck home.

For the moment Socrates was free, but a few weeks later the tyrants decided to implicate him in their tyranny by ordering him and four others to arrest Leon of Salamis, a wealthy man whom the Thirty had decided to murder in order to obtain possession of his property. In similar ways the Thirty were able to implicate hundreds and perhaps thousands of citizens in their own crimes. Socrates received the order, but instead of going to Salamis with the four others who were ordered to make the arrest, he simply went to his own home, well knowing the penalty of disobedience to the commands of the tyrants; and he would himself have been arrested and put to death if the tyrants had not been overthrown soon afterward.

The rule of the Thirty lasted for eight months, from September, 404, to May, 403. Horrified by the endless bloodletting, the Athenians finally rose up in arms under their democratic leaders, Thrasybulus and Anytus. Critias and his army were destroyed on the fortress hill of Munychia overlooking Piraeus. Gradually peace settled on Athens.

For Socrates there was no peace. The leaders of the restored democracy distrusted him, and his notorious friendship with Alcibiades, Critias, and Charmides made him suspect. Anytus in particular disliked him, for he had once taken the democratic leader to task, saying: "Now that you have reached the highest positions which the city can offer you, it is wrong of you to bring up your son as a tanner." Socrates did not despise the tanner's trade. It was simply that he believed the dignity of the city would be upheld if the boy devoted himself to more intellectual attainments or if he became a government servant. According to Xenophon, Socrates believed that with this remark he signed his own death warrant.

In February, 399, a young Athenian poet called Meletus wrote the formal indictment:

Meletus, son of Meletus, of the deme of Pitthus, indicts Socrates, son of Sophroniscus, of the deme Alopece, witnessing on oath that Socrates does not worship the gods worshiped by the state, but he has introduced new and unfamiliar gods, and furthermore he is guilty of corrupting the young. The prosecutor demands that the punishment be death.

(Diogenes Laertius, *Socrates*, XIX)

For some five hundred years this document survived in the Temple of Cybele. There is no reason to believe that it was written by Meletus. Anytus and the orator Lycon were the forces behind the indictment; Meletus seems to have been introduced merely as a puppet. Asked what he knew about Meletus, Socrates could only say: "He is young and unknown, and I have scarcely any acquaintance with him. I remember he has long straight hair, a hook nose, and not much of a beard."

But Socrates had only to read the indictment carefully to realize that the trap had been sprung. No more damning indictment could have been prepared: it was both true and false, and there was suffi-cient truth to outweigh its falsity. He knew—he could not help know-ing—that the charges were unanswerable. They were too vague to stand up to logical examination, but they could not be laughed away. The man in the street, who had suffered at the hands of Socrates' corrupt pupils and watched the old philosopher as he cleverly de-molished every argument that was presented to him, could easily be convinced that Socrates was a dangerous and evil force. Years later men were to say openly that Socrates was condemned for having once been a friend of Critias.

At the trial Socrates made only a halfhearted defense. He spoke of his services to the state, denied that he worshiped strange gods, called upon the prosecution to prove one single case of corruption for which he was responsible, and explained that the whole purpose of his life was to question all accepted ideas and to make men dissatis-fied with themselves until they had examined themselves and found what was wanting. He told about Chaerophon's visit to the Delphic oracle, and how the youth had returned to Athens with the reply that no one was wiser than Socrates. He claimed that the oracle had spoken truly, because he alone was certain of his ignorance, while the politicians, poets, and workmen he met in his daily travels all claimed knowledge over matters they knew nothing about. By demolishing their pretensions he had made enemies for himself, but was it a crime to make enemies? He summoned Meletus to the bar of the court, and asked what was meant by that general accusation of impiety and cor-ruption, and demolished one by one the young poet's arguments. Un-happily, they would come to life again after being demolished. Meletus had only to say: "I swear by Zeus that you believe in abso-lutely nothing at all!" for the audience to shout their approbation. It was the picture they had formed of Socrates: the corrupter of youth, the atheist who mocked at the gods, the Sophist who could destroy all arguments, leaving nothing in their place. They feared his irony and his wit, and he did nothing to dispel their fears, for the wit sparkled all the more brilliantly now that he was close to death:

Men of Athens, I am not defending myself for my own sake, as you may believe, but for your sakes, that you may not lose God's gift by condemning me. For if you put me to death you may not easily find another like me. I am like one of those gadflies which fasten themselves to horses—it is a ludicrous image, but that is how I cling to this city at God's command: this city which is like a large and lazy thoroughbred which needs to be stirred up. And God, I believe, has set me here for this purpose. All day long and in all places I am that gadfly who fastens himself upon you, arousing and persuading and reproaching you. You will not easily find another like me, and therefore I advise you to spare me. I daresay you have been annoyed, as drowsy sleepers are when they are suddenly awakened from sleep, and then it might please you to slap me down and finish with me, and in this way you would be able to sleep on for the remainder of your lives, unless God in his care of you sent you another gadfly.

That I am what I say I am—a person sent to this city by God—becomes clear when I tell you that I have neglected all my own affairs and have been enduring this neglect for many years so that I can go about your business, coming to each of you individually like a father or an elder brother, bidding you to seek after virtue. This is not ordinary human behavior. If I had gained anything, if I had received payment for my exhortations, there would have been something to be said for it, but you can observe for yourselves how my otherwise shameless accusers have not committed the supremely shameful act of producing witnesses to say that I accepted money from any man, or ever asked for it. I myself shall bring forth an honest witness— my poverty.

(*Apology*, XVIII)

Previously the famous orator Lysias had been asked to compose a speech in his defense. Lysias completed the speech and gave it to Socrates, who handed it back with the words: "That's a lawyer's speech, not a philosopher's. It suits me no better than well-made shoes or fine clothes." So he prepared his own speech, full of those ironies which were like the grace notes of his conversations with his pupils, and most of his arguments must have passed over the heads of the five hundred judges, who continually interrupted and shouted insults, so that he had to remind them of the respect due to a man on trial for his life. At one point Plato jumped up on the rostrum and shouted: "Men of Athens, I am the youngest of those who have mounted the rostrum—" He got no farther. The judges ordered him down, and Socrates continued his defense, which was no defense, but a kind of apologia for his whole life. When the vote was taken, he was condemned to death by a majority of some sixty votes, and when he was asked, as the law provided, to suggest an alternative sentence, he offered to pay a fine of twenty-five drachmas, a derisory sum which the judges rejected out of hand. He was asked again to suggest an alternative punishment—it seems fairly certain that a large fine or banishment would have been acceptable—but he was in no mood for these frivolities. He suggested that instead of being punished he should be rewarded like the victors at the Olympic games with a pension for the rest of his life. When the final vote was taken, he was condemned to death by a majority of one hundred and forty votes, being eighty more than the votes by which he had been found guilty.

A month later, after days spent in meditation and conversation with his friends, he drank the hemlock. He could have escaped from prison, but this he refused to do on the grounds that it was his duty to be obedient to the laws of Athens. Like the Spartans at Thermopylae, he died in obedience to the laws of the state.

Soon after his death, so Diogenes Laertius tells us, the Athenians repented of their action, and closed the gymnasia as a sign of mourning. Some years later a bronze statue by Lysippus was erected "in the place where the sacred vessels were kept," which was perhaps the Erechtheum. He was not forgotten. Plato, Xenophon, Aeschines and Phaedo, and perhaps twenty others, wrote dialogues in which they attempted to capture the peculiar quality they had detected in Socrates' conversations. Men saw in him what they wanted to see. Xenophon saw his own platitudes, Plato his own brilliance, but both saw the real man behind the ironic mask. Like Jesus, Socrates was a mirror reflecting the world's passions, but so brightly polished that it was blinding to ordinary eyes.

When Socrates died he left no school, no body of doctrine, no records of any kind. There was, as far as we know, no will and no testament describing how he wanted his small possessions distributed, and presumably they were inherited by his family, by Xanthippe and his children. The state, if it wanted to, could sequester his possessions, for a condemned man had no rights to any property and was without any of the privileges of citizenship. Dying, he belonged to no state, and he did not even have the right to be buried in Athens. He had given dignity to the city by wandering about its dusty streets, and now there remained of him nothing but a small heap of ashes.

Yet Socrates dead was still a force to be reckoned with. It was not only that he had hammered out a new way of looking at life, asking those questions which sometimes forced men and even inanimate things to reveal their secrets, but he had invented a new way of dying, and such men quickly become legends. His words were remembered, gathering power long after his death, and so was his physical appearance, the way he walked and talked, the way he rolled his eyes and strutted like a waterfowl and held his liquor and resembled a satyr, not one of those satyrs who run wild through the woodlands lustily pursuing women but one who pursues Perfect Beauty and is content with nothing less. His memory haunted Athens, as it continues to haunt us to this day.

After his death few of those who had known him dared to remain in Athens. Plato was in hiding—he speaks of being ill during the last days of Socrates, but it was clearly a diplomatic illness. Soon we hear, on the testimony of Plato's pupil Hermodorus, that the close-knit group around Socrates had made their way safely to Megara, where they gathered around the philosopher Euclides. Here the *Phaedo* may have been composed, for that minute-by-minute account of the last hours of Socrates has too much freshness to permit us to believe that it was long delayed. Here, too, there may have been gathered the shorthand notes of the dialogues which Plato in later years would edit and embroider. About this time someone may have carved the statue of Socrates which survives today in a Hellenistic copy. It is just such a statue as people made in commemoration of the dead, standing in an attitude of calm, the old flesh refined to youthfulness, the gown arranged in methodical folds, the philosopher himself wearing an air of abstraction and remoteness as though about to vanish into smoke and air. This statue in the British Museum stands only a few inches high, but it is the most lifelike of all those that have come down to us, and the most completely credible; but it is not the ugly, satyrlike Socrates of *The Banquet*. The white hair falls heavy over his ears, the forehead juts up like the prow of a ship over the deep-set eyes, while the coiled beard ripples like cascades of frost over the muscular chest. Such a portrait could only be fashioned by an artist with an overwhelming affection for him at a time when he was still vividly remembered. It may be a copy of the bronze statue by Lysippus erected in the place where the sacred vessels were kept.

Though Socrates was remembered, there was never at any time a desire to found a school of philosophy in his name. He had hinted that he desired nothing of the kind, and such a school would have had no meaning without his physical presence. All that men could do was to continue in the path he had opened for them.

25 ⸕ XENOPHON

OF ALL the followers of Socrates of whom we have any record, Xenophon is the most puzzling. Born near Athens of a respectable family about 430 and meeting Socrates for the first time when he was about sixteen, he was in close association with Socrates for at least ten years: yet the philosopher left no deep impress on his mind. Dutifully, Xenophon took notes on Socrates' conversations. He listened attentively and contemplated a history of philosophy: an odd choice, for he had no talent for philosophy at all. Among the barren wastes of his Socratic notebooks there is little sign of life. He was chiefly interested in virtue and the art of government, and he was inclined to record the more sententious utterances of Socrates on these subjects. Occasionally we hear the authentic voice of the master. Once he was asked whether a dung basket could be beautiful, and replied: "Yes, by Jupiter, and a golden shield can be an ugly thing if it is not beautifully formed for its appropriate task!" On another occasion Socrates saw a man beating his slave, and asked what crime the slave had committed. "I'm beating him because he is stupid, and idle, and gluttonous!" the man said, and Socrates commented mildly: "Have you ever wondered who deserves the greater number of stripes, you or your slave?" We learn of Socrates' likes and dislikes. He disliked rich food, paintings on public buildings, gaudy costumes, men who sought power, and all cosmological speculations, for, as he said, the gods disapprove of inquiry into things which they do not wish to have known, and that is why men cannot gaze on the sun or see the winds or look into their own souls. Xenophon reports a number of conversations with the young Pericles, the son of

Pericles, who was later put to death by the Athenians after his failure at the battle of Arginusae, and with a certain Euthydemus, "the handsome one," who seems to be Xenophon himself. These conversations are often pedestrian, and suggest the scraps thrown from a great man's table.

Restless, indolent, with no hope of a high government appointment in Athens, Xenophon decided to try his chances overseas. From Sardis there came an invitation from his young philosophical friend Proxenus to enter the court of Cyrus, Prince of Persia. Xenophon showed the letter to Socrates and asked his advice. Socrates cautiously suggested that he should consult the oracle at Delphi, and Xenophon did so, only taking care not to ask Apollo whether the journey was advisable but only what gods he should sacrifice and pray to during his travels. Socrates was annoyed and pointed out that Xenophon had committed an act of duplicity. Xenophon went off to Sardis, where his modesty, beauty, and intelligence found favor in the eyes of the prince, who was at that time secretly planning rebellion against his elder brother, Artaxerxes II.

Cyrus was everything Xenophon expected a Persian prince to be. With his upturned nose, he looked more Greek than Persian, and he was generous to excess to those who were loyal to him. He was a hard-riding soldier who enjoyed fighting and singlehanded combats with wild beasts, and bore the marks of a bear's claws on his face. Xenophon's passion for royalty thrived in the court at Sardis, where Proxenus, his thirty-year-old Boeotian friend, was high in the prince's affections. And when Cyrus recruited an army of Greek mercenaries, saying he intended to put down a revolt of the wild hill tribes of Pisidia, Proxenus was appointed to the command of one of the five columns and Xenophon was invited to accompany the expedition as an observer. So in the spring of 401 an army of about 14,000 Greeks, a great number of them from Sparta, set out across Asia Minor.

Gradually it became clear that they were all the victims of a ruse. The hill tribes were left in peace. Cyrus planned nothing less than an attack on Babylon, the heart of the Persian Empire, 1,500 miles from Sardis. The Greeks grumbled, but Cyrus was in no mood to see his mercenaries leave his service, and by pleas and bribes and the promise of Persian booty he was able to keep them together. By the early summer they had passed through the Cilician Gates, and soon they were riding along the banks of the Euphrates. At the beginning of September they had reached the small village of Cunaxa, only sixty miles north of Babylon, where a huge Persian army was waiting for them. The Greeks attacked and would have carried the day if Cyrus had not ridden out against the imperial guard, determined to kill his brother, and been killed. If he had lived, he might have ascended the throne and by surrounding himself with Greek mercenaries he might have brought about the marriage of Greece and Persia some forty-five years before Alexander the Great was born. With his death the expedition lost whatever meaning it had ever possessed.

The Greeks were confronted with two simple alternatives: they could surrender to the Persians or fight their way back to Greece. When their leaders, including Proxenus, were treacherously killed while seeking terms, they realized they would have to fight their way back. To the west lay deserts, and to the north unknown mountains inhabited by wild and hostile tribes. They had no maps, no guides, no knowledge of the country or its language, no food, no supply columns, and winter was coming on. They decided to march north along the banks of the Tigris and try to reach the Black Sea. Hard on their heels was a Persian army estimated at 400,000 men. Their worst enemies were hunger, cold, distrust of one another, the sense of being lost in the vast emptiness of a foreign land. They were mercenaries who obeyed no laws except those they invented on the march, responsible to no one except themselves, electing their own leaders, pillaging as they went. Xenophon was elected one of the generals of the army, and as might be expected he kept a diary, which he later edited under the title of *Anabasis*, or "The March Up-country."

The *Anabasis* accomplishes perfectly what it sets out to do. Xenophon tells the story swiftly and almost artlessly, in such a way that we are convinced that it happened as he relates it. A very human and frightened army made its way through the mountains of Kurdistan and Armenia to the Black Sea. They forded rivers, crossed mountain passes ten feet deep in snow, and battled continually with guerrillas and marauding tribesmen. They were perpetually offering sacrifices and pouring libations in the hope that the gods would fight at their side. There were weeks when they fought every day, other weeks when the land seemed strangely empty, menacing and beautiful, with no enemies in sight. Here Xenophon recounts the adventures of a single morning:

Xenophon was having his breakfast when two men came running up to him. Everyone knew he could be approached, whether he was at breakfast or supper, and even when he was fast asleep, they knew they could wake him up and talk to him, so long as what they had to say had a bearing on the fighting. The two men told him they had been gathering kindling for their campfires, and had seen on the other side of the river, among some rocks which went right down to the water, an old man and a woman and some girls storing away what looked like bundles of clothing in a cave. Watching these people, they concluded that this was a safe place to cross, for at least the enemy's horsemen could not come near. So they undressed and waded naked into the water, holding their long knives in their hands and expecting they would have to swim. However they were able to get across without the water reaching up to the crotch, and once they were across they made off with the clothing and came back.

When he heard this Xenophon immediately poured a libation and ordered the young men to fill their cups and pray to the gods who had shown them the ford, so that the enterprise should come to a happy fulfillment. And as soon as the libation was made, he brought the young men straight to Cheirisophus, and they told him their story. Afterwards Cheirisophus also offered a libation, and then a general order went out to the troops to start packing for the journey, and then the captains were called in to discuss how they could best make the crossing, so as to overpower the enemy in front without suffering any losses in the rear. It was decided that Cheirisophus should go first with half the army, while the other half stayed behind with Xenophon, while the baggage animals and the camp followers should go across in the middle.

When everything was ready, they marched off, keeping the river on the left. The two young men acted as guides. It was rather less than half a mile to the ford, and as they moved along the bank, the enemy's cavalry on the opposite shore kept pace with them.

On reaching the bank of the river where the ford was, they grounded arms, and then Cheirisophus himself put a wreath on his head and threw off his cloak and took up his arms, ordering everyone else to do the same. Then he commanded the captains to form their companies in open order in deep columns, some to the left and others to the right of him. At this point the soothsayers cut the throats of the animals over the river. Meanwhile the enemy were shooting with

*arrows and slings, but they were still out of range. The appearance of
the omens was favorable, and all the soldiers chanted the battle hymn
and cheered, and the women too broke into a song of triumph; for
the soldiers had brought many women with them.*

(Anabasis, IV, 3)

We never learn why the old man, the woman, and the girls hid
their clothing in a cave, and that is as it should be, for Xenophon
simply relates what he has seen or known in all its casual and un-
predictable variety. There is no attempt to impose a pattern on the
journey. They discover a village buried underground, they come upon
melted patches in the snow and learn that these patches are caused by
hot springs, and they learn to protect their eyes from the snow glare.
All this, and much more, Xenophon relates as effortlessly as though
he were telling a story by the fireside. He remembers the women he
encounters, and he shows war for what it is—the aimless wandering
followed by short intervals of dreadful fear. For the first and last
time we are permitted to accompany a Greek army on the march,
for nowhere else is there to be found such a complete account of
what it was like, with a minute and loving attention to detail. When
finally in the early months of 400 they reached the town of Trapezus
(Trebizond) on the Black Sea, having lost 5,000 men on the way but
the army still intact, they could congratulate themselves on accomplishing a feat unparalleled in the history of Greece. They had fought
their way into the very heart of the Persian Empire, which no Greek
army had ever seen before, and they had come out of the adventure
relatively unscathed. They had shown that the Persians could be
defeated on their own ground by a properly trained Greek army,
and the lessons of the march of the ten thousand were learned by
Alexander the Great.

Xenophon was no philosopher, but he had all the makings of a
great novelist. He was a master of the convincing detail. The famous
account of how the Greeks came in sight of the sea is told with exactly
the right details—raw oxhide shields, silver cups, Persian robes, and
finger rings—so that we are brought into immediate physical presence
with the scene in all its strangeness:

*Xenophon was with the rearguard when he heard the clamor in
front, and he thought there were some more enemies attacking ahead,
for some ravaging natives had gathered behind them and the rear-*

*guard had picked some of them off and made prisoners of others in an
ambush, capturing some twenty raw oxhide shields with the hair still
on. However, when the clamor grew louder and nearer, and those who
were going up front were running in the direction of those who were
shouting, and the more there was of them the louder the shouting,
then it struck Xenophon that something serious was afoot. So he
mounted his horse and took Lycius and the cavalry with him, and gal-
loped forward. Soon he heard soldiers shouting: "The sea! The sea!"
and he passed the word along the column. Then they were all running,
even the rearguard; pack animals and horses were driven at full speed.
And when they arrived at the top of the hill, they all embraced one
another, the men, the generals, and the captains, all weeping.*

*Then someone suggested they gather stones and make a great
cairn of them, and on top of the cairn they put a lot of raw oxhides
and staves and shields, all captured. The guide cut the shields to shreds,
and urged us to do the same. Not long afterward the Greeks sent
him on his way, giving him a horse, a silver cup, a Persian robe, and
ten darics for his pains, taking these treasures out of the common
store; but what he especially wanted were the soldiers' finger rings,
and he acquired a considerable number of them. He showed them a
village where they should encamp, and told them about the road
which would lead them to the country of the Macrones. By this time
it was evening; and that night he left us.*

(Anabasis, IV, 7)

Xenophon's art approaches artlessness, and sometimes it is difficult to decide whether he is being disingenuous or superbly skillful.
He had a photographic memory. He met some obscure tribesmen
called the Mossynoici, and described them as vividly as though they
were Persians in full battle array, telling about their white oxhide
shields shaped like ivy leaves, their short tunics which reached down
to their knees "and were about as thick as a linen clothes' bag," and
their leather helmets "with tufts of hair wound round the middle to
produce the effect of a tiara." As a good soldier, he records their
military equipment—iron battle-axes, and spears nine feet long "with
a sharp point on one end and a wooden knob on the other." He admired their fat babies fed on chestnut meal, and calmly noted their
habit of cutting off the heads of their enemies and parading with
them while dancing and singing "some sort of tune."

Though the army had reached the sea, its adventures were far from over. For fourteen long months the Greeks pillaged and raided and fought their way westward, never certain whether they were among friends or enemies even when they had reached Thrace. For a while Xenophon thought of founding a colony on the shores of the Black Sea, and it amused him to think of himself as the philosopher-king, commanding the destinies of his soldiers. They were battle-hardened men from all the provinces of Greece, their only loyalty during the march being to the army itself, and even this loyalty was weakening. At Chalcedon they were prepared to offer their services to anyone who paid them, and they might have sold themselves to the Persians who commanded the Hellespontine province if Pharnabazus, the local satrap, had not induced a Spartan admiral to ship them to Europe, where they succeeded in selling themselves to a Thracian prince whose main object in life was to murder all the men of the Thracian hill tribes and sell their women into slavery, in this way acquiring the money to pay soldiers to murder more tribesmen and destroy more villages. Xenophon paints a distressing picture of his own dealings with the prince. On the verge of disintegration, the army was acquired by the Spartans, who were establishing themselves in Asia Minor and preparing for war against Persia.

Xenophon had not finished with fighting; there were a few more desultory campaigns, but his heart was not in it. Banished from Athens, he acquired an estate at Scillus near Olympia, where he lived the life of a country gentleman. Money acquired from the sale of prisoners during the long march had been invested for him in the temple of Artemis at Ephesus, and when at last the money reached him he built a temple on the estate, inviting all the townspeople to attend the festivals of the goddess. His faith in omens and goddesses continued unabated. There was a river called the Selinus running through the estate, and since there was another river with the same name running through Ephesus, he regarded himself as the lord of another Ephesus. He was a kindly and scrupulous host, and a gentle taskmaster to his tenants. He liked his estate so much that he inserted an account of it in the middle of the *Anabasis:*

There were fish and shellfish in the rivers, and much good hunting, and all kinds of game on the estate. When Xenophon received the holy money, he built an altar and a temple, and he set aside a tenth

part of the income from the estate for the service of the goddess. All
the townfolk and all the men and women in the neighborhood came
to take part in the festival, and the goddess provided those who
camped on the estate with barley, bread, wine and cakes, and a share
of the animals from the sacred herd after they were sacrificed, and
such other animals as were brought down by huntsmen; and of these
there were many, for Xenophon's sons and the sons of the townfolk
went out hunting especially for the festival, and invited any one else
who wanted to to join them. Pigs, antelopes, and stags were hunted,
partly on holy ground and partly on Mount Pholoe. This land is on
the road from Sparta to Olympia, about two miles from the temple of
Zeus. The ground holy to Artemis consists of meadows and thickly
wooded hills, good breeding country for pigs and goats and horses,
and so it is possible to provide fodder for all those who attend the
festival. Round the temple itself stood a plantation of fruit trees, pro-
ducing fruit in all seasons. The temple is a small-scale model of the
great temple at Ephesus, and the image of the goddess is exactly the
same except that it is of cypress wood, and not of gold.

(Anabasis, V, 3)

The brilliant commander settled down to the life of a country
gentleman as though he were made for it. For twenty years he farmed
and wrote his books. He was on terms of friendship with the Spartan
king, and wrote his life. He liked the company of kings, celebrating
them as passionately and impersonally as any Elizabethan in the service of his queen. He had the Elizabethan temper even to his casual
treacheries and his delight in living on an estate with his hunting dogs
and a host of servants.

He wrote dryly, modestly, almost casually. The *Anabasis* was
his masterpiece, filled with the sensations of vivid life, but no masterpieces followed. He continued Thucydides' history of Greek affairs,
bringing the story down to the battle of Mantinea, but in three hundred pages there are perhaps ten which crackle and blaze with life,
and the rest is a misery of monotony. He wrote a curious essay on
education called the *Cyropaedia*, which exalts the virtues of the self-
denying Persians and Spartans: Xenophon denied himself nothing.
There were books on hunting, on the art of horsemanship, on the
functions of the cavalry commander. There was a lengthy treatise on
household management, and there were his collected notes on Socrates,
all oddly dry and filtered through a mind incapable of excitement.

The passion withered, and the life went out of him. Once he had been beautiful, talented, included among the small circle of Socrates' faithful adherents. He had known Plato, Chaerophon, Simmias, Cebes, Phaedo, Hermocrates, and all the rest of that small group which gathered around Socrates, and by baiting him, and asking interminable questions, and by following in his footsteps had made themselves philosophers. But there is no trace of philosophy in Xenophon. To the end he remained the pleasant gentleman.

26 ≪ PLATO

THERE WERE men like Pericles who succeeded in living quietly with their genius. They never seemed to exert themselves, but passed through life with astonishing ease like unruffled swans flying through tempests. Aeschylus roars; Euripides weeps; Sophocles remains calm, and like Pericles he walks with a strange assurance through the tumult of the market place. One cannot imagine them ever being afraid. So it was with Socrates, studying the world with ironical calm, always walking at a leisurely pace, while the demons boiled in his brain and his mind moved like greased lightning. We call such men Apollonian, for they have a god-given quietness.

Of such men was Plato, the young aristocrat who abandoned poetry for philosophy when he became the pupil of Socrates. All the gifts were showered on him at his birth. He was physically strong, handsome, superbly intelligent. He painted, wrote poems and tragedies, wrestled at the Isthmian games, acquired a vast library, and studied all the known sciences in turn. His mind was speculative and poetic. Unlike Aristotle, who sometimes wrote abominably, Plato wrote with an angelic gift for style.

For ten or eleven years after the death of Socrates he became a wanderer. He traveled through Egypt and Libya, and visited Italy. Of the Italianate Greeks he wrote: "They find their happiness in continual feasts, glut themselves twice a day and never sleep alone. I say nothing of the other practices that accompany this way of living. No man upon earth, engaging in such practices from his youth up, could ever, after forming these habits, attain to wisdom." At Tarentum he met Archytas, the rich founder of a Pythagorean school, and a man with a wide-ranging mind, for at different times he was a general, a statesman, and a teacher of mathematics. Dionysius I, tyrant of Syracuse, hearing that he was in Tarentum, summoned him to Sicily, and Plato seems to have assented more for the prospect of visiting Mount Etna than for the pleasure of listening to the tyrant discourse on poetry, for Dionysius thought highly of his own poetic tragedies and even arranged for them to be heard in Greece.

Dionysius was handsome, gifted and superbly arrogant. He had ravaged southern Italy and waged victorious war against the Carthaginians; he had made Syracuse the greatest power in the central Mediterranean, and he was relentlessly determined to maintain his power. And when Plato, seizing the opportunity to teach virtue to a tyrant, spoke of justice and the need to grant a measure of contentment to the people, Dionysius, who never permitted anyone to discuss his rule, flew into a rage and shouted: "You talk like an old fool!" Plato replied: "You talk like a tyrant!" According to Diogenes Laertius, Dionysius would have had Plato killed if a better idea had not occurred to him. Pollis, the Spartan ambassador, was leaving for Greece and it amused the tyrant to offer the philosopher to the ambassador as a slave. So, in shackles, Plato was taken onto the Spartan ship, and when the ship put in at Aegina Pollis had him led ashore, knowing—as he must have known—that the Aeginetans were determined to kill any Athenian who landed there. Plato was calmly waiting to be killed when the Aeginetans decided there was some advantage to be gained by selling him, and put him up for public auction. He was sold to Anniceris of Cyrene for twenty minae, which is perhaps $400 of our money. Anniceris arranged for Plato's return to Athens, and some time later he received the twenty minae from Plato's friends. He refused the money, saying that he too was entitled to have a high regard for Plato. There is a pleasant story that the grove of Academe among the pinewoods of the Outer Cerameicus was bought with the ransom money which Anniceris refused to accept.

In due course Dionysius heard what had happened, and wrote an apologetic letter to Plato, begging him not to say anything evil about him. Plato, with his usual tartness, wrote back that he had no time to think of Dionysius at all.

For the next twenty years Plato lived for the school he founded. It was not a college for training students in the arts and sciences; it was quite simply and deliberately a school for the training of states-men, for encouraging discussion on the principles of government. Most, perhaps all, of the students were young men of high birth, who could expect to have a career in government before them. Plato be-lieved, as Socrates had believed before him, that good government could come only from good laws, and that the best administrators of these laws were youths with clear minds and with a love for truth and beauty; it was no disadvantage if they were handsome and rich. They were the true philosophers, for they lived in the world and were apart from it, being "the spectators of all time and all existence." "Courage, magnificence, intelligence, memory" were their natural gifts, and the order in which Plato arranged the requisite virtues for statesmanship was in descending order. Socrates would probably have been uncomfortable in the Academe: the institution was altogether too self-consciously directed toward the encouragement and training of benevolent tyrants.

There was a hall where the students and teachers ate in common, and small huts where built in the neighboring woodland where they could give themselves up to solitary meditation. At the nearby gym-nasium they would exercise, for Plato insisted on the cultivation of the body as much as on the cultivation of the mind. Most of the students probably stayed in the grounds of the Academe, and some may have made the short journey through the Dipylon Gate and along the Street of Tombs to the famous olive grove where the sacred olives were plucked, and beyond this lay the school, which took the form of a *thiasos*, or religious community, ostensibly founded for the ob-servance of the cult of the tutelary deity Academus, whose altar stood in the grove. There was also an altar to the Muses, somewhere near the library. Academus, though long dead, was regarded as the perma-nent legal owner, and the Academe was consequently administered in his name.

To the Academe came pupils from all over the Greek world. We know some of their names and some of their accomplishments. Eu-doxus of Cnidus, a former pupil of Archytas, studied there: he be-longed to an older generation, and had already discovered the theory of proportions. Theaetetus of Sunium, who was to die later in the Corinthian War, continued his studies of solid geometry there, and the young Speusippus, the son of Plato's sister, worked on the defini-tion and classification of plants and animals. These were presumably research students, for the main concern of the school was constitutional law, while the laws of biology and mathematics took second place. Of the law students we hear of Phormio from Elis, Menedemus from Pyrrha, Euphraeus from Oreus, and Delius from Ephesus, all of whom went on to become lawgivers and the advisers of tyrants and kings. Euphraeus, for example, went to live in the court of King Perdiccas III of Macedon, and enjoyed a position of great influence in the country, while Delius became the trusted adviser of King Philip, and served his son Alexander in the same capacity. Aristotle and Demosthenes also were pupils at the school.

If we can believe the comic poets, Plato ruled over the school with unsmiling gravity, deeply concerned with his high and serious purpose. He was "gloomy Plato," living on a frugal diet of olives and endlessly pacing up and down as he discoursed on virtue and justice. He was proud and fastidious, and had no gift for small talk. Once he saw some people throwing dice and reproached them for it. "It is only a trifle," they said. He answered: "The habit is not a trifle." He rarely drank, and slept as little as possible, for as he observed in *The Laws:* "No one while sleeping is good for anything."

He had been teaching and writing dialogues for twenty years when he was summoned to Sicily again. Dionysius I had died—it was believed that he was poisoned by his physician—and his son Dionysius II had come to the throne. He was a weak and amiable youth, and Dion, his uncle and chief minister, thought that some advantage might be gained by putting the young prince in the care of Plato. Dion had met Plato during his first visit to Sicily, and been deeply influenced by him; and during the intervening years they had maintained their friendship by correspondence. The young Dionysius had spent all of his life within the palace, forbidden to meet anyone not completely subordinate to his father, finding his amusement in amateur carpentry, "making little model wagons and lamp shades and wooden chairs and tables." Dion wrote an impassioned letter to Plato, saying that a heaven-sent opportunity had arrived for bringing about an ideal state, for the young ruler had all the makings of a philosopher-king.

Plato had some experience of the impulsiveness of youth, and was in no hurry to leave Athens for Syracuse. More letters were exchanged, and at last the young Dionysius offered to place himself unreservedly at Plato's service. Taking with him the young Xenocrates of Chalcedon, who was destined to become the president of the Academe after his death, Plato at last set out for Syracuse, which he reached in the early autumn of 367. He was greeted with the honors usually reserved for royalty. "One of the royal chariots came to take him from the ship," says Plutarch, "and Dionysius sacrificed to the gods in thanksgiving for the great blessing granted during his reign. The citizens had high hopes of the reformation of the tyrant when they observed the modesty of the banquets and the decorum of the court and the gentle and humane behavior of the tyrant in all matters that came to his attention."

At first Dionysius was an apt pupil, taking lessons in law and mathematics. Plutarch speaks of all the floors of the palace being covered in fine sand, to allow the courtiers to work on problems of mathematics and geometry. Gradually Dionysius lost interest. He abandoned philosophy, lawmaking, and mathematics for Gargantuan banquets—one banquet over which he presided is supposed to have lasted uninterruptedly for ninety days. Suddenly Dion was arrested and Plato placed under house arrest, where he might have remained indefinitely if war had not broken out. Then, having spent only a few turbulent months in Syracuse, he was allowed to return to Athens, taking Dion with him. Six years later he made his third and last journey to Syracuse, Dionysius promising once more to devote himself to philosophy. Plato was now about sixty-five, and his chief interest in Syracuse was to ensure the succession to the throne of Dion, his friend for thirty years. Archytas, too, was insisting that everything would be gained by Plato's coming. Plato had no very high hopes of accomplishing his purpose: he feared the intractability of the tyrant, and even more the intrigues of the court. "I was very frightened, full of foreboding," Plato wrote, and he mentions an attempt to kill him which was prevented by Dionysius, who treated him with the honors due to a king and showed himself for the first time to be a genuine student of philosophy, though Plato was puzzled by his facility. Dionysius knew the proper words, but it was not at all certain that he knew the meanings behind the words or whether he really understood what he was saying. Plato put him to the test. It was a very simple test, and amounted to nothing less than a searching examination about whether Dionysius was prepared to surrender himself wholly to philosophy, dedicating his life every moment of the day to the highest moral principles and so regulating the state that every action flowed out of philosophy: "otherwise his fine principles were no more than the tan which a sun-bather gets on his body."

Dionysius failed to pass the test. He knew the right words and

spoke them in the proper order, but conviction was missing. Regret-
fully Plato came to the conclusion that conviction could not be
taught: it could come only after a long and impassioned communion
with philosophy, and then suddenly it would "blaze up as though
kindled by a leaping spark." No such blaze was kindled in Dionysius'
soul. Plato decided that nothing further could be done with him, and
once more he became an unwilling prisoner in the court, until at long
last he was rescued by Archytas who sent a galley from Tarentum;
Plato slipped aboard and made his way safely back to Athens.

As far as we know, Plato never again sat close to the seat of
power. Even when Dion launched an expedition against Syracuse
and succeeded in wresting power from Dionysius, Plato rejected all
offers to join him. He loved the man this side of idolatry, but feared
the ruler; and though Dion had spent many years at the Academe
and seemed to possess "the conviction of philosophy," he showed
himself to be an even worse tyrant than Dionysius, arrogant and over-
bearing, ruling by naked force, and always suspecting that his courtiers were plotting against him. He was murdered by some Zakyn-
thian soldiers who entered his room unarmed, thinking to tear him to
pieces with their bare hands; but failing in this, they called for a
sword, which was slipped through the window, and cut his throat.
Dionysius was luckier. Captured by the great Corinthian general
Timoleon, he was permitted to spend the rest of his days in exile in
Corinth, where he loitered in the fish markets and amused himself by
debating with chorus girls about their singing. Years later, when someone asked him whether the society of philosophers had been rewarding to him, he answered: "Yes, indeed, for through them I have
acquired the wisdom to bear my present fate."

Plato found no reward in the society of tyrants: he had even
lost a good deal of his prestige in meddling with Syracusan affairs.
His long *Seventh Letter*—the only one of the surviving letters that is
indisputably genuine—recounts with wearisome detail exactly how
ineffective he was, and there is an oddly unpleasant note of special
pleading. He was too blunt, too proud, too self-contained to be a
diplomat. He could not tolerate tyrannical follies, and he had very
little understanding of the practical affairs of government, perhaps
because he was obsessed by the ideal government of the philosopher-
king.

He spent his last years in Athens, ruling over the Academe.

There in old age he wrote *The Laws*, the longest and most didactic of his works, written in a kind of brooding anger against the follies of men and governments, remembering the hurts he had received in Syracuse and somehow interweaving them so keenly into the body of his work that we are constantly reminded of Dion and Dionysius. Again and again he thunders against "the many monstrous impieties of those who rose from humble beginnings to positions of supreme eminence." Again and again he celebrates, against all the evidence, the resourceful young tyrant who has received the gift of intelligence and has acquired "the conviction of philosophy." God will attend him, Justice will be the handmaiden walking by his side, and he will rule over a loyal and obedient population, which knows that its best interest lies in loyalty and obedience—preferably a small population, numbering some 5,040 souls, since 5,040 is divisible by all the integers between 1 and 10, and therefore they can be grouped more easily according to the mathematical purposes of the tyrant. In this state there will be no wrestling, no poetry, no fornication. No one will possess gold or silver, or wear flamboyant clothes. The entire population, under the watchful eyes of the thirty-seven law wardens, will behave in a respectful and modest manner, no man exhibiting any advantage over another. One searches in *The Laws* in vain for any realization of the ordinary desires and aspirations of the great mass of mankind. Plato seems to be writing against the grain, wearily, knowing that there is no salvation for mankind and that the tyrants will never obey his mathematical rules. *The Laws* provides the second of his projected constitutions—*The Republic*, a far more brilliant work, being the first. He thought of writing a third, but did not live long enough to do more than sketch out a brief introduction in a work which has come down to us under the title of *Epinomis*, or "Beyond the Laws." He died in 347 at the age of eighty, having outlived Socrates by more than fifty years. More than a hundred and twenty years passed between the birth of Socrates and the death of Plato.

He left a will in which he disposed of a silver goblet, an earring, a gold finger ring, a few pieces of furniture, and two small pieces of property. Artemis, a female slave, was given her freedom, but four male slaves were kept in bondage. It is the will of a man born into wealth, who at the end of his days possesses no more than a small farmer might possess.

But if Plato left very little money, he left a vast treasure in the dialogues in which he re-created the life and thought of Socrates over a long period of years. Without Plato, we should know Socrates only through the two-dimensional versions of Xenophon, Aeschines of Sphettus, Diogenes Laertius, and a few others. With Plato, we see Socrates plain. We see him in the flesh, and we see the brightly lit mind and we are made aware of a character combining an extraordinary strength with an almost feminine subtlety. The portrait rings true. Just as a painter will attempt to suggest many moods in a single portrait, and inevitably introduces something of himself into the finished painting, so Plato does not attempt a stenographer's report (though often utilizing such reports), but instead he attempts a poetic interpretation on a vast canvas. Sometimes we hear the authentic words of Socrates; at other times the words have filtered so slowly through Plato's imagination that accretions of his own thought, and the thought of many others, have been added. The dominant image, the face, the voice, the gestures, the way the sentences are put together, are always consistent.

Let us take for example the dialogue always placed at the head of the dialogues in the belief that it was the first written by Plato. The *Euthyphro* is a discussion on holiness supposed to have taken place during the weeks when Socrates was under indictment for impiety, but not yet brought to trial. Euthyphro, too, is under a kind of indictment for impiety, though totally unaware of it. He tells Socrates that he has come from the island of Naxos to prosecute his own father, who killed a farm laborer for murdering a servant. The father threw the murderer into a pit where he perished of hunger and cold. Euthyphro claims that it is an act of piety to prosecute murderers, even if the murderer happens to be your own father, and such an act is protected by divine sanction. Socrates asks a few questions. What is holiness? What is especially pleasing to the gods about indicting one's own father? Is it an unholy thing for a son to prosecute his father? Soon Euthyphro is complaining that all his certainties are crumbling, for Socrates has the power to make fixed things seem to move away.

SOCRATES

What you are saying, Euthyphro, reminds me of the statues made by my ancestor Daedalus.[1] *Now if I were the one who carved*

---

[1] The legendary hero Daedalus was said to have made sculptures that moved of their own accord.

*them or made them move about, you might well have laughed at me
for the family resemblance you saw in them, saying that my words
too go running about and don't stay still. But as it happens, you are
the one who made the statements, and so some other jest is needed.
Your statements don't stand still, as you can see.*

EUTHYPHRO

*I think your jest is very much to the point, for it is not I who
made those statements wander about and never remain in the same
place. You are the Daedalus. They would have stayed still if it had
depended on me.*

SOCRATES

*Apparently then, my friend, I am a more clever artist than Dae-
dalus, inasmuch as he was only able to make his own works move,
while I, so it appears, can give motion to the works of others as well
as my own. And the most exquisite part of it is that I am wise against
my will, for I would rather have my arguments stay fixed and stable
than possess the wisdom of Daedalus or possess all the wealth of Tan-
talus. Enough of this! Since you seem to be indolent, I will make bold
to suggest a way in which you can instruct me on the nature of holiness . . .*

(Euthyphro, 11 C)

Already nearly all the peculiar characteristics of the Socratic
dialogue are present. We see Socrates looking at ideas, holding them
up to the light, turning them round and round, examining them with
the care of a jeweler who must sooner or later make up his mind
whether he is dealing with diamonds or paste, and always there is the
hint of mockery, the sheer delight in reducing his opponent's argument to nonsense. And what is remarkable is that he accomplishes all
this without the least offense, with a gaiety which is the demonstrable
sign of his generosity and humanity. He brought joy to philosophy;
and philosophers since Socrates have usually forgotten that this was
his greatest claim to our affections.

In such passages we hear the authentic voice of Socrates, who
believed in the living voice and had no great faith in the written word,
for he said:

*Writing has a very strange quality indeed, which it shares with
painting; for the creations of an artist appear to be alive, but if you
ask them a question they preserve a solemn silence. So it is with written*

words: you imagine they would give an intelligible account of them-
selves, but should you question them about their meaning, they in-
variably come up with the same answer. Every word, once it is writ-
ten down, is at the mercy of those who understand it and those who
have not the least inkling of what it is about; and it doesn't know
whom to speak to, and whom not to speak to, and when it is ill-treated
and reviled, it cannot run to its father for help, and it can neither
protect nor defend itself.

(*Phaedrus*, 275 D)

It is not necessary, of course, to believe that Socrates was being
wholly serious. What he chiefly objected to about writing was that
it was a patchwork carefully pieced together: it did not have the
spontaneity and the fire of the spoken word. He could not bring himself to believe that writing could touch the soul. Only the voice of the
teacher could inculcate virtue and nobility in the young, or so Socrates thought. The *Phaedrus* is a superb vindication of the power of
conversation to arrive at ultimate truths, but only if it is conducted
with a passionate desire for the truth and aided by divine inspiration.

There is a story told of Heracleitus that some visitors, finding
him alone in his hut and warming himself by his stove, drew back for
fear of interrupting his thoughts. Heracleitus smiled and beckoned to
them, saying: "Here also the gods are present." Socrates would have
said the gods were present whenever men undertook to debate on
ultimate things. He was like a painter in water colors who can never
erase any color once it has been put down on paper: he must be right
the first time. Plato, on the contrary, was the conscious artist who
revised continually, never content until he had found the perfect
word.

The miracle, then, is that so much of the living voice of Socrates
rings through those dialogues written so laboriously and over such a
long period of time. Throughout the *Apology*, the *Crito*, and the
Phaedo, the three dialogues concerned with the trial and execution of
Socrates, we see Socrates living quietly but with astonishing intensity,
confronting death gaily, rejoicing to the very end in the gift of conversation. When the jailer during the last hours suggested that he
should not talk so much, because the excitement of talking would
hinder the effect of the hemlock, Socrates said: "Tell him to mind his
own business," and went on talking cheerfully. In *The Frogs* Aristophanes said that Talk was his god. If it was not his god, it was at least

the joy of his life.

And what talk it was! As Plato records it, it came in great spates or in sudden coruscating fountains: it was like a dance. From being coldly logical, it would take wing and soar into a cloud of rainbow-colored myths and legends, and hover there, surveying the world below with eyes of enchantment, before plummeting down to earth to continue to throw a net of logic over its prey. It was conversation raised to the power of music, with no more system than you will find in a Mozart symphony, which is to say there was a good deal of system, but it was carefully concealed in an effortless display of virtuosity. Not for him the patient catalogues of Aristotle, nor the vast embroideries of Plato's work on the laws. The sudden glance, the lightning stroke, are his weapons. He wields a rapier, never a two-handed sword.

Yet always the purposes are serious, even desperately serious. To the end he was involved in a love affair with the moral law. That he should be sentenced to death for corrupting the young was the final irony granted to a life devoted to virtue. He saw men as the vehicles of the moral law, and they were all the more majestic because morality weighed heavily on their shoulders.

Plato's reasons for recording the dialogues are stated clearly in the *Seventh Letter*, where he tells how "my aged friend Socrates" was haled before the courts and tried on a charge so outrageously ill-founded that it made him despair of the state and all its laws and customs. Henceforward Plato was dedicated to the service of the state, not the state as it existed but as it should be: the state in which such crimes are no longer possible. All the dialogues therefore feed into *The Republic*, the long and closely argued portrait of a state founded on the moral law.

The Republic is an extraordinary document, for so many strands are woven into it, so many arguments are pursued, and so many facets of Socrates and Plato are displayed that the reader is likely to be overwhelmed by its variety. Here the Socratic dialogue is painted in all the colors of the spectrum of thought. There is no suggestion that anything is held back: everything must be said, all experiences must be examined, and all the combinations and permutations of the moral law must be clearly laid out. To permit himself to write freely and to give an air of authenticity to the scene, Plato employs deliberate ruses never employed previously. As in all the previous dialogues,

Socrates is the principal speaker, but in *The Republic* for the first and last time he appears as the author of the work, relating the conversations in the first person. It is a subtle ruse, designed to bring Socrates into the foreground. Plato himself makes no appearance, but his two older brothers Adimantus and Glaucon are conveniently present to ask the questions which Plato would like to ask, and by dividing himself among his brothers, Plato, while remaining wholly invisible, emphasizes his own role in the composition of this immense and prolific argument.

The strange thing about *The Republic* is that, deep down in his heart, Socrates is shown to be a man who is not fundamentally interested in the Republic. Socrates, or rather Plato, who occasionally wears the mask of the master, appears to be so disgusted by the human spectacle that he can scarcely contain himself with fury. There are moments when the detached intelligence quails in the face of human vulgarity, human stupidity, and the abysmal wretchedness of the human race. Why, he seems to be asking—why build a Republic for such *canaille?* The complaint is stated most eloquently in a passage toward the end of the book:

"Those who have no knowledge of wisdom and virtue, but spend their days in feasting and similar occupations, are borne downwards, and so they wander through life. They have never raised their eyes to the true world above them, they have never been lifted up to taste the real and perfect pleasures; but like cattle they look down and bow their heads to the earth and to their tables, and feed and fill themselves and copulate, and in their greed for more they kick and butt one another with horns and hooves of iron, and kill one another because they cannot be satisfied. Nor can they ever be satisfied, so long as they feed on unreality the portion of themselves which is itself unreal and insatiable."

"My dear Socrates," replied Glaucon, *"you sound as though you are giving a sermon on the common herd."*

(*Republic*, IX, 586 A)

There is no doubt that Plato means exactly what he says, but there is some doubt whether he says what Socrates thought. His private prejudices are mingled with the public utterances of Socrates, and his own fears are sometimes put into the mouth of a man who was always fearless.

Yet one of the main themes of *The Republic* is the insatiable ignorance of humanity, its absolute perplexity unless in some manner it can reach out to the divine forces which move the universe. Humanity does not know what it is, or where it is, or what it is doing. It is rudderless, and there are no maps, no shores in sight. Stesichorus told the story of how the ten-year siege of Troy was fundamentally an exercise in meaningless barbarism, because it was completely pointless: there was no Helen to be rescued, only a wraith, a phantom, a "something" that resembled the real Helen who spent those years quietly in Egypt, waiting for Menelaus. In much the same way, according to Plato, do men live out their lives in an anguished desire for the unobtainable, striving toward a goal which is continually vanishing into the distance.

In the famous parable of the cave Plato paints a dark and almost hopeless picture of our sublunary world; but it is not the anguish of the cave dwellers that affects us so much as the greater anguish of those who strive to escape from the cave into the real world outside:

Imagine a cave with the entrance opening into the light and running a long way underground. Imagine that inside the cave there are men who have been imprisoned there since childhood, their heads and legs clamped in such a way that they cannot turn their heads. Some way above them and behind them a fire is burning, and between the fire and the prisoners there runs a road. Imagine a curtain-wall built along this road, like the parapet on which puppets are shown. Imagine too that people are carrying all kinds of articles behind the curtain-wall, shapes of men and animals in wood and stone and other materials, and some of these people are speaking, and some are silent. The prisoners, seeing the shadows on the wall, and hearing the voices, would surely imagine that the voices belonged to the shadows.

Imagine that one of the prisoners were set free, and suddenly compelled to stand up and turn his head and look and walk toward the fire; all these actions would be painful to him, and he would be too dazzled to see clearly the objects of which he had formerly seen only the shadows. So if he were told that what he had formerly seen was only an illusion, and that he was now closer to reality and seeing more accurately, because the objects he was observing were themselves closer to reality, and if in addition he was compelled to describe each of these moving objects as they were pointed out to him, surely

Kouros of Anavysos.

Archaic Kore.

Caryatidis of Erechtheum.

Head of a Girl from Chios. Height 14½ inches.

Head of a Girl from Cyprus. Height 2¼ inches.

Head of a Youth from Marathon.

Head of a Man from Delos.

Head of a Philosopher from the sea off Anticythera.

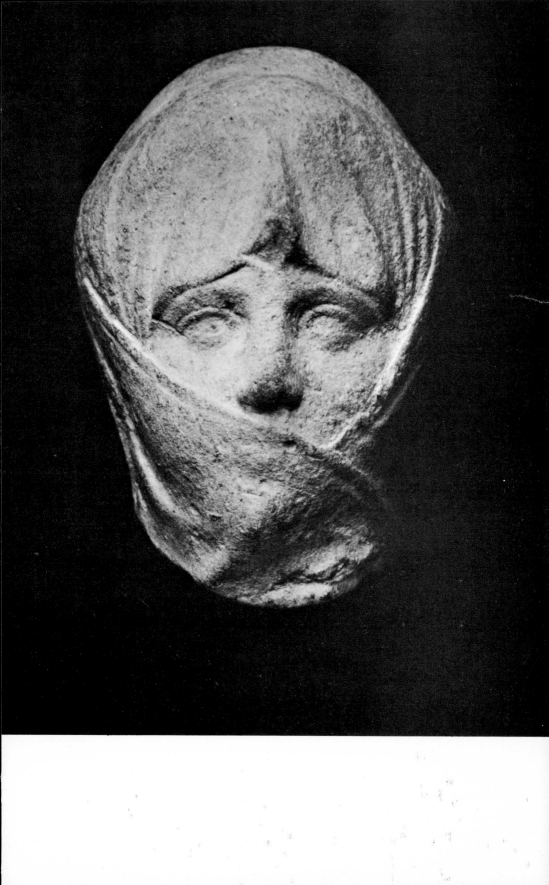

he would be deeply disturbed, imagining that the shadows were more real than the objects he now saw.

And then, too, if he were made to look directly into the light of the fire, it would hurt his eyes and he would turn back and take refuge in the things he could see, and these would appear to him to be clearer than the things that were shown to him. And if finally he were dragged up the steep and rugged ascent, and not let loose until he came into the sunlight, surely the process would be painful and he would be filled with indignation, and when he emerged into the light he would be overwhelmed with its splendor, and he would be unable to recognize a single one of the things which were now called real. At first he would find it easier to perceive shadows, and afterwards he would recognize the reflections of men and other objects in water, and only much later would he recognize things themselves. And then, too, he would find it easier to recognize the heavenly bodies in the night sky, the moon and the stars, rather than the sun and the daylight. Only at the very end would he be able to contemplate the sun, not by its reflection in water, nor in images, but as it truly is.

(Republic, 514–517)

Plato has, of course, loaded the dice against humanity. He has made the cave so deep that no glimmer of sunlight can ever penetrate, and to make doubly sure that the prisoners will never even suspect the existence of the sun, a fire and a wall stand between them and the mouth of the cave. The prisoners are trapped in such a way that they can only face the wall at the bottom of the cave, and they cannot even step backwards for a better look at the shadow play. Plato's cave is a machine for torturing humanity.

The invention of the cave has all the hallmarks of Plato rather than of Socrates. It is brilliantly designed to show the painful stages of awakening to reality. The unfastening of the chains, the stiff turn of the head, the recognition of the puppet show, the immense fire blocking out the light of the sun, and then the violent ascent and the discovery of a world so bright that at first it can only be tolerated at night and in reflected light, all these correspond to stages of initiation into reality. Each stage is accompanied by intense pain, and by a kind of progressive bafflement, for at every stage there are unsuspected terrors. Until the very last moment, when the initiate is bathed in the sun's glow, there is no alleviation from the anguish of being human.

With this portrait of the human condition, Plato removes himself completely from any recognizable Socrates. In the *Phaedrus* Socrates is made to say that the recognition of the supreme reality is accompanied by pain, but it is not an unbearable pain. At the spectacle of Perfect Beauty a man grows wings, "which are of all corporeal things most akin to the divine," and though these wings are invisible, being attached to the soul, nevertheless their growth is accompanied by pain, "a sensation similar to that experienced by children when cutting their teeth, attended by itching and soreness about the mouth." It is perhaps the measure of the difference between Plato and Socrates that where one imagines the approach to godhead to be fairly painless the other imagines it to be so tortured and painful that it is scarcely worth the effort. There is something to be said for remaining quietly at the bottom of the cave and enjoying the shadow play.

Everything we know about Socrates suggests that he invented the happy parable of the wings, while everything we know about Plato suggests that he invented the joyless parable of the cave.

Not that Plato was joyless; but there was deep within him an awareness of the sinister forces at work in the human soul, and this awareness seems to have been very largely lacking in Socrates, whose gaiety was proverbial. One cannot imagine Plato saying: "I have a passion for friends, and I would rather have a good friend than the best cock or quail in the world; I would even go further, and say the best horse or dog; and by the dog of Egypt, I would go still further and say I would prefer a good friend to all the gold of Persia!" It rings true, and we feel that Plato has recorded the words accurately in the dialogue on friendship called *Lysis*. And when Socrates goes on to say: "Poor creature as I am, I have one talent: I can recognize, at first sight, the lover and the beloved," this, too, rings true, and we are aware that he is saying something which is very central to his philosophy of life. Plato's preoccupations were of another order altogether. There is a sense in which he is a more troubled and profounder philosopher than his master.

It is necessary to distinguish Plato from Socrates, for though they move together and sometimes wear the aspect of a single person, there are rare moments when they seem to veer wildly apart. Plato, for good reasons, was preoccupied by the nature of tyranny, and nearly all the passages on tyranny seem to come from his hand. It is Plato, not Socrates, who speaks of "the terrible, savage, and lawless desires which exist in every man," and who compared the waking tyrant with the sleeper, bloated with wine, who dreams of having intercourse "with his mother or with any man or god or beast," because in his nightmares he sees no reason why he should not commit terrible crimes.

So here and there we discover elements in the dialogues which are essentially Platonic, and other elements which are essentially Socratic. It is Plato, not Socrates, for example, who tells the story of Gyges and the ring, telling it so artfully that we can well believe Dionysius of Halicarnassus who reported that when Plato died there were found among his belongings many tablets showing how often he had worked over the opening sentences of *The Republic* until he finally achieved the simple, flowing sentences which recount how Socrates met Glaucon during a festival at Piraeus. The story of Gyges and the ring tells how the earth opened during a thunderstorm, and a shepherd made his way into the chasm and discovered a bronze horse hollowed out and with a door through which he saw a corpse of more than human size. The shepherd slipped into the horse and removed a gold ring from the corpse, and stole away. Once a month the shepherds reported to the king on the state of his flocks, and while he was attending the meeting with his companions, the shepherd absentmindedly turned the bezel of the ring toward the inside of his hand. It was a magic ring, and he became invisible. He turned the bezel outward, and became visible again. A stupendous power had been granted to him. He waited until he came into the king's presence before becoming invisible once more. He knew he could commit any crime he pleased and go unscathed, and so he seduced the queen, and with her help he murdered the king and ascended the throne.

It is one more of the many parables on the nature of the tyrant, and we recognize the same handwriting which appeared in the parable of the cave. It smacks of Plato, who was in love with caves and introduced them wherever possible. There are more caves in his story of Er, the Pamphylian soldier who was killed in battle and ten days later his body was lifted on a funeral pyre, where he came to life and told the story of what he had seen in the other world. He said he had traveled in company of many others until he came to a strange place where two immense caves opened into the sky and two more opened into the earth. Here was the judgment seat: the good were sent into the cave which opened into the heavens, while the evil were dealt with unmercifully. The punishment for Ardiaeus the Great, tyrant of

Pamphilia, who was perhaps Dionysius in disguise, was to be bound hand and foot and neck, and then flayed, and then impaled on thorns. After the souls had been punished or received their rewards, they were brought to a great Pillar of Light, and there they were allowed to choose their next lives. They could choose whatever they pleased. They could even if they wished choose to become tyrants, though the moment they had so chosen they were informed of the penalty— by order of the Judge they must eat their own children. They could become birds or animals, and it was in this way that Orpheus became a swan, Ajax a lion, Agamemnon an eagle, Thersites a baboon, and Odysseus became what he had always wanted to become—an ordinary man. Having chosen their destinies, they were led to the River of Forgetfulness to drink its waters. At midnight they were awakened by an earthquake and a thunderclap, and suddenly they were all hurled into their new births "like shooting stars."

According to the parable, Er was for some reason excluded from the ranks of the dead and he was forbidden to drink from the River of Forgetfulness. When he opened his eyes it was dawn and he was lying on his own funeral pyre.

Plato tells the intricate fate reserved for men at their deaths, but we hear the authentic voice of Socrates at the conclusion:

"So we should believe the soul to be immortal, able to endure all evil and all good, and we should always hold to the road that leads above, and in every way pursue justice and wisdom. In this way we shall be at peace with God and with ourselves, both in our life here and when, like the victors in the games receiving their rewards, we receive the prize that is given to us; and so it is that in this life and in the thousand-year journey of the soul all will be well with us."

27 ≪ THE SCIENTIFIC TEMPER

ABOUT the year 550 B.C. it began to dawn on the Greeks that the universe was not irrational, obedient to the whims of the gods, but obeyed the law, the *logos*, by which all things were governed. The gods remained, for it was their function to remain, just as it was their function to change their shapes and characters and continually absorb influences from abroad, but high above them, invisible and changeless, stood the *logos* in solitary splendor. The *logos* did not have the bearded face of Zeus, and there were no oak leaves around its head. It did not speak in the thunderstorm, or in dreams, or in prophecies. Its words were silent, its deeds unseen. Out of the heart of the *logos* there flowed the power that moved all universes. The winds poured out of it, the tides rose at its command, and all time and space came streaming from it.

At first the Greeks tended to describe the *logos* tentatively, recognizing that it was beyond description. Xenophanes spoke of "one god, greatest among gods and men, in no way similar to mortals either in body or in thought." He deplored the entire body of the works of Homer and Hesiod, saying they were a reproach among men, for they showed the gods stealing and committing adultery and deceiving one another. The *logos* did not commit adultery, did not steal, did not deceive. It was as far remote from human passions as the farthest star, being pure and passionless and wholly without any appetites. Pythagoras thought it might be represented by the perfect number, or by a musical scale. "The Pythagoreans," wrote Aristotle, "believe the elements of number to be the elements of all things, and the entire universe to be a musical scale and a number." Parmenides spoke of the One, which was perhaps only the Decad of Pythagoras under another name. So the Greeks moved merrily among abstractions, leaping from one to another, until it occurred to them that the architecture of the universe must be logical and rigorous, possessing some of the qualities of a machine, a *mechanê*, like a ship or the human body, with their countless parts moving together in concert.

So it came about that the Greeks were the first to inquire into the laws of the universe and develop the techniques by which these laws could be made known. These techniques were never, or rarely, concerned with experiments alone, for they regarded experimental knowledge as only a small part of the available knowledge about the workings of the universe, men's speculations being at least as real as the discoveries of the scientist working in his laboratory, or of the anatomist dissecting the corpse of an animal.

Around 500 B.C. we begin to hear of extraordinary advances in technical knowledge, and the deliberate use of mathematics to solve engineering problems. Alcmaeon of Croton, a Pythagorean physician, is carefully dissecting animals. New navigational instruments are coming into use. Hecataeus is studying the histories of all the countries around the Mediterranean and traveling westward as far as the Gulf of Genoa and the coast of Spain, while Xenophanes is observing the phenomenon of raised beaches in the presence of shells and marine fossils inland, and Alcmaeon is discovering the optic nerve and the Eustachian tubes. Suddenly the eyes are growing keener, the hand steadier. The painted curtains with the mythological figures rise to reveal a stage where everything is still mysterious, still shining in the divine light, but no longer diffuse. Suddenly the shapes of the world are sharply outlined, brilliantly colored, and more wonderful than ever now that they can be known.

On the island of Samos especially there were great advances. Here Eupalinus of Megara constructed a conduit to bring water into the city by boring a tunnel nearly a mile long, eight feet wide, and eight feet high. The engineers bored from both sides of a hill and the archaeologists who excavated the tunnel in 1878 discovered that the borings fell short of coincidence by only three feet. This is only one of the engineering feats which Herodotus ascribed to the Samians: they built the biggest of all known temples, and an artificial harbor enclosed by a breakwater running into twenty fathoms of water. All these constructions depended upon mathematical knowledge and precise calculations. Herodotus was a little awed by the Samians, and he explains that he told their history at length because he was so impressed with their technical skills.

The world of science came to birth at the same time as democracy. They came hand in hand, for they sprang from the same cause. Tyranny is always an expression of mythology, and now at last, before the fierce eyes of reason, tyranny was compelled to withdraw into the shadows. Democracy, according to Aristotle, was "to govern and to be governed." It was an experimental science, and like many experiments it proved not to be infallible. Tyranny was lawlessness, and to a generation that believed the universe obeyed the law of the *logos* the very irrationality and incoherence of tyranny proved that it was, of all disciplines, the least conducive to the happiness of men.

In the space of a hundred years the Greek scientists opened out whole new territories never explored before. The mathematicians set the pace. The rigorous Pythagorean discipline bore fruit in the astonishing achievements of Hippocrates of Chios, who showed that a lune bounded by an arc of 90°, and by a semicircle upon its chord, is equal in area to the corresponding chord with the center as its apex. For the first time an area enclosed by straight lines had been equated to an area enclosed by segments of a circle. He had not squared the circle, but he had found a relationship between squares and circles which suggested that all the curving shapes of nature could be accurately measured: the curling leaf, the flow of water, the billowing of a woman's draperies, all these were subject to measurement, to the law of the *logos*.

After the mathematicians came the geographers, mapmakers, biologists, physicists, and physicians. There was almost no area of human endeavor in which the Greeks did not make astonishing advances. By common consent two Greek scientists towered above the rest. One founded the science of medicine. The other, trained as a marine biologist, took for his province nearly all the remaining sciences.

Of the man Hippocrates we know almost nothing except that he was born about 460 B.C. and led a wandering life, living at various times in Thrace and on the islands of Delos and Thasos, in Athens and at Abdera, always returning to his birthplace on the island of Cos, where he presided over the hospital attached to the temple of Asclepius. He was descended from a long line of physicians, and his two sons followed in his profession. He died at Larissa about 377 B.C. in extreme old age. Of his appearance we can only guess that he had some resemblance to the busts which later generations carved of him, showing him as an old man with a high, furrowed forehead, deep lines scored on a narrow face, and a neatly trimmed beard: the idealized portrait of a physician weighed down with anxieties and cares.

But if the man escapes us, the quality of his mind is abundantly revealed in his writings, which were grave and austere, with a certain hard definiteness, as of a man who has pondered deeply and watched much suffering and seen many men die, but who has come in the end to some unshakable conclusions. Perhaps there are only six books in the Hippocratic corpus which can be unreservedly credited to him— *Ancient Medicine* (an early work), *On Wounds in the Head*, *Prognostic*, *Regimen in Acute Diseases*, *Airs Waters Places* and the *Aphorisms*, which most clearly reveal the nature of the man.

He did not write the Hippocratic oath as it has come down to us, for it shows signs of having been written at a later date, but he must have written an oath very like this, and the substance of the oath clearly derives from him:

I swear by Apollo the Healer, by Asclepius, by Health and all the powers of healing, and I call to witness all the gods and goddesses that I may keep this oath and promise to the best of my power and judgment.

To my master in the healing art I shall pay the same respect as to my parents, and I will share my life with him and pay all my debts to him. I will regard his sons as my brothers and teach them the art if they desire to learn it, without fee or covenant. I will hand on precepts, lectures, and all other learning to my sons, to my master's sons, and to those pupils who are duly apprenticed and sworn, and to no others.

I will use my power to help the sick to the best of my ability and judgment. I will abstain from harming or wronging any man by it.

I will not give a fatal draught to anyone, even if it is demanded of me; nor will I suggest the giving of the draught. I will give no woman the means of procuring an abortion.

In my life and my art I shall behave with purity and holiness.

I will not cut, even for the stone, but I will leave all cutting to the practitioners of the craft.

Whatever houses I enter, I will enter for the benefit of the sick and will abstain from every voluntary act of mischief and corruption, making no sexual contact of male or female, bond or free.

Whatever I see or hear, either in my profession or in private, I shall never divulge, keeping silence upon such things as though they were religious secrets.

If I keep this oath and do not violate it, may it be granted to me to enjoy my life and in my profession to earn the good repute of men at all times; but may the contrary befall me if I transgress and violate my oath.

This extraordinary oath must rank with the Funeral Speech of Pericles and Plato's *Phaedo* among the great documents of Greek civilization. There hovers over it a sense of Apollonian calm, a divine propriety and gentleness, and a quiet duty to men and the gods. The physician demands of himself the same arduous discipline which is expected of the highly trained athlete.

Hippocrates was concerned to keep careful watch over his patients, noting all the changes that take place during the course of an illness, establishing the *pattern* of a disease. He believed that illness had physical causes: it was not a visitation of the gods. Since men were only a little removed from the gods they were all the more worthy of being cured of their afflictions. He is interested in everything that happens to his patients—how they breathe, how they walk, how they stand, how they speak and smile, what they think, and the kind of dreams they have. It is not enough to examine the skin, the temperature, the stools, urine, sputum, and vomit, all the evident signs of disease. The entire man must be seen and understood, and then after prolonged examination and after interpreting a hundred different signs it might be possible to come to some elemental conclusions. "The examination of the body," he wrote, "is a serious business, requiring good sight, good hearing, and smell, and touch, and taste, and reasoning."

The great achievement of Hippocrates lay in his power to sweep away the legends and present man as an infinitely complex system, each part of the system being subservient to law. He was not afraid of anatomy, and there is a story that he presented a perfect skeleton made entirely of gold to the Temple of Apollo at Delphi. When Plato came to compare the great men of his time it occurred to him to place Hippocrates with the great sculptors Polyclitus and Phidias, for did not Hippocrates also shape the features of men?

Among the glories of the Hippocratic corpus are forty-two case histories. Some are brief, some are of considerable length, but all of them testify to close and accurate observation. We have to wait for nearly two thousand years before the compilation of case histories like these became the accepted practice:

In Thasos, the wife of Delearces, living on the plain, was seized after great sorrow with an acute fever together with shivering. From the beginning she always wrapped herself up in her bedclothes, and remained silent. She fumbled, picked, scratched, plucked hairs from the bedclothes, wept and laughed. She had no sleep. Her bowels were irritable, but passed nothing. When urged, she drank a little. Her urine was thin and scanty, her fever was slight to the touch, and there was coldness in her extremities.

Ninth day. *A good deal of incoherent talk, and then silence.*

Fourteenth day. *Respiration rare and heavy, with long intervals, and then hurried.*

Seventeenth day. *Bowels after being stimulated passed disordered matters, then whatever she drank passed unchanged; nothing coagulated. The patient was totally insensible, the skin parched and tense.*

Twentieth day. *Much rambling talk, but afterwards she became composed, then speechless, and her respiration was hurried.*

Twenty-first day. *Death.*

Throughout the patient's respiration was rare and heavy; she took no notice of anything; she was always wrapped up in her bedclothes, and she either talked incoherently or was completely silent.

(*Epidemion,* XV)

The unknown doctor who wrote this case history has given an accurate account of a patient suffering from typhoid fever. The "rare and heavy breathing" was evidently the type of breathing known as "Cheyne-Stokes respiration," common among the dying. There is no evidence of treatment; perhaps there was none. There is simply the record which could be compared with similar records until the norm of the disease could be discovered, and its effects discerned over a wide range of cases.

Again and again in the writings of the Hippocratic school we come upon references to the need for careful observation. The *Apho-*

risms describe the symptoms of many diseases as they were learned from countless observations, and if some of them seem rudimentary to us now, they were not rudimentary in the fifth century B.C.:

> *Consumption occurs chiefly between the ages of eighteen and thirty-five.*
>
> *When sleep puts an end to delirium it is a good sign.*
>
> *Old men endure fasting more easily than middle-aged men, youths endure fasting badly, and worst of all children, especially those who are possessed of unusual vitality.*
>
> *If a convalescent eats well, but fails to put on flesh, it is a bad sign.*
>
> *The old generally have fewer complaints than the young, but when they have chronic diseases, they usually end fatally.*
>
> *All diseases occur at all seasons, but some are more apt to occur and to be aggravated at certain seasons.*
>
> *A spasm supervening on a wound is fatal.*
>
> *If there is no swelling after severe and grave wounds, it is very serious.*
>
> *Do not disturb a patient either during or just after a crisis, and do not attempt experiments with purges or diuretics.*
>
> *For extreme diseases, extreme methods of cure.*
>
> *We must attend to the appearance of the eyes in sleep as seen from below; for if a portion of the white can be seen between the closing eyelids, and if this is not connected with diarrhea or severe purging, then it is a bad and fatal sign.*

So, with patience and art, and with increasing skill in recognizing symptoms, the ancient doctors studied their patients and began to map out a system of medication and treatment which was the best in their time. They believed the human body was composed of four "humors"—blood, phlegm, yellow bile, and black vile—and they sometimes erected wonderfully complex theories to explain the predominance of one humor over another. But on the whole the scientific method was in effective command.

"Life is short and art is long," Hippocrates wrote, adding sorrowfully: "The opportunities are fleeting, experiments are dangerous, and judgment is always difficult."

28 ⫷ ARIST⦿TLE

"**A**LL MEN possess by nature the desire to know," wrote Aristotle at the beginning of the *Metaphysics,* and with that statement, dubious in relation to all men but perfectly true in relation to Aristotle, he depicts himself as completely as a man can in a single sentence. He was, as Dante said, the master of them that know—*il maestro di color che sanno.* His chosen field was nothing less than all the accumulated knowledge of the universe, and he had no doubt that a painstaking philosopher could reduce it to intelligible terms. There were no mysteries that could not be solved, no secrets that could not eventually be made to reveal themselves. He believed that the Greek language with the extraordinary richness and flexibility of its constructions provided the perfect instrument for describing all the arts, sciences and skills known to man. The depths of the sea and the heights of the heavens would submit themselves to the genius of the language, and in the end all knowledge would be embraced in a net of words.

The aim of Aristotle was therefore knowledge and the orderly arrangement of it. Everything would be examined, defined, compared, and placed in its proper order in an orderly universe. In his view the human intelligence had suffered too long a mysterious attachment to poetry: it had thought to take Heaven by storm, whereas the proper technique was a careful study of the minute weaknesses of the heavenly defenses. Heaven, too, if it were sufficiently studied, could be carried away in a net of words. So it happens that nearly all of Aristotle's surviving works suggest an implied rebuke against Plato, who wanted to transform the state before he had understood its workings, and who postulated a Heaven filled with Ideas which could never be submitted to rigid analysis because they were articles of faith. Aristotle had no belief in the realm of the Ideas, though from time to time he might pay them a passing tribute. What he believed in with single-minded passion was the intelligibility of the universe.

If we can trust the surviving works, which appear to be based largely on stenographic records, he had no particular gift of style, no sense of the music running through the universe. He was down-to-earth, cautious, superbly in love with facts, and incapable of constructing theories until he had arranged the facts in the proper order, though the proper order might occasionally be that order which best illustrated his theories. Mythology and poetry were subjects he regarded warily, and it was characteristic of him that when he discussed the nature of poetic tragedy, he discovered simple concrete rules which in his view all tragedies should follow, though in fact none of the extant tragedies obey his rules except *Oedipus the King*. Sometimes his net of words becomes a strait jacket.

For nearly two thousand years Aristotle occupied a place of overwhelming eminence in European thought. He was "the philosopher," as though there were no others. He left his stamp on the minds of countless generations of scholars, who appealed to his authority as formerly the Greeks had appealed to the authority of the Delphic oracle.

He was born in Stagira, an Ionian colony in Thrace, his father being the physician of King Amyntas of Macedon. He claimed descent from the great physician Asclepius whose two sons, according to Homer, ministered to the Greeks at Troy, and since Asclepius by common consent was the son of Apollo, Aristotle could therefore claim to be descended from Apollo. He grew up at the court of King Amyntas and seems to have been on friendly terms with his son, Philip. He was about eighteen when he left northern Greece to study in Plato's Academe, where he remained, according to the legend, for twenty years, first as a student and then as a teacher, being known as "the scholar" from his addiction to reading and acquiring manuscripts.

He remained in Athens until about the time of Plato's death, and there is some reason for believing that he hoped to become the president of the Academe, and when the presidency fell to Plato's nephew Speusippus, Aristotle left Athens for twelve years of wandering, first staying at the court of Hermeias, tyrant of Assos, near Troy, where he pursued his studies in politics and biology and married the tyrant's niece, and then to Mytilene, where he taught and acquired the reputation of a patriot devoted to the destruction of the growing power of Persia, and then at Pella, the capital of Macedonia, where he became the tutor of Alexander, son of Philip of Macedon. An enduring friendship sprang up between the prince and the philosopher. There were occasional periods of coolness, but when Alexander was riding in triumph through Asia he took care to send biological specimens to his old teacher.

About 335 Aristotle returned to Athens, and set up school in a grove sacred to Apollo Lyceius and the Muses; the grove seems to have been near the river Ilissus at the foot of Mount Lycabettus. There were several lecture rooms, a library, a map room, an altar, and a building called the Temple of the Muses. A large grant from Alexander the Great provided for the purchase of books and maps. Aristotle would teach in the Peripatus, a covered walk, from which the name of "peripatetic" was given to the school. In the morning he lectured on logic and first principles to a select group of students, and during the afternoon there were public lectures on rhetoric, politics, ethics, and indeed on all fields of knowledge. Unlike the Academe, the Lyceum resembled a modern university with a complex curriculum and a program of postgraduate studies.

Aristotle taught at the Lyceum for twelve years, but when Alexander the Great died in 323 the protection he had received from the Macedonian regent Antipater came to an end, and with the rise of anti-Macedonian feeling in Athens he fled to Chalcis, "lest," he is reported to have said, "the Athenians sin twice against philosophy." He died the following year of a stomach ailment aggravated by overwork, at the age of sixty-two. Plato's will was short, and he left few possessions. Aristotle's will, which has survived, was long and suggested considerable wealth. Antipater was made executor. Aristotle asked that a statue be erected to his mother at Nemea, and that some stone animals be erected at Stagira "in honor of Zeus the Savior and Athena the Savior" in memory of a vow he had made with Nicanor, the prospective husband of his daughter. He asked that his mistress Herpyllis be well cared for, and that a husband be found for her; she was to receive a silver talent, four maidservants, and a boy slave. She could have his father's house at Stagira or remain in the house at Chalcis, whichever she pleased. He asked, too, that the bones of his wife Pythias, the niece of Hermeias, be dug up and buried beside him. The will is written with great care, and leaves no doubt about his affection for his wife, his mistress, and his daughter.

Of the appearance of Aristotle we know very little. Diogenes Laertius tells us that he had a bald head, small eyes, thin legs, and a pronounced lisp, and that he was inclined to wear costly gowns and finger rings and dressed his hair carefully, thus showing himself to be a typical Ionian. He seems to have had a dry wit, and some pleasant anecdotes are told of him. Once when he was asked why beautiful people are so much sought after, he answered: "That is a question fit for a blind man to ask." On another occasion he was asked what advantage he gained from the study of philosophy, and he replied: "That I do without compulsion what others do from fear of the law." Of education he said: "The roots are bitter, but the fruit is sweet." Hearing that someone had abused him, he laughed and said: "He can hit me too, if he likes, in my absence."

Aristotle wrote over two hundred books: their titles are preserved in three lists which have come down to us, but some of the more inviting titles are lost. He wrote books called *On being given in Marriage*, *On Divine Happiness*, *On Melancholy*, *On Fainting Spells*, *On Drunkenness*, *On Vertigo and Sudden Dimness of Sight*, *On Flattery*, *On Enthusiasm*, *On the Praises to the Gods*, and *On Alexander*. None of these have survived. He compiled or edited summaries of 158 political constitutions in preparation for the writing of the *Politics*, and all these are lost except for a fragment of *The Constitution of Athens* which was recovered from the Egyptian sands in 1890. He wrote two volumes of poetry, and his total works comprised, according to Diogenes Laertius who apparently counted them, 445,270 lines. Of these perhaps one twentieth survive.

We understand Aristotle best by remembering his ancestry: that long line of doctors descended from Asclepius and Apollo. He has the physician's approach to things, the physician's desire to know the complex workings of all living organisms, seeing the concrete particular rather than the universal forms, and studying things as they are, not as he hoped they might be. About a quarter of his surviving work consists of studies in natural history rooted in observation and experiment. He had a special affection for the beginnings of things. The reproductive process in particular fascinated him, for he saw the mating of two animals, however small, not as an isolated act but as one involving the powers of the entire universe, the work of the divine economy being continued by these creatures subject to decay. Infinity lay within the embryo; eternity opened wide to receive the young chick. When he writes about the birth of animals and birds, he assumes the air of the detached observer, but there is no escaping the excitement in the voice. Here he describes the chick as it comes to birth:

About the twentieth day, if you open the egg and touch the chick, it moves inside and chirps; and it is already coming to be covered with down, when, after the twentieth day is past, the chick begins to break the shell. The head lies over the right wing close to the flank, and the wing lies over the head; and about this time there can plainly be seen the membrane resembling an afterbirth which comes next after the outermost membrane of the shell, into which membrane one of the navel strings was described as leading (and, by the way, the chick in its entirety is now within it), and so also is the other membrane resembling an afterbirth, namely that surrounding the yolk, into which the second navel string was described as leading; and both of them were described as being connected with the heart and the big vein. At this conjuncture the navel string that leads to the outer afterbirth collapses and becomes detached from the chick, and the membrane that leads into the yolk is fastened onto the thin gut of the creature, and by this time a considerable amount of the yolk is inside the chick and a yellow sediment is in its stomach. About this time it discharges residuum in the direction of the outer afterbirth, and has residuum inside its stomach; and the outer residuum is white. By and by the yolk, diminishing gradually in size, at length becomes entirely used up and comprehended within the chick (so that, ten days after hatching, if you cut open the chick, a small remnant of the yolk is still left in connection with the gut), but it is detached from the navel, and there is nothing in the interval between, but it has been used up entirely. During this period the chick sleeps, makes a move and looks up and chirps; and the heart and the navel together palpitate as though the creature were respiring.

(Historia Animalium, VI)

Aristotle is not always as accurate and poetical as this; sometimes poetry and old wives' tales take over the function which should have been reserved for science. He says that the female heron screams during sexual union, blood drips from her eyes, and she lays her eggs in an awkward manner as though attended by pain. The *Historia Animalium* is a treasure house of incongruities, fables and scientific investigations lying cheek by jowl. He thought goats breathed through their ears and vultures were impregnated by the wind. He believed that mice die if they drink in summer, that music will snare a stag, and that eels are generated spontaneously. He was fond of salamanders that walk through fire, and wrote learnedly about unicorns and manticores without having seen them or apparently known anyone who had. But when he writes about what he knows he has an angelic accuracy. He is the first scientist and a fine spinner of tales.

Aristotle, then, was an experimental scientist, but he was also many other things. He was a superb logician. In his treatises on logic he showed an astonishing capacity to split hairs in all possible ways, and to continue splitting them long after they had become invisible. His treatises on logic were the special delight of the medieval Schoolmen, who also enjoyed the compendious splitting of hairs, but to stress his interest in logic is to underestimate his essential humanity.

He believed that everything in creation had been fashioned for a deliberate purpose, and this belief in a teleological universe gave him insights he would not otherwise have possessed. All things were arrows: all were aimed at some mysterious and invisible target which lay just below the horizon. Of the nature of the target he could only guess. Was it God? Was it Beauty? Was it the Best? He did not know, but sometimes while he was studying the parts of animals or the generation and corruption of living forms he would interrupt his discourse with some startling pronouncement on the nature of the universe. So we find him writing in *De Partibus Animalium*: "All the realms of Nature are marvelous. Purpose and design in their highest degree are to be found everywhere in Nature, and the ultimate end of her workings and generations is a form of the beautiful." And in *De Generatione et Corruptione* he declares that "God fulfilled the perfection of the universe by creating a perpetual becoming, because this is the closest approximation to eternal being."

These are not logical statements: they grew out of his study of animal life, his affection and understanding of living creatures. And it is characteristic of him that he will speak sometimes as though Nature herself was God, and at other times he will say that "Nature always acts like an intelligent workman."

When Aristotle writes about the nature of man or about politics, there is the same fundamentally human approach. He is not so much concerned with the ideal man or the ideal state as with the infinite variety of man and the infinite variety of states. He delights in the eccentric, the unfamiliar, the strange. Here, for example, is his brief description of Hippodamus, the first town planner:

Hippodamus, the son of Euryphon, a native of Miletus, who first invented the art of planning cities and who was responsible for laying out the Piraeus, was a strange man whose desire for fame led him to acquire a reputation for eccentricity. Some thought him affected, for he wore his hair down to his shoulders and covered himself with expensive ornaments, though never wearing anything but cheap clothes in summer and winter. He took care that these clothes should be very warm. He desired to know the secrets of Nature, and without being a politician, he was the first to inquire about the best form of government.

(Politics, II, viii)

So again in the *Nicomachean Ethics*, when he writes about the various "characters" who form the community of men, describing one by one the temperate, the courageous, the envious, the free spender, the niggardly, and many others, he will employ the cunning of a novelist to give point to the special features he wants to emphasize. Aristotle's portrait of the *megalopsychos*, "the great-souled man," is justly famous. The *megalopsychos* is the man who dares to live alone in the secret worship of his own soul. "The man who lives alone," wrote Plato, "would partake of the character of a god or of a beast." Aristotle attempts to show that he partakes of neither and that his desires, instead of being easily satisfied or productive of despair, are indeed insatiable. Aeschylus remarked sadly in *The Persians*: "If you have lived alone, you know how bare is the furniture." Aristotle's *megalopsychos* answers gravely that in the interior of the soul there is very little need for furniture. It is a voice of extreme gentleness and cultivated ennui, and the portrait is delicately painted, so delicately indeed that we begin to suspect that Aristotle is engaged in a mocking self-portrait, though Hegel unaccountably suggested that he was engaged in drawing the features of Alexander the Great. The portrait as it finally emerges shows every crack and wrinkle on the face of the sitter:

The megalopsychos *is especially concerned with honor and dishonor. Great honors conferred by persons of worth give him only a moderate pleasure, for he believes he is only receiving what is due to him, or even less, for no honor can be adequate to the merits of perfect virtue. Nevertheless, he will deign to accept such honors, because they have nothing greater to bestow upon him. Honor rendered by common people, or on trifling grounds, he will utterly despise, since he feels he does not deserve the honor. He will also despise dishonor, for no dishonor can justly attach to a man of great soul . . .*

It is characteristic of such a man that he will never ask help from anyone, or only with reluctance, but he will render it willingly, and he will be haughty toward men of position and fortune, while being courteous to those of moderate station, because it is a difficult and lofty thing to be superior to the great, but easy to outdo the lowly. A lofty bearing toward the strong is not a sign of ill-breeding, but to act in such a way toward common people comports a vulgar display of strength against the weak.

He will not compete for the common objects of ambition, or go where other people take the first place, and he will be idle and slow to action except where great honors or great achievements are at stake, and he will not engage in many undertakings, but only in such as are important and distinguished. He will be open both in love and in hate, since he will regard concealment as cowardice, and he will care more for the truth than what people think, and he will speak and act openly, for being contemptuous of others he will be perfectly frank and outspoken unless he is amusing himself ironically with the common people. He will be incapable of living in anyone's shadow, unless it is a friend; nor is he given to admiration, for nothing is great to him. He bears no grudges and is no gossip, and he will neither speak about himself nor about others. He likes to own useless and beautiful things rather than useful things that bring a profit to him. He has a slow gait, a deep voice, and a deliberate utterance.

(*Nicomachean Ethics*, 1124)

One should not forget that this superb portrait of the exotic *megalopsychos* is the result of acute observation. The pieces fit together. Aristotle is here a scientist, minutely observing a rare specimen of the human race, analyzing it, looking for its source of sustenance, defining its functions and the role it plays in creation, and relating the separate parts to each other.

In much the same way, seeking after causes and characteristics and principles and welding them into a single portrait, he discusses the nature of tragic drama or the nature of the democratic state. There is a *wholeness* in his descriptive passages, and far more art than he is usually given credit for. Here for example is his description of a tyrant maintaining his power in a way which has become all too familiar:

If anyone raises his head too high, then the tyrant must cut it off, and he must destroy all men of spirit, and forbid common meals, clubs, education, and the like, and he must guard against anything which inspires courage and confidence among his subjects. He is bound to prohibit literary assemblies or any other meetings where discussions take place, and he must do his utmost to prevent people from knowing one another (for their acquaintance with one another brings about mutual confidence). He must compel all people staying in the city to appear in public and live at his gates; then he will know what they are doing. If he can keep them underfoot, they will learn humility. In this way he must contrive to be master of those arts which have been learned by the Persians and the barbarians, and for the same end. A tyrant should know what all his subjects are saying and doing, and he should use spies, like the "female detectives" at Syracuse, and the eavesdroppers sent by Hiero to resorts and meetings, for the fear of informers prevents people from speaking their minds, and if they do, they are more easily discovered. Another art of the tyrant is to sow quarrels among his subjects; friends should be made to attack friends, the people with the gentry, and the gentry with one another. Also he should take care to impoverish his subjects; in this way the people, kept at their hard labors, are prevented from conspiring against him.

(Politics, V, ii)

The reading of Aristotle's *Politics* can be an alarming experience, for he discusses forms of tyranny only too prevalent in our own time and we realize how little we have progressed during all these centuries. The only crumb of comfort he can offer is that the most enduring tyranny known to him lasted for two generations, and many were short-lived. He noted that the Peisistratids lasted for thirty-five years, and the tyrannies of Hiero and Gelon in Syracuse for seventeen years.

Of democracy he spoke with detachment and some envy, for he spent many years of his life under tyrannies; and no one has ever improved on his statement that the essence of democracy was "to govern and to be governed." He knew the many dangers of democracy, but he also knew how they could be guarded against: by giving the people as much liberty as possible, by preventing unjust punishments which arouse grievance and hatred, and by limiting the tenure of office of high officials to the shortest possible term—he thought a six-month tenure of office was sufficient for any official. Plato wrote that it was "impossible for the masses to be philosophical," and therefore he found it intolerable that they should form the government of a state. Aristotle with greater wisdom acknowledged that in the ideal state there would be no government at all, but since the ideal was unattainable, there was merit in a democracy which permitted the people "to govern and to be governed," and he found no merit in tyrannies unless they were ruled by tyrants whose sole aim was to serve the people. He found no evidence that such a tyranny had ever existed.

"The master of them that know" threw his net over all the sciences of his time. He was so greedy for knowledge that he left nothing untouched, and everything he touched he illuminated. For twenty centuries he was regarded as the first of scientists, the intellectual champion of the Western world, the acknowledged mentor through the realms of matter and of the spirit. St. Thomas of Aquinas harnessed Aristotelian philosophy to Christian dogmatics, while atheists found sustenance in his pervading rationalism. Our philosophical concepts, our religions, and our sciences are still subtly influenced by him. Of all the Greeks he threw the longest shadow.

29 ⋘ THE RISE OF PHILIP

WHEN Aristotle in the *Politics* described the nature of tyranny he noted that to preserve his power there was no wickedness the tyrant would not commit. Every conceivable means of intimidation and subversion was regarded as lawful as long as he could maintain his grip on the people and reduce them to subjection. "The entire policy of the tyrant," he wrote, "may be summed up in three sentences. First, he sows distrust among his subjects. Then he removes their power. Then he humbles them."

The classic example of a tyranny—though for obvious reasons Aristotle never referred to it—was the northern kingdom of Macedon inhabited by half-savage Illyrian tribesmen with a scattering of Thessalians and ruled by a dynasty of kings who claimed descent from the gods and the legendary heroes. The kings of Macedon ruled by fear, and by fear alone. They were almost untouched by the intellectual awakening of Ionia, Athens, and the Greek colonies in Italy and Sicily. The Greeks were content to regard them as barbarians, strange interlopers from a world of forests and marshes. No one would ever have guessed that out of Macedonia there would come a completely civilized man who would conquer the world.

When Philip II came to the throne of Macedon in 359 B.C. his chances of survival were excessively remote. His brother Alexander had reigned for only a few months before being murdered by one of the nobles, Ptolemy of Olorus, who seized the throne. Three years later Ptolemy was murdered by Alexander's younger brother Perdiccas. Six years later an army of Illyrian hill tribes swept down on Macedonia, and Perdiccas was slain. His infant son Amyntas came to the throne, and soon he too was murdered by Alexander's youngest brother. In fourteen years four kings had ruled over Macedonia, and there seemed no reason to believe that Philip would rule for more than a few months. In fact he ruled for twenty-three years, and in the course of a series of brilliant and terrifying raids he brought all of Greece under his power. The Greeks, who had fought off the Persians, were conquered by the despised barbarians in the north.

Philip was twenty-three or twenty-four when he came to the throne. He was a heavy-built man, loving laughter and wine and boys, and some women, and most of all he loved glory. "I am at peace with those who are willing to obey me," he wrote once, and so it was. At the age of fifteen he had been sent as a hostage to Thebes, where he remained for three years, studying at the Theban military academy under Epaminondas, the great general who had converted Boeotia into an armed camp. Philip was the pure soldier, never happier than when he was taking part in military exercises. From Epaminondas he learned discipline and the uses of the phalanx, from his half-savage Illyrian ancestors he derived his courage and ferocious temper. He had little diplomatic skill, and indeed he had very little need for it.

The original Theban phalanx consisted of a line eight men deep, armed with spears about eighteen feet long. Philip lengthened the spears to twenty-one feet, and he lengthened the line to sixteen men or any number he pleased, so that there were times when the line might be a hundred and sixty men deep. The phalanx had the effect of a tank: it could cut and destroy everything in its path. The Macedonian phalanx was never defeated until it met the Roman legion more than a century later.

When Philip took power, his country was being attacked on all sides. Illyrian and Paeonian tribesmen were still coming down from the north, the Thracians were pouring in from the east, the Thessalians were restless in the south, and there were revolts among the hill tribes in the west. The Paeonians seemed to be the least dangerous and the most amenable to bribery; these he bought off until the hard northern winter came down, and for a few months all campaigns came to a stop. During these winter months he was busily training his tribesmen and teaching them the art of forming phalanges. The winter maneuvers set the foundations for his power, for when the springtide came round he wheeled against all his enemies in turn and defeated them. In one battle against the Illyrians he suffered scarcely any casualties, while 7,000 Illyrians were left on the field. Then he drove against the Thracians and pushed back his eastern frontier to include Mount Pangaeus, which was rich in gold. With an almost unlimited supply of gold and with a small army of battle-hardened troops, he turned his attention to the conquest of Greece.

Philip went about the business of conquering Greece with the cunning of a fox. Occasionally he would send diplomatic notes to cities which thought themselves in danger, promising that no harm would come to them; and when they were lulled into a sense of security, he would appear outside their gates with a formidable force of cavalry and with the tightly packed phalanx, which no obstacle could withstand for long. Sometimes cities surrendered out of fear, even when his armies were not in sight. He took Amphipolis, Pydna, Potidaea, and Methone, annihilated the Phocian army, and during his downward march through Greece he was only stopped at the Pass of Thermopylae. So dreadful was his power that he was invited to assume the presidency of the Pythian games held at Delphi in 346 B.C. It was a political victory of the first magnitude, and he sent off a message to Athens notifying the Athenians of this latest victory. It was almost an ultimatum.

Athens was being led by the wise and careful Eubulus, more famous for his dexterity with finances than for any desire to send armies into the field, though he had checked Philip at Thermopylae. Like many other Athenians, he seemed to believe that Philip was an adventurer who would eventually destroy himself. Philip protested strongly that he wanted peace with Athens, and he was continually pouring large sums of money into the hands of Athenian demagogues who may even have believed in his protestations. There was one young lawyer who believed none of them. His name was Demosthenes, and he had recognized very early that Philip was a man who would not stop until he was checked by a superior force; and when in 351 B.C. the Athenians spoke of sending a small token force against him, he answered logically in a speech known as the *First Philippic* that nothing could be gained by play-acting:

One thing is clear: he will not stop unless someone opposes him. Are we to wait for him? Are we to dispatch empty galleys and send after him the curses of this or that person, and will all be well? Should we not go down to the ships? Should we not sail with at least a part of our national army now, before it is too late? Should we not land somewhere along the coast? Someone says, "Where shall we land?" The war itself, men of Athens, will discover the rotten parts of his empire, if we make a trial: but if we sit at home, hearing the orators accuse and malign one another, no good can ever be achieved.

Demosthenes went on to fight Philip with all the weapons of his oratorical skill. It was an unequal combat, for Philip's weapons were cunning and terror, and the best equipped and largest army in Greece. One was the champion of Greek freedom, the other of tyranny.

They had almost nothing in common except that they were human beings. Philip was coarse, brutal, handsome, possessed of immense physical strength, capable of carousing all night and then at dawn leading his army onto the field of battle. Demosthenes was pale, sickly, ugly, very small and thin. Philip was happiest in a crowd, Demosthenes was by nature reserved and quiet, and happiest when alone.

His father was a wealthy swordmaker, who died when he was seven, leaving him in the hands of guardians who defrauded him of his inheritance—the estate amounted to fifteen talents, corresponding to perhaps $30,000 in our money. He grew up to be an unprepossessing youth with a burning desire to punish his guardians, who kept him and his family in enforced poverty. He was often ill and was kept away from school, where he was nicknamed Battalus after a famous effeminate flute player of the time. Loneliness and misery gave him a quick wit and a biting tongue, and for this he received another nickname, Argas, meaning a venomous serpent. Very early in his life he determined to become a lawyer in order to bring his guardians to court, but he had no natural talent for oratory, and suffered from a pronounced stammer. He cured himself of his stammer by making long speeches with his mouth full of pebbles, and he cured his weak voice by declaiming verses while running uphill. He had an ungainly posture, and he did his best to cure it by studying his appearance in a mirror. He had no gift of style, and so he immersed himself in a cellar, endlessly copying out Thucydides' *History of the Peloponnesian War*. He became the greatest orator Greece had ever known, and perhaps the greatest orator of all time, but it was a triumph of will over native ability.

He was twenty before he was able to bring suit against his guardians. Three of these early speeches survive: they are vigorous, but oddly unconvincing. The guardians charged that his grandfather was a traitor to Athens who fled to the Bosporus after betraying to the enemy a harbor in the Chersonese; his grandfather then married a wealthy Scythian woman. Demosthenes pointed out that he was not being charged for the sins of his grandfather, and in fact he was not being charged at all. He was bringing suit against the men who had squandered his patrimony, insulted him at every opportunity, and acted as though they were determined to squeeze every last ounce of money and treasure from the family property. Demosthenes won the case and was awarded ten talents, but the guardians fled the country, and there is some doubt whether he was able to collect the money.

To earn a living he became a speech-writer, preparing briefs for lawyers or for private individuals intent on pressing a suit. His uncle Demo was a banker who made a profitable living by lending money to shipowners and grain merchants. A certain Protus, an Athenian, borrowed money from Demo against grain he was importing from Sicily on a ship belonging to Hegestratus. The ship sailed to Syracuse, and grain was loaded into the hold. Thereupon Hegestratus and his shipboard companion Zenothemis went to the bankers in Syracuse, raising loans on the grain, pretending it was theirs, and sending the money to safekeeping in Massilia (Marseilles). Then they set sail for Athens, and on a dark night after they had been two or three days at sea, and were not far from Cephallenia, Hegestratus slipped down into the hold with a handsaw and cut a hole in the ship's bottom. It must have been a rusty handsaw, or he bungled the job, for the passengers heard the noise below decks and started to investigate. Hegestratus, caught redhanded, panicked, rushed on deck, and jumped overboard, hoping to swim to the ship's dinghy which was being towed behind, but he drowned, "thus receiving," as Demosthenes observed, "a very well-merited end." Zenothemis, who was also in the conspiracy, did not panic. Thinking quickly, he went round the deck shouting that the ship was sinking and all the passengers must take to the dinghy. Protus kept his head. He offered the crew a large reward if they would bring the ship to port, but even when they reached Cephallenia Zenothemis was still plotting to prevent the ship from reaching Athens, claiming that the shipowner and the loan which covered the cost of the grain belonged to Massilia, and he was himself a man from Massilia, and therefore the ship should turn about and make for the western

Mediterranean. The matter was brought to court, and the judge ordered the ship to proceed to Athens, but even then Zenothemis was not finished, for in Piraeus he claimed that he had sailed on his own ship with his own grain, and that Protus was an impostor.

Such was the story which Demosthenes related in court, or wrote down so that it could be spoken by his uncle Demo. The story was told skillfully, with an eye for relevant detail, but one is left with the feeling that Demosthenes is only flexing his muscles. Gradually he was acquiring a reputation as a gifted, if not greatly talented speaker, who could be ironically persuasive in court. He was also acquiring a reputation for being capriciously generous with his money and for taking bribes, but it is unlikely that he was either generous or bribable. He had always been ambitious, and soon he was making speeches before the Assembly on public affairs. When he was about thirty, a new note appears in the speeches. The softness goes out of them. Instead, we begin to hear the sound of rolling thunder. Previously he had been the lawyer calmly debating the sordid affairs of the market place: theft, embezzlement, misappropriation of funds. Now with a kind of soaring inner violence he was debating the fate of nations.

In 354 B.C. rumors reached Athens that the Persians were preparing to invade Greece: hotheads called for an immediate mobilization and declaration of war. Demosthenes urged calm in a speech called *On the Naval Boards*; there was no need to provoke an unnecessary war; Athens had enough enemies without inventing another, and besides she was ill-prepared. There were rumors that the Persian king was advancing toward Greece with twelve hundred camelloads of gold. Demosthenes laughed the rumors to scorn, and suggested that it would be better to enlarge the fleet to three hundred men-of-war, and to be in a state of preparation, than to dream about those camelloads of gold which would scarcely survive the long journey. If money was needed, it would be found when the attack came. If allies were needed, they too would be found when the attack came and not before. The watchword was vigorous caution. Calmly, succinctly, remembering the battles of long ago, Demosthenes was all for maintaining a strong peace and then waiting upon events. There were dangers closer than Persia, and against these too the Athenians must be prepared.

The greatest danger was the rise of Macedonia to a position of power and eminence, threatening the entire fabric of the Athenian alliances. The Greeks were stunned by the sudden rise of this man who possessed the gold mines of Mount Pangaeus and the revenues from all the rich ports he had captured, and who was honored and celebrated by men who remained unaware that he was determined to conquer them, and then to conquer the whole of the known world. He possessed the means to accomplish any purpose he desired.

In the *First Philippic* Demosthenes had raged helplessly against the inactivity of the Athenians. He had hoped a large force would be sent to Thrace under capable officers, but in fact the officers were held in reserve in Athens. "You choose your captains not to fight but to be displayed like dolls in the market place," Demosthenes said bitterly. It was not quite true. Eubulus knew the dangers of Philip's rise to power as well as any man, and he was quietly preparing to increase the military strength of Athens with a new arsenal and a new fleet. Athens was still the strongest naval power in the Aegean, and she could still protect her commercial interests.

In the following year Philip threatened Olynthus, a town of Chalcidice in alliance with Athens. Once again Demosthenes called for the immediate formation of a citizen army to be sent to the defense of the ally. He asked why nothing was being done, why everyone was so terrified of the armed might of Philip. In the speech known as the *Second Olynthiac* he declared:

Do not believe, men of Athens, that Philip and the people he rules over have the same likings. He desires glory, and this is his passion, and he is ready for any adventure, any peril, preferring to a life of safety the honor of achieving what no Macedonian king has ever done before. The people have no share in the glory; they are exhausted by these long marches up and down the country; they suffer and toil incessantly; and they are allowed no leisure for their work or for their private concerns, and they are unable to spend their hardearned money, for all the markets of the country are closed because of the war.

So you can see how the Macedonians themselves are disposed toward Philip. They say his mercenaries and guardsmen are admirable and well-trained soldiers, but as I have heard from a man who has been in their country, one who is incapable of falsehood, they are no better than others. If there are any who are experienced in battles and campaigns, Philip is jealous of them and drives them away—so my in-

formant tells me—because he desires to keep the glory to himself, his jealousy of others being the greatest of his many failings. And if there are any good and virtuous men in his service, men who refuse to share his daily intemperances, drunkenness, and licentiousness, these are simply pushed aside and counted as nobodies. All the rest of the men around him are brigands and parasites, who will get drunk and perform such dances around him as I dare not name to you.

With the *Second Olynthiac* Demosthenes declared a personal war against Philip, knowing well the cost if he should ever fall into the king's hands. He had hoped a large army would go to the relief of Olynthus, but only a trickle was sent, and the town fell, with disastrous consequences to Athenian power in the north.

Every day the power of Philip was increasing, and that of Athens was waning. Two years after the capture of Olynthus, the Athenians sent out peace feelers, and Demosthenes was included in the embassy which went to wait on Philip in his hillside capital. To his avowed enemy Philip showed only a dangerous cordiality, but Demosthenes had the opportunity to study the king at close quarters. He was confirmed in his beliefs. The king was harsh, unscrupulous, capable of any falsehoods; he was also so powerful that his demands had to be accepted. Affably, the king said he would be content to make a treaty of peace providing that Athens and Macedon should each retain the territories they occupied at the time of the peace treaty; and he made a private promise to the ambassadors that he would not attack Phocis. This private promise was not included in the draft treaty.

The ambassadors returned to Athens with the feeling that they had accomplished a peace which might be lasting and that Philip had a healthy respect for Athenian sea power. As it happened, the peace did not last more than a few weeks, and Philip had no respect for anyone or anything. "Every king and tyrant is an enemy to freedom, an antagonist to laws," Demosthenes said in the *Second Philippic*, and it was no more than the truth. Philip forgot his promise not to attack Phocis. Instead, he hurled his armies against it, razed the towns, scattered the townsfolk among the villages, demanded an annual tribute of sixty talents, and quartered troops in the country to make sure it was paid. To Demosthenes this was no more than the expected treachery. "From the day he attacked Phocis dates the real opening of hostilities," he declared, and so it was. From that moment Philip was determined to reduce Athens to subjection.

Philip went about the task slowly and carefully, sending a continual stream of spies to Athens and wherever possible buying off Athenian statesmen and orators. He transformed Thrace into a satellite state after dethroning its king, thus extending Macedonian power almost to the Chersonese. Just in time Demosthenes hurried to Byzantium and successfully weaned the citizens from any desire to swear allegiance to Macedon. Philip was infuriated. He sent an army against Byzantium, hoping to destroy the city in the course of a few days' brisk fighting, but two Athenian fleets converged on it and the attack was beaten off. Ruefully Philip was compelled to admit Athenian naval supremacy.

But if Athens possessed power over the sea, Philip had power over the land. He assembled an army and determined once and for all to put an end to any opposition, wherever it arose in Greece. He had lost an eye in battle, he had a broken collarbone, one arm mangled, and a leg deformed by wounds, but he was still capable of leading an army. He drove south to the Pass of Thermopylae and captured Elatea, and from there sent ambassadors to explore the intentions of the Thebans. The news threw Athens into consternation. It seemed likely that the Thebans would join with the Macedonians in an all-out attack on Athens. It was a time of horror and bafflement. No one seemed to know what could be done to stave off the threatened attack. Several years later Demosthenes gave an extraordinary account of those hours:

It was evening. A person came with a message to the presidents that Elatea was taken. They rose from supper immediately, drove off the people from their market stalls, and set fire to the wicker frames; [1] *others sent for the generals and called the trumpeter; and the city was full of commotion. The next morning at daybreak the presidents summoned the council to their hall, and you went to the Assembly, and before you could introduce or prepare the question, the whole people were up in their seats. When the council had entered, and the presidents had reported their intelligence and presented the courier, and he had made his statement, the crier asked, "Who wishes to speak?" and no one came forward. The crier put the question repeatedly. Still no man rose, though all the generals were present and all the*

[1] It is thought that the wicker frames of the stalls in the market place were set alight as a fire signal, to attract the people from the countryside into the city.

*orators, and our country with her common voice called for someone
to speak and save her—for when the crier raises his voice according
to law, it may justly be deemed the common voice of our country. . . .*

   *Well, then, I was the man called for upon that day. I came for-
ward and addressed you. I said that those who were alarmed because
Philip had the Thebans with him did not really understand the state
of affairs; if this had happened, Philip would have driven far beyond
Elatea to our own borders. No, he was sending to Thebes to draw the
Thebans into alliance with him. "This," said I, "is how I believe the
matter stands. All the Thebans whom it was possible to bribe or deceive he has already under his command; those who have resisted him
from the first and still oppose him he cannot prevail upon. So what
does he intend to do, and why has he seized Elatea? He intends to
encourage and embolden his friends, to intimidate his adversaries, so
that they may either concede from fear what they now refuse, or be
compelled to submit to him, and he is doing this by displaying a force
in the neighborhood and by bringing up troops. Now," said I, "if we
determine on the present occasion to remember any unkindness which
the Thebans have done us, and to regard them in the character of
enemies with distrust, then we shall be doing exactly what Philip
wants of us, and then it will happen that those Thebans who now hate
him will join forces with him, and altogether they will march on
Athens. But if you will listen to me, and be pleased to examine what
I say, I believe it will meet with your approval, and I shall dispel the
danger hanging over Athens. What I advise is that you forget your
fears. Fear for the Thebans—they are nearer harm than we are—the
peril is all round them. Then I urge you to march to Eleusis all the
fighting men and the cavalry, and show yourselves to the world in
arms, so that your partisans in Thebes may have equal liberty to speak
up for the good cause."*

   No Athenian was ever likely to forget that morning when Demosthenes held the city in the palms of his hands. The people agreed to his
demands, and that day ambassadors set out from Athens to Thebes.
Demosthenes won his greatest diplomatic victory, for he convinced
the Thebans to join in an alliance with Athens. And when a few days
later Philip marched into Boeotia from the west, he found the army
of the allies waiting for him. He had 30,000 foot soldiers and 2,000

horse, and the allies had about the same number.

The battle which took place at Chaeronea was soon over. The Macedonians were tougher, more skillful, and more highly trained than the allies, and they had better generals. The Greek generals failed to take advantage of an initial success by the Athenians on the left. They advanced rapidly—too rapidly—and the Macedonians poured through the gap. The Sacred Band of Thebes fought to the last man. Among the Athenians who fled was Demosthenes, who had fought as a hoplite in the ranks.

Philip was now master of Greece, and Athens was no more than a Macedonian colony.

All the work of Demosthenes had come to ruin, but even in defeat he was still the acknowledged leader, whose counsels prevailed without a dissenting voice. In the hearts of the Athenians he held the place once occupied by Pericles. So they called upon him to deliver the funeral oration over the heroic dead of Chaeronea and made him commissioner to repair the walls for the defense of the city. Philip had been unexpectedly lenient to the Athenians, perhaps because he still hoped to use their fleet for the conquest of Persia. He ravaged Sparta, placed his garrisons in Thebes, Corinth, and Chalcis, but never led his army into Athenian territory.

Eight months after Chaeronea a certain Ctesiphon suggested that the time had come to offer Demosthenes the golden crown for his services to the state. The orator Aeschines, a tortuous braggart, gave notice that he would prosecute Ctesiphon for proposing so illegal an offer, and for seven years the crown was withheld. The great battle of the orators was fought in 330 B.C., when Aeschines delivered an immensely long and vituperative speech in which he accused Demosthenes of being a traitor, a perjurer, and an embezzler, and not content with these charges went on to accuse him of all kinds of improprieties in his private life. Demosthenes replied with the greatest speech he ever delivered, known as the *Oration on the Crown*, in which he ridiculed the charges and justified his entire political career. He had been attacked violently; he attacked violently. He tore Aeschines to shreds, ridiculed his manner of speaking, his birth, his upbringing, everything about him, asserting that he had no claims to distinction except the claim of impudence, and then launched into passionate justification of his own actions in defense of the freedom of Greece. It is a long speech, but it is on fire throughout. Philip was dead, and now Alexander ruled the world from Asia, and Demosthenes raged against them both for all the harm they had done to freedom. Philip and then Alexander had become masters of Greece, but the Athenians were confirmed in their liberties because he had protected them:

I say that Athens is by all mankind acquitted, owing to my counsels; and I am acquitted by you. And if you ask me, Aeschines, why I deserve the crown, I answer in this way. When, beginning with Aeschines, all the statesmen of Greece were corrupted formerly by Philip and now by Alexander, I was never tempted and never induced to betray what I considered just and benevolent to my country. Neither opportunity, nor fair speeches, nor hope, nor large promises, nor fear, nor anything in the wide world led me from the path of duty. I never leaned on the side of profit. All I did sprang from a soul which was upright, honest, and incorruptible. Entrusted with affairs of greater magnitude than any of my contemporaries, I administered them all honestly and faithfully. Therefore I claim to be honored.

If any other man had spoken these words, he would have been laughed out of court; but Demosthenes spoke with grave authority, and what he said was true. The jubilant Athenians gave him the crown.

He survived Philip, and he survived Alexander. He had grown old and worn in the service of the state, but he had lost none of his oratorical power, and when Alexander died in 323 B.C., Demosthenes was one of those who called upon the Greeks to throw off the Macedonian yoke. All over Greece there were revolts, which were ruthlessly quelled. Antipater, the Macedonian viceroy, demanded the surrender of the Athenian orators, who escaped to Aegina. Leaving his friends, Demosthenes sailed to the island of Calauria and took refuge in the temple of Poseidon. There Antipater's vindictive manhunter found him. Before he could be arrested, he swallowed poison which he had hidden in his pen.

Aᴸᴸ THOSE who ever saw him marked his extraordinary grace and beauty. He had a delicate white skin which reddened all over his body when he had been drinking or when he was excited, and he habitually held his head a little to the left side as though he suffered from some stiffness of the neck, and his eyes were deep blue and piercing, though sometimes they grew soft and melting. It was observed that there was something peculiar about his eyes: they were too large and they turned upward and did not seem to focus on the person he was talking to. His hair was reddish-gold, usually in tangles, and in his youth he wore it down to his shoulders. He was not tall, but well-proportioned, with carved cameolike features, a broad smooth forehead, a sculptured mouth, and a firm chin. Even at the very end, when he had conquered most of the known world, he had the look of a youth.

We know him as Alexander the Great. His soldiers knew him simply as *basileus*, the king, for he destroyed so many kings that there were almost no others left to share the title, and there were none of his commanding eminence. After his death at the age of thirty-two, legends were told about him: how he had gone down into the underworld, how he had unlocked the secrets of the universe hidden in a high cave in the mountains of the Caucasus, and he had flown to the midnight stars and returned with the lamp of Heaven, but there was no need to invent legends. The youth with the strange smile and the red-gold hair was legendary enough while he walked the earth.

He was born in 356, the son of Philip of Macedon and the Epirote princess Olympias, who met her future husband at the celebration

418

of the mysteries at Samothrace. Neither was wholly Greek, and Olympias may have had no Greek blood in her veins. She was a proud and passionate woman, ruthlessly determined to secure her power, and much feared because she was reputed to be a sorceress. Philip was constitutionally incapable of fearing anyone, not even his wife. The young Alexander was brought up in a court dominated by these two rapacious rulers, and the wonder is that he retained his sanity. He was closer to Olympias than to Philip, and all his life he retained her love.

There is a story recounted by Plutarch that on a single day Philip won a battle at Potidaea, heard that his general Parmenio had won a decisive victory over Illyrian tribesmen, and learned that his race horse had won at the Olympic games. Finally there came news that Olympias had been delivered of a son, Alexander. The diviners not unreasonably announced that a child born on such a day could scarcely avoid being invincible.

Alexander grew up in the palace at Pella under the stern regimen thought suitable for Macedonian princes. He was thirteen when Philip invited Aristotle to be his tutor; for the next three years Alexander sat at Aristotle's feet, learning political theory and ethics and the geography of Asia, and perhaps being admitted into the laboratories where Aristotle pursued his studies of flowers, birds, and animals. Aristotle wrote for him a treatise on the art of government and another called *The Alexander, or an Essay on Colonists*, which may belong to a later time. Geography especially fascinated Alexander, and when some Persian envoys arrived at the court and were received by him in the absence of his father, he entertained them by questioning them about the roads of Asia and the distances run by the royal couriers. He had no great affection for sports, except hunting. Because he could run very fast, someone suggested that he should compete in the Olympic games. He answered that he would only compete if all the other runners were princes.

At sixteen he governed Macedonia as regent while his father went off to fight the Byzantines. A few months later a revolt broke out among the Thracian tribesmen. Alexander gathered an army, took their towns by storm, drove out the tribesmen, and settled colonists in a new town which he called Alexandropolis, the first of many towns and cities which were to bear his name. Significantly these colonists were assembled, as Plutarch tells us, "from many nations." From a very early period of his life Alexander was experimenting in the deliberate breakdown of national loyalties.

At the battle of Chaeronea in 338 Alexander distinguished himself by commanding Philip's left and leading an attack against the Sacred Band of Thebes. Five hundred years later men were still pointing to an old oak near the river Cephisus, calling it "Alexander's oak" because he had pitched his tent under it. But though Alexander at eighteen had saved the day for Philip, family dissension broke out almost immediately. Philip had decided to divorce Olympias and marry in her stead Cleopatra, the niece of his general Attalus. Alexander attended the marriage feast, and all might have gone well if Attalus, drinking too deeply, had not offered up a prayer for a grandson who would inherit the throne. Alexander hurled a wine-cup at the general and shouted: "Then am I a bastard!" Philip, in a hot rage, drew his sword and would have killed Alexander on the spot if he had not slipped between two chairs. Alexander had the last word. Looking at the drunken king sprawling on the floor, he shouted: "So there's the man who thinks he will go over to Asia, but he cannot go safely from one chair to another!" Such taunts were mortally dangerous. He slipped out of the room, found his mother, and fled with her to Illyricum. His companions, the chosen playmates of his youth, were then sent into banishment.

These companions were to play an important role in Alexander's subsequent career. Among them was Ptolemy, his quick-witted and hook-nosed half brother, the son of Philip and a concubine called Arsinoë. It was rumored that he was not the son of Philip but of an obscure Macedonian called Lagus, but he bore the title of a royal prince and was treated accordingly by the king. Though he was a year older than Alexander, he survived him by fifty years. Then there was Nearchus, a levelheaded young Cretan from a family that had settled in Amphipolis, a born cavalryman who was to become grand admiral of the fleet. There was Harpalus prince of Elimyotis, with the club-foot and the expression of deep seriousness, weak and sickly, whom Alexander admired for his learning: he was to be made treasurer of the empire and to abscond with as much of the treasure as he could lay hands upon. Most impressive of all the companions was Hephaestion, who resembled a taller, more robust Alexander with his easy grace, his serene courage, and his flute playing. They shared one tent, drank from one cup, fought side by side; if he had survived he would have inherited the empire.

The companions of Alexander were not exiled for long. A certain Demaratus of Corinth took it upon himself to reprove Philip for permitting a feud in his own household while embarking on so many great plans for Greece. Philip had faith in Demaratus, and immediately recalled the exiles. For a few more months a precarious peace existed between Alexander and Philip, who was preparing to invade Persia. He was attending the wedding feast following the marriage of his daughter to Alexander, King of Epirus, when he was stabbed to death by a young nobleman called Pausanias. Olympias seems to have been privy to the plot; the Persians may have been implicated. Alexander was far away, and knew nothing of these events until the news was brought to him by messenger. He hurried to the capital, to find the court given over to intrigues. On the king's death the choice of the new king was vested in the army. The army, led by Antipater and Parmenio, declared for Alexander, and from that moment there was no more doubt that Alexander would inherit the throne. All those who were suspected of having had anything to do with the plot were summarily executed. Alexander came to the throne after a short and savage bloodbath in which all other contenders perished.

Philip had made himself captain of Greece, but only the Macedonians took pleasure in being ruled by him. All over Greece his death was celebrated with feasts and celebrations and public prayers in honor of his murderer; and the northern tribes celebrated their release from Macedonian tyranny by rising in open revolt. Alexander inherited an empire in ruins: his effective rule extended only over a few square miles around his capital. If he had been cautious he would have sent an expedition against the tribesmen and then attempted by means of bribery and diplomatic skill to revive his father's hegemony over the Greeks in the south, but it was not in him to be cautious. In the late summer of 336, only a few weeks after coming to the throne, he led his army south, leaving the subjugation of the tribesmen to a later time. He soon regained control of Thessaly, terrified Thebes into submission, received an Athenian delegation promising loyalty, and presented himself at Corinth as the general of the Corinthian League in the place of his father. Returning to Macedonia through Delphi, he heard, with no outward show of surprise, that he was blessed by Apollo.

Having, in this lightning raid, subdued the Greeks, Alexander returned his attention to the wild tribesmen of the northern frontiers.

Once again there were swift raids into territories which no one believed he could penetrate, sudden ambushes, forced night marches.
He reached the Danube, made an alliance with the Celts, and went
on to destroy so many tribes over such a long period of time that the
Greeks came to imagine that he had died of his wounds in the frontier
lands, and for the second time Athens rejoiced and Thebes celebrated
the death of a Macedonian king. He was on Mount Pelion in eastern
Thrace when he heard that the Thebans were in revolt. Fourteen days
later he stood under the walls of Thebes, demanding that the leaders
of the revolt be surrendered to him. The Thebans demanded that
Alexander surrender two of his generals, Antipater and Philotas, and
they proclaimed war against Alexander in the name of all the Greek
cities which loved their freedom. Alexander decided to teach the
Greeks a lesson they would never forget, and ordered the destruction
of Thebes, the entire population being sold into slavery and every
house leveled to the ground. Only one house was spared: this was
the house once occupied by Pindar.

He would have done the same to Athens and destroyed the
Parthenon if the Athenians had not hurriedly submitted to him; for
there was no mercy in him. To the Athenian envoys he made a parade
of forgiveness, and Plutarch relates that he warned the Athenians to
keep close watch on events, for if his plans miscarried they might find
themselves the arbiters of Greece. His plans were well known, and
they were especially well known to the Persians. His aim was nothing
less than to bring all of Asia Minor into the Macedonian empire in
revenge for the Persian invasion of Greece a hundred and fifty years
before. He had as yet no intention of attacking the heartland of
Persia.

In the spring of the following year he crossed the Hellespont
into Asia at the head of an army of some 30,000 foot and 5,000 horse.
Of these only about 12,000 were Macedonians, and another 12,000
were Greeks, the remainder of the army being composed of Thracian
tribesmen, Cretan archers, and Agrianian javelin throwers. Halfway
across the Hellespont he sacrificed a bull to Poseidon and from a
golden goblet poured a libation into the sea. They said he was the
the first of the army to step onto the shores of Asia. He never saw
Greece again.

Alone except for a small retinue he made the journey to ancient
Troy, where he poured a libation on the tomb of his ancestor Achil-

les and as a further act of homage he ran naked round it, while Hephaestion performed the same offices for the tomb of Patroclus. They sacrificed in the old temple of Athena and from its walls took down the holy shield, which was to accompany them through all their journeys. Then he summoned the Trojans before him, declared the city a free democracy, and abolished the tribute they had paid regularly to the Persians.

The small army marched south toward the river Granicus, where an army of 20,000 Asiatic horse and 20,000 Greek mercenaries under Memnon of Rhodes was waiting for him on the steep southern bank of the river. It was now early summer, and the river, though there was a strong current, could be forded. Alexander threw his cavalry across and somehow succeeded in establishing a foothold on the high ground, being himself always in the thick of the combat, conspicuous in his armor and a helmet fashioned out of electrum with its double crest of white plumes. The slope was slippery with mud—it had evidently been raining heavily—and in the course of the confused battle he was very nearly killed by a blow from a battle-ax wielded by the Persian Spithridates: the ax penetrated his helmet and would have pierced his brain if it had gone an inch deeper. Finally the Persians broke, and the Greek mercenaries were surrounded, all but 2,000 being butchered. By evening the battle had been won. It was the first of his four major victories, and the only one in which the odds were heavily against him. In honor of his victory he sent three hundred suits of Persian armor to be hung in the Acropolis as a votive offering to Athena with the inscription: "Alexander, son of Philip, and all the Greeks except the Spartans, present this offering from the spoils taken from the barbarians inhabiting Asia." To Olympias he sent all the gold plate and purple raiment found on the battlefield.

Granicus was the wedge which was eventually to split Persia wide open. One by one the Greek cities on the coast of Asia Minor revolted against their Persian satraps and declared for Alexander. The whole of Hellespontine Phrygia surrendered to him. Sardis capitulated; then it was the turn of Ephesus; Miletus held out under a strong Persian garrison, but by July he had forced it to surrender; there remained Halicarnassus, which resisted stubbornly. He needed Halicarnassus because it was an important port, and his grand strategy involved the destruction of the Persian fleet by the destruction of its bases: he would reduce it to impotence by cutting it off from its supplies. He attached so much importance to Halicarnassus that he left Ptolemy with 3,000 foot and 200 horse to besiege it, while he went on to Gordium, pressing forward with two columns, one under Parmenio moving through Lydia while he led his own column along the Lycian coast. He was relieved to leave Halicarnassus behind, for while he was in camp a swallow had fluttered into his tent and flown round and round his head, twittering loudly in a way which suggested that it was trying to warn him of coming dangers, and it kept settling on various parts of the bed where Alexander was lying. He was only half awake when the swallow came into the tent, and he tried to shoo it away softly. Finally the swallow perched on his head.

Like all Greeks, Alexander regarded birds as messengers of the gods. He consulted the soothsayers, and it was agreed that the insistent swallow had come to warn him of treachery by a friend, and that the conspiracy would prove unsuccessful, for swallows are domestic and talkative birds and the warning had evidently come in time. Alexander decided that the traitor was a certain Alexander of Lyncestis, who was one of his chosen companions and had been placed in charge of the Thessalian cavalry, a young man possessed of great boldness, for he had accompanied Alexander fully armed into his father's palace after Philip's murder and helped Alexander to power though his own brothers were implicated in the crime. There were rumors, perhaps more than rumors, that the Persian king had offered Alexander of Lyncestis the throne of Macedon and a gift of 1,000 gold talents to kill him. Alexander immediately ordered the arrest of the Lyncestian.

The swallow in the tent was only one of the many omens that accompanied his progress. The air was thick with the voices of the gods chattering away in a language only understood by soothsayers and necromancers. About the same time a spring near Xanthus in Lycia swelled over its banks and threw up a copper plate on which in ancient characters could be read words which seemed to indicate that the time would soon come when the Greeks would overthrow the Persians. Such omens abounded, becoming more numerous as the hour of decision approached. Alexander was Aristotle's clearsighted pupil, but he was also a credulous student of the miraculous, his mind moving delightedly in the realm where birds and thunderclaps and copper plates long buried in the earth assumed prophetic meaning.

At Gordium he unloosened the sacred knot made from the bark of a cornel tree, which roped together the wagon and the yoke belonging to Midas, the founder of the Gordian dynasty. What kind of knot it was, and how he unloosened it, are mysteries which may never be solved. There was a widely held belief that anyone who succeeded in unloosening it would become the conqueror of the world. Alexander therefore was compelled to unloosen it. The story that he cut the knot with his sword is certainly untrue; he would acquire no merit by such a childish solution to the problem. It is more likely, as Aristobulus believed, that he was able to separate the wagon from the yoke by pulling out the wooden peg joining the shaft to the yoke, and then drawing off the yoke from below: in this way the heavily encrusted knot with the ends hidden within it would come loose, and he could unravel it at his leisure. "That very night," says Arrian in his *Life of Alexander*, "there was lightning and thunder—a further sign from Heaven, and accordingly on the following day Alexander offered sacrifices to the gods who had sent this sign and proclaimed the Loosing of the Knot."

Delphi had once pronounced him *aniketos*, "the invincible"; Gordium proclaimed him the world conqueror; a hundred omens had warned him of victories to come. Now as he marched through Galatia and Cappadocia, he began to realize the inevitability of conflict with Persia, not merely with the Persian garrisons and satraps in Asia Minor, but with the Great King himself, who came to the throne in the same year as Alexander. Darius (Daryavush) was a worthy opponent of the young king who had already conquered Greece and was fast conquering Asia Minor. He, too, had the habits of a conqueror and was at home among intrigues. He was tall and elegant, with large eyes, an aquiline nose, and a short bristling beard; he had murdered more than one man with his bare hands. Day after day the Persian couriers had brought to his palace at Susa alarming reports of Alexander's victories. At last, fearing further delay, Darius led his army into Syria with the intention of destroying Alexander as soon as he emerged through the Syrian Gates. Alexander was in Tarsus, having reached the city only just in time to prevent it from being put to the flames by the Persians. A few days later he had gone bathing in the ice-cold waters of the river Cydnus, and caught such a severe chill that his life was despaired of. The doctors scarcely knew what to do, for if their treatment failed they were likely to be torn to pieces by the Macedonian soldiers. At last, taking his courage in his hands, Philip the Acarnanian, his chief physician, decided to give him a strong purgative, and he was preparing the draught when a letter arrived from Parmenio. Alexander read the letter and calmly placed it under his pillow until Philip entered the room with the draught. Alexander took the goblet and showed Philip the letter, which read: "Beware of Philip. I am informed that he has been bribed by Darius to poison you." The doctor was still reading the letter as Alexander drank the purgative. Alexander never referred to the letter. Slowly, with Philip attending him, he regained his health and resumed command of the army.

Darius had brought his army up to Sochi in Syria, two days' march from the gates of Amanus, and hearing reports that Alexander was on the other side of the hills, he decided to attack at once; but while Darius was leading his forces through the pass, Alexander, now fully recovered, was leading his forces through a pass a few miles to the south. The intelligence services of both kings had broken down. As soon as he realized that Darius had left Sochi, Alexander retraced his steps, for unless he offered immediate battle and destroyed the Persian forces he would be cut off from his supply bases, separated from Greece by the entire length of Asia Minor. He had no ships, and almost no allies. He was trapped, and he had no alternative but to fight his way out of the trap.

When Alexander reached the small plain of Issus at dawn and found the army of Darius arranged in formation behind the river Pinarus between the mountains and the sea, he confronted the largest army he had ever seen. There were 30,000 Persian cavalry near the sea, the same number of Greek mercenaries in the center, and the light-armed troops were strung along the foothills. Darius had about 90,000 soldiers, and Alexander less than a third of that number. So, while the Persians waited, Alexander spent the morning making his dispositions, and when the battle was joined in the afternoon he had decided to bring his most powerful forces against the center, where Darius and the imperial guards were to be found. The battle was a confused affair, with Parmenio's cavalry retreating along the seashore, and the Greek mercenaries fighting with very little heart in the center. Alexander and the Companions hurled themselves in the

direction of Darius and the close-knit formation of the imperial
guards. They broke through the outer ring, and there appears to
have been a moment when Alexander and Darius confronted one
another in combat. Then the ring closed again, and Darius was lost
from sight. Toward evening, at a time when his troops seemed to
have the upper hand, he panicked and fled the battlefield, driving
in his chariot to the foothills and there abandoning it.

At the moment when he left the battlefield Darius had decided
the fate of the Persian Empire.

The fame of Alexander had been spread abroad; his former
victories were known; his ruthlessness and determination to avenge
the invasion of Xerxes had already given him a stature greater than
he yet deserved. The very fact that he was the only king remaining
on the battlefield gave him the victory; and the remnants of the Persian army fled into the hills and vanished into the night.

Alexander spent the night in the golden tent of Darius amid the
heaps of treasure which Persian kings customarily carried with them
in their travels. Plutarch tells a circumstantial story of Alexander's
doffing his armor and saying: "Let us go and wash off the sweat of
battle in the bath of Darius." "No," said one of the Companions,
"but rather in that of Alexander." When Alexander saw the ba-
sins and pitchers and caskets, all gleaming with gold and curiously
wrought, and all lying where Darius had left them in the many-
roomed tent heavily scented with spices and unguents, he turned to
his Companions and said: "Now I know what it is like to be a king."

Later, when he was dining, he heard the weeping of women,
and learned that Darius' mother, wife, and two unmarried daughters
were mourning his death. Darius' chariot had been found in the foothills, together with his shield and bow and royal cloak, but there
was no reason to believe that he was dead. So Alexander sent word
that, as far as he knew, Darius was still alive, and they should have
no fear for themselves: they would be treated with the respect due
to their rank. It was generally believed that Darius' wife was the
most beautiful woman in Asia: Alexander refused to set eyes on her,
and he refused any discussion of her beauty in his presence. He had
no love for women, his private affections being centered upon Hephaestion, the companion of his childhood.

On the following day Alexander and Hephaestion paid a visit
to the mother of Darius. She immediately assumed the taller of the

two was the king, and prostrated herself before Hephaestion, who drew back. When one of her attendants pointed to Alexander, saying he was the king, she was confused and made an effort to withdraw. Alexander smiled, and said: "Hephaestion is also Alexander." In time he seems to have developed a considerable affection for the old woman, and once when she petitioned him to spare some Persian tribesmen he granted her wish. There is no record that he ever granted any other similar petition.

With the battle won and the Persian army in flight, Alexander was still far from having won an empire. The Persian Empire was so vast, its resources so much greater than the resources of any other country, that it could fight twenty pitched battles of the scale of Issus without too much harm. Marching across Persia, Alexander's army could be exhausted in a hundred skirmishes. This he knew, and he therefore set about the conquest of the Persian home fleet based on Tyre as a preliminary to securing his Mediterranean flank. Tyre was a Phoenician city built on an island. Its ships were manned by Phoenician sailors, but the command was in the hands of the Persians. With the destruction of Tyre, the most powerful naval base in the eastern Mediterranean, he could go on to conquer the rest of the Palestinian coast without any fear that armies would be landed by sea to thwart his progress. His eyes were on Egypt, and his aim was to conquer the western crescent of the Persian Empire.

For a year and a half he remained close to the sea. He was not yet ready to plunge across the deserts of Asia.

The Tyrians proved to be disappointingly stubborn. They were in league with the Carthaginians; they were rich and powerful; and they were so contemptuous of Alexander's small army that they murdered the envoys sent to demand the submission of the island city. For seven weary months the siege of Tyre continued. When it fell in July, 332, the exhausted and exasperated Macedonians simply massacred the male population and sold the women and children into slavery. It was not the first time Alexander had exacted a terrible vengeance.

His next objective was Egypt. Except at Gaza, he found no obstacles to his southward march; and Egypt surrendered without a blow. The four or five months spent in Egypt assumed the nature of a royal progress. There was no fighting at any time. Afterward he would be fighting continually almost to the day of his death.

He founded Alexandria. According to Arrian, the second century A.D. historian who was able to draw heavily on contemporary sources, Alexander walked around the site while a soldier followed him, sprinkling meal taken from the soldiers' packs. Within a few days walls began to rise where the meal fell. He needed a capital for his new Egyptian kingdom, and to link it with Greece the capital had to be on the seacoast. He was still thinking in terms of ships, and still obsessed by the neccessity of naval domination over the Mediterranean.

His next care was to visit the oasis of Siwa in the Libyan Desert, the seat of the oracle of Zeus Ammon, regarded by the Greeks as of very nearly equal importance with the oracle of Apollo at Delphi. There was another purpose to the dangerous journey across the desert: the need to safeguard his communications, for knowledge about the Libyan Desert was meager and it was necessary to know whether the Libyan tribesmen, who had plagued the Pharaohs for a thousand years, would rise in revolt. The inevitable question was put to the god, who answered with the inevitable reply. Henceforth Alexander regarded himself as one especially blessed by Zeus Ammon. No one knows the actual words exchanged between the young king and the ancient oracle. Writing to his mother in Macedonia he said he received messages which must remain secret until he could communicate them to her with his own lips. He never returned to Macedonia, and Olympias never heard the secret messages.

He had not lost his taste for philosophy; and now, being at leisure, he sought out Egyptian philosophers. He especially approved of the teachings of the philosopher Psammon, who spoke of the kingship of God over all the races of mankind, a doctrine which went back a thousand years to the time of the heretic-king Akhnaton. Plutarch observed that Alexander's rewording of the doctrine was even more philosophical, for he said: "God is the common father of all mankind, and makes peculiarly His own the very best of men." In time the doctrine was to bear fruit in the vision of the final *homonoia*, the reconciliation under one Father of all the races of the world.

But the time for *homonoia* had not yet come. There were still battles to be fought and a world to be conquered. In July, 331, a year after the massacre at Tyre, he led his army across the Tigris to search out the army of Darius, which he found at Gaugamela not far from the ruins of Nineveh. A vast unwieldy army, with elephants and

scythe-sided chariots, stretched across the plain as far as the eye
could see. We know the orders for disposal of the various corps, because the official lists were captured and preserved, but we know re-
markably little about the course of the battle. Neither the elephants
nor the scythed chariots put fear into the hearts of the Macedonians.
Alexander repeated the tactics employed at Issus by directing the
attack on Darius and his escort of imperial guards; and once again
Darius fled in panic at a time when the rest of his army was gaining
ground. His inexplicable flight proved to the Persians that he had
forfeited the right to be an emperor. Instead of pursuing Darius,
Alexander marched on to Babylon and Susa, both cities surrendering
even before he came in sight of them; then he marched on to Persepolis, the holy city of the Persian emperors, remarkable for the
beautiful palaces which lay in the shadow of the hills where the
Achaemenid kings were buried.

There is a curious story that Alexander was holding a feast in
one of the palaces when Thais, an Athenian courtesan, demanded the
privilege of setting fire to it. "It will pay me for all the toils I have
undergone following the camp all over Asia," she said. "Nothing
would give me greater pleasure than to do this with the king looking
on, for then it would be recorded by posterity that the women who
accompanied Alexander took a more severe revenge on the Persians
for the injuries inflicted on Greece than all the famous commanders
by sea or by land." Plutarch tells the story in considerable detail. He
gives a dramatic account of a drunken mob wildly applauding the
courtesan, and of Alexander, crowned with flowers, leading the mob
and setting light to everything within reach, only to repent of his
action a little while later, when he ordered the fires extinguished.

The capture of Persepolis was Alexander's supreme achievement
as a conqueror. He had no need to make further conquests, for by
the physical occupation of the holy city he became the dominant
power in the Persian Empire. Until the time of Augustus Caesar no
one ever had so much power over so many people as the man who
was King of Kings, King of Macedon, and Pharaoh of Egypt, and
who called himself quite simply "the Lord of Asia." He was twenty-
five years old.

Because he was so young, and because he suffered from the terrible restlessness of the Greeks to see and to know, he left Persepolis
in the spring of 330 and spent the remaining seven years of his life in

a series of lightning campaigns. He pursued Darius to the shores of the Caspian, only to find the emperor stabbed to death a few minutes before he arrived on the scene: the murderer was the emperor's cousin Bessus, who seems to have thought that by killing Darius he would find favor in the eyes of Alexander. Instead, he was caught and suffered the indignity of having his nose and the tips of his ears cut off before he was finally executed in Ecbatana.

Restless, Alexander set about those further conquests which would come to an end only with his death. He swung north against Bactria and Sogdiana, stamping out all resistance among those obscure tribesmen who had never threatened his power, until he came close to the frontiers of China. He built perhaps a hundred cities and towns to remain as milestones of his progress, and of these no more than four or five survived to become centers of Greek influence in Central Asia. He had an obscure idea that somewhere in Asia he would find the source of the Nile, and he was certain he would come upon the great Stream of Ocean which encircled the habitable earth. He told his soldiers he would not rest until he had overrun all Asia: then he would send them home with more wealth than they could ever dream of. But he never found the great Stream of Ocean, and the hardships of the journey led to mutinies. He was no longer simply "the Lord of Asia." He represented in his person a great revolutionary process bringing Greek civilization to the East; and it is in the nature of revolutions to devour their own parents. One by one his lieutenants and advisers, Philotas, Parmenio, Cleitus, Callisthenes, and many others, fell victim to his fury. He stood on that dangerous eminence where treacheries are commonplace, and mutinies are to be expected. He drove his men mercilessly into India, and would have gone on to conquer the whole of the subcontinent if his soldiers had not threatened to revolt: then he led them across the desert of Baluchistan back to Persepolis and his capital in Babylon. Five years were spent on these interminable campaigns on the borders of the empire.

In Egypt he had appointed Egyptian governors; in Persia he gave high offices to Persians. Increasingly he came to regard himself as a ruler removed from the prejudices of nationalism, owing loyalty not to one nation but to all. From Aristotle, from the Egyptian philosopher Psammon, and from his own thinking there had come the vision of a universal state, a commonwealth in which all were to be partners rather than subjects. Already he regarded himself as the first among

Persians, as previously he had regarded himself as the first among Greeks. He followed Persian court ceremonial, and was attended by Persian magi as well as by the Greek seers who accompanied him in all his battles to offer the proper sacrifices and to study the auguries. Gradually a common Macedonian-Persian culture was emerging. Peace was being organized by Macedonians and Persians acting together; and even if he had wanted to, Alexander would have been unable to prevent the fusion of cultures.

The fusion was going on quietly, almost mechanically, when a strange incident brought it out into the open. At Opis, a few miles north of Babylon, he summoned his Macedonian troops and announced that he was discharging old and disabled soldiers and sending them back to Greece with suitable gifts and rewards for their services. He seemed to have no other thought except to please the soldiers by giving them gifts and bounty. To his surprise the army received the news with an outburst of ferocious anger. All the accumulated resentments, all the memory of wounds suffered and long marches endured, came to the surface when Alexander used the word "discharge." The men shouted: "Discharge all of us! Send us all away! Next time go campaigning with your father!" Probably, suggests Arrian, who records the incident, they meant that he should go campaigning with Zeus Ammon, who in the silence of his shrine in the Libyan Desert was popularly supposed to have addressed Alexander as his son. But it is just as likely that they meant Philip, who was dead.

This was mutiny, and Alexander already had considerable experience of quelling mutinies. He leaped down from the platform, and pointed out thirteen of the ringleaders to his officers, ordering that they should be led off to execution. Then he returned to the platform and delivered a long speech in which he alternately praised and blamed the Macedonians, and offered to abide by their desire. If they wanted to be discharged, he would not stand in their way. He had suffered as many wounds as any of them, paid their debts, attended their marriages, made them all viceroys, generals, and captains, and now, having given them golden crowns and led them to the world's end, retaining for himself out of all the treasure of countless cities only the purple and the crown, he was ready to see them depart. "Go, all of you, and when you reach your homes, tell them how you deserted your king who led you from victory to victory across the world, and abandoned him to the conquered barbarians! No doubt your words will win you the praises of men and the rewards of Heaven. Go!"

For two days Alexander shut himself up in his tent, while his troops retired sullenly to their quarters. The Persian officers were summoned to his tent: he told them that henceforward the army would be captained only by Persians. When the Macedonians heard this, they ran to Alexander and begged for mercy. Then he stood before them, weeping, for they were like beggars crouching there, until a cavalry officer called Callines said: "My lord, what hurts the Macedonians most is that you have made the Persians your kinsmen. They kiss you, but no Macedonian is allowed to kiss you!"

"No," said Alexander, "you are all my kinsmen, and so I shall call you!"

At this there was a wild burst of cheering, and soon the soldiers returned to their own tents singing lustily.

The love-match between Alexander and his Macedonians was renewed, and so too was his love-match with the Persians. To seal the compact a vast banquet was held, where Macedonians and Persians sat together and drank from the same loving cup, a huge silver *krater* that had once belonged to Darius, while the trumpets sounded and libations were poured to the gods of Greece and Persia. According to Arrian, nine thousand people attended that banquet, where Alexander prayed solemnly to the gods that Persians and Macedonians might rule together in harmony. With that prayer he announced the beginning of a new dispensation of time, an end to conquests, and the reign of unity and concord among men.

The prayer crowned his life. Nothing he had ever done, nothing he did in the few remaining months of his life was of greater moment than the banquet at which he spoke fervently of the duty of mixing all men as in a loving cup. So, in much the same tones, St. Paul would speak of the time when there would be "neither Greek nor Jew, barbarian nor Scythian, bond nor free."

Alexander died, and the vision faded; for it is in the nature of visions to fade. A strange youthful emperor had come into the world, claiming to be the son of Zeus Ammon and the descendant of Heracles, but in fact he was descended from Socrates by way of Plato and Aristotle. He resembled neither Zeus nor Heracles; he was like Apollo in his wisdom and his peculiar rages. So, resembling Apollo, the sculptors portrayed him, and by one of the curious accidents of history his statues became the models of the images of Buddha, at first in Gandhara and then over India and the Far East, so that to this day all the representations of Buddha preserve, however remotely, the features of Alexander. In the temples of Malaya, Burma, Siam, Java, and Japan, we see the heroic Alexander at his meditations. The Buddha, who believed only in the peace of the soul, wears the face of the Great Reconciler, who prayed that all men should be mixed as in a loving cup and all the people of the world should live in harmony under the fatherhood of God.

The Greeks gave to the world their purity and grace, their ease and joy of life, their physical beauty, their intellectual fire, and their sense of the dignity of man under the heavens, but they gave far more. They gave us a way of life which we have largely followed, often without realizing that we are treading in their footsteps. They were the superb artificers of a civilization which has endured for so long that we are in danger of forgetting that they are our parents. They thought the thoughts we are still thinking, and dreamed the dreams we are still dreaming. They throw their long shadows over us, and to our surprise we discover that these shadows are made of beams of intense light; for they came at the dawn, and we are still far from high noon.

≫ BIBLIOGRAPHICAL NOTE ≪

There are, I imagine, five indispensable works needed for a study of Greek civilization. A good classical atlas, a good classical dictionary, Liddell and Scott's Greek-English lexicon, J. B. Bury's *A History of Greece*, and the entire collection of the Loeb classics in the familiar green covers. This is, of course, only the beginning, for there is no end to the number of special studies and translations and scholarly papers on various facets of Greek culture; nor is there ever likely to be an end. So any book list can be no more than the skeleton of a skeleton.

I have listed here some of the books which have been most useful to me. They are the books I have and want to keep, rather than the books I consulted in libraries. In addition there are three books which seem to me to deserve a place apart, being so close to indispensability that it would seem to be almost impossible to write about Greece without them. They are Werner Jaeger's *Paideia: The Ideals of Greek Culture*, translated by Gilbert Highet (New York, Oxford University Press, 1945) in three volumes, and the two volumes of Moses Hadas, *A History of Greek Literature* and *Ancilla to Classical Reading*, both published by the Columbia University Press in 1962.

THE BARREN LAND

FRAZER, SIR JAMES. *Greece and Rome*. London, Macmillan & Co., 1937.
LIDDELL, ROBERT. *Aegean Greece*. London: Jonathan Cape, 1955.
PAYNE, ROBERT. *The Splendor of Greece*. New York: Harper & Brothers, 1960.
WIGRAM, W. A. *Hellenic Travel*. London: Faber & Faber, 1957.

THE FERTILE ISLAND

HUTCHINSON, R. W. *Prehistoric Crete*. Harmondsworth: Penguin Books, 1962.
MARINATOS, SPYRIDON. *Crete and Mycenae*. New York: Harry N. Abrams, 1960.
PLATON, N. *A Guide to the Archaeological Museum of Heraclion*. Heraclion: Andreas Kalokairinos, 1955.

ANCIENT GREECE

THE MYCENAEANS

CHADWICK, JOHN. *The Decipherment of Linear B*. Harmondsworth: Penguin Books, 1961.

MYLONAS, GEORGE E. *Ancient Mycenae*. London: Routledge & Kegan Paul, 1957.

PAYNE, ROBERT. *The Gold of Troy*. New York: Funk & Wagnalls, 1958.

VENTRIS, MICHAEL, and CHADWICK, JOHN. *Documents in Mycenaean Greek*. Cambridge: Cambridge University Press, 1956.

WACE, HELEN. *Ivories from Mycenae*. Athens: National Museum, 1939.

THE COMING OF THE GODS

FESTUGIÈRE, ANDRÉ-JEAN. *Personal Religion among the Greeks*. Berkeley: University of California Press, 1954.

HARRISON, JANE ELLEN. *Themis*. New York: Meridian Books, 1962.

———. *Prolegomena to the Study of Greek Religion*. New York: Meridian Books, 1955.

KERÉNYI, CARL. *The Gods of the Greeks*. Harmondsworth: Penguin Books, 1958.

———. *The Religion of the Greeks and Romans*. New York: E. P. Dutton, 1962.

MYLONAS, GEORGE E. *Eleusis and the Eleusinian Mysteries*. Princeton: Princeton University Press, 1961.

NILSSON, MARTIN P. *Greek Folk Religion*. New York: Harper & Brothers, 1961.

OTTO, WALTER F. *The Homeric Gods*. New York: Pantheon, 1954.

THE BITTER HARVEST

LATTIMORE, RICHMOND. *Hesiod: Works and Days, Theogony, The Shield of Herakles*. Ann Arbor: University of Michigan Press, 1959.

THE FAR-FLUNG SETTLEMENTS

MATT, LEONARD VON, and LUIGI PARETI. *Ancient Sicily*. New York: Universe Books, 1960.

MATT, LEONARD VON, and UMBERTO ZANOTTI-BIANCO. *Magna Graecia*. New York: Universe Books, 1962.

THE EARLY SONGS

LATTIMORE, RICHMOND. *Greek Lyrics*. Chicago: University of Chicago Press, 1955.

SYMONDS, JOHN ADDINGTON. *Studies of the Greek Poets*. London: Adam and Charles Black, 1902.

THE SPLENDID CONTESTS

FRAZER, SIR JAMES. *Pausanias's Description of Greece*. 5 vols. Cambridge: Harvard University Press, 1918–1935.

THE RESOUNDING SONGS

FAGLES, ROBERT. *Bacchylides: Complete Poems*. New Haven: Yale University Press, 1961.
LATTIMORE, RICHMOND. *The Odes of Pindar*. Chicago: University of Chicago Press, 1947.

TOWARD AN INTELLIGIBLE UNIVERSE

BURNET, JOHN. *Early Greek Philosophy*. New York: Meridian Books, 1960.
GUTHRIE, W. K. C. *The Greek Philosophers*. New York: Harper & Brothers, 1960.
ZELLER, EDUARD. *Outlines of the History of Greek Philosophy*. New York: Meridian Books, 1955.

THE REIGN OF THE TYRANTS

SINCLAIR, T. A. *A History of Greek Political Thought*. London: Routledge and Kegan Paul, 1951.
WOODHOUSE, W. J. *Solon the Liberator*. Oxford: Clarendon Press, 1938.

THE SOVEREIGN PEOPLE

BARKER, SIR ERNEST. *Greek Political Theory*. New York: Barnes and Noble, 1960.
TOYNBEE, ARNOLD J. *Greek Historical Thought*. New York: New American Library, 1962.

THE COMING OF THE PERSIANS

OLMSTEAD, A. T. *History of the Persian Empire*. Chicago: University of Chicago Press, 1948.

THE TRAGIC TRIUMPH

KITTO, H. D. F. *Greek Tragedy*. New York: Doubleday, 1954.
NORWOOD, GILBERT. *Greek Tragedy*. New York: Hill and Wang, 1960.
THOMSON, GEORGE. *Aeschylus and Athens*. London: Lawrence and Wishart, 1950.

THE WORLD WIDE OPEN

GREEN, PETER. *Essays in Antiquity*. New York: World, 1960.
MYERS, J. L. *Herodotus, Father of History*. Oxford: Clarendon Press, 1953.

PERICLES

BURN, A. R. *Pericles and Athens*. New York: Collier Books, 1962.

THE GOLDEN AGE

ASHMOLE, BERNARD. *The Sculptures of the Parthenon*. London: The British Museum, 1961.

ANCIENT GREECE

LAWRENCE, A. W. *Greek Architecture*. Harmondsworth: Penguin Books, 1957.
RICHTER, GISELA M. A. *A Handbook of Greek Art*. New York: Graphic, 1960.
SELTMAN, CHARLES. *An Approach to Greek Art*. New York: E. P. Dutton, 1960.
THOMPSON, HOMER A. *The Athenian Agora*. Athens: American School of Classical Studies, 1954.

SOPHOCLES

BATES, WILLIAM NICKERSON. *Sophocles, Poet and Dramatist*. New York: A. S. Barnes, 1961.

EURIPIDES

BATES, WILLIAM NICKERSON. *Euripides, A Student of Human Nature*. New York: A. S. Barnes, 1961.
HADAS, MOSES. *Euripides, Ten Plays*. New York: Bantam Books, 1960.
MURRAY, GILBERT. *Euripides and His Age*. New York: Oxford University Press, 1946.

ARISTOPHANES

CORNFORD, FRANCIS MACDONALD. *The Origin of Attic Comedy*. New York: Doubleday Anchor Books, 1961.
EHRENBERG, VICTOR. *The People of Aristophanes*. New York: Schocken Books, 1962.
MURRAY, GILBERT. *Aristophanes*. Oxford: Clarendon Press, 1933.

THE RISE OF SPARTA

JOWETT, BENJAMIN (trans.). *Thucydides: The Peloponnesian War*. New York: Bantam Books, 1960.
MITCHELL, H. *Sparta*. Cambridge: Cambridge University Press, 1952.

SOCRATES

TAYLOR, A. E. *Socrates: The Man and His Thought*. New York: Doubleday Anchor Books, 1956.

XENOPHON

WARNER, REX (trans.). *Xenophon: The Persian Expedition*. Harmondsworth: Penguin Books, 1961.

PLATO

LEVY, G. R. *Plato in Sicily*. Hollywood-by-the-Sea, Fla.: Transatlantic, 1959.
PATER, WALTER. *Plato and Platonism*. London: Macmillan & Co., 1934.
TAYLOR, A. E. *Plato: The Man and His Work*. New York: Meridian Books, 1960.

THE SCIENTIFIC TEMPER

FARRINGTON, BENJAMIN. *Greek Science*. Harmondsworth: Penguin Books, 1961.
ROSS, W. D. *Aristotle*. New York: Meridian Books, 1959.

SANTILLANA, GIORGIO DE. *The Origins of Scientific Thought*. New York: New American Library, 1961.

THE RISE OF PHILIP

HOGARTH, D. G. *Philip and Alexander of Macedon*. London: John Murray, 1897.

THE CONQUEST OF THE WORLD

TARN, W. W. *Alexander the Great*. New York: Beacon Press, 1956.
————. *Hellenistic Civilisation*. New York: Meridian Books, 1961.

☞ CHRONOLOGICAL TABLE ☜

c. 3000   Beginning of Bronze Age in countries bordering the Aegean.
c. 2000   First waves of Greek immigration.
c. 1600   Mycenaeans established in Mycenae, Tiryns, Pylos, and Thebes.
c. 1500   Linear B script comes into existence.
c. 1450   Collapse of Minoan Crete.
c. 1230   Theseus King of Athens.
c. 1184   Fall of Troy.
c. 1100   Dorians in northern Greece.
c. 1050   Ionian colonization of Asia Minor.
c. 850   Birth of Greek alphabet in Ionia. Homer's *Iliad* and *Odyssey*. Greek Pantheon nearly complete.
c. 750–650   Greek colonization of Italy and Sicily.
c. 776   First Olympic Games.
c. 700–500   Ionian school of philosophy.
c. 594   Reforms of Solon in Athens.
561   Peisistratus becomes tyrant of Athens.
546   Cyrus conquers Sardis.
527   Death of Peisistratus.
514   Harmodius and Aristogeiton assassinate Hipparchus.
507   Cleisthenes brings democracy to Athens.
499   Ionia revolts from Persian Empire. First play of Aeschylus.
497   Ionian Greeks burn Sardis.
493   Themistocles archon of Athens. Collapse of Ionian revolt.
492   Beginning of Persian Wars.
490   Battle of Marathon. Temple of Aphaea at Aegina.
485   Xerxes becomes emperor of Persia. Gelon becomes tyrant of Syracuse.
483   Discovery of silver at Laurium.
480   Battles of Thermopylae, Artemisium and Salamis. Sicilians defeat Carthaginians at Himera.
479   Battles of Plataea and Mycale.
478   Hiero I becomes tyrant of Syracuse.
477   Formation of Confederacy of Delos.
476   Athens and her allies take the offensive against Persian positions in the Mediterranean.
472   Production of Aeschylus' *Persians*.
469   Birth of Socrates. Third actor introduced by Sophocles. Naxos revolts from Confederacy of Delos.
468   Aeschylus defeated by Sophocles in dramatic contest. Cimon defeats Persians at Eurymedon.
467   Production of Aeschylus' *Seven against Thebes*.

465 Sculptures and metopes of Temple of Zeus at Olympia.
464 Earthquake in Sparta. Revolt of helots. Siege of Ithome.
463–429 Public career of Pericles.
461 Assassination of Ephialtes.
460 Birth of Thucydides. Production of Aeschylus' *Prometheus Bound.*
459–454 Athenian expedition against Egypt, which ends in failure.
458 Production of Aeschylus' *Oresteia.*
457 Spartans defeat Athenians at Tanagra.
456 Completion of Temple of Zeus at Olympia. Death of Aeschylus.
455 Production of Euripides' first tragedy.
454 Treasury of Confederacy of Delos removed to Athens.
451–446 Truce between Athens and Sparta.
448 Peace of Callias. End of Persian Wars.
447–432 The Parthenon.
445 Birth of Aristophanes. Peace with Sparta.
443 Herodotus joins colonists founding Thurii.
442 Production of Sophocles' *Antigone.* Frieze of Parthenon begun.
440 Expedition against Samos.
438 Phidias carves Athena Parthenos, and begins pedimental sculptures of the Parthenon.
437–432 The Propylaea.
432 Prosecutions of Phidias, Anaxagoras and Aspasia.
431–404 Peloponnesian War.
430 Plague at Athens. Trial of Pericles.
429 Death of Pericles. Cleon in power. Production of Sophocles' *Oedipus the King.*
428 Revolt of Mytilene. Death of Anaxagoras. Birth of Plato.
427 Production of Aristophanes' first comedy.
425 Death of Herodotus.
424 Battle of Delium.
423 Production of Aristophanes' *Clouds.*
422 Battle of Amphipolis. Brasidas and Cleon killed.
421 Peace of Nicias. Production of Aristophanes' *Peace.*
420–405 The Erechtheum.
418 Spartan victory at Mantinea. Athens and Argos allies against Sparta.
416 Trial of Protagoras. Massacre at Melos.
415–413 Athenian expedition to Syracuse.
415 Mutilation of Herms. Production of Euripides' *Trojan Women.*
411 The Four Hundred in power in Athens. Recall of Alcibiades. Production of Aristophanes' *Lysistrata.*
406 Athenian victory at Arginusae. Death of Sophocles and Euripides.
404 Fall of Athens. Assassination of Alcibiades in Phrygia. Rule of the Thirty.
403 The Thirty expelled. Restoration of the democracy.
401 Production of Sophocles' *Oedipus in Colonus.* Retreat of Xenophon's Ten Thousand.
c. 400 Death of Thucydides.
399 Trial and death of Socrates. Plato goes to Megara.
394 Long walls rebuilt by Conon.
387 Plato founds the Academe in Athens.
378 Second Athenian Confederacy. Alliance of Athens and Thebes.

371 Epaminondas defeats Spartans at Leuctra. Peace of Callias between Athens and Sparta.

367 Death of Dionysius of Syracuse.

362 Epaminondas killed at Mantinea.

357 Dion captures Syracuse.

c. 354 Death of Xenophon.

351 Demosthenes' *First Philippic*.

347 Death of Plato.

343 Aristotle goes to Pella as tutor of Alexander.

338 Battle of Chaeronea. Philip of Macedon supreme in Greece.

336 Philip assassinated. Alexander becomes King of Macedon. Darius III becomes emperor of Persia.

335 Alexander razes Thebes. Aristotle founds Lyceum in Athens.

334 Alexander enters Asia.

333 Alexander at Gordium. Battle of Issus.

332 Siege of Tyre. Alexander becomes Pharaoh of Egypt.

331 Alexandria founded. Battle of Gaugamela.

330 Alexander enters Persepolis. Assassination of Darius III.

327 Alexander begins his expedition against India.

324 Alexander at Opis. Death of Hephaestion.

322 Death of Aristotle and Demosthenes.

⇒ INDEX ⇐